Spreading the News

SPREADING
THE NEWS

. . .

*The American Postal System
from Franklin to Morse*

Richard R. John

HARVARD UNIVERSITY PRESS
Cambridge, Massachusetts
London, England
1995

To my family

Library of Congress Cataloging-in-Publication Data
John, Richard R., 1959–
Spreading the news: the American postal system from Franklin to
Morse / Richard R. John.
p.   cm.
Includes bibliographical references and index.
ISBN 0-674-83338-4 (cloth : alk. paper)
1. Postal service—United States—History.   I. Title.
HE6185.J634   1995
383'.4973—dc20
95-20067

CONTENTS

PREFACE

This book is a history of the American postal system in the seventy-year period between its establishment in 1775 and the commercialization of the electric telegraph in 1844. During these seven decades, the postal system spurred a communications revolution that was as profound in its consequences for American public life as the subsequent revolutions that have come to be associated with the telegraph, the telephone, and the computer. This book tells the story of this communications revolution and, more broadly, of the challenge it posed for American business, politics, and cultural life.

Today, of course, the postal system is but one of many institutions that transmit information from place to place. During the early republic, however, the situation was quite different. Telegraphs, telephones, and all of the other modes of long-distance communication with which we today are so familiar were in the future, while the postal system was widely hailed as one of the most important institutions of the day. And with good reason. No other institution had the capacity to transmit such large volume of information on such a regular basis over such an enormous geographical expanse. Few were faster, making the stagecoaches and the riders who conveyed the mail synonymous with speed. Though the postal system suffered several setbacks during the 1830s, it remained the linchpin of the American communications infrastructure until the following decade when, with the advent of commercial telegraphy, it lost its preeminent position in the transmission of information relating to commerce and public affairs.

This book is very different from the one I originally planned. My initial interest in the postal system was spurred less by its role in the transmission of information than by its supposed importance as one of the first bureaucracies in the United States. Intrigued by the antibureaucratic ethos that has become such a pervasive feature of contemporary life, I hoped to explore how, where, and why this ethos had first emerged. Given my interests, the postal system seemed a sensible choice. After all, for almost thirty years historians have traced the beginnings of bureaucracy in the United States to a series of organizational innovations in the postal system introduced shortly after the inauguration of President Andrew Jackson.[1] Prior to Jackson, so these historians contend, the postal system was prebureaucratic. Following his inauguration—and, above all, following the passage of the Post Office Act of 1836—the Jacksonians are credited with having rapidly transformed the institution into a recognizably modern bureaucracy, complete with job categories, organization charts, and accounting checks, making it the precursor of the large-scale, hierarchical organizations that have come to dominate so many sectors of American government, business, and professions. "There has," one of the leading students of the subject grandly declares, "perhaps been no more sweeping and fundamental change in all of American history."[2]

Given the pivotal role that so many historians assigned to the Jacksonians in this transformation, it seemed to me that the history of the postal system during the Jackson administration would be a good place to begin. Accordingly, I read through the correspondence of Jacksonian postmaster general Amos Kendall for the months immediately preceding and following the passage of the Post Office Act of 1836. If this piece of legislation was indeed the landmark in American bureaucratic history that it was claimed to be, then Kendall's correspondence should be filled with references to the dramatic changes that the act had introduced. However, to my surprise, though Kendall dealt with a number of pressing administrative challenges during this time, his correspondence failed to reveal any hint of the momentous changes that he had supposedly overseen. Subsequent research into the history of postal administration confirmed my findings. Without exception, every one of the ostensibly epochal innovations in postal administration that the Jacksonians had purportedly introduced had in fact originated prior to Jackson's inauguration. Thus, if the postal system was bureaucratic at the close of Andrew Jackson's administration in 1837, it was bureaucratic at its start in 1829.

Having failed to find the origins of American bureaucracy in the Jacksonian postal system, I decided to rethink my project. Kendall's correspondence may not have revealed much about the beginnings of American bureaucracy, but it did provide an intriguing glimpse of the day-to-day workings of one of the largest and most influential institutions of the day. The rise of bureaucracy in the postal system, I now came to see, was far less important—and far less interesting—than the role of the institution in facilitating the transmission of information throughout the United States. In this country—to a greater extent, perhaps, than in any other—the unimpeded transmission of information has long been hailed as a cherished ideal. Just as social mobility has been sought by the ambitious, informational mobility has been prized by merchants, politicians, editors, and the cultural elite. Could American postal policy help to explain why this was so? Could it have shaped the development of such information-intensive institutions as the national market, the voluntary association, and the mass party? Could it have worked to create an enduring national society out of a fragile union of confederated states?

Questions such as these have led me to give this inquiry its present form. The resulting book is neither an exhaustive chronicle of the internal dynamics of postal administration nor an analytical essay on the role of informational mobility in American life. Rather, it is an interpretative biography of the life and times of an important American institution during a critical epoch in its history. By exploring the role of the postal system in American public life in the period between 1775 and 1844, I hope we may gain a fresh perspective not only on an important chapter in the American past, but also on the origins of some of the most distinctive features of American life today.

ACKNOWLEDGMENTS

Scholarship is a collective endeavor, and I have accumulated many debts in the course of preparing this book. Of the many archivists, librarians, and administrators who have helped to facilitate my research, I would especially like to thank the staffs of the American Antiquarian Society, the American Philatelic Research Library, and the National Postal Museum at the Smithsonian Institution. Of particular assistance have been James H. Bruns, Nathaniel Bunker, Nancy H. Burkett, Herbert Collins, Robert W. Coren, Virginia L. Horn, David R. Kepley, Kathy Kilian, Carol Linton, John J. McDonough, Aloha South, and Joyce Tracy. Thanks also to Joseph Simonetti, who tracked down a number of elusive documents, and Jim McNeill, who helped edit the text.

This book originated as a doctoral dissertation, and I am grateful to my advisors, David Herbert Donald and Alfred D. Chandler, Jr., for the care with which they oversaw my graduate education. From the outset, both encouraged me to pursue what seemed to many a decidedly unorthodox topic; and, notwithstanding my stubborn determination to expand the scope of the project beyond its original confines, both stuck with me to the end. Only those who have been fortunate enough to have had the opportunity to work closely with these two outstanding teachers, scholars, and gentlemen can fully appreciate the high standards they have set for the rising generation.

In the best tradition of academic collegiality, many scholars have kindly shared ideas about how my project might be improved. Of the countless individuals who have assisted me in this regard, I should like to single out the following: Bernard Bailyn, James M. Banner, Jr., Michael Les Benedict, Burton J. Bledstein, Menachem Blondheim, Geoffrey Bowker, Richard D. Brown, Joan E. Cashin, Daniel A. Cohen, Michael Kent Curtis, Konstantin Diercks, Colleen A. Dunlavy, Karl Eschbach, Lacy K. Ford, Jr., Ronald P. Formisano, William E. Gienapp, William J. Gilmore-Lehne, Edward G. Gray, Robert A. Gross, Thomas L. Haskell, Daniel Walker Howe, Nancy G. Isenberg, Richard J. Jensen, Richard B. Kielbowicz, Michael Lacey, Naomi R. Lamoreaux, Richard B. Latner, Thomas C. Leonard, Michael Lienesch, Thomas K. McCraw, John C. Nerone, David Paul Nord, Karen Orren, Jeffrey L. Pasley, Mark A. Peterson, Robert V. Remini, David Riesman, Michael Schudson, Elaine K. Swift, and Bertram Wyatt-Brown. In addition, I am much indebted to Yale graduate student Robert P. Forbes, who gave the entire manuscript a close and careful reading, and who shared with me his own research on antiabolitionist politics.

Among the unexpected pleasures of my research was the chance it gave me to exchange information and ideas with philatelists, who in recent years have expanded their interests well beyond the study of individual stamps and postal markings. For special favors, I am grateful to Stanley M. Bierman, Richard C. Frajola, Richard B. Graham, Douglas A. Kelsey, Michael Laurence, Steven M. Roth, and Harvey S. Teal. I am particularly grateful to Robert J. Stets, a meticulous scholar who has graciously shared with me his encyclopedic knowledge of American postal history in the decades preceding the War of 1812. And in a class all by themselves are Robert Dalton Harris and Diane DeBlois. In the year since I stumbled upon their remarkable postal history journal, *P.S.*, at the American Philatelic Research Library, I have profited greatly from their renowned hospitality, their extraordinary collection of postal ephemera, and their provocative ruminations on the role of the postal system in the making of the modern world. Few young scholars can be so fortunate as to have encountered such enthusiastic and knowledgeable kindred spirits.

On a more personal note, I would like to extend a word of thanks to my family, who have helped me in countless ways over the years: my father, who inspired in me an abiding interest in American history; my mother, who backed my decision to go to graduate school at a time when job prospects for humanities Ph.D.s seemed unusually grim; my sister, who prayed when I got bogged down; and my brother, who has repeatedly displayed an uncanny knack for figuring out just what it was I was trying to say. Special thanks to Martha Burns, who, in addition to helping edit the text, brought to my attention several documents I would otherwise have missed. No one did more to keep up my spirits as I went through the various rounds of revision. Thanks also to Andrea L. Charters, who heard a good deal about the project in its early stages; to William Braverman, who boosted my spirits during the three memorable years we served together as resident tutors at Mather House; to Bill McKibben, who gave me good advice about how to improve my prose; to Barbara Vance, who helped run down a number of citations; to Kate Layzer, who kept wondering when it would be done; to Nancy L. Reimer, who pitched in at the end; and to Stephan and Abigail M. Thernstrom, who have watched over my academic progress since my freshman year in college and who have cheered me on with good advice and a supportive home away from home. Donna Bouvier expertly edited the manuscript, and Aïda Donald made some sage suggestions as to how it might be improved. Of course, none of these individuals should be held responsible for errors of fact or interpretation, which are mine alone.

Partial funding for my research was provided by the committee on the History of American Civilization travel fund at Harvard University; the Frances Hiatt Fellowship at the American Antiquarian Society; the Western Postal History Museum; the John E. Rovensky Fellowship of the Lincoln Educational Foundation; and the Humanities Institute of the University of Illinois at Chicago. I am particularly indebted to the Commonwealth Center for the Study of American Culture at the College of William and Mary, which gave me the opportunity to refine my ideas in an ideal academic setting as a postdoctoral fellow. Accordingly, I would like to close by expressing my gratitude to Thad Tate and Chandos Brown of the Commonwealth Center for the professionalism with which they oversaw my stay. Without their assistance, and that of the College of William and Mary, it would have been far more difficult to complete the research and writing that has made it possible to expand my dissertation into a book.

A note on the quotations: I have modernized the capitalization, punctuation, and spelling and silently corrected obvious errors in orthography.

· 1 ·

The Postal System as an Agent of Change

"THERE IS AN astonishing circulation of letters and newspapers among these savage woods . . . I do not think that in the most enlightened rural districts of France there is intellectual movement either so rapid or on such a scale as in this wilderness." So wrote the French traveler Alexis de Tocqueville in 1831 as he journeyed by stagecoach through the transappalachian hinterland of Kentucky and Tennessee.[1] Back in France, Tocqueville made a number of calculations, which he included in a footnote to *Democracy in America,* his celebrated survey of American public life. The results confirmed his initial impression. Using postal revenue as an index of intellectual movement, Tocqueville found that the average inhabitant of Michigan territory received a greater volume of nonlocal information than the average inhabitant of the Département du Nord.[2] This discovery was startling because at the time Michigan territory was a thinly populated agricultural district on the extreme western fringe of European settlement while the Département du Nord was a bustling commercial center in the very heart of France. The conclusion seemed inescapable: "There is no French province in which the inhabitants knew each other as well as did the thirteen million men spread over the extent of the United States."[3] Almost in spite of himself, Tocqueville was drawn to the deceptively simple proposition that communication could create culture, that the movement of information could spark the movement of ideas.

Tocqueville's discovery forced him to rethink some of his most basic assumptions. Before arriving in the United States, Tocqueville later recalled, he had assumed that in the United States, as in France, there would be a direct relationship between the wealth, size, and physical endowment of a given locality, and the familiarity of its inhabitants with the wider world. Along the Atlantic seaboard, he thought the population would possess a level of cultural attainment roughly comparable to that of the French bourgeoisie. In the interior, however, the inhabitants would be even more provincial than the peasantry of France. Tocqueville anticipated, in short, that as he traveled from the Atlantic seaboard to the transappalachian West he would be able to journey backward in time, recapitulating in reverse, as it were, the upward ascendancy of humanity from savagery to civilization.[4]

He could not have been more mistaken. When he first arrived in Michigan territory, Tocqueville had fully imagined that the crude log cabins he had glimpsed from his stagecoach window sheltered some "rude and ignorant folk." To his surprise, however, he soon discovered that in all but the most superficial respects the Michigan backwoodsman bore a striking resemblance to the most urbane of the sophisticates that he had encountered back East. The Michigan backwoodsman might live in a simple log cabin at the very edge of European settlement, yet he wore the clothes and spoke the language of the town and was "aware of the past, curious about the future, and ready to argue about the present." Fortified by his Bible, handy with an ax, and—by no means least important—regularly supplied with newspapers to keep him informed of late-breaking developments in the wider world, he was rapidly replicating on the fringes of European settlement the very civilization that he remembered from his youth. He was, in short, neither an ignorant peasant nor some primitive savage, but a "very civilized man" who had temporarily taken up residence in the "wildernesses of the New World." It was, Tocqueville felt sure, a juxtaposition that would have been inconceivable in France.[5]

To impress his French readers with his discovery, Tocqueville appended to *Democracy in America* a vivid description of a ride he took in the stagecoach that brought the Michigan backwoodsman his mail. "We went at a great pace," Tocqueville reminisced, during the night as well as the day, along recently cleared paths that passed through immense forests of evergreens. When the darkness became impenetrable, the stagecoach driver lit a larch branch to illumine the way. From time to time, the driver paused for a moment to drop an enormous bundle at a hut in the forest. The hut, Tocqueville laconically explained, was the post office, and the bundle was the mail. Before long it would be morning, and the backwoodsman would arise and repair to the post office so that he might "fetch his share of that treasure."[6]

*   *   *

2

TOCQUEVILLE'S observations highlight a feature of American public life in the early republic that is too often overlooked. By 1831, two decades before the completion of the first major east-west railroad and thirteen years before the establishment of the first successful electric telegraph, the United States had already been transformed by a communications revolution whose implications had yet to be felt in France.[7]

This communications revolution was a highly complicated event. Like so many of the epochal transformations that have shaped the pattern of everyday life, it was a long revolution: it occurred in an extended territory over an extended period of time. And, like so many of the large-scale processes that have figured conspicuously in the making of the modern world, it was a latent revolution: its full implications went all but unnoticed to the vast majority of the millions of people whose lives it shaped. Still, certain of its features can be described with a fair degree of precision. Most obviously, it involved the transmission of an unprecedented volume of newspapers, letters, and other kinds of information through time and over space. In addition, it was dependent upon the stagecoach, as well as various other horsepowered means of conveyance, to transmit this information. And last but not least, it was set in motion by the postal system, that "great link between minds," as Tocqueville described it, that "penetrates" into the "heart of the wilderness," bringing enlightenment to palace and hovel alike.[8]

The importance of the postal system in Tocqueville's America can be measured in a variety of ways. Consider its size. In 1831, the postal system, with more than 8,700 postmasters, employed just over three-quarters of the *entire* federal civilian work force, mostly as part-time postmasters in villages and towns scattered throughout the countryside (see Table 1.1).[9] The federal army, in contrast, consisted of a mere 6,332 men, most of whom were located at isolated army posts in the transap-

Table 1.1 Postmasters in the federal civilian work force, 1816–1841

Year	Postal officers	All federal officers	Percentage
1816	3,341	4,837	69.1
1821	4,766	6,914	68.9
1831	8,764	11,491	76.3
1841	14,290	18,038	79.2

Source: Historical Statistics of the United States: Colonial Times to 1970 (Washington, D.C.: Government Printing Office, 1975), pt. 2, p. 1103.

Note: Federal officers include civilian employees of the army and navy, but exclude military personnel.

palachian West.[10] In addition, the postal system transmitted 13.8 million letters and 16 million newspapers at a cost of $1.9 million through a network that extended over 116,000 square miles (see Table 1.2).[11] No other branch of the central government penetrated so deeply into the hinterland or played such a conspicuous role in shaping the pattern of everyday life. Indeed, it would hardly be an exaggeration to suggest that for the vast majority of Americans the postal system *was* the central government. Many contemporaries agreed. The enterprise, declared postal authority and onetime postal clerk Pliny Miles, was of more importance to the people, while its daily operations were felt to a "wider extent" and affected a "larger share" of the public at large than the other departments of the central government "all put together."[12]

The importance of the postal system within the American government owed a good deal to the peculiar structure of the American state. In keeping with the intentions of the Founding Fathers, the American political order was federal in the sense that its administration was divided between the central government and the individual states. Under this arrangement, the central government was responsible for a relatively small number of tasks, mostly confined to foreign affairs, while the individual states retained jurisdiction over a wide variety of activities that ranged from the supervision of public morality to the construction

Table 1.2 Letters and newspapers transmitted by the postal system, 1790–1840

Year	Letters (millions)	Letters per capita	Newspapers (millions)	Newspapers per capita
1790	0.3	0.1	0.5	0.2
1800	2.0	0.5	1.9	0.4
1810	3.9	0.7	n.a.	n.a.
1820	8.9	1.1	6.0	0.7
1830	13.8	1.3	16.0	1.5
1840	40.9	2.9	39.0	2.7

Source: letters: Pliny Miles, "History of the Post Office," *Bankers' Magazine,* 7 (1857): 363–364; *newspapers: 1790: Dunlap's American Daily Advertiser* (Philadelphia), Feb. 9, 1792; *1800:* Richard B. Kielbowicz, "The Press, the Post Office, and the Flow of News in the Early Republic," *Journal of the Early Republic,* 3 (1983): 271; *1820, 1830, 1840:* Kielbowicz, *News in the Mail: The Press, Post Office, and Public Information, 1700–1860s* (New York: Greenwood Press, 1989), p. 71; *population: Historical Statistics,* vol. 1, pp. 8, 14.

Note: Population excludes Indians and slaves. All totals are estimates. The newspaper total for 1790 is based on data for 1791; the newspaper total for 1800 is based on data for 1799.

of public works. Following the victory of Thomas Jefferson in the election of 1800, the central government did not even collect any direct taxes, relying instead on the revenue that it obtained from land sales and duties on imported goods.

The anomalous position of the postal system within the American political order can be illustrated by the public clamor that often accompanied the dismissal of a local postmaster. "There is a kind of sleight o'hand and mystery about it," observed the disillusioned Jacksonian John Barton Derby shortly after the large-scale partisan dismissal of postmasters that followed Jackson's inauguration in March 1829, "which for months presses on the hearts of the villagers like an incubus. They go about the streets and . . . seem to be saying to themselves, 'E'cod!—there *is* a United States government, or I'm darned!' For so beautiful is the system of government continued by our wise forefathers, that while the general government of the United States poises and holds together the whole, no man *in the country* ever feels its *direct* action (when it is peacefully and constitutionally administered), excepting in the appointment of a postmaster of his village. And it is only by some irregularity in the system, that he becomes conscious of subjection to higher powers than his own paternal state government."[13]

Perhaps the best way to appreciate the enormous size of the American postal system is by comparing it with postal systems in other parts of the world. By 1828, the American postal system had almost twice as many offices as the postal system in Great Britain and over five times as many offices as the postal system in France. This translated into 74 post offices for every 100,000 inhabitants in comparison with 17 for Great Britain and 4 for France.[14]

Outside of western Europe, the contrast was even more marked. In British North America, or what is now Canada, the postal system provided such a limited level of service that merchants and even public officers grew accustomed to routing their interprovincial mail via the United States.[15] And in Russia the postal system was so restricted that as late as 1896 it consisted of a mere 3 post offices for every 100,000 inhabitants, which was smaller than the comparable total for the United States at the time of the adoption of the federal Constitution in 1788.[16]

No less anomalous than the position of the postal system within the American political order was its position within the economy as a whole. At the time Tocqueville took his stagecoach ride through Michigan territory, the postal work force, with its army of 8,700 postmasters, far exceeded that of any other enterprise in the country. Few of the myriad enterprises that dotted the countryside employed more than a dozen workers, while even the largest textile mills rarely employed more than 300 operatives. Not until the completion of a rudimentary trans-appalachian railroad network in the 1850s would another enterprise emerge whose work force was even remotely comparable. And not until the 1870s, following the reorganization of the Pennsylvania Railroad, would a nongovernmental enterprise decisively outstrip the postal system in size.[17]

Given the size of the American postal system, the scale of its operations, and the volume of mail that it transmitted, it should come as no surprise that its division of labor was unusually complex. Had the enterprise not possessed a sophisticated division of labor, it is hard to imagine how postal officers could possibly have transmitted such an enormous volume of mail.

At the core of this division of labor was a rudimentary three-level administrative hierarchy. At the upper level were the senior clerks who staffed the postal headquarters in Washington; at the middle level the distributing postmasters who staffed the specially designated distribution centers where the bulk of the sorting was done; and at the lower level the local postmasters who staffed the branch depots at which postal patrons sent and received their mail. Far more complicated administrative hierarchies already existed in the burgeoning military and civilian bureaucracies of the major European states. Yet the division of labor in the American postal system was by far the most elaborate to have been established in the early nineteenth-century United States. Even the Bank of the United States, which is often considered the first multi-unit enterprise in the country, had no more than twenty-five branch offices at its peak in 1831, none of which processed, on a regular basis, a volume of transactions that was in any way comparable to the volume of transactions that the postal distribution centers had been processing for thirty years.[18]

The consequences of this division of labor were far reaching. By facilitating the regular transmission of information throughout the length and breadth of the United States, the postal system provided ordinary Americans with information about the wider world that they could obtain in no other way. Of course, in no sense were ordinary Americans exclusively dependent on the postal system for nonlocal information. The Michigan backwoodsman might have learned a good deal from peddlers, merchants, and other sojourners who were in the vicinity or passing through. He might have profited from the chance to read the myriad pamphlets, handbills, broadsides, and religious tracts that made their way into the hinterland. And, if he were lucky, he might even have received a letter that had been hand carried by a family member, a friend, or perhaps even a perfect stranger. But in one crucial respect, the information that the backwoodsman received from the postal system was unique. In Tocqueville's America, the postal system and the postal system alone had the capacity to broadcast regularly and throughout the length and breadth of the United States the time-specific information about the wider world that was commonly called news. Just as the tolling of the village bell introduced the peasantry of Europe to the linear logic of the mechanical clock, so the regular arrival of the mail extended this linear logic to the farthest reaches of the transappalachian West. News, after all, is a perishable commodity; like meat, eggs, or cheese, it quickly goes stale. Indeed, it may well be the periodical character of the information that the postal system transmitted that most sharply differentiated the information that Americans received in this way from the other kinds of information that were available to them at the time.[19]

Just as the form of the information that the postal system transmitted was novel, so too was its content. Thanks to a variety of generous government subsidies, a large percentage of the total volume of the mail consisted of newspapers, magazines, and public documents that described the proceedings of Congress and the routine workings of the central government. This steady flow of information in turn helped to introduce a widely scattered population to two key ideas: that the boundaries of the community in which they lived extended well beyond the confines of their individual locality, state, or region, and coincided more or less with the territorial limits of the United States; and that the central government might come to shape the pattern of everyday life. In our own media-saturated age, it may require a willing suspension of disbelief to understand how the postal system could once have played such a role. Yet only if we take this step will it become possible to understand Tocqueville's America, a world in which the press was the principal mass medium, the stagecoach an important form of public transportation, and the postal system a powerful agent of change.

IN AN ENCYCLOPEDIA article published in 1832, the celebrated political theorist Francis Lieber made a remarkable claim. The postal system, Lieber declared, deserved to be ranked with the printing press and the mariner's compass as "one of the most effective elements of civilization."[20] In an age that venerated the printed word and in which the mariner's compass remained a vital navigational aid, it would be hard to imagine how anyone might have described the enterprise in a more favorable light.

From a contemporary standpoint, Lieber's claim may strike us as more than a little odd. After all, we have grown accustomed to relying upon postelectronic norms in estimating the relationship between time, space, and speed, and are rightly skeptical of the inflated claims that are sometimes made for mass communications as an agent of change. Yet Lieber was not trying to be provocative. Rather he was merely repeating what was fast becoming a nineteenth-century truism. By the time Tocqueville arrived in the United States, it had become something of a commonplace to hail the rapid expansion of the postal system as one of the most notable features of American public life. "Among the improvements in the United States," declared one commentator in 1809, none had advanced more rapidly, or proved "more extensively useful" than the transportation of the mail.[21] Its "great business," reported mail contractor Isaac Hill, after having visited postal headquarters in 1818, was "managed with the regularity of the machinery of a clock," while the network itself was by then so extensive that there was scarcely a town in the country, no matter how remote, whose inhabitants could not communicate with the most distant parts of the Union through this new "medium."[22] The expansion of the postal system, agreed a Washington newspaper editor a few years later, was "well calculated to excite our wonder . . . Its progress . . . has been so rapid as almost to stagger belief, and did we not know its history to be true, it might pass and be received as a romantic tale, having no foundation but in the regions of fancy, in the wanderings of imagination."[23]

For many commentators, the single most notable feature of the American postal system was the extent to which it had come to surpass the postal systems of the much-admired ancient civilizations of Greece and Rome. Today, of course, few would find it particularly surprising that the moderns had surpassed the ancients in this regard: it is, after all, no longer fashionable to invest modern enterprises with an ancient pedigree.[24] In the early republic, however, many Americans found it important to highlight the superiority of the American postal system to its Greek and Roman predecessors, if only because so many accounts of the enterprise—including Lieber's—prefaced their discussion of the modern postal system with a survey of the postal systems of the ancients. Like the dynastic genealogies of the Bible, one postal system begat another in a seemingly endless procession of names, places, and dates.

One of the first notable accounts to stress the superiority of the moderns over the ancients appeared in 1820 in a popular woman's magazine. After briefly surveying the history of the postal systems of the world, the author claimed to be "astonished" to recall that the Greeks and Romans had never established a postal system open to the public at large.[25] Before long, commentators began to draw attention to the absence of a public postal system in the ancient world as evidence of the superiority of the modern age. Should the ancient Greek historian Herodotus visit the present-day United States, predicted the Congregationalist minister Leonard Bacon in 1843, he would find "hardly anything" more "wonderful" than its postal system. After all, Bacon added, the postal system transmitted, reliably and at great speed, the correspondence not only of emperors and kings, as had all the postal systems with which Herodotus would have been familiar, but also of the public at large. As a minister, Bacon found it particularly noteworthy that Paul, the early Christian apostle, had sent all of his celebrated epistles by private conveyance. Not even Jesus, Bacon mused, had ever sent a letter through the mail.[26]

To highlight the distinctiveness of this state of affairs, Bacon modified Lieber's well known characterization of the postal system. The postal system, Bacon now contended, was not merely an "element of civilization," but an "element of modern civilization," that is, an element that was distinctive to the particular historical epoch within which he lived. The Romans, agreed Pliny Miles, may well have possessed a fine road network, yet they lacked a postal system that penetrated into the hinterland and that was open to the public. The postal system, he concluded, was "essentially" modern.[27] "Athens had her Parthenon," reflected Yale undergraduate Albert Bigelow, yet no modern postal system. The antecedents of this important enterprise, Bigelow added, might well be coextensive with civilization itself, yet the enterprise itself was still "in the vigor and bloom of youth . . . As we listen in vain amid the many voices of the past for the whoop of the locomotive, and the rattling of the steam press, so, fruitless will be our search for the myriad boxes of the post office, and for the vast system of agencies established to give them efficacy."[28]

Once contemporaries concluded that the modern postal system had no real counterpart in the ancient world, they found themselves scrambling to devise an appropriate language to describe its operations. Some turned, plausibly enough, to the other large-scale institutions of the day. When he entered postal headquarters, reported Maine Congressman Francis O. J. Smith in 1835, he immediately discovered an "immensity of detail and labor" that exceeded the annual operations of "almost any state government in the Union." The division of labor within the general post office, Smith added, reminded him of nothing so much as a Lowell textile mill.[29] For Bacon, its "wonderful machinery" reminded him of the railroad and the pin factory, two of the technological marvels of the age. After all, Bacon explained, the postal system took up a letter when you dropped it into one of its ten thousand hoppers, transmitted it hundreds of miles with a speed and security that would be otherwise impracticable, and delivered it to the very individual to whom it had been addressed: "Why this is a machinery which, in a sense, extends your presence over the whole country, even to the edge of the wilderness, where the last traces of government and of civilized life disappear."[30]

Many compared the postal system to parts of the human body. For one *New York Times* correspondent, it was that "mighty arm of civil government" without whose cooperation the press would be "crippled and disabled."[31] For Maryland Congressman William D. Merrick, it was the circulatory system that transmitted the "knowledge" that was necessary to keep "pure republicanism" alive.[32] And for South Carolina Congressman John C. Calhoun, it was the nervous system of the "body politic" that, in conjunction with the press, transmitted sensory impressions from the extremities to the brain: "By them, the slightest impression made on the most remote parts is communicated to the whole system."[33]

A surprising number of contemporaries compared the transmission of information through the postal system with the movement of electricity. Long before the electric telegraph was credited with having "annihilated" time and space, the postal system had been described in precisely the same way. "A few days," reported a country curate in 1820, carries a communication with "mathematical certainty" throughout the United States. "Distance is thus reduced almost to contiguity; and the ink is scarcely dry, or the wax cold on the paper, before we find in our hands, even at a distance of hundreds of miles, a transcript of our dearest friend's mind." Others were even more effusive in describing the effects that the postal system had brought about. "Time and distance are annihilated," exclaimed one writer in 1831, describing the effects of the receipt of a letter from a childhood friend, and "we are *there*."[34] The information the postal system transmitted, reflected Bacon in 1843, was like "the electric stream."[35] Indeed, it would be hard to isolate a single bit of figurative language that commentators used to describe the electric telegraph in the period following its commercialization in 1844 that had not already been deployed to describe the postal system. The convention persisted, curiously enough, even after 1844. "Touch the wire at one end," declared letter carrier James Rees in 1866, in reference to a recent improvement in international mail, "and its vibration may tend to enlighten even the land of the heathen."[36]

Most common of all were comparisons rooted in literary theory, and, above all, in the distinctive literary idiom that the eighteenth-century moral philosopher Edmund Burke termed the sublime. Indeed, it would hardly be an exaggeration to say that by midcentury a rhetoric of the bureaucratic sublime—with its curious mingling of pity and terror, wonder and dread—had firmly established itself as a dominant motif in popular discussions of the postal system in the press. Perhaps not surprisingly, this motif appeared repeatedly in the writings of the men who had devoted a good deal of their working lives to the enterprise. In no other country, declared Postmaster General John McLean in 1828, did there exist a "civil branch of governmental operation" that could equal the American postal system in its extent, or that embraced "so great a variety of interests."[37] The history of the enterprise, exulted postal agent James Holbrook a few years later, had by this time become "interwoven" with the whole social life of civilized man: "How society in the nineteenth century could exist without mail routes and the regular delivery of letters, it is impossible to conceive. Imagine a town without a post office! a community without letters! 'friends, Romans, countrymen, and lovers,' particularly the lovers, cut off from correspondence, bereft of newspapers, buried alive from the light of intelligence, and the busy stir of the great world! What an appalling picture!"[38] What would happen, wondered Pliny Miles around the same time, if the postal system should suspend its operations for one short month? "How disastrous would be the result, in a mercantile community! How much, often times, is depending on a single letter! What heart-burnings, what losses and calamities, sometimes occur in consequence of a delay of a single day! Of what importance, then, is every wheel and axle in this vast machine! What a type of perpetual motion!"[39]

Postal officers may have been among the most energetic popularizers of the rhetoric of the bureaucratic sublime, yet they were hardly alone.

For Ohio editor John S. Williams, the very sight of a table of postal statistics was enough to inspire him with an almost religious awe. "Are you not mute in astonishment?" Williams exclaimed. "And do you not tremble lest some mighty jar with one tremendous crash will tumble all to ruins?"[40] For German-born journalist Francis Grund, the postal system had, in conjunction with the periodical press, done more to change the "face of the world" than "half a million of philosophers" or "the bayonets of all the nations of Europe"; while, in conjunction with the periodical press and the spirit of Christianity, it had "revolutionized the world."[41] And for Georgia congressman Absalom H. Chappell, the power of the enterprise had become "so great, so growing, so penetrating and pervading" that had the Founding Fathers not specifically entrusted its administration to the central government, it would be dangerous for the government to administer it at all. After all, Chappell added, its administration involved the government in the carrying trade on a "vast scale" and required the organization of a "huge and distinct administrative department," which, in its operations, touched "daily and intimately the private affairs as well as public interests of the people."[42]

Not to be outdone was Francis Lieber, who returned to the theme in a magazine article in 1841. The postal system, Lieber now declared, deserved to be classed as the "most striking example" of the "immense effects" of the "division and union of labor." As such, Lieber observed, it was one of the "most deeply interesting subjects," whether considered in light of history, political economy, politics, ethics, or as the "truest handmaid of writing and printing."[43] To illustrate his point, Lieber pondered the historical significance of an ordinary letter that a postal patron had sent from Germany to an immigrant family in the interior of the United States. Such a letter, Lieber explained, with its arcane postal markings in a variety of languages, was a fitting emblem of the kinds of changes that the postal system was helping to bring about. After all, Lieber added, during the entire course of its journey, the letter had been completely outside the control of both its sender and its recipient, the only people who had the slightest personal interest in its delivery. Yet, like millions of similar letters that had been sent in the same way, it reached its destination. All things considered, Lieber concluded, this was a remarkable achievement: "What order, what a chain of trust and confidence in one another, what degree of international good-will, how vast and systematic an arrangement—indeed, how gigantic must not an institution be to bring about such an effect, and which, extending over whole families of nations, is nevertheless able to carry its blessings into the meanest cottage!"[44] In a private letter to Postmaster General Charles Wickliffe, Lieber underscored his basic point. The postal system, Lieber grandly declared, was one of the "most powerful agents of civilization" whose significance could be denied by "no one who pays the least attention to history."[45]

However suggestive these accounts may have appeared to contemporaries, they left many issues unresolved. How, precisely, did the postal system bring about its much-vaunted effects? Here, too, contemporaries had a good deal to say. For Grund, the key to its historical significance lay less in the content of the information that it conveyed than in its form. A given newspaper article, Grund conceded, might not exert as great an influence as a particularly moving speech. But if the message were repeated again and again, its effect was sure to be far more profound.[46]

For William Ellery Channing, the significance of the enterprise lay in its role in linking together the far-flung population of the United States. Many Americans, Channing conceded in 1829, probably considered the role of the postal system in facilitating the transmission of information between the government and the citizenry to be its most important "national service." But such a conclusion overlooks its "highest benefit." However important the postal system may be for the government, it does "incomparably more for us as a community." No other channel of intercourse can so effectively bind the "whole country" in a "chain of sympathies" and in this way transform it from a confederation of separate states into "one great neighborhood."[47] In this way, Channing anticipated by over a century the well known aphorism of media critic Marshall McLuhan that communications technology was fast transforming the world into a global village. Yet had Channing written a few years later, it is highly unlikely that he would have been so sanguine. By 1835, with the interdiction of the periodicals that abolitionists had attempted to send through the postal system by slaveholders intent upon preserving their own sectional community from outside assault, the very process that Channing had hoped would bring Americans together became a potent engine for driving them apart, setting the country on a collision course that would culminate in civil war.

Most commentators were content, like Channing and Grund, to confine their discussion of the postal system to a sentence or two in a work that was primarily devoted to some other theme. For Eli Bowen, however, the subject called for considerably more elaboration. A journalist and onetime postal clerk with a flair for literary exposition, Bowen combined an abiding faith in the postal system as an agent of change with a fervent admiration for Henry Clay, the statesman who had dedicated his public career to mobilizing the resources of the central government to strengthen the bonds of the Union. Like Channing, Bowen looked to the postal system to help unite the country. Notwithstanding the growing sectional rift between North and South, Bowen declared in 1851, "'Uncle Sam's' mail routes" still linked with "iron bonds" the "citadel of abolitionism in the North" and the "hot-bed of secession in the South."[48] In addition, Bowen stressed the role of the postal system in facilitating the direct participation of a far-flung citizenry in public affairs.

To make his point, Bowen compared public life in the modern United States with public life in ancient Greece and Rome. "We hear nothing," Bowen observed, of the "free and independent yeomanry" of antiquity; that is, of that class of landowning citizen-farmers who could participate in public life without ever leaving the farm. How could this be? The answer lay in the failure of the Greeks and Romans to establish a postal system that was open, like the American postal system, to the public at large. Given this failure of the imagination, the Greeks and Romans had no choice but to establish democratic regimes in which the major political decisions were made by that portion of the citizenry that had the necessary means to take part directly in public affairs, rather than republican regimes in which the citizenry participated indirectly in the political process through the periodic election of representatives. Should a Greek or Roman citizen-farmer wish to take part in public affairs, he had no choice but to leave his farm and move to the city, since he needed a good deal of information to participate effectively in public affairs, while this information was necessarily restricted to those individuals who lived in close physical proximity to the seat of power. It was for this reason, Bowen added, that no Greek or Roman political philosopher had ever invented the idea of representative government. The "sole reason" they had never come up with this idea, Bowen explained, was because they lacked a "sufficient *medium* of communication." Had such a medium existed, they would have thought of the idea at once: they were, after all, "as wise as we are." But under the circumstances, no ancient political philosopher could possibly have imagined that the interests of a rural landowner could be represented by someone a "thousand miles off." And had by some fluke such a scheme been adopted, it would have proved an "utter abortion

. . . The government would have rotted down in five years." A similar fate, Bowen added, would have long ago befallen the government of the United States had this "important defect" not been "abundantly supplied" by the postal system and the press.[49]

Luckily for the United States, the situation was quite different. Thanks to the postal system, the citizen-farmer had no trouble securing access to a steady flow of information on public affairs, making it possible for him to participate in national politics without leaving the farm. In the short term, Bowen predicted, this guaranteed that the postal system would foster geographical expansion, economic prosperity, and political stability, notwithstanding the looming sectional conflict between the slaveholding and the nonslaveholding states. And in the long term, Bowen added, it would spread these benefits to all the peoples of the world: "While printing held forth a flaming torch, to guide the steps of man to a higher and nobler destiny than he had previously known, the establishment of posts, in systematic order, conveyed its benignant rays to the four quarters of the globe, penetrating its darkened regions, and equalizing, elevating, and harmonizing . . . the social position and geographical distribution of the people."[50] Not even Francis Lieber ever offered a more enthusiastic tribute to the postal system as an agent of change.

GIVEN THE VOLUME of praise that nineteenth-century commentators heaped on the postal system, one might suppose that its history would occupy a prominent place in modern accounts of the making of the modern United States. After all, historians customarily heed the judgment of informed contemporaries and organize their narratives around themes rooted in the language of the day.

In the case of the postal system, however, this has yet to occur. To a surprising degree, its history has been entirely overlooked, with most general accounts including no more than a token sentence or two about the role of the postal system in American public life. With the exception of a number of specialized studies of particular topics, the postal system remains the "important," yet "virtually unknown," institution that one historian proclaimed it to be in 1974.[51]

This neglect is all the more surprising given the frequency with which historians have been called upon to rectify the situation. "It is well known," declared the compiler of a collection of postal documents as long ago as 1838, "that little has been systematically published on the past history of the post office department in our country."[52] "Our schoolbooks contain no allusions to it," reported letter carrier James Rees three decades later, "nor are its officers mentioned with any marks of commendation in any of our national works."[53] Almost a century later, surprisingly little had changed. In 1951, the respected economic historian George Rogers Taylor lamented the absence of a "detailed scholarly study" of the Jacksonian postal system, while many others have urged their peers to chronicle the role of the enterprise in American public life.[54] "One wonders how a meaningful history of American business can be written," observed one in 1960, "without an understanding of the contribution of the postal service."[55] Historians need to pay more attention, added another in 1975, to the "mechanisms of print dissemination" as they became "increasingly larger and more complex."[56] "We need many more institutional histories of these early bureaucracies," declared a third a few years later.[57] "An adequate general theory of modern historical development," agreed a fourth more recently still, must give more weight to "nationalist sentiments, 'reasons of state,' and the independent concerns of governmental elites and bureaucracies."[58]

In explaining why the history of the postal system has been so neglected, a variety of considerations come to mind. Perhaps the most obvious is the challenge of gaining at least a rudimentary mastery over the enormous volume of primary source material, much of which is widely scattered. In the period between 1789 and 1840, the letterbooks of the postmaster general alone occupy over twelve feet of shelf space at the National Archives in Washington, D.C., while over five hundred congressional documents detail its routine operations and a hundred pamphlets describe the various controversies with which it became embroiled. In addition, over one hundred fifty manuscript collections scattered in twenty-four states and the District of Columbia provide important insights into the workings of the postal system at the local level. So overwhelming is the sheer bulk of information that a century ago postal historian Carl A. Ernst noted that it has served to deter rather than attract historians who might otherwise have been intrigued by the theme.[59] In the intervening years, little has changed. Indeed, it may well be this single circumstance that best explains why so many projected histories of the American postal system have never appeared in the form in which they had been originally planned. Prior to the invention of microfilm and the photocopier, few historians had the necessary resources to complete the work.

Yet even had historians flocked to the topic, they might well have found themselves discouraged by a pair of misconceptions that have obscured the full significance of the role of the postal system in the American past. The first concerns the character of long-distance communication in the pre-electronic era, the second the role of the central government in American public life.

From the standpoint of the postelectronic present, it is easy to understand why so many historians have characterized long-distance communication in the early republic as notoriously poor. Complaints about poor mail delivery abound in the personal correspondence from the period as well as in the press. Rarely, however, have historians paused to consider the interpretative questions that are raised by these complaints. How representative are they? Are they truly indicative of a genuinely low level of service? Or, alternatively, might they not reflect the degree to which a comparatively high level of service had come to be taken for granted?

Similar questions are raised by the issue of speed. By present-day standards, the movement of the mail in the early republic was unbelievably slow. Even the fastest mounted horse express, after all, almost never exceeded an average speed of twelve miles per hour. Yet is this the relevant comparison? No one in Tocqueville's America, after all, could possibly have imagined that it would one day be feasible to routinely transmit information at the speed of light. Indeed, even to speak of a pre-electronic period—or, for that matter, of a time lag in the transmission of information—is to risk perpetuating a myth, since it presupposes that there is a single, transhistorical standard against which the movement of information ought to be judged.

Informed contemporaries saw things quite differently. Impressed by the magnitude of the improvements that the government had introduced, they contrasted the high level of service that Americans enjoyed in the present with the far more limited facilities that had existed in the period before 1788. " 'Old Times'—Or Seventy Years Ago," ran the headline for a New Jersey newspaper article in 1825 that compared postal schedules of the colonial period with postal schedules of the present day.[60] The recent improvements in mail arrangements, observed jurist Joseph Story in 1833, reminded him of nothing so much as the "wonders of magic" in comparison with the "imbecile expedients of former times."[61] Fifty years ago, recorded postal clerk Jesse Dow in 1839, it took forty days to receive a reply to a letter sent from Portland, Maine, to Savannah, Georgia, and thirty-two days to receive a reply to a letter sent from Philadelphia to Lexington, Kentucky. By 1810, however, the government had reduced the Portland-Savannah reply time to twenty-seven days and the Philadelphia-Lexington reply time to sixteen days; and by 1839, to a mere twelve and eight days respectively, an improvement on the Philadelphia-Lexington route of a staggering 400 percent.[62] During the War of Independence, reported the editor of the *Farmers' Monthly Visitor* in 1852, the local post office had been open only twice a week, "but now our go-ahead-ativeness is hardly satisfied with three mails a day . . . Of a surety this is an age of progress!"[63]

Few contemporaries left a more revealing account of these improvements than Eliza Quincy, a Massachusetts matron with a keen eye for detail. To highlight the contrast between past and present, Quincy described a trip that she took in the 1780s across New Jersey with the postrider, one Mr. Martin, or, as Quincy called him, "the Post." Mr. Martin, Quincy explained, was a remarkable old man who projected a "sort of military appearance," outfitted as he was in a brightly colored uniform that included a blue coat with yellow buttons, a scarlet waistcoat, blue yarn stockings, and a red wig topped by a cocked hat. Yet what Quincy found most remarkable about Mr. Martin was not his appearance, but his pace. So slowly did Martin ride from office to office, Quincy reminisced, that he balanced his horse between his knees, freeing up his hands so that he could knit himself a pair of socks. "He certainly did not ride *post*," Quincy added, or at least he did not do so according to the "present meaning of that term," by which she meant not only that Mr. Martin had failed to adjust his movements to fit the rhythms of the horse, but also that his conduct bore little resemblance to the speed-conscious postriders with which the American postal system in the early republic had become inextricably linked.[64]

Just as historians have underestimated the importance of improvements in the means of communication in the pre-electronic past, so too they have neglected the role of the central government as an agent of change.[65] Examples of this neglect recur with predictable regularity in the writings of many of the leading historians of the period. In the early republic, one historian has wryly observed, the central government was a "midget institution in a giant land."[66] At no point in American history, declared another, was it "more feeble."[67] Its "weakness," added a third, was "pathetic."[68] By any "candid view," conceded a fourth, it was not "one of the important institutions in American society."[69] "National administration," concluded a fifth, had "little effect on the social, economic, religious, and intellectual developments that were shaping American civilization."[70]

While the neglect of the central government has been particularly widespread in recent years, it is by no means confined to the recent past. After all, over a century and a half ago Alexis de Tocqueville ventured a remarkably similar assessment in his *Democracy in America*. "Nothing strikes a European traveler in the United States more," Tocqueville declared, in one of the most oft-quoted passages of an oft-quoted work, "than the absence of what we would call government or administration. One knows that there are written laws there and sees them put into execution every day; everything is in motion around you, but the motive force is nowhere apparent. The hand directing the social machine constantly slips from notice."[71] Tocqueville may have been impressed with the influence of the postal system on the Michigan frontier, yet when he came to writing his conclusions, he failed to discuss the system in a chapter of its own, relegating it instead to footnotes, though he did manage to find room in his text for chapters on newspapers, literature, and even parliamentary eloquence.

Tocqueville's dismissive account of the role of the central government in American public life has often been cited approvingly even by historians who are critical of other features of his work. Only rarely, however, have these historians paused to consider just how atypical a view it was among the leading public men of the day. Francis Lieber may have been unusually forthright in his stress upon the central government as an agent of change, yet he was hardly alone. Throughout the United States, public figures brooded darkly about the growing role of the central government in shifting the delicate balance of power between the central government and the states. Even Tocqueville admitted as much. Anxiety about the recent expansion of the central government, Tocqueville observed, was the "one great fear" that preoccupied virtually all of the public figures with whom he met.[72] Tocqueville found it impossible to take this anxiety seriously, given the relatively decentralized character of the American political order in comparison with that of France. Yet Tocqueville's own discussion of long-distance communication in *Democracy in America* undercuts his analysis by highlighting the role of the postal system in shaping the pattern of everyday life. Here was one instance in which Tocqueville's oft-disparaged gift for observation outpaced his celebrated power of analysis; here Francis Lieber proved to be the more perceptive student of American public life.

The reasons for this general neglect of the role of the central government in American public life are complex. In large measure, it is a product of the sea change in historical sensibility that accompanied the emergence of the United States as a world power. In comparison with the formidable military-industrial complex that has emerged since the Second World War, the central government in the early republic has almost inevitably come to seem puny, unimportant, almost quaint. But once again, one wonders if this is the relevant frame of reference. The inhabitants of the early republic could not possibly have anticipated the changes that were yet to occur. From their standpoint, the relevant comparison was the far weaker administrative apparatus that had existed prior to the adoption of the federal Constitution in 1788.

Another reason for this neglect has been the common presumption among recent historians that the engines of historical change are large-scale social processes, such as commercialization and demographic expansion, in which public policy has played at best an incidental role. For these historians, as a trio of sociologists have perceptively declared, it has become virtually an article of faith that at some fundamental level social processes originating in the realm of family and work must have "absolute causal primacy" over social processes set in motion by public policy, or, put more broadly, that changes originating in the realm of society are necessarily more fundamental than changes originating in the realm of the state.[73]

The influence of these society-centered premises on historians of the early republic has been particularly marked. Unwilling to consider the possibility that public policy may have been a historical agent in its own right, these writers have shifted our attention away from the history of government and toward the history of the supposedly underlying sources of social change. As one such historian put it, in summarizing this now common view, it would be a serious mistake to subordinate the analysis of these "social structures and relations" to the study of mere "political institutions."[74] As a consequence, they have dismissed altogether, almost as a point of pride, the possibility that political institutions such as the postal system might have played an important role in shaping the pattern of the past. This is doubly unfortunate. In addition to assuming away the very phenomenon whose insignificance they ought to prove, these historians have popularized the highly misleading belief that the many public figures in the early republic who were deeply disturbed by the growing role of the central government in American public life had profoundly misunderstood the most pressing public issues of the day.

*   *   *

20

To BE SURE, the history of the postal system has not been entirely neglected. Over the course of the past century and a half, a number of individuals have made valuable contributions to our understanding of the role of the postal system in American public life. Generally speaking, these works fall into three categories: internalist studies, which chronicle the major developments in postal administration; externalist studies, which link the institution to its environment; and contextualist studies, which locate the institution within its political, cultural, and economic setting.

The internalist studies are by far the oldest of the three, and can be said to go back as far back as 1831, when postal clerk Edmund F. Brown announced the impending publication of his "Annals of the Post Office Department of the United States from the year 1677 to 1831." Had Brown published his book in the form that he had originally intended, it would have been the most elaborate survey of American postal history to have appeared in the antebellum period. According to the preliminary announcements that Brown issued to generate publicity for the work, it was to consist of over four hundred pages of text and was to include an overview of the principal events in American postal history as well as a sampling of the most important public documents bearing on postal affairs. Such a mass of information, Brown confidently proclaimed, would assuredly be of interest to all who wished to become acquainted with "one of the most important institutions of the country."[75] Unfortunately for the cause of American postal history, Brown abandoned the project and his "Annals" never found its way into print. All that remains is a disappointingly brief manuscript in the Library of Congress, the bulk of which was published in 1842 in an Ohio historical magazine.[76]

Notably more successful was Brown's fellow clerk Jesse Dow, who published an informative article on the history of the postal system in the *United States Magazine and Democratic Review* in 1839. Though Dow's article had a decidedly Jacksonian slant — it underplayed the major postal finance scandal that followed the inauguration of Andrew Jackson in 1829 and exaggerated the role of Postmaster General Amos Kendall in the ensuing reforms — it remains a valuable firsthand account of postal administration in the half-century following the adoption of the federal Constitution.[77] In the next few years, Dow was joined by a trio of postal colleagues — Peter G. Washington, Pliny Miles, and Daniel D. T. Leech — each of whom published highly detailed studies that, like Dow's, drew on their own firsthand experience with postal affairs.[78]

This tradition reached its culmination in 1872 with the publication of the *Autobiography of Amos Kendall,* a seven-hundred-page biography of the Jacksonian postmaster general that Kendall's son-in-law William Stickney published three years after Kendall's death.[79] Notwithstanding its length, the *Autobiography* is surprisingly sketchy in its treatment of several key episodes in Kendall's postal career and extremely partisan in its overall approach. Unfortunately, these limitations have only slowly been appreciated by historians, leading in some cases to the popularization of a highly distorted account of the course of events.

With the publication of Kendall's *Autobiography,* the first phase of historical writing on the postal system came to a close. And for a generation, the topic was largely forgotten. Not until the First World War would the history of the enterprise in the early republic once again command attention, this time by academically trained social scientists interested in the role of political institutions in American public life. The most important figures in this second phase of historical writing were Wesley Everett Rich, a promising Harvard-trained economist who died prematurely of influenza at the age of twenty-nine, and Leonard D. White, a University of Chicago political scientist and a leading student of the history of public administration in the United States. Rich's contribution took the form of a monograph on the history of postal policy in the two and a half centuries preceding the inauguration of Andrew Jackson, while White's consisted of a series of chapters in his magisterial history of American public administration between 1787 and 1900.[80] To this day, they remain the necessary starting point for serious students of the early history of postal administration in the United States.

When Rich received his Ph.D. in 1917, the preparation of tightly focused, empirically based monographs on political institutions remained a standard rite of passage for graduate students in history, economics, and political science. During the past few decades, however, the study of political institutions has been relegated to the margins of historical scholarship. Convinced that previous scholars had greatly exaggerated the role of public policy in shaping the pattern of the past, and intent upon expanding the range of historical inquiry to embrace the study of society as a whole, an entire generation of scholars has turned its attention away from the study of political institutions, almost to the point of proscribing altogether the very area of inquiry that had once been such a prominent focus of scholarly concern.

Given the widespread disdain among many scholars today for the study of political institutions, it should come as no surprise that much of the most influential recent scholarship on the history of the postal system focuses on the relationship of the enterprise to the external environment. Key figures in this externalist tradition include social historian Lynn L. Marshall, political scientist Matthew A. Crenson, and historical geographer Allan R. Pred. For Marshall, changes in postal policy are the product of the "bureaucratization" of American society; for Crenson, they are a response to the collapse of traditional structures of social relations; and for Pred, they are an artifact of the dynamics of urban growth.[81] While these conclusions are often suggestive, they have proved to be of limited assistance to me in the preparation of this book since they are predicated upon a number of highly questionable assumptions about the nature of social change.

Less sweeping in its conclusions, yet far better grounded in the relevant sources, is the growing body of scholarship that locates the postal system within its historical context. Major recent studies include Richard B. Kielbowicz's lucid exploration of the relationship of the postal system and the newspaper press and Oliver W. Holmes and Peter T. Rohrbach's engaging survey of the relationship of the postal system and the stagecoach industry.[82] Particularly notable for its breadth of vision is Wayne E. Fuller's *American Mail,* a deftly written survey of the entire sweep of American postal history published in 1972; to this day, it remains the best general introduction to the role of the enterprise in American public life. To a far greater extent than the internalists, Fuller is sensitive to the complex interrelationship between the postal system and the wider world, and to a far greater extent than the externalists, he has chosen to make the postal system his primary focus of concern. Yet even Fuller is ultimately less interested in the role of the postal system as an agent of change than he is in its role in creating an arena within which various social groups—the South and West versus the North and East and, more broadly, the "people" versus "business"—struggled for control of the American state.[83]

SPREADING THE NEWS is intended as a contribution to this contextualist tradition. Central to my inquiry is the conviction that the American postal system in its first seventy years was much more than an arena within which various social groups struggled for control of the levers of power. Like all large-scale enterprises the American postal system was firmly embedded in its social context. Yet given its size, scale, and administrative complexity, it is highly implausible that it would merely be a mirror for changes originating in some other realm. No less than the highway system or the industrial corporation, the postal system itself was an agent of change. My intention, in short, is not merely to locate the postal system *in* the social process, but to explore its role *as* a social process, and, in particular, to consider some of the ways in which the communications revolution that it set in motion transformed American public life.

In no sense was this transformation foreordained. No one in 1775, or even 1788, could possibly have anticipated the full magnitude of the changes that were about to occur. And only in part were these changes the product of monster abstractions like commercialization or demographic expansion. No less important was the reconstitution of American postal policy that the Founding Fathers set in motion with the passage of the Post Office Act of 1792. So far reaching were the implications of this landmark piece of legislation that it is worth considering whether the single most revolutionary era in the entire history of American communications may well have taken place in the half-century *preceding* the commercialization of the electric telegraph in 1844.

The chapters that follow elaborate on this theme. Chapters 2, 3, and 4 consider the challenge that the communications revolution posed for American public life, focusing, respectively, on the passage of the Post Office Act of 1792, the completion of the national postal network that the act brought into existence, and the implications of this achievement for the millions of Americans scattered throughout the United States.[84] The remaining three chapters focus, respectively, on the challenge to postal policy posed by the Sabbatarians, who were opposed to the transmission of the mail on the Sabbath; the Jacksonians, who were hostile to the growing influence of the postmaster general in national politics; and the slaveholders, who were outraged by the determination of abolitionists to organize a mass mailing to transform public attitudes toward slavery. In each of these controversies, the postal system was far more than the arena within which the action was staged. Rather, in a variety of subtle and not-so-subtle ways, it shaped the public issues that these controversies raised and the social divisions that they spawned. And in the course of this complicated drama of challenge and response, the political persuasion that has come to be known as Jacksonian Democracy was born and, with it, some of the most enduring features of American public life.[85]

· 2 ·

The Communications Revolution

IN THE FOUR DECADES between the adoption of the federal Constitution in 1788 and the victory of Andrew Jackson in the election of 1828, the American postal system expanded from the minor adjunct of a neo-colonial bureaucracy to the central administrative apparatus of an independent state. This remarkable transformation was set in motion with the Post Office Act of 1792, a landmark in American communications policy and one of the most important single pieces of legislation to have been enacted by Congress in the early republic. Prior to 1792, the American postal system remained constrained by the assumptions that had shaped royal postal policy for British North America in the period prior to the War of Independence. After 1792, it was rapidly transformed into a dynamic institution that would exert a major influence on American commerce, politics, and political thought.

IN THE SEVENTEEN-YEAR period between 1775 and 1792, the American postal system was little more than a mirror image of the royal postal system for British North America as it had existed in the period prior to 1775.[1] Like the royal postal system, it was expected to generate a revenue that could help the central government defray its routine expenses; like the royal postal system, it was confined to a chain of offices that linked the major port towns along the Atlantic seaboard; and like the royal postal system, it offered no special facilities for the press. The similarities between the two institutions were highlighted by a rate chart listing the cost of mailing a letter from office to office that Benjamin Franklin issued shortly after his appointment as the first postmaster general of the soon-to-be-independent United States in 1775. In all but the most superficial respects, Franklin's chart was identical to a similar chart that he had prepared ten years earlier as deputy postmaster general for the royal postal system under the Crown.[2]

The fiscal rationale for postal policy received classic expression in William Blackstone's influential *Commentaries on the Law of England,* first published in 1765. "There cannot be devised," Blackstone observed, a "more eligible method . . . of raising money."[3] Long after the break with Great Britain, this rationale remained influential in the United States, with public figures taking it more or less for granted that postage, like the duties on imported goods, should be treated as a tax. Postage, explained New York financier Gouverneur Morris in 1777, echoing Blackstone almost word for word, was the "most agreeable tax ever invented," since it constituted payment for a service that the taxpayer could conveniently secure in no other way.[4] Though postal revenue never contributed as much to the treasury in the United States as it did in Great Britain, and while the fiscal rationale was soon challenged by congressmen eager to reinvest postal revenue to improve the level of service, the fiscal rationale would continue to shape American postal policy for decades to come. Not until 1801 would a president shift the postal system out of the treasury department, and not until the 1830s would a prominent congressman challenge the assumption that, at the very least, the postal system should remain self supporting, an assumption firmly rooted in the experience of the eighteenth-century past.[5]

Equally notable were similarities in the level of service.[6] By 1765, the royal postal system in British North America provided postal patrons with a remarkably high level of service by the standards of the day. The northern district alone included sixty-seven offices that stretched along the Atlantic seaboard in an arc from Canada to Virginia, which worked out in per capita terms to approximately one office for every 22,000 free inhabitants, or almost precisely the ratio as in England and Wales.[7] The royal postal system also provided patrons with regular packet service between New York and Charleston and Falmouth, England, transforming these three port towns into funnels for the transmission of information between the British North American hinterland and the wider world.[8]

Following the break with Great Britain, American postal officers did their best to replicate the level of service that the royal postal system had provided postal patrons prior to the war. This did not prove to be easy. Notwithstanding the appointment of former royal postal officer Benjamin Franklin as its head, the enterprise went into a steep decline from which it would not entirely recover until after the end of the War of Independence in 1781.

Much of this decline can be explained by the vicissitudes of war. Prior to 1775, the heaviest users of the postal system had been merchants active in overseas trade. During the war, their trade was significantly curtailed. Deprived of their customary access to the British mail packets and hemmed in by the British naval blockade, merchants had little occasion to write the same number of letters that they had prior to the war, and as a consequence postal revenue—and, with it, postal service—dramatically declined. The post was "very regular," reported congressional delegate John Adams to Thomas Jefferson in 1777, yet the mail came but "once a week," in contrast to the prewar period, when three weekly deliveries had been the norm.[9] The bulk of the letters, Adams added, was written by members of Congress, which spoke well for the industry of the delegates, but which did nothing to generate the necessary revenue for improvements in service, since the delegates had the right to transmit their correspondence free of charge.[10]

No less important in explaining this decline was the incompetence of Postmaster General Richard Bache, who Franklin designated as his successor when Franklin left the United States in 1776 to oversee diplomatic negotiations with France. Had Bache exerted himself, the congressional postal system might have matched or even exceeded the level of service that the royal postal system had attained prior to the war. Wartime, after all, is often a catalyst for innovation, and the fledgling American government was desperately in need of a means of communication to link it to its armies in the field. Here was an excellent opportunity to establish a postal network to link East and West as well as North and South. Yet Bache failed to rise to the challenge and soon lost de facto control of military communication to army commanders George Washington and Nathanael Greene, who promptly established their own independent teams of postriders to maintain a line of communication between their armies and the seat of power.

The end of the war in 1781 brought surprisingly little in the way of improvement. As late as 1788, thirteen years after the establishment of the American postal system and seven years after the adoption of the Articles of Confederation, the American postal system included only sixty-nine offices, just two more than the sixty-seven offices in the northern district of the royal postal system in 1765.[11] The failure of the postal system to expand is particularly striking given the rapid expansion in the area of settlement. In the years immediately following the end of the war in 1781, enterprising pioneers pushed farther into the hinterland than their forebears had during the entire course of the previous one hundred fifty years. Yet in 1788, as in 1781—or, for that matter, 1765—the American postal system remained huddled along the Atlantic seaboard. To be sure, the confederation period was not entirely bereft of improvement. In 1785 postal officers contracted for the first time with stagecoach proprietors to carry the mail on certain portions of the North-South post route, and in 1788 Congress established its first major East-West post route, a 250-mile line of posts between Philadelphia and Pittsburgh.[12] In addition, several state legislatures established their own state-run postal systems, while countless entrepreneurs established their own private posts.[13] But these improvements did little to serve the great mass of the public at large. Notwithstanding the expansion in the area of settlement, American postal officers had failed to meet the needs of the day. Little wonder, then, that James Madison could declare as late as 1788 that the clause granting Congress the authority to establish post roads, while potentially of "great public conveniency," was a "harmless" power unlikely to play a major role in American public life.[14]

IN THE PREAMBLE to the federal Constitution, the Founding Fathers declared the "people" of the United States to be the sovereign power. Precisely what they meant by this declaration was by no means evident then, and it remains controversial today. But one thing seemed certain. If the people were truly sovereign—that is, if they were the final, indivisible, and supreme source of political authority—then no one could plausibly deny the citizenry the right to secure uninterrupted access to up-to-date information about the ongoing affairs of state. Long before the War of Independence, backwoods evangelicals had joined with the seaboard gentry to challenge all monopolies of knowledge that strengthened the authority of church and state. But only after the adoption of the federal Constitution would public figures commit themselves to keeping the citizenry well informed. Only then would they authorize the routine publication of the ongoing proceedings of the federal Congress, a service that had been unknown prior to 1788.[15] And only then would they put aside their conviction that public access to political information might prove dangerous or even subversive, a conviction that would remain intellectually respectable in Great Britain for decades to come.[16]

Few documents better illustrate the prevailing assumptions with regard to the informational environment than the *Federalist* essays that

James Madison prepared in 1787 and 1788 to build public support for the adoption of the federal Constitution. Though Madison's essays have long been hailed as a notable contribution to American political thought, they are predicated upon a surprisingly limited conception of the role of political information in American public life. Nowhere in these essays did Madison imagine the possibility that printers might establish newspapers that would report continuously on the proceedings of Congress. Nowhere did he predict that public figures might one day possess the technical means to create durable mass-based political parties that would transcend the boundaries of the individual states. Nowhere did he imagine that the citizenry might soon begin to communicate with each other in voluntary associations, bypassing the government altogether. Indeed, at no point did Madison even go so far as to envision the emergence of public opinion as a political force. On the contrary, Madison predicated his defense of the federal Constitution on the confident expectation that the United States was so geographically extended that its far-flung citizenry could not possibly secure access to the information necessary to monitor the government's ongoing affairs. Only when the representatives returned to their home districts to meet with their constituents face-to-face would the citizenry have the opportunity to catch up on the latest news. Once the representatives returned to the capital, they would once again be on their own.

Critics of the federal Constitution, such as Elbridge Gerry of Massachusetts, found this assumption highly disturbing. How, Gerry wondered, could liberty be preserved in a country where the citizenry had no way of keeping abreast of the ongoing affairs of state? Madison was well aware of this objection and did his best to turn it to his advantage. The very *inability* of the citizenry to secure the necessary information to create durable factional alliances, Madison explained, constituted an important key to its survival. Unable to secure access to information, the citizenry would find it impossible to establish enduring institutions that might contravene the common good.[17]

Madison's expectations may have accurately reflected the political status quo, yet they were a poor guide to the future. Far more prescient in this regard was Madison's good friend Benjamin Rush, an Edinburgh-trained physician who developed his ideas in a remarkable "Address to the People of the United States," published in 1787. As a physician, Rush favored heroic treatments, such as the copious bleeding of patients; as a political analyst, Rush advocated an equally dramatic augmentation in the capacity of the central government. With a calm self-assurance surpassed by none of the other Founding Fathers, Rush hailed the adoption of the federal Constitution—and, with it, the augmentation in the capacity of the central government—as a fitting culmination to the radical changes in American public life that had been set in motion with the Declaration of Independence in 1776. "There is nothing more common," Rush declared, "than to confound the terms of the American revolution with those of the late American war. The American war is over: but this is far from being the case with the American revolution. On the contrary, nothing but the first act of the great drama is closed."[18]

Central to Rush's vision was his conviction that the central government ought to play a major role in shaping the values and beliefs of the public at large. To adapt the "principles, morals, and manners of our citizens to our republican forms of government," Rush explained, it was "absolutely necessary" that the government circulate "knowledge of every kind . . . through every part of the United States." To bring about this anticipated moral reform, Rush looked to the postal system, the "true non-electric wire of government" and the "only means" of "conveying light and heat to every individual in the federal commonwealth." In particular, Rush recommended that Congress admit newspapers into the mail free of charge and expand the chain of seaboard offices into an integrated network embracing every city, town, and village in the country.[19] From the standpoint of his day, Rush's recommendation had a bold, almost utopian cast. In the space of a few sentences, he had supplanted Blackstone's fiscal rationale for postal policy with an educational rationale that was far more ambitious than anything that any other public figure had contemplated prior to that time. Rarely before had any public figure envisioned such an expansive role for the postal system. And with the passage of the Post Office Act of 1792, Rush's educational rationale for postal policy became firmly enshrined in the law of the land.

HISTORIANS have long puzzled over the failure of Congress to enact a major piece of postal legislation until 1792, four years after the adoption of the federal Constitution and halfway through the first session of the second federal Congress. For one historian, this delay was a sure sign of the decidedly minor importance of the postal system in American public life.[20] For another, it was indicative of the fundamental continuity in postal policy from the eighteenth century to the present day. By 1789, or so this historian claimed, the modern postal system already existed "in embryo": "Its main lines of policy had nearly all been laid down and its basic rules established."[21]

In fact, the history of American postal policy in the period between 1789 and 1792 was a good deal more complex. Congress waited three years to formally incorporate the postal system into the newly established central government not because it had more important things to do, but because of sharp disagreements as to how it ought best to proceed. The adoption of the federal Constitution had created new expectations for the central government, and it took time for these expectations to work their way into law.

The Post Office Act of 1792 shaped American postal policy in three major ways. First, it admitted newspapers into the mail on unusually favorable terms, hastening the rapid growth of the press. Second, it prohibited public officers from using their control over the means of communication as a surveillance technique. And third, it established a set of procedures that facilitated the extraordinarily rapid expansion of the postal network from the Atlantic seaboard into the transappalachian West. While the full implications of these changes would only become clear with the passage of time, taken together, they were much more than merely an incremental modification of the status quo. Notwithstanding the inevitable persistence of certain features of the informational ancien régime, the passage of the Post Office Act of 1792 broke radically and irrevocably with the inherited traditions of the past.

PRIOR TO 1792, Congress had never enacted legislation to formally admit newspapers into the mail. Though postriders had frequently carried newspapers prior to this time, they did so, as one well-informed printer explained in 1791, "at their pleasure" and on their "own private account."[22] For John Holt, a newspaper printer and former royal postal officer, this was deeply frustrating. Why, Holt implored Massachusetts delegate Samuel Adams in 1776, did Congress refuse to provide this vital service to the public at large? After all, Holt added, for the vast majority of the citizenry, newspapers were far more important than the letters that the government already transmitted in the mail.[23]

The principal exceptions to this ban were the newspapers that individual congressmen sent to their constituents and the newspapers that printers exchanged with each other. The first of these exceptions was a corollary to the privilege that Congress granted itself to transmit, or "frank," an unlimited number of posted items through the postal system in order to keep its constituents informed of its ongoing affairs. Before long, Congress grew accustomed to conducting a large volume of correspondence in this way—including, in addition to newspapers, letters, pamphlets, and government documents—making the postal system, as Madison observed in 1782, the "principal channel" through which the citizenry secured its "general knowledge" of public affairs.[24] Like all franked items, the newspapers that Congress transmitted to their constituents were conveyed by the postriders in a special satchel, known as the official portmanteau, that they mounted on the horse's rump, rather than in the saddlebags that they slung from their side, which were used to carry their personal effects. The placement of the newspapers in the official portmanteau greatly increased the likelihood that they would reach their intended destination. Not only were they safely out of sight in a locked container to which only postal officers had the key, but they also had the protection of the moral strictures that stigmatized mail robbery as a crime. "Even along the post roads," one congressman explained, "the common packets of newspapers are not safe from depredation, but when once they get into the interior parts of the country, there is hardly any chance of their escaping, whereas under cover of a frank, they are sure to reach their destination in safety."[25] For this reason, congressmen came to regard it as their duty to transmit newspapers to their constituents, making them, in effect, newsbrokers for the public at large.

The only other class of newspapers that enjoyed such a highly favored status were the exchange papers that postal officers permitted printers to exchange with each other, continuing a custom that antedated the war. Long before the establishment of the American postal system, postal officers had encouraged postriders to permit printers to exchange one copy of their newspaper with fellow printers and in this way to provide their journalistic peers with the nonlocal information on which they relied to fill their pages. Sometimes these newspapers were transmitted in the official portmanteau; more commonly, however, they were transmitted along with the rest of the newspapers in the riders' personal saddlebags. Shortly after the introduction of stagecoach service in 1785, Postmaster General Ebenezer Hazard expanded this privilege by permitting printers to include their exchange papers in the official portmanteau on those segments of the post road over which stagecoaches carried the mail. On those segments of the post road still served by postrider, however, the exchange papers would continue to be transmitted in the saddlebags, just as they had been before, giving the postrider the option of leaving them behind should their weight prove too great. When Hazard was pressed by a group of Philadelphia printers to relax this restriction, Hazard stood firm. If he were to expand the privilege to include those portions of the post road that were still served by postriders, Hazard explained, the increased weight of the mail might well overburden the postriders and retard the transmission of the mail.[26] Taking the moral high ground, Hazard reminded the printers that he had no obligation to provide them with any special services at all. The postal system, Hazard lectured the printers, had been established by Congress "for the purpose of facilitating commercial correspondence" and thus had, "properly speaking, no connection with the press."[27] "Even in England," Hazard added, in a letter to a friend, postal officers did not regard newspapers as a regular part of the mail.[28]

Hazard's tilt with the printers provides a revealing glimpse at the prevailing assumptions regarding the proper relationship of the postal system and the press in the years immediately preceding the passage of the Post Office Act of 1792. During the entire course of Hazard's controversy with the Philadelphia printers, not even the most outspoken of Hazard's critics sought anything more than an extension of their customary privilege to exchange their papers with each other. None went so far as to propose that the government admit into the mail those newspapers that they transmitted to their ordinary subscribers. As late as 1788, then, it was by no means inevitable that the central government would soon transmit newspapers intended for ordinary subscribers or, for that matter, that it would even transmit the printers' exchange papers as a matter of right.[29]

Only gradually would these assumptions change, largely as the product of the full and vigorous debate that took place in Congress between 1789 and 1792 over the proper relationship of the postal system and the press. In the first phase of this debate, Congress considered the propriety of admitting certain newspapers into the mail. When this proved unworkable, Congress shifted, in the second phase of the debate, to consider the propriety of admitting *every* newspaper into the mail, a proposal that it eventually incorporated into the Post Office Act of 1792.

The selective admission of newspapers into the mail had several advantages. Not only would it increase public access to information on public affairs and relieve congressmen of the time-consuming burden of franking newspapers for their constituents, but in addition it would prevent the informational deluge that postal officers feared would overwhelm the postal system should Congress admit *every* newspaper into the mail. Though the details of this proposal remain obscure, it was almost certainly intended to help boost the circulation of John Fenno's *Gazette of the United States,* the semiofficial organ of the Washington administration. Had Congress enacted this proposal, Fenno would presumably have been authorized to admit his newspaper into the postal system at highly preferential rates and in this way to reach subscribers throughout the United States.

However expansive this proposal may have seemed to congressmen familiar with the far more limited facilities of communication that had prevailed prior to this time, it met almost immediately with a stinging rebuke. Among its principal critics were Elbridge Gerry of Massachusetts and Aedaneus Burke of South Carolina. Neither Gerry nor Burke doubted the advisability of admitting newspapers into the mail. They feared, rather, that if Congress awarded this privilege selectively, it would greatly increase the ability of the government to manipulate the electorate. From their standpoint, what might have seemed like a harmless bill actually contained the "plainest outlines" of an insidious plan to establish a "court press and court gazette," an institution that, like the government-subsidized newspapers in Great Britain, would flood the public with information sympathetic to the existing regime.[30]

Gerry and Burke carried the day, and the selective policy was dropped. The need it had sought to address, however, remained unmet, and so, in the second federal Congress, the subject came up again. The key figures in this second phase of the debate included John Fenno of the *Gazette* and Benjamin Franklin Bache of the *General Advertiser.* Though Fenno and Bache stood at different points on the political spectrum—Fenno backed the Washington administration, while Bache was soon to emerge as one of its most outspoken critics—they shared the conviction that the central government had an obligation to greatly increase the facilities that it provided the newspaper press. The main purpose of his *Gazette,* Fenno reminded Congress in March 1791, was to "diffuse information to all parts of the Union from the seat of government, as from a common center." Should Congress fail to act, this worthy goal would prove impossible to attain.[31]

Most congressmen agreed that something should be done. But questions remained. Should Congress admit newspapers into the mail absolutely free of charge, or should it charge newspapers a modest fee? Leading the charge for the restrictionists was James Madison of Virginia. Better acquainted than most with the intricacies of postal finance,

Madison stressed that the imposition of a small fee would secure newspapers against the "casualties to which they are now exposed." If the fees were imposed on the recipient, Madison explained, this would give the postmasters who collected them an incentive to oversee their delivery, since, in accordance with a venerable tradition, they received a commission on every item they delivered.[32]

Others warned about the effects of the proposed policy change on the structure of the periodical press. The admission of newspapers into the mail free of charge, Fenno warned, would provide a major boost for printers in the North and East, since, other things being equal, most Americans preferred to read newspapers that originated in the large commercial towns, and few of these towns could be found in the South.[33] As a consequence, Fenno explained, the unrestricted admission of newspapers into the mail free of charge would put southern printers in a "very disadvantageous position" since, by providing northern and eastern printers with a national market, it would enable them to pour their newspapers into the southern states at a price "greatly below which the same work can possibly be executed there."[34]

The antirestrictionists, in contrast, urged Congress to admit every newspaper into the mail absolutely free of charge. "Wherever information is freely circulated," Gerry declared, in a notable defense of this view, "there slavery cannot exist; or if it does, it will vanish, as soon as information has been generally diffused." But should Congress impose any tax whatever on the press, the tax might well prove to be the "surest mode" of "introducing a system of despotism" into the United States.[35]

Expanding on Gerry's position was Benjamin Franklin Bache, the son of former postmaster general Richard Bache and the grandson of Benjamin Franklin. Bache articulated his views in a remarkable series of editorials published in November and December 1791. Firmly convinced that the status quo was "ruinous" for printers and that something must be done, Bache sketched a vision of the role of the postal system in American public life far more expansive than anything that either Bache's father had proposed during his stint as postmaster general or, for that matter, that Bache's grandfather had contemplated during his long postal career.[36]

Bache's approach to postal policy was rooted in his understanding of the proper role of the central government in American public life. In the United States, Bache observed—adopting a position that would have been heartily seconded by Benjamin Rush—the central government had an almost sacred obligation to publicize its ongoing affairs, since its very existence was predicated upon the "enlightened approbation" of the citizenry in the conduct of its elected representatives. But how was the government to attain this laudable goal? One answer lay in the postage-free admission of newspapers into the postal system, the "only channels" through which this information—the "necessary ground of enlightened confidence"—could flow.[37] Such a policy, Bache explained, would permit the "rays from this focus" to reach "every part of the empire."[38] In addition, the communication channel between the government and the citizenry that these newspapers would establish would create "pores" through which individuals living at a distance from the seat of power could "perspire" and in this way, he contended—in a curious mixing of metaphors—transform the newspaper press into a "kind of chimney to the federal edifice."[39] To illustrate his point, Bache drew attention to the recently enacted amendments to the federal Constitution that have come to be known as the Bill of Rights. No one could deny, Bache declared, that the American people possessed as their birthright not only ten but "ten thousand rights." But until the newspaper press undertook to broadcast this information to the public at large, how could this legacy shape the course of events?[40]

Notwithstanding the best efforts of antirestrictionists such as Gerry and Bache, Congress sided in the end with Madison and, in the Post Office Act of 1792, charged every newspaper admitted into the mail a modest fee. The legislation itself had two principal features. First, it admitted *every* newspaper into the mail, provided only that it pay the nominal fee of one cent if it traveled fewer than one hundred miles and one and a half cents if it traveled a greater distance. And second, it put the newspaper printers' exchange policy on a legal footing, codifying a custom that had its roots in the colonial past.

Few regarded the new rates as unduly high. According to Fenno, the fees were in many cases a quarter of the cost he had formerly paid private carriers to deliver his *Gazette*.[41] Even Bache was forced to conclude that the fee was "trifling." But Bache remained troubled about what the future might bring: "May it not be said that this trifling duty is laid on newspapers not for the revenue which it will raise, but to establish a principle which once introduced may be proceeded on so as greatly to check if not entirely put a stop to the circulation of periodical publications."[42] For the moment, however, everyone agreed that the law would provide postmasters an incentive to deliver the newspapers that they received in a timely manner as well as give southern printers the necessary protection to keep them from being overwhelmed by competitors in the North and East.

"NO PROPHETIC GENIUS," declared one journalist in 1851, could possibly have imagined the "future consequence, and almost illimitable circulation of newspapers through the mails" that Congress had set in motion when it admitted newspapers into the postal system with the Post Office Act of 1792.[43] There is good reason to suppose that the journalist may have been right. For printers as well as the public at large, this act transformed the role of the newspaper press in American public life.

Few features of the Post Office Act of 1792 were more important to newspaper printers—and, in particular, to those printers located outside of the national capital—than the codification of the printers' customary exchange privilege. "Postmasters are now bound by law," explained one Boston newspaper editor shortly after the act went into effect, to forward all exchange papers to the printers, while "before they were not." As a consequence, the circulation of exchange papers was now more "certain and extensive" than it had been at any point in the past.[44] Many of these newspapers were quickly discarded as waste. Some, however, provided printers with the information that they needed to keep their subscribers in touch with the wider world. By all accounts, the total volume was impressive. By the 1820s, these newspapers sometimes made up between one-third and one-half of the total weight of the mail.[45] By the 1840s, every newspaper published in the United States received free of charge an average of 4,300 different exchange newspapers every year.[46] No less important, the policy provided a major boost for what would quickly come to be known as the "country press." By guaranteeing printers located throughout the United States regular access to the information that they needed to fill their pages, it ended the monopoly that had formerly been enjoyed by printers located in close physical proximity to the seat of power, and in this way created the "country editor" as an occupational class.

Just as printers benefited from the exchange privilege, so too they benefited from the admission of subscribers' newspapers into the mail.[47] By underwriting the low-cost transmission of newspapers throughout the United States, the central government established a national market for information sixty years before a comparable national market would emerge for goods. Not until the 1850s, with the completion of a rudimentary transappalachian railroad network, would merchants in other lines of trade have the chance to reach the national market that newspaper printers had been tapping since 1792. And not until the 1880s would manufacturers begin to transmit perishable products other than newspapers on a regular basis throughout the United States. In the 1790s, the primary beneficiaries of this policy were Philadelphia-based printers like Fenno and Bache. Following the relocation of the capital to Washington in 1800, they were joined by Samuel Harrison Smith, William Seaton, and Joseph Gales, Jr., of the Washington-based *National Intelligencer* and Hezekiah Niles of the Baltimore-based *Niles's Weekly Register*. By the 1840s, Horace Greeley took advantage of the highly favorable newspaper rates to transmit the country edition of his influential *New York Tribune* throughout large portions of the North and the West.

By all accounts, the total volume of newspapers that printers sent to subscribers through the postal system was enormous. By 1800, the postal system transmitted 1.9 million newspapers a year; by 1820, 6 million; by 1830, 16 million; by 1840, 39 million (see Table 1.2). In absolute terms, these totals probably constituted no more than 10 percent of the total number of newspapers printed in any given year, with the bulk of the remainder being distributed by private carriers, newsboys, and other private vendors, including stagecoach drivers, who often carried them, as the phrase went, "outside of the mail."[48] Yet if one considers the special country editions of weekly newspapers that metropolitan printers such as Horace Greeley prepared for rural subscribers, the percentage may be higher still. According to one estimate, the postal system at midcentury transmitted some 65 percent of *all* the country editions in the United States.[49] Even in thickly settled Massachusetts, with its excellent network of private carriers, the percentage could be as high as 40 percent.[50] In the more thinly settled South and West, the percentage would doubtless have been higher still.

Perhaps the easiest way to appreciate the implications of this newspaper subsidy is to compare the weight of the newspapers that printers sent through the postal system with the revenue that they brought in. In 1794, newspapers generated a mere 3 percent of postal revenue, while making up fully 70 percent of the weight.[51] Forty years later, little had changed. In 1832, newspapers generated no more than 15 percent of total postal revenue, while making up as much as 95 percent of the weight.[52] On a typical day, reported the New Hampshire mail contractor turned senator Isaac Hill, the incoming mail at the Washington post office contained one tidy packet of letters and twenty-one enormous sacks of newspapers, each of which weighed between 150 and 200 pounds.[53]

No other class of mailable items enjoyed such favorable rates. Letters were so much more expensive to send that one postal officer estimated that if newspapers were charged a comparable rate the cost of their transmission would increase by almost 700 percent.[54] Similarly, though magazines enjoyed lower rates than letters following their admission into the mail in 1794, they remained far more expensive than newspapers and, unlike letters and newspapers, could always be excluded if they should prove burdensome.[55] Charleston postmaster Thomas W. Bacot articulated this rule in a letter to a postal colleague in 1814. Postal officers, Bacot decreed, could transmit the popular Philadelphia magazine the *Port Folio* through the postal system, though, Bacot added, postal patrons "cannot claim it as a right."[56]

Even more daunting constraints limited the transmission of books and parcels. Prior to 1851, postal regulations excluded books from the mail altogether; even after this date, postal officers regarded their transmission as an unusual event.[57] And not until the twentieth century would the government begin to transmit parcels through the mail. In Great Britain, in contrast, their transmission was well established by 1815 and was commonly regarded as a lucrative branch of the business.[58] In the United States, however, no such service existed. Consequently, it was far easier in the early republic to transmit a parcel from the United States to Great Britain than it was to transmit it fifty miles into the interior of the United States.[59] Predictably enough, given these constraints, enterprising printers of all kinds quickly adapted their publications to a newspaper format, leading in short order to the publication of religious newspapers, agricultural newspapers, reform newspapers, and even literary newspapers that reprinted entire novels for transmission at the low newspaper rate. In the early 1840s, one Boston publisher offered subscribers 104 square feet of reading matter for a nickel—not including the additional penny or two in postage that it would cost to transmit these "mammoth monsters" to any location within the United States.[60]

Who paid for the newspaper subsidy? Not the central government: while few expected the postal system to return a revenue, everyone agreed that at the very least it should remain self-supporting. Rather, the subsidy was paid for by letter writers, of whom the vast majority were merchants. To reduce the cost of securing political information for citizen-farmers, many of whom lived in the South and West, Congress increased the cost of doing business for merchants, most of whom lived in the North and East. In the broadest sense, then, this policy was not distributive, but regulatory or, more precisely, redistributive. So skewed was the rate structure that beginning in the 1830s certain public figures—including the Jacksonian postmaster general, Amos Kendall—formally proposed that Congress increase the newspaper rate to prevent the urban newspapers in the North and East from swamping the country papers in the South and West.[61]

For others, the whole policy seemed more than a little unfair. With what justification, wondered Congregationalist minister Leonard Bacon in 1843, did the government lavish on the newspaper press more privileges than a Methodist circuit rider?[62] To Bacon's chagrin, however, Congress seemed unwilling to contemplate a change. "There does not appear to have been a man in Congress," fumed Bacon two years later, "who suspected that newspapers had not a divine right to some exclusive privilege at the post-office."[63] Even some postal patrons in the South and West found cause to complain. Outraged that postal officers charged the high letter rates for the printed market lists known as "price currents" that merchants exchanged with each other, the chambers of commerce in Mobile, Alabama, and Savannah, Georgia, formally protested the newspaper subsidy. In 1842, the latter went so far as to urge Congress to ban newspapers altogether from the mails.[64]

Few events better illustrate the importance of the newspaper subsidy in shaping the informational environment than the alarm with which country editors greeted the prospect that Congress might follow Gerry's advice and admit every newspaper into the mail absolutely free of charge. Such a policy, these hinterland editors feared, would swamp the country with newspapers originating in the major commercial centers and force them out of business. Sensitive to the printers' concern, Postmaster General Joseph Habersham touched on it directly in the 1800 edition of the *Post-Office Law*. Henceforth, Habersham decreed, local postmasters should encourage postal patrons to subscribe to newspapers published in their own states and neighborhoods in preference to those published at a distance. The establishment of country presses, Habersham explained, was of "great public use," since it would extend the "knowledge of letters" by encouraging a multitude of small enterprises to publish not only newspapers, but also books and other useful items. In addition, it would prevent from spreading throughout the countryside the "rage of party" that the highly partisan political newspapers in the major commercial centers did so much to incite.[65]

The relationship between postal policy and the expansion of the newspaper press occasioned a good deal of discussion on the part of contemporaries familiar with postal policy in other parts of the world. British travelers in particular were quick to stress how the absence in the United States of the various newspaper taxes that the British government imposed on its newspaper press worked to boost that press in the United States.[66] Not everyone agreed. According to Alexis de Tocqueville, newspapers circulated so widely in the United States not because they were cheap, but rather because they provided the citizenry with the necessary information to fill the multitude of local offices that were such a distinctive feature of American public life. Had the government not expected the citizenry to participate in local politics, Tocqueville reasoned, newspaper readership would have been far smaller regardless of the cost, since in the absence of a compelling demand for local news ordinary Americans would have had little reason to subscribe.[67] Had Tocqueville paused to sample the American press, however, he would have discovered that the vast majority of American newspapers were preoccupied not with local news, as Tocqueville's analysis would lead one to expect, but rather with national and international affairs. Only in the 1850s would the country press turn its attention to local affairs, more than sixty years after it had come into existence with the passage of the Post Office Act of 1792.[68]

Just as postal policy hastened the quantitative expansion of the press, so too it hastened its geographical penetration into the hinterland. Particularly important in this regard was the absence of administrative constraints upon the transmission of newspapers from printer to subscriber.[69] By subsidizing the transmission of *every* newspaper—rather than, say, a special class of newspapers originating in the national capital, such as Fenno's *Gazette*—Congress created a highly decentralized informational environment. Perhaps the best evidence for the distinctiveness of this policy can be found in the simple fact that, following the transfer of the national capital from Philadelphia to Washington in 1800, the national capital quickly faded in importance as a publishing center, a circumstance that would have been inconceivable in Great Britain or France. Equally notable was the absence of a special class of postal clerks to monitor the contents of newspapers sent in the mail. In Great Britain, every newspaper that postal officers transmitted fell under the direct supervision of the "clerks of the road," who were expected to monitor its contents and who had full authority to exclude it from the mail should it fall outside the permissible boundaries of dissent. In the United States, the absence of a comparable institution effectively prevented the establishment of a government-controlled "court press" of the kind that had so worried Gerry and Burke.[70]

The refusal of American public figures to establish formal controls to monitor the press did not, of course, eliminate the possibility of abuse. During times of great political turmoil, such as the War of 1812, postal officers interfered so regularly with the transmission of newspapers that contemporaries regarded the practice as widespread.[71] Yet this practice was always presumed to be abnormal and was rarely tolerated for long. Far more notable is the fact that prior to the abolitionist mails controversy in 1835 no public figure seriously questioned the avowedly educational rationale for American postal policy that Benjamin Rush had so eloquently articulated on the eve of the adoption of the federal Constitution in 1788 and that Congress had institutionalized with the Post Office Act of 1792.

JUST AS THE Post Office Act of 1792 protected newspapers from official surveillance by transmitting every newspaper on an equal basis, so, too, it prohibited postal officers from opening letters that postal patrons had sent.[72] The only exceptions were letters that postal officers found impossible to deliver. These, in accordance with a long-standing postal procedure, postmasters were required to return to postal headquarters, where they were opened by a special class of postal officers known as dead letter clerks. If the letters contained valuables or other enclosures, they were returned to the sender; if not, they were summarily burned.

For many Americans, the refusal of the government to sanction the opening of its citizens' correspondence became yet one more sign of the moral superiority of its much-heralded experiment in republicanism. A fundamental tenet of American postal policy, as one postal officer earnestly intoned, was that "silence"—the privilege to commit one's thoughts to paper without fear of official surveillance—is as "great a privilege as speech."[73] Nowhere, observed Francis Lieber, with the possible exception of Great Britain, was the inviolability of a posted letter more respected than in the United States.[74] In an absolute government, Lieber added, the government might deem it important for the postmaster general to inquire into private letters. In a "free nation" such as the United States, however, the government possessed no such right, since the citizenry expected its postmaster general to be not a "political officer"—as he might be, for example, in an "absolute government"—but merely the "chief conductor of the simple business of transmitting their correspondence."[75]

To be sure, in some cases this prohibition was almost certainly ignored. Virtually every major public figure in the early republic complained at one point or other about the perils of sending letters through the mail. Given the volume of these complaints, it would strain credulity to suppose that postal officers refrained altogether from opening the letters of administration critics and contriving ways to leak their contents to the public at large. Thomas Jefferson was so disgusted with the frequency with which the contents of his supposedly private correspondence found their way into the opposition press that he resolved in 1801 "never to write another sentence of politics in a letter."[76] Even relatively unknown individuals sometimes had cause for complaint. In 1820, for example, one citizen petitioned Congress to seek restitution for the "corruption" of postal officers who allegedly opened a letter that had been sent to him from Germany twenty years before.[77]

Still, the law was plain. In 1798, for example, many congressmen were disturbed by the activities of George Logan, a Quaker merchant who had undertaken as a private citizen to correspond with the government of France. Had Logan lived in France, government censors would almost certainly have inspected his correspondence as a matter of course. Since Logan lived in the United States, however, Congress found it necessary to enact a special law, dubbed the Logan Act, to prohibit private citizens from conducting diplomatic negotiations with a foreign government on their own account. Lacking an administrative mechanism to monitor Logan's conduct, Congress found that it had no alternative but to ban it outright.

A far different situation prevailed in Great Britain and France. Lieber may have praised the British for their commitment to postal inviolability, yet, in fact, the British government maintained a "secrets office" well into the nineteenth century, whose staff routinely opened correspondence that the government considered potentially subversive. Though the practice was regulated, it was by no means unknown. Between 1798 and 1844, British judges issued no fewer than 372 separate search warrants authorizing the opening of letters; at one point, they went so far as to empower surveyors to travel through the north of the country with a general warrant to open the letters of virtually anyone they pleased.[78] In France, the counterpart of the British secrets office was the notorious *cabinet noir*. So efficient was this institution that during the War of Independence virtually every American diplomat who served in that country found occasion to complain. The willingness of the French government to spy even on its military allies was so notorious that many American diplomats—including three future presidents, Thomas Jefferson, James Madison, and James Monroe—were said to have grown accustomed to preparing their dispatches in code.[79] According to John Jay, every letter that he had received during his tour of duty as minister to France bore the characteristic "marks of inspection."[80] Even ordinary Americans were warned of the need to take appropriate precautions. As one editorialist quipped:

> In writing to France, it is better and safer
> To write on thin paper and seal with a wafer;
> If the paper is thick, there's high postage to pay,
> And wax can be melted to learn what they say.[81]

In the rest of Europe, the security of the mail was, if anything, even more precarious. German postal censors were reputed to be so clumsy that they routinely destroyed the letters that came to their attention. To minimize the possibility that a given letter might be mutilated beyond recognition, popular magazines enjoined postal patrons sending letters to the German states to summarize their contents on the back cover.[82] In Russia, the insatiable appetite of the secret police for information was common knowledge. "Since my arrival in this city," wrote Russian foreign minister James Buchanan to secretary of state Edward Livingston in 1833, "I have not received a single communication of any kind, either through the post office or foreign office, whether public or private, which has not been violated . . . The Post Office American Eagle here is a sorry bird."[83] Foreigners would be well advised to proceed with caution, one business journalist warned. "No seal is held sacred, and unless foreigners are particularly guarded in their allusions to political events, they are likely to involve their friends in serious embarrassments."[84] Under the circumstances, had the Russian government enacted a variant of the Logan Act to discourage Russian subjects from corresponding with foreigners, it might well have been opposed as a constraint upon the ability of its secret police to monitor the country's internal affairs.

OF ALL THE CHANGES that Congress set in motion with the Post Office Act of 1792, by far the most radical was its assumption of the power to designate the routes over which the government would carry the mail. Prior to 1792, this power had rested with the executive; after 1792, Congress decreed that it and it alone would determine how the postal system would expand. Though this decision was seemingly a minor administrative matter, in fact it had major implications for the pattern of everyday life, since it virtually guaranteed that the postal network would expand rapidly into the transappalachian West well in advance of commercial demand.

Prior to 1792, the expansion of the postal network was limited by a number of constraints. Among the most important was the considerable confusion about just who had the authority to establish post routes that lay entirely within the boundaries of the individual states. Everyone agreed that the central government had the authority to establish the principal North-South post route; questions remained, however, about whether it also had the right to establish post routes that did not cross state lines.[85] This uncertainty was greatly exacerbated following the end of the war, when the authority of the central government went into a steep decline. Frustrated by these shortcomings, and intent upon improving communication facilities within their boundaries, the legislatures of a number of states, including Maryland and New Hampshire as well as the district of Vermont, went so far as to establish their own postal systems and to appoint their own postmasters general.

A further constraint upon the expansion of the postal network had its origin in the prevailing assumptions regarding postal finance. In theory, Congress might have authorized postal officers to finance postal expansion out of general revenue. In practice, however, it remained committed to the assumption that every post route should remain self-supporting, a legacy of the fiscal rationale for postal policy that was carried over from the Crown. Most important was the bedrock assumption that the principal market for postal communication lay along the Atlantic seaboard. As long as these assumptions prevailed, postal officers found it extremely difficult to imagine a world in which the Atlantic seaboard would become less a back door to Europe than a gateway between Europe and the transappalachian West.

Few events better symbolized the persistence of this Atlantic-centered worldview than the installation of a wooden statue over the entryway to the Boston post office in July 1792. The work of the well known Boston woodcarver Simeon Skillin, the statue depicted Mercury, the messenger to the gods of ancient Rome, in the act of bounding from the globe. In his left hand, Mercury held aloft his traditional winged staff; in his right hand, he displayed a letter directed to *"Thomas Rus-*

sell, Esq., Merchant, Boston—per post." According to a contemporary newspaper account, the statue conveyed a "handsome compliment" to the "mercantile interest" of the town and, in particular, to Russell, a public-spirited merchant who was active in the overseas trade and who may have commissioned the statue himself. The statue, the editor added with evident satisfaction, was sure to impress overseas visitors to Boston with "favorable ideas" of the "wealth and consequence of the town."[86]

Though Skillin completed his statue four years after the adoption of the federal Constitution, its installation revealed less about the radical changes in postal policy that were about to occur than it did about the continuing weight of traditions rooted in the past. Most obviously, it provided a telling reminder of the extent to which even after the War of Independence the postal system remained identified with overseas trade, just as it had been under the Crown. The statue was located on State Street, down by the wharves, and it honored a merchant active in the overseas trade. Even more revealing was Skillin's reliance upon a classical motif and the Boston editor's stress on the importance of the statue for foreign visitors to the town. Just as Europe remained the market, so too European norms continued to provide postal patrons with their principal ideas of how a postal system ought to be run. For Skillin, as for so many of his contemporaries, the wisdom of the ancients remained a far more important source of inspiration than the novel circumstances that would soon link the postal system with the burgeoning settlements to the West.

THE GRADUAL reorientation of the American postal system from the seaboard and toward the hinterland was decisively shaped by the outcome of a series of important congressional debates on American postal policy that took place between 1789 and 1792. The first of these debates ended in a stalemate between the House and the Senate. In the House, the majority tried to wrest control over the power to designate new postal routes away from the executive; in the Senate, the majority favored the status quo.[87] It was for this reason, reported Connecticut congressman Roger Sherman—who, as the chairman of the House Committee on the Post Office and Post Roads, was in a position to know—that Congress failed to enact a major piece of postal legislation in the first federal Congress following the adoption of the federal Constitution in 1788.[88]

This stalemate was finally resolved in the second federal Congress, though not before yet another extended debate. In this debate, which took place entirely within the House, the chief protagonists were North Carolina congressmen Hugh Williamson and John Steele and the issue was the route to be followed by the main North-South post road. At bottom, the controversy pitted the interests of the seaboard against those of the hinterland. Williamson, the representative of the seaboard, was determined to keep the post road along the coast; Steele, the representative of the hinterland, sought to relocate it to the middle of the state.[89] Williamson acknowledged that the existing route was roundabout and that it served but a small fraction of the citizenry. But he saw no reason why the postal system should provide the fastest means of transmission or serve the majority. He contended, on the contrary, that it should continue to serve the seaboard, where it could facilitate the collection of the revenue upon which the treasury department levied its tariff on imported goods.[90] Steele, in contrast, stressed that relocating the route would increase the utility of the postal system for the majority of the population of the state. Well aware that the precise location of this route was likely to prove contentious, Steele further recommended that Congress designate President Washington himself to make a tour of the area in order to settle the point.[91]

As long as Congress framed the issue in these terms, there was no obvious way in which the disagreement between Williamson and Steele might be resolved. Should Congress shift the post road to the hinterland, it would reduce the level of service along the coast. Yet should Congress uphold the status quo, the needs of the majority would go unmet. The Post Office Act of 1792 neatly solved this dilemma by changing the rules of the game. Henceforth, Congress decreed, it would grant itself the authority to designate every postal route in the United States, rather than confining itself to designating the route of the principal North-South post road, as it had prior to this time. No longer, in short, would Congress have to choose between Williamson and Steele. Henceforth, both could have the level of service that they desired.

More than any other single event, the assumption of control by Congress over the designation of new post routes doomed any attempt to revive the fiscal rationale for postal policy and guaranteed the rapid expansion of the system into the West. By 1795, even such stalwart fiscal conservatives as Alexander Hamilton admitted as much. Bowing to congressional pressure, Hamilton reluctantly conceded that, should Congress wish to earmark the entire postal surplus to postal purposes, rather than returning it to the general treasury, he had no objection to shifting the jurisdiction of the system from the treasury secretary to the secretary of state.[92]

Hamilton's recommendation marked something of a landmark in the history of American public life. Now that even Alexander Hamilton had rejected the fiscal rationale for postal policy, it was highly unlikely that anyone else would have the temerity to champion the cause. Postal officers might continue to return a portion of their annual surplus to the government, as they would for another forty years, yet few regarded this as the major rationale for the enterprise as a whole.

Nowhere was this repudiation of the fiscal rationale more evident than in Congress. During the various postal debates that took place between 1795 and 1834, the pivotal issue was never whether the postal surplus should be returned to the treasury but rather how the postal surplus ought best to be spent.[93] Only in 1834, when Congress confronted for the first time the looming specter of a permanent postal deficit, would the issue of postal finance reemerge. And when it did, Congress chose merely to guarantee that the enterprise would remain self supporting, rather than to divert postal revenue to some other end.

Few events better symbolized the reluctance of Congress to revive the fiscal rationale for postal policy than its refusal to ban private individuals from carrying letters on the routes over which the government carried the mail.[94] In no other "civilized country," marveled Francis Lieber in 1835, did the postal system rest on such a precarious legal foundation. Should Congress try to prohibit private individuals from carrying letters in this way, Lieber added, it would be immediately opposed as a "strange interference" with "private concerns."[95] On some routes in the 1790s, stagecoach passengers were said to carry more letters on their own account than postal patrons transmitted via the mail.[96] Had Congress intended to raise revenue from the postal system, it is hard to believe that this practice would not have been prohibited by law, as it was in Great Britain and France.[97] But from 1792 to 1845, Congress refused to ban private mail carriage outright. The principal exception was the lucrative stretches of post road in the thickly settled regions of the North and the East, where postal officers used the courts to block the establishment of regular private mail delivery firms to compete with the government. "Between our great cities, from Boston to Baltimore," observed one congressman in 1833, "contracts could be obtained to carry the mail for a cent a letter. Why, then, were the rates still continued so high? That other routes through the interior might be sustained. The government had the monopoly, and carriers dare not enter into competition with the post office department."⁹⁸ For a brief period between 1839 and 1845, it seemed that even this limited ban was about to give way. Spurred by the new communications channel created by the railroad, as well as by the decline in the level of service that followed the ascendancy of Jacksonians, entrepreneurs established a host of nongovernmental mail delivery firms—the so-called "private expresses"—to compete directly with the government in the North and the East. In the end, however, Congress refused to relax the ban, choosing instead to drive the private expresses out of business by simultaneously tightening the postal monopoly and lowering the basic letter rate, which it did with the Post Office Acts of 1845 and 1851.⁹⁹

The abandonment of the fiscal rationale for postal policy had important implications for American public life. Prior to 1792, the expansion of the postal network remained constrained by the assumption that every new route should be self supporting. After 1792, however, this constraint no longer applied.¹⁰⁰ As a consequence, Congress soon established dozens of new routes that could not possibly break even, a circumstance that would have been inconceivable prior to 1792. Before long, the practice became commonplace. Congress had grown so accustomed to expanding the postal network in this way, explained one congressman in 1797, that many of these new routes did not bear "one-hundredth" of their expense.¹⁰¹ By 1840, postal officers were routinely transferring to postal operations in the South Atlantic, the Northwest, and the Southwest 12 cents of every dollar in revenue that they generated in New England and almost 50 cents of every dollar in revenue that they generated in the Mid-Atlantic states.¹⁰²

The impetus for the expansion of the postal network owed a good deal to the structure of the House. Since congressional apportionment was based on population and constituents were constantly clamoring for new routes, there existed a built-in bias in favor of expanding the postal network on the basis of population rather than on the basis of the existing pattern of commercial demand. For a time, every state was given a single seat on the House Committee on the Post Office and Post Roads, virtually guaranteeing that post routes would be established in this way.¹⁰³

To facilitate the expansion of the postal network, Congress devised a relatively simple technique. In order to demonstrate the existence of popular support for the establishment of a new route, congressmen encouraged their constituents to prepare an official request in the form of a petition. In the ensuing decades—beginning almost immediately after the passage of the Post Office Act of 1792 and continuing until the Civil War and beyond—thousands of these petitions found their way to Congress. Petition after petition and year after year, ordinary Americans declared their support for public policies that linked them more closely to the central government—and, with it, to the market economy—than anything that their forebears could have even remotely conceived. Only on the rarest of occasions did anyone recommend the elimination of an unprofitable route or even a reduction in the existing level of service.[104] None opposed the expansion of the postal network outright. "We recommend that a post be established to our district and county towns," declared one group of South Carolina petitioners in 1793, since "such communications" were the "soul of commerce!" Lacking such a "direct, regular, and immediate communication by posts," the petitioners explained, they were "kept in ignorance" and "know not anything which concerns us, either as men or planters."[105] It was "incalculably advantageous," observed another group of petitioners from Connecticut in 1809, for "every well regulated government" to keep its citizenry well informed by "disseminating every species of useful information among them." This was true, the petitioners added, even though the town consisted primarily of "agriculturists," a few merchants, and "many mechanics."[106] Improved postal service, reported a group of petitioners from South Carolina in 1821, would facilitate the transmission not only of political newspapers, but also of the reform periodicals published by voluntary associations intent upon ameliorating the condition of the Indians and the slaves. Though the South Carolina petitioners took a "lively interest" in these voluntary associations, lacking a convenient post office they found it impossible to maintain an "immediate connexion" with their aims. After all, the petitioners added, the "privilege" of having any periodical publication circulating among them would "entirely depend on the location of our contemplated post office."[107]

Though it is impossible to know for certain, it seems likely that a large percentage of these petitions achieved their desired result. Few measures, after all, were less controversial. Between 1792 and 1828, Congress established 2,476 different post routes and discontinued a mere 181 (see Table 2.1).[108] Even Nathaniel Macon, a legendary scourge of governmental largesse, conceded that he routinely voted for every single post route bill that came up for debate.[109] According to one contemporary, the post route bill was kept in a special desk, where it could be examined by congressmen interested in the post roads in their own

Table 2.1 The expansion and geographical penetration of the postal network, 1790–1840

Year	Post offices	Population per post office	Settled area per post office (thousands of square miles)
1790	75	43,084	3492.7
1800	903	4,876	339.3
1810	2,300	2,623	180.2
1820	4,500	1,796	116.3
1830	8,450	1,289	75.5
1840	13,468	1,087	61.4

Source: population and post offices: Historical Statistics, vol. 1, pp. 8, 14, vol. 2, p. 805; *settled area:* Carville Earle and Changyong Cao, "Frontier Closure and the Involution of American Society, 1840–1890," *Journal of the Early Republic,* 13 (1993): 166.

Note: Population excludes Indians and slaves.

states. The bill was typically very long and was rarely printed. In the 1850s, one Michigan congressman remarked that in the twenty-five years he had been in Congress, not a single application for a new mail route had been denied.[110]

Some public figures were willing to see the postal network extended almost without limit. Its recent expansion, acknowledged North Carolina congressman Lewis Williams in 1829, may have been "very great," yet he hoped that this expansion might continue " 'til every neighborhood, nay almost every citizen should be accommodated with a post office at his door, if he should think proper to have it so."[111] Not everyone was so expansive. Was it really necessary, brooded the Richmond *Enquirer* in 1823, to establish post offices in thinly peopled districts of Virginia that were a mere seven miles apart?[112] The policy, remarked ex-President James Monroe two years later, could sometimes produce absurd results. "It has been reported to me," Monroe observed, that there were many instances in which postmasters had been appointed to offices in localities that were so remote that "not a single letter is ever sent there, to any person, but themselves."[113] Even sympathetic observers wondered if perhaps Congress was going a bit too far. "We hear continually of new offices established within a mile or two of other offices," reported postal authority Peter G. Washington in 1852, "and where, of course, there can be no real occasion for them, unless we indeed aim at a sort of post-millennium, where every man may have a post-office at his own door or in his own house."[114]

The distinctiveness of this state of affairs is highlighted by comparing

American postal policy with its counterparts in Great Britain and France. During the opening decades of the nineteenth century, neither the British nor the French government had a comparable commitment to extending postal service into the hinterland. In Great Britain, the postal system continued to return a considerable surplus to the Crown long after the American postal system had routinely begun to run into debt.[115] The consequences of this policy were predictable. As late as 1840, British postal officers had yet to establish post offices in 400 of the 2,100 registrar's districts that the Church of England maintained, while large portions of the country lacked any postal service whatsoever.[116] According to journalist Richard Cobden, one such village could be found a mere fifty miles from London, a situation that would have been inconceivable in the United States.[117] Even more striking was the contrast with France. Under French law, postal officers had the authority to establish new post offices only in those localities that could guarantee an annual postal revenue of $200 a year.[118] If the same principle had been adopted in the United States, over 90 percent of all the post offices in the country would have been forced to shut their doors.[119]

The changes that the expansion of the American postal network set in motion hastened not only a quantitative increase in the level of service, but also a qualitative reorientation in the character of American public life. Slowly but surely, postal policy was helping to transform the eighteenth-century Atlantic community of the Founding Fathers into the nineteenth-century national community that hundreds of thousands of Americans would fight and die for during the Civil War.

Perhaps the best way to appreciate the magnitude of this transformation is by turning to a contemporary work of fiction. In 1842, the writer Nathaniel Hawthorne published a lighthearted sketch called "A Virtuoso's Collection," which consisted of an artful description of the curious items that an eccentric antiquarian had brought together in a Boston museum. At the entrance to this museum was a handsome statue that "wore such a look of earnest invitation" that it impressed the narrator "like a summons to enter the hall." Though the virtuoso insisted the statue to be the "original statue of Opportunity, by the ancient sculptor Lysippus," readers familiar with Hawthorne's Boston would have immediately recognized it instead as the very same Mercury that Thomas Russell had commissioned for the Boston post office in 1792.[120] By 1842, however, the original purpose of the statue had long since been forgotten, along with the vision of an Atlantic community that it had been intended to promote. Indeed, it was precisely for this reason that the virtuoso could pass it off as a relic of classical antiquity, confident that few Bostonians would call his bluff. Few circumstances better illustrate the sea change in American postal policy that had taken place in the intervening years. No longer was the Boston post office the back door to Europe; it had become instead a gateway between Europe and the transappalachian West. And in the course of this remarkable transformation, an institution that would have been familiar to the ancients had been transformed into an enterprise that was quite literally without precedent in the history of the world.

IN *DEMOCRACY IN AMERICA*, Alexis de Tocqueville warned against the danger of exaggerating the significance of public policy in shaping the pattern of the past. Too much importance, Tocqueville observed, is attributed to laws, too little to custom, habit, and mores. A century and a half later, Tocqueville's warning remains sound advice. No student of American civilization can fail to be impressed by the extent to which many of the most distinctive features of American public life can trace their origins to values and beliefs that owed little to deliberate political acts such as the adoption of the federal Constitution in 1788.

Yet it would be equally misleading to assume that legislation can never exert a major influence upon the course of events. In certain cases, a deliberate political act such as the passage of a piece of legislation can hasten or hinder the formation of certain groups and ideas. Occasionally, it can even exert a palpable influence on the pattern of everyday life. One such piece of legislation was the Post Office Act of 1792. More directly than any other law that Congress passed during the 1790s, this act hastened the establishment of a national market to link the Atlantic seaboard and the transappalachian West as well as the creation of a public sphere to link the national capital to the rest of the United States.

The role of postal policy in the establishment of this national market would be hard to exaggerate. In the period between 1792 and 1828 — when, following over thirty years of rapid expansion, the national postal network was more or less complete — the postal system provided merchants with the only reliable means for transmitting information, bills of exchange, and money throughout the United States. Only the central government had the necessary resources to finance the establishment of such an extensive network; only the central government had the administrative capacity to guarantee that this network would remain in operation year in and year out; and only the central government had the moral authority to resolve the legal disputes that would inevitably arise from its routine operations, spanning as these operations did a multitude of separate jurisdictions. Had a private competitor emerged, it would seem highly unlikely that it could have commanded the necessary measure of trust. Even to suggest such a possibility is to run the risk of anachronism: Not until the 1830s, *after* the national market had been established, would private entrepreneurs begin to compete against the government in an organized way.

By all accounts, the volume of money that the postal system transmitted was large. "The mail has become the channel of remittance for the commercial interest of the country," reported Postmaster General Gideon Granger in 1802, "and in some measure, for the government."[121] "An enormous amount of money in banknotes" was transmitted in this way, reminisced postal clerk Thomas Brown in looking back on his stint in the Richmond post office around 1810.[122] "Security in the transmission of banknotes and valuable papers through the mail," declared Postmaster General John McLean in 1825, was of "great importance to the community at large, and particularly to the commercial part of it."[123] After all, McLean added a few years later, "no inconsiderable amount of the active capital in the country, in one form or another" was transmitted through the postal system every year.[124] Though quantitative estimates are hard to come by, postal journalist Pliny Miles offered up one estimate in 1855. In a given year, Miles estimated, merchants transmitted as much as $100 million in this way—a sum that, while small by present-day standards, was almost double the federal budget for that year. Miles was in a particularly good position to venture such an estimate, since a few years earlier he had served a stint in the dead letter office, where he had been permitted to open letters that had for some reason failed to reach their intended recipients. During the course of one year, Miles calculated, over $2 million had passed through his hands alone. "Not unfrequently would there be say ten, twenty, and sometimes fifty thousand dollars in one draft, and in a single letter."[125] Prior to the rise of the express industry in the 1830s, which gradually took over the task of transmitting money and other valuable items, the total might well have been larger still.

Sometimes the money that merchants entrusted to the mail was lost en route. "Robbery of the mail is very frequent in the United States," reported British traveler John M. Duncan, "yet all things considered, not so much as might be expected. Remittances from one part of the Union to another, even of large sums, are generally made by transmitting banknotes in letters by the post office; scarcely a letter bag is made up for any of the larger cities, which does not contain in this way large sums of money. The mail is totally unprotected; there is no guard, and the driver carries no arms."[126] Of the various sums that he had entrusted to the postal system, Miles estimated in 1855, fully one-third had miscarried. For the country as a whole, Miles added, the total was probably between $500,000 and $1 million. Though these totals were hardly trivial, they were, by Miles's own reckoning, no more than 1 percent of all the money that had been transmitted in this way.[127] Baltimore postmaster Thomas Finlay provided an even more flattering estimate in 1843. Should the government undertake to insure money in the mail, Finlay calculated, and should it confine its guarantee to those portions of the postal network that were served by railroad and steamboat, the government could prudently insure it at the extremely low rate of one-tenth of 1 percent.[128]

Had miscarriage been endemic, of course, it would seem highly unlikely that merchants would have entrusted so much money to the postal system in the first place, particularly since the government refused to reimburse them for money lost in the mail.[129] Yet for many merchants, it was a risk that they were plainly willing to take. During the past fourteen years, recorded one Philadelphia merchant in 1833, he had sent over $3 million in banknotes, checks, and drafts through the mail between Philadelphia, Cincinnati, and New Orleans. During all this time, the merchant added, he had "never lost a dollar or a letter by miscarriage."[130] The practice of sending money through the mail, reported Lexington, Kentucky, postmaster Benjamin Ficklin a few years later, had become so common that it seemed as if there *"was no risk* in it."[131] There were thousands of merchants, testified postal special agent James Holbrook in 1855, who, if called upon, would declare that during the many years they had relied on the postal system to transmit money to distant creditors—involving, in many cases, the collection and disbursement of millions of dollars—they had lost or suffered the delay of no part of their correspondence, valuable or otherwise, through any fault of its staff. To make his point, Holbrook recounted the experience with the postal system of one New York–based manufacturing firm. For many years, the firm had remitted through the mail nothing but checks, third-party drafts, and other "representatives of money." Since everything arrived safe and sound, the firm then began sending actual banknotes "whenever convenience required, without bestowing a thought upon the insecurity or danger of such a course."[132]

Just as the Post Office Act of 1792 hastened the establishment of a national market—and, in this way, provided a major boost to the economy—so, too, it created a new kind of public sphere that was soon destined to transform the boundaries of American public life. Prior to 1792, the public sphere had been largely limited to government officers and merchants living in the principal port towns along the Atlantic seaboard. In the language of the sociologist, it was patrimonial; that is, it revolved around the activities of individuals who resided in close physical proximity to the seat of power. Little had changed since the days of the Greeks and the Romans, when it was taken for granted that if a citizen wished to participate in public life he had no choice but to leave the countryside and move to the city. With the passage of the Post Office Act of 1792—and, in particular, with the greatly expanded coverage of national politics that it encouraged—the public sphere became disembodied, that is, it became identified with a process that existed not in a particular place but rather in the imaginations of millions of people, most of whom would never meet face–to–face. By the time Tocqueville visited the United States in 1831, this transformation was complete. For the first time in world history, a government whose territorial confines extended well beyond the limits of an individual city had created a national community that extended to every citizen living within its boundaries an invitation to participate in public affairs.

The creation of this national community was one of the most important events in American history in the half century between the adoption of the federal Constitution in 1788 and the Panic of 1837. No event—not the introduction of universal male suffrage, not the rise of the mass party, not the advent of industrialism, and not even the settlement of the transappalachian West—did more to divide the neoclassical world of the Founding Fathers from the romantic world of Jacksonian Democracy. Significantly, this event owed little to social changes in commerce, population, literacy rates, or technological improvements in the means of communication, such as the electric telegraph or the penny press. And in no sense was it foreordained. Ever since the widespread commercialization of the printing press in the sixteenth century, it had been technically feasible to transmit time-specific political information on the ongoing affairs of state on a regular basis and on a continental scale. And ever since the Puritans had landed in New England in 1630, there had existed a population in the territory that would become the United States that possessed the necessary cultural attributes to participate in an ongoing discussion of public affairs. Yet it was not until the eighteenth century that public figures came to hail this potentiality as a cherished ideal. Far more than any putative combination of social or technological circumstances, it was this cultural transformation that explains this epochal event.[133]

Few institutions were more profoundly shaped by this event than Congress. No longer could the representatives remain largely insulated from the public at large. No longer could congressmen assume, as James Madison had in his *Federalist* essays in 1787 and 1788, that the citizenry would interact with their representatives only during the periodic visits of the latter to their home districts. On the contrary, after 1792 these representatives increasingly found themselves preoccupied with the task of keeping the sovereign people continuously informed of their ongoing affairs.

Once Congress committed itself to providing the citizenry with a steady flow of information, it threw itself into the task. Beginning shortly after the passage of the Post Office Act of 1792, and accelerating in 1813 with the reorganization of the printing of government documents, Congress bombarded the public with newspaper accounts of its proceedings, pamphlets, reprinted speeches, and reports and documents of all kinds. By 1830, these publications, along with the publications issued by the governments of the individual states, made up fully 30 percent of all the imprints in the United States.[134] So great was the demand for news that by the 1820s congressmen began to grow accustomed to delivering speeches for "Bunkum"—speeches, that is, that they intended less as verbal performances for their Washington colleagues than as published texts for their constituents back home. The chief object of these speeches, remarked an astonished British observer in 1839, was to give congressmen the chance to fill a number of columns in the local newspaper and, in this way, to convince his constituents that he was energetically at work on their behalf.[135] To fill up the necessary space in the newspapers, reported another British observer at roughly the same time, speakers quite literally found themselves "speaking against time."[136]

Inevitably, the preparation of these printed speeches became divorced from their actual delivery. So adept was *Intelligencer* editor William Seaton at transforming the rambling productions of Congress into language that was "interesting to read," remarked one bemused British visitor in 1808, that he filled his newspaper with eloquent orations, "a sentence of which never passed in the House."[137] By the 1820s, it had become increasingly difficult to know who had actually said what. Rejecting the traditional assumption that speeches should be highly polished, extemporaneous verbal performances, Kentucky congressman Richard M. Johnson delivered a pair of reports in 1829 and 1830 that had been ghostwritten by a postal clerk, while in the following years President Andrew Jackson routinely delivered major state papers that had been prepared by a small circle of journalistic advisors. Few congressmen did more to exploit the growing gap between the spoken and the written word than David Crockett of Tennessee. Prior to his death at the Alamo, Crockett collaborated with various Washington insiders to produce a number of topical surveys of American public life that, while basically faithful to his ideas, were deliberately contrived for popular effect. If a ghostwriter could improve upon his spoken performance, Crockett reasoned, this was all to the good.[138]

The final step in the complicated process of translating the spoken performance into the published text was the actual transmission of the speech itself. Many of these printed speeches reached the hinterland in the exchange newspapers from the Washington press that non-Washington printers relied on as their principal source of information on national affairs. Others were packaged in pamphlets that congressmen sent to selected constituents under the cover of their frank. By law, congressmen were supposed to sign their name to every document that went out under their frank. Often, this regulation was evaded by hiring substitutes to complete the work. Occasionally, however, a congressman did his best to uphold the letter of the law. The incorruptible Silas Wright of New York, for example, was said to spend an average of three hours every afternoon when Congress was in session personally signing government documents, at a rate of three thousand items a day.[139] So important had the practice become that in 1844 Maine Congressman Francis O. J. Smith hailed the franking privilege as the "galvanic current" that "animates the organization of both political parties." Almost every member of Congress, Smith added—in the Senate as well as the House—"feels that his reelection is more or less dependent on an active exercise of it."[140]

Congress kept no statistics on the volume of franked mail, forestalling the criticisms that such statistics would inevitably have spawned. Yet there can be little question that it was large. According to one informed estimate, by the 1850s the franking privilege accounted for somewhere between one-quarter to one-half of the total weight of the mail that left Washington on any given day.[141] In addition to speeches and government documents, congressmen got into the habit of franking all manner of things, including books, dirty laundry, and even pianos.[142] Others gave out franked envelopes to friends, an abuse that was widely practiced as late as 1852.[143]

British observers found all this highly irrational. Why, they wondered, did congressmen deliver speeches to which no one paid the slightest attention so that they might be packaged and transmitted hundreds of miles to gratify the curiosity of their constituents? Some responded that the existence of the practice was clear proof that Congress had little to do, since the real business of the country was conducted in the individual states. In large measure, of course, this was perfectly true. Throughout the nineteenth century, Americans customarily looked to their state legislatures, and not to the federal Congress, for the services that government could provide. But it would be a mistake to assume that the transmission of such a large volume of information had no influence on the course of events. In the early republic, one of the most important activities of the central government was publicity. Long before the advent of commercial telegraphy, Congress had created a national community that existed in the collective imagination of the citizenry. And to keep this community properly supplied with information, Congress found that it had no choice but to broadcast its proceedings throughout the length and breadth of the United States.

THE IMPLICATIONS of the Post Office Act of 1792 extended well beyond its role in the establishment of a national market and the creation of a disembodied public sphere. No less important was its role in shifting the contours of American political thought. Once Congress had committed itself to transforming the informational environment, it was only a matter of time before public figures pondered the significance of this transformation for American public life. In the 1790s, the political implications of this transformation spurred George Washington and James Madison to articulate two related but distinct rationales for American postal policy. For Washington, the rationale was logistical: by broadcasting information to the public at large, the postal system would help to secure the allegiance of a far-flung population. For Madison, it was civic: by providing the citizenry with the means to monitor its elected representatives, the postal system could help to check the abuse of power.

Washington's stress upon logistics was profoundly influenced by his long experience as commander-in-chief. Just as Washington had lobbied Congress during the War of Independence to improve the lines of communication between the government and the armies in the field, so now he urged it to improve the flow of information between the government and the citizenry. There is "no resource so firm for the government of the United States," Washington explained in 1793, in advocating the outright repeal of postage on newspapers sent through the mail, as "the affections of the people governed by an enlightened policy; and to this primary good, nothing can conduce more, than a faithful representation of public proceedings, diffused without restraint throughout the United States."[144]

Few public figures articulated Washington's logistical rationale for postal policy with greater conviction than Rufus Putnam, a former comrade-in-arms who had emerged in the postwar period as a major figure in the settlement of the transappalachian West. Committed to binding East and West, Putnam hailed the transmission of political information from the capital to the hinterland as a means toward this end. Should the government regard the expansion of the postal network in a "political light only," Putnam informed Postmaster General Timothy Pickering in 1794, the "knowledge" that it could "diffuse" among the people living in "these remote parts of the American empire" might well be of "infinite consequence to the government." Nothing could be more fatal, Putnam added, in a government constituted like that of the United States, than the ignorance of its citizens with regard to public affairs, since this would make them the "easy dupes of designing men" who would be prone to "flock in thousands after a demagogue" and challenge the authority of the recently established central government in the transappalachian West.[145]

If Washington and Putnam were primarily concerned with broadcasting political information from the government to the citizenry, Madison was primarily concerned with encouraging the citizenry to participate in public affairs by consulting with its representatives with regard to the ongoing affairs of state. In a brief yet notable essay on public opinion that he published in the months preceding the passage of the Post Office Act of 1792, Madison explored this idea in a systematic way. Madison's "Public Opinion" never became as celebrated as the essays he had written for the *Federalist* in 1787 and 1788. Yet in at least one respect, it provided a far better guide to the future course of events. For it was in this essay, and not in the *Federalist,* that Madison explored for the first time the momentous role that the postal system was soon to play in American public life.

Madison opened his essay with an arresting claim. "Public opinion," he declared, "sets bounds to every government" and was the "real sovereign in every free one." Readers familiar with Madison's *Federalist* essays would have found this claim intriguing, since as recently as 1788, the concept of public opinion had figured little in Madison's political thought. Now, however, on the eve of the passage of the Post Office Act of 1792 and in anticipation of the far reaching changes that it was about to set in motion, Madison hailed public opinion as a key element in his political thought. Madison predicated his discussion on certain theoretical assumptions about the relationship between the physical size of a government and the facilities of communication that the government provided. Whatever facilitated the "general intercourse of sentiments," Madison predicted, was equivalent to a "contraction" of the territorial limits of the country. And should the country be too large for effective government, these improvements would be "favorable to liberty." Since Madison assumed that this was currently the predicament of the United States, he further posited that improvements in the means of communication would more or less automatically promote the public good. Accordingly, he urged Congress to greatly improve these facilities of communication through the encouragement of commerce, the construction of a national program of internal improvements, the encouragement of an opposition press, and, most important of all, the *"circulation of newspapers through the entire body of the people"* with the passage of the Post Office Act of 1792.[146]

Madison was of course by no means the only public figure to support the admission of newspapers into the mail. Washington hoped Congress would eliminate newspaper postage altogether, a position Madison rejected as impractical, while administration publicist John Fenno had publicly proclaimed that the government had an obligation not only to provide the citizenry with the administration's position on the leading issues of the day, but also to provide it with the views of the opposition. In this way, Fenno noted approvingly in a revealing turn of phrase, the press "enlightens, satisfies, and tranquilizes the public mind" even as it empowers ordinary citizens to "compare the publications which appear against and for the administration of their open government, and to judge for themselves."[147]

But few administration supporters were as willing as Madison to encourage the widespread transmission of information for purposes that went beyond criticizing particular government policies to challenging the legitimacy of the party in power. Here lay the crux of the difference between Washington and Madison. For Washington, the newspaper press remained an extension of the authority of the government. For Madison, it became a rallying point that opposition leaders could rely on to mobilize the citizenry through the creation of organizations like the Republican party. Though Madison did not regard the Republican party as a party in the modern sense—an organization, that is, with a life of its own—he did hope that in time it might take control of the levers of power. In addition, Madison praised the press for its role in facilitating the widest possible circulation of information regarding the recently ratified Bill of Rights. Like Bache, Madison had come by 1791 to conclude that it mattered little whether Americans had been born with ten rights or ten thousand if the press did not constantly remind them of the fact.[148]

Madison expanded on his position in an address to President Washington that he prepared shortly after the passage of the Post Office Act of 1792. Praising the improved facilities of communication that the act had brought about, Madison hailed these facilities as "justly reckoned" among the "surest means" of preventing the "degeneracy of a free government," since they would be certain to recommend "every salutary public measure" to the "confidence and cooperation of all virtuous citizens."[149] By describing the role of the postal system and the press in this way, Madison subtly expanded upon Washington's commitment to facilitating the widest possible transmission of political information, since Madison clearly implied that if the citizenry found a given piece of legislation to be less than "salutary" it might legitimately take steps to oppose its enforcement.

Madison may have been committed to expanding the facilities of communication for the public at large, but he was far too searching a thinker to regard this prospect as an unqualified good. Few public figures, after all, had more reason to question the wisdom of permitting the citizenry to engage in a completely unrestricted discussion of public affairs. Like most well informed Americans, Madison remained deeply troubled by the prospect that organized groups might one day use the facilities of communication to stir up religious and ethnic hatreds just as countless religious and ethnic groups had in Europe during the Reformation, and just as the Baptists, Presbyterians, and Anglicans had in Virginia during the 1780s, even to the point of threatening to block the adoption of the federal Constitution in that state. Should the government expand the facilities of communication for the public at large, Madison quite understandably feared that analogous conflicts might well imperil the United States.

Madison touched on these fears in a remarkable memorandum that he prepared, but never published, during the same months that he wrote his notable essay on public opinion. Whatever facilitated the "general intercommunication" of sentiments and ideas, Madison posited, borrowing a metaphor from astronomy, tended to contract the "orbit" within which the government revolved. In a nation that was too geographically extended to permit easy communication among the public at large, this contraction would be favorable to liberty. Should the orbit of the government become too small, however, it would inexorably "hasten its violent death."[150]

In 1792 Madison remained little more than a prophet crying in the wilderness. Few contemporaries, after all, were perceptive enough to understand how, as the facilities of communication expanded, the "orbit" of the government might soon become so small as to embroil the country in civil war. By 1835, however, the situation had been radically transformed. Thanks in large measure to the communications revolution set in motion by the Post Office Act of 1792, ordinary Americans now found it possible for the first time to actively participate in a truly open-ended national discussion on the leading events of the day, rather than merely to receive periodic broadcasts from the seat of power, as Washington had envisioned, or to engage in carefully structured two-way consultations with their elected representatives, as Madison had hoped. Given the enormous political, economic, and cultural diversity of the United States—and, above all, the differences between the slaveholding and the nonslaveholding states—this was a recipe for disaster. Just as Madison had feared, the same informational mobility that had worked to bring the country together could work to drive it apart. Such was the unintended consequence of Madison's civic rationale for postal policy. For in the end, it was not isolation, but familiarity, that posed the gravest threat to the Union.

· 3 ·

Completing the Network

IN HIS ANNUAL message to Congress in December 1827, President John Quincy Adams made a remarkable prediction. The day was not far off, Adams declared, when the American postal system would extend the "facilities of intercourse" to every villager in the Union. Having witnessed the rapid expansion of the postal system that had taken place in the years since his youth, Adams had good reason to be impressed. When he graduated from college in 1787, the postal system consisted of little more than a chain of offices that linked the major Atlantic seaboard port towns and offered no special facilities for the press. Now, a mere four decades later, it had expanded into an integrated network that embraced virtually every city, town, and village in the United States and that hastened the regular transmission of a wide variety of newspapers and magazines. In addition, by 1827 the postal system not only transmitted information, but also subsidized the stagecoach industry, making it possible for passengers with the time, money, and inclination to travel overland throughout the vast hinterland of the South and West. Proud of this achievement, President Adams took pains to highlight its import. Thanks to the recent increase in the stagecoach subsidy, he reflected, it would soon become possible for ordinary Americans to communicate either "by correspondence" or "in person" throughout the length and breadth of the United States.[1]

The completion of the national postal network and the establishment of a national stagecoach network under postal auspices are two of the notable events of the early republic, yet their history remains surprisingly obscure. This chapter and the next take up this neglected theme. This chapter considers the history of the postal network from the standpoint of the postal headquarters, or what was then known as the general post office; the next chapter shifts the angle of vision to the post offices in the field. My intention is to identify those features of the postal network that played the most prominent role in American public life. While my discussion ranges widely over space and time, it takes as a convenient point of departure the administration of the general post office in 1828, the year in which, for all intents and purposes, the national postal network was finally complete.[2]

IN 1828, the general post office occupied a suite of offices on the first floor of a 120,000 square-foot brick building in Washington, D.C., that was located roughly halfway between the White House and the Capitol. Originally built in 1793 by real estate speculator Samuel Blodget as a public hotel, the building had served as the general post office since 1810 and had been greatly expanded in 1828 to provide additional room for the city post office, a matter of great importance to Congress since it provided the representatives with a vital link to their constituents back home.[3] Though the building was rarely described by the many visitors who flocked to the national capital to see a republican government at work, one British traveler did take the trouble to draw attention to its remarkable size, adding that its brick facade had been sadly marred by a coat of bright yellow paint.[4]

Heading the enterprise in 1828 was John McLean, an earnest, energetic, and politically ambitious forty-three-year-old lawyer who secretly yearned to be president of the United States.[5] McLean first came to public notice during the War of 1812 when, as an Ohio congressman, he provided valuable support for the war effort in the West. Following the war, McLean served briefly as a judge on the Ohio Supreme Court before securing the commissionership of public lands in 1822 and the postmaster generalship in 1823. Among his competitors for the postmaster generalship were four United States senators, including Richard M. Johnson of Kentucky, a likable yet somewhat unscrupulous political entrepreneur whose close ties with the stagecoach industry helped to win him a reputation as one of the most influential political wire-pullers in the United States.[6] McLean remained postmaster general until March 1829 when, shortly after the inauguration of Andrew Jackson, he resigned to take a vacant seat on the United States Supreme Court.

McLean owed his appointment as postmaster general to the timely intervention of John C. Calhoun, Monroe's capable secretary of war.[7] By securing McLean the postmaster generalship, Calhoun cemented a political alliance with an up-and-coming public figure whom he hoped might soon rival Henry Clay as a spokesman for the West. McLean, for his part, was grateful for Calhoun's support and consistently deployed the considerable patronage that was at his disposal to bolster Calhoun's political base, confident that in the end Calhoun's political ascendancy would work to his own benefit as well. When Calhoun went into the opposition during the middle of Adams's administration, McLean secretly did so too, even though he continued to profess his loyalty to Adams in public right up to the election of 1828.

McLean's approach to public administration—like that of Calhoun, John Quincy Adams, and Henry Clay—is best described as "national republican": *national* in the sense that he supported the expansion of the central government, and *republican* in the sense that he was sensitive to the aspirations of the great mass of ordinary Americans, in particular those Americans who hailed, like McLean, from the transappalachian West. Under Monroe, McLean remained constrained by the conservative administrative principles that Monroe inherited from Jefferson and Madison. Following the inauguration of the more progressive Adams, however, McLean quickly introduced a number of notable administrative innovations that did much to expand the role of the postal system in American public life.[8]

From a political standpoint, McLean's tenure as postmaster general was a major success.[9] When McLean took over as postmaster general in 1823, he was all but unknown to the public. By the time of his resignation in 1829, he had emerged as one of the leading statesmen of the day, a distinction he retained for the next thirty years. By October 1831, McLean had emerged as a credible opposition candidate in the upcoming presidential election and, according to seasoned political insiders like Martin Van Buren, he might well have carried the politically pivotal state of New York.[10] Eager to capitalize on McLean's political popularity, the leaders of the newly established Anti-Masonic Party offered McLean the Anti-Masonic presidential nomination in the election of 1832, which McLean declined, unwilling to enter into a three-way race with Andrew Jackson and Henry Clay.[11] Two decades later, McLean remained a viable presidential contender, even though, as a Supreme Court justice, he had supposedly removed himself from the electoral realm. In the first Republican national convention in 1856, McLean secured 34 percent of the vote on the first ballot, including that of the little-known Illinois lawyer Abraham Lincoln. In the second Republican national convention in 1860, McLean remained a potential contender, even though by this time he was over seventy years old.[12]

McLean never did become president or even the nominee of a major party. Yet his rapid rise to public prominence reveals the growing importance of the postal system in American public life. Prior to McLean's appointment, few journalists had granted the postal system more than a passing mention, while public figures were quick to ridicule the notion that a mere postmaster general could ever hope one day to become a candidate for president.[13] By the end of McLean's tenure in office, the postal system had become a frequent subject of discussion in the press, and McLean had emerged as one of the most highly respected public figures of the day. In tribute to McLean's achievement, and in recognition of the growing importance of the enterprise over which he presided, President Andrew Jackson took the notable step of elevating the postmaster generalship to Cabinet-level status at the beginning of his administration in 1829, ranking it third in standing, ahead of the secretary of the navy, the secretary of war, and the attorney general, and behind only the treasury secretary and the secretary of state. Though this ranking was purely honorific and lacked any formal standing in law, it aptly symbolized the emergence of the postal system as the central administrative apparatus of the American state.[14]

McLean's remarkable popularity owed a good deal to circumstances that were only obliquely related to his official performance. By no means the least important of these was his celebrated religiosity. Not only did McLean go to church every Sunday, but he saw to it that his family did too.[15] In an age in which the electorate was decidedly more pious than most of the men who sought its support, this could be a major asset. In addition, McLean had the good fortune to belong to the Methodist church, an organization that was rapidly emerging as one of the largest, fastest growing, and most influential denominations in the country. Few public figures were better positioned to reap the political rewards of the remarkable upsurge in evangelical fervor that has come to be known as the Second Great Awakening. McLean's religiosity impressed even Anne Royall, the maverick political journalist who was well known for her strident attack on the sectarian orthodoxies of the day. Notwithstanding Royall's anticlericalism, she had nothing but praise for McLean, whom she hailed as a public-spirited statesman "immaculate as the virgin snow."[16]

No less important in explaining McLean's popularity was his mastery of the subtle art of self-promotion. Intent upon thrusting himself into the national political arena, McLean issued an unprecedented number of open letters, official circulars, and reports. By far the most successful of McLean's publicity ventures were his annual reports of the postmaster general to the president, an innovation that, characteristically, McLean introduced. Widely reprinted in newspapers from Maine to Missouri, these reports helped make McLean a household name throughout the United States. Well aware of their potential importance in boosting his reputation, McLean took care to prepare them in a spare, lean style that contrasted markedly with the florid prose of the public oratory of the day and to include a variety of interesting statistics documenting the scale of the enterprise over which he presided. In his annual report for 1828, for example, McLean took the trouble to calculate that the general post office employed no fewer than 17,584 horses, 2,879 carriages, and 243 sulkies and wagons to carry the mail.[17]

However important McLean's religiosity may have been in consolidating his public reputation, and however successful his publicity campaign may have been in boosting his personal popularity, neither can fully explain his rapid rise to national prominence. Even more important was McLean's solid record of achievement as head of the largest and most complicated branch of the central government. To properly administer the American postal system demanded a fair knowledge of human nature, a solid measure of tact, and an almost herculean appetite for administrative detail. McLean possessed these traits in abundance and brought to the work of his office the self-discipline, personal ambition, and entrepreneurial vision that had so distinguished the tenure of his mentor John C. Calhoun as secretary of war.

Among the most notable features of McLean's postal career was his stamina. McLean could bear any administrative challenge that could be "imposed upon his shoulders," declared one admiring contemporary, and could thrive under a daily work regimen that would have killed Henry Clay.[18] In a similar spirit, Anne Royall hailed him as one of the "most indefatigable men in the world."[19] So committed was McLean to mastering the routine details of his office that during the annual contract season he refused to leave his desk for weeks at a time, even going so far as to have his meals sent up. It was a performance that Adams considered so unusual that he duly recorded it in his diary.[20] North Carolina congressman John Branch found particularly impressive McLean's refusal to take an extended summer vacation, and drew attention to this fact in an ultimately successful motion to grant McLean a major salary increase.[21] Today, of course, such sustained bursts of administrative energy have come to be regarded as almost routine. In the 1820s, however, they were far more rare. Few merchants worked at a desk for more than a few hours at a time, while most public figures left Washington for months at a stretch during the hot, dusty summers.

McLean's administration of the postal system earned him many plaudits from public figures familiar with his work. President Adams praised him as the most capable postmaster general in the history of the republic, even though Adams strongly suspected—correctly, as it turned out—that McLean was secretly maneuvering to help bring about his defeat in the election of 1828.[22] Postal officer Phineas Bradley hailed McLean for having improved the level of service to a degree that exceeded his "fondest expectations."[23] And Kentucky journalist and future postmaster general Amos Kendall credited him with having singlehandedly elevated the enterprise from "comparative insignificance" to a prominent place in American public life.[24] Not to be outdone was the editor of the politically influential *Albany Argus,* who observed matter-of-factly shortly after McLean's resignation that the former postmaster general had already received such an enormous barrage of favorable commentary in the press that for him to add to the wave of adulation would be like trying to "swell still higher the already overflowing Mississippi" by "casting into it a particle of water drawn from a neighboring streamlet."[25] McLean was understandably proud of his sterling reputation, and did everything he could to keep it in public view. Should he one day become a candidate for president, McLean informed Adams in 1831, he would pledge to run the country on the same principles by which he had run the general post office when it had been under his charge.[26]

McLean's senior assistant in 1828 was Abraham Bradley, Jr., a Connecticut lawyer and topographer who had served in the general post office for thirty-seven years and who had been first assistant postmaster general since 1800, when he had helped to relocate the office from Philadelphia to Washington.[27] Bradley hailed from Litchfield, Connecticut, where he had trained as a lawyer in the celebrated law school run by Tapping Reeve. After serving briefly as a district judge in western Pennsylvania, Bradley came to the attention of Postmaster General Timothy Pickering, who appointed him to office in 1791. By all accounts, Bradley was well advised to make the switch. Stiff and formal in demeanor, he lacked the easy conviviality that was so necessary in a frontier judge and found it next to impossible to deliver the impromptu harangues that the office demanded.[28]

However deficient Bradley may have been as a judge, he proved to be an excellent clerk. Diligent and conscientious, he was widely respected as a leading authority on the scheduling arrangements that the general post office had introduced for the stagecoach industry, most of which he had committed to memory and many of which he himself had devised. In 1828, Bradley's primary operational responsibility lay in the realm of postal finance, having been relieved of control over mail contracting a few years earlier in an office reshuffling that McLean had instituted to increase his flexibility in making advantageous arrangements.[29]

Among Bradley's notable accomplishments was his authorship in 1796 and again in 1804 of an innovative set of maps of the United States.[30] In addition to portraying every single post route in the country, the best known of these maps included an extraordinarily detailed chart listing the arrival and departure times for the stagecoaches that carried the mail from post office to post office along the principal North-South route. Bradley's maps were displayed in many of the country's larger post offices and, in addition, reached a broad public audience through their inclusion by Jedediah Morse in his celebrated *Geography* of the United States.[31] More than almost any other document from the period, Bradley's maps helped stamp the public imagination with an image of the geographical extent of the United States and so hastened the transformation of the ill-defined northern, western, and southern frontier into a clearly demarcated border. As late as 1822, Bradley's work was singled out for praise by writer John Melish in the introduction to his *Traveler's Directory through the United States*.[32] To this day, his maps are admired by students of the period as a major departure in the history of American cartography and as the single best source of geographical information on the United States during the 1790s.[33]

Although as first assistant postmaster general Bradley was technically responsible for all aspects of postal finance, in practice he delegated the time-consuming auditing of the postmasters' and mail contractors' accounts to Obadiah Brown. Bradley and Brown were a study in contrasts. Bradley was a close-mouthed lawyer with an almost obsessive commitment to upholding the existing rules and regulations. Even his closest friends seem to have customarily referred to him as "Mr. Bradley." Brown, in contrast, was a gregarious Baptist preacher who was more than willing to cut corners if he thought it would help get the job done. Notably free of clerical pretension, he was said to be uniformly cheerful except when he was actually praying or preaching in the pulpit.[34] Even Anne Royall, that notorious scourge of clerical pretension, numbered him among her personal friends.[35] Characteristically, Brown was known around the office as Obadiah, the Parson, or even, by one account, as Beeswax, a reference, presumably, to his good-natured propensity to poke his nose into his colleagues' affairs.[36]

The contrast between Bradley and Brown extended well beyond their official demeanor. Though Bradley cultivated a studious indifference to the vagaries of partisan politics, it was no secret that he supported John Quincy Adams in the election of 1828, just as he had supported Adams's father John in his unsuccessful bid for reelection twenty-eight years before. Brown, in contrast, was not only an enthusiastic Jacksonian, but also the close friend of Congressman Richard M. Johnson, the Kentucky Jacksonian who would later emerge as the vice presidential running mate of Martin Van Buren in the election of 1836. When Johnson was in Washington attending Congress, he boarded at Brown's E Street home and very probably worshiped at his church.[37]

Though Brown was hardly the only postal clerk to fraternize with members of Congress, Bradley viewed Brown's special relationship with Johnson with alarm. Johnson's close ties to mail contractors like James Reeside of Philadelphia were notorious among political insiders familiar with postal affairs. When Johnson visited Philadelphia, he and Reeside were known to stroll arm in arm through the streets, both sporting identical red vests and red cravats that Johnson had bought to dramatize his special relationship with one of the most important stagecoach proprietors of his day.[38] For insiders familiar with the workings of the postal contracting office, the point was unmistakable: the vests and cravats were precisely the same color as Reeside's stagecoaches. Given Brown's easygoing ways, Bradley quite naturally feared that Johnson might persuade Brown to lavish lucrative mail contracts on his personal friends. As long as McLean remained in charge of the enterprise, there was little cause for concern. Following McLean's resignation, however, Bradley's fears were fully realized when in 1835 Brown was forced to resign in disgrace following a humiliating postal finance scandal during which his irregular dealings were exposed to public view.

In addition to Bradley and Brown, the senior staff of the general post office in 1828 included Phineas Bradley, Andrew Coyle, and Charles K. Gardner. Bradley, the second assistant postmaster general, oversaw the contracting arrangements, a job he had learned from his brother, Abraham, but which he performed with far greater flexibility and tact. Coyle, the chief clerk, was responsible for coordinating the relationship between the general post office, the treasury department, and Congress, and was well known in official circles as an upwardly mobile overachiever who, through dint of hard work, had risen step by step through the postal hierarchy over the course of a dozen years.[39] Gardner, McLean's principal assistant in making postal appointments, was a New York Calhounite and a veteran of the War of 1812 who had published a highly regarded textbook on military tactics in 1819.[40]

The Bradley brothers, Brown, Coyle, and Gardner oversaw a staff that consisted of thirty clerks, a considerable work force in an age when few enterprises employed more than a dozen individuals at any one site. By all accounts, the staff labored diligently and well. Most spent at least part of the six-hour workday engaged in the laborious task of copying out in longhand the steady volume of letters, reports, and requests for information that the general post office prepared for Congress, the other executive departments, and the officers in the field. By far the most important prerequisite for a clerkship was mastery of the rudiments of good penmanship, or what was then known as the possession of an elegant hand. Clerks took great pride in their mastery of the niceties of calligraphy and devoted an extraordinary amount of time to the crafting of impressive-looking documents. Upon receiving one such document, Massachusetts congressman Daniel Webster is reputed to have expressed surprise that it had not been engraved. Characteristically, this was an anecdote that postal clerks repeated with pride.[41] In addition, the clerks sent out countless instructions to postmasters and contractors and maintained over thirty separate account books. Though few of these account books have survived, those that have provide little support for Tocqueville's contention that, in the United States, public record-keeping was primitive and poorly understood.[42] If anything, they suggest that the staff of the general post office was so preoccupied with the preservation of good order that it may well have risked losing sight of the larger goals that the enterprise was intended to serve.

Among the most notable features of these postal clerkships was their financial security. By 1828, it was more or less taken for granted that postal clerks, like federal judges, were entitled to remain in office for as long as they continued to perform their various responsibilities in a satisfactory way.[43] The general rule, scrupulously observed, was that no one was to be dismissed—or, as the phrase went, "removed"—without a fair hearing. No clerk enjoyed a legally enforceable right to his office, as did, for example, some of his counterparts in Great Britain and France; and appointments had always been based at least partly on partisan grounds. But arbitrary dismissals were virtually unknown. Once a clerk secured his appointment, barring the grossest and most obvious derelictions of duty he was set for life. In addition, and no less important, each clerk was salaried, and all were well paid. In a period when $300 was assumed to be the minimum necessary income to maintain a family, McLean earned $6,000, his two principal assistants made $2,500 each, and his clerks made between $800 and $1,300. Most were married, had children, and owned slaves, often a young girl who presumably served as a cook.[44]

The significance of the clerks' job security is easily overlooked. In more recent times it has been taken for granted that a steady salary is a hallmark of middle-class life; in the early republic, however, it was far more rare. Apart from ministers in the more prestigious denominations, few Americans could count on such a reliable form of support. A small number of wealthy Americans may have been able to insulate themselves from sudden fluctuations in the economy, but for everyone else the specter of downward mobility was very real, and with it all the dependency, degradation, and misery that it entailed. Little wonder, then, that clerkships were eagerly—indeed, almost frenetically—sought, and that they were restricted to white men, the single most privileged class of Americans of the day. In a highly uncertain age, a postal clerkship was one of the few forms of employment at once financially lucrative and economically secure.

WHILE THE STAFF of the general post office engaged in a wide variety of tasks, virtually everything it did involved the coordination of one of three great administrative circuits: a communication circuit, which regulated the transmission of the letters, newspapers, and other items that filled the official portmanteau; a transportation circuit, which regulated the conveyance of the mail from office to office; and a financial circuit, which regulated the circulation of postal revenue from postal patrons to the postal agents who carried the mail. Though these three administrative circuits were obviously related, they are best considered separately, since each involved the mastery of a very different combination of skills.

In 1828, the communication circuit was administered in keeping with procedures that were almost thirty years old. At its core was the sorting scheme that postal officers had devised in 1800 to simplify the transmission of the mail. Henceforth, every post office in the United States was divided into one of two classes: the "distributing" offices, or distribution centers; and the "common" offices, or branch depots.[45] In visual terms, this scheme can be depicted as a constellation of rimless spoked wheels each joined at the hub, with the distribution centers as the hubs and the branch depots as the spokes. If everything went as planned, postal officers sorted every item twice: once at the distribution center nearest the branch depot from which it had been sent, and once again at the distribution center nearest the branch depot to which it was addressed. At the distribution centers, of which there were forty-eight in 1828, postal officers were required to sort the mail into separate packets for each office to which it was directed, or to the distribution center closest to its final destination. At the branch depots, they were required merely to sort the mail by its general direction, north, south, east, or west.[46]

While the establishment of the hub-and-spoke sorting scheme is sometimes credited to Thomas Jefferson's postmaster general, Gideon Granger, in fact it was the work of John Adams's postmaster general, Joseph Habersham, a Georgia merchant with an unusually fine grasp of the rudiments of postal administration and the ablest individual to hold the office in the period prior to McLean. The scheme was briefly opposed by Granger, who only slowly came to appreciate its role in simplifying the sorting of the mail.[47] For this reason, the hub-and-spoke sorting scheme, like the establishment of the Bank of the United States, deserves to be remembered as a notable administrative achievement of the Federalists and, in particular, as a response to the challenge for postal policy that had been set in motion with the passage of the Post Office Act of 1792.

Prior to Habersham's reform the general post office required postmasters to sort every packet of letters and newspapers that arrived at their respective offices. As long as the postal system remained little more than a single chain of offices strung along the Atlantic seaboard, this procedure made sense. As the enterprise expanded, however, this arrangement became increasingly impractical. The crux of the problem was that too many people sorted too many letters too many times. In part, the trouble stemmed from the enormous demand for information required of the general post office. As Habersham explained to Augusta, Georgia, postmaster William Hobby in 1800, the scheme obliged Habersham, as the chief executive officer in the postal system, to maintain a correspondence with every post office in the country. In addition, it greatly increased the likelihood that a given piece of mail might be improperly tampered with en route to its destination. As long as every packet of letters was opened in every office along the line, it was virtually impossible to prevent *someone* from improperly peeking into the correspondence of public figures, merchants, and other well known users of the enterprise. Habersham hoped his "new system," as he termed it, would solve both of these perplexing problems at a single stroke.[48]

The hub-and-spoke sorting scheme brought into existence an entirely new class of postal officers: the distributing postmasters. The distributing postmasters performed many of the tasks that have come to be identified with middle management, making them a harbinger of one of the most notable institutional innovations in the modern world. Like the modern middle manager, the distributing postmaster acted as the principal intermediary between the general office and the offices in the field. For this he received a steady income, though technically not a salary. The letterbook of Thomas W. Bacot, the postmaster of Charleston, South Carolina, in the second decade of the nineteenth century, documents the kind of tasks that a distributing postmaster performed. In addition to relaying information from the general post office to the postmasters at the branch depots, Bacot oversaw the appointment of postal officers in his immediate vicinity, monitored the postal agents to make sure they maintained their assigned schedule, and in general encouraged his "brother postmasters" to get on with their work.[49]

The establishment of the hub-and-spoke sorting scheme was a notable turning point in the history of American postal policy because it marked the moment at which postal officers began to differentiate the transmission of information from sender to recipient from its physical conveyance from place to place. The physical conveyance of the mail from office to office, of course, remained dependent on the postal agents who carried the mail, yet its *regular transmission* from sender to recipient depended far less upon the *speed* with which the stagecoaches, postriders, and other mail carriers traveled from post office to post office than upon the *administrative coordination* of these mail carriers by the middle-level postal officers who managed the mail.[50]

The hub-and-spoke sorting scheme remained a standard feature of postal policy from 1800 until the Civil War, when it was finally supplanted by the continuous sorting scheme on specially outfitted railroad cars that has come to be known as railway mail. Prior to the Civil War, the coming of the railroad had little effect on postal policy even though the general post office had been relying on the railroad to carry the mail on certain routes for almost thirty years. Here was one instance in which

American postal policy clearly lagged behind its counterpart in Great Britain, providing a revealing index of the stubborn conservatism of postal administrators in the decades immediately following the resignation of John McLean.

Habersham's sorting scheme may have greatly simplified the work of the general post office, yet it by no means eliminated the administrative challenge of managing the mail. By 1828, this challenge had become formidable indeed. Notwithstanding the delegation of many key tasks to the distributing postmasters, the postmaster general remained responsible for a staggering volume of work. On an average work day, McLean might personally attend to as many as three hundred different letters from contractors, postal patrons, and postal officers in the field.[51] In theory, McLean could have decentralized postal administration by establishing a branch office somewhere in the West, an idea that was floated as early as 1818 and that resurfaced repeatedly in the years to come.[52] In practice, however, McLean insisted on retaining tight control over his far-flung staff. "If the department were ten times as large as it now is," observed postal authority Peter G. Washington in 1851, "we should still . . . deplore the division, or the coordinate authority over it, of a plural number of officers, as a great evil."[53] It was a sentiment with which every senior postal officer in the antebellum period, including McLean, would have heartily approved.

To maintain contact with his staff, McLean sent out a steady stream of information. In 1825 and again in 1828, he issued updated editions of *Post-Office Laws, Instructions, and Forms,* the standard operating manual for postal officers. The 1828 edition of this manual ran to no fewer than fifty-three densely packed pages of text, to which McLean appended nine pages of sample forms.[54] In addition, McLean sent out innumerable handwritten letters and printed circulars and took care to insure that every major new postal regulation found its way into *Niles's Weekly Register,* the most authoritative periodical of the day.

To make sure that all this information had the desired effect, McLean monitored his staff in a variety of ways. In addition to requiring regular financial reports from his postmasters in the field, McLean subscribed to a large number of newspapers, since it was often from newspaper articles that he received his first notice that something had gone wrong in the field. For special assignments, McLean relied on his trusted special agent, Michael Simpson, who performed a variety of tasks, including the supervision of the Philadelphia post office following the discovery of the financial irregularities of postmaster Richard Bache, Jr., and the initiation of secret political negotiations on McLean's behalf with Andrew Jackson at his Tennessee estate.[55]

By 1828, the employment of special agents was a standard feature of postal operations. Hailed as the "invisible agents" of the general post office, they were among the most highly regarded of all public officers, precursors of the private eye.[56] Special agents were particularly celebrated for their role in ferreting out postal officers who had stolen bank notes that had been sent through the mail. One proven technique for trapping these culprits involved the use of carefully prepared decoy letters that contained specially marked bank notes. While some postal officers criticized this technique as contemptible, since it tempted their peers to break the law, others praised it for its deterrent effect. Special agent James Holbrook took the latter view and, in a notable memoir published in 1855, described a number of the more common surveillance techniques in an effort, he declared, to fortify postal officers against the "peculiar temptations" to which they were exposed. Holbrook's memoir—waggishly titled *Ten Years among the Mail Bags,* in a play on Richard Henry Dana's *Two Years Before the Mast*—is among the first books published by a subordinate officer of the central government and has the further distinction of helping to establish the genre of the modern detective story, which emerged at roughly the same time.[57]

When McLean found a postal officer guilty of robbing the mail, he was likely to press for conviction, convinced that this was the most effective way to prevent others from emulating the crime. Mail robbery was severely punished under federal law, and McLean was determined to use every means at his disposal to increase the security of the mail. President Adams fully shared McLean's concern. Though Adams was often urged to pardon postal officers guilty of robbing the mail, he invariably refused. Postal embezzlement, Adams moralized in 1828, upon being urged to pardon a Tennessee postmaster who had been sentenced to ten years in prison for stealing a winning lottery ticket from a letter, was a crime that was "so dangerous in its consequences" and to which there was "so great exposure of temptation" that "society has scarcely any guard against it excepting in the severity of the punishment."[58]

If a given letter had been properly routed through the system yet still failed to reach its proper destination, it ended up at the dead letter office, a curious institution that generated a good deal of attention in the press. The origins of the institution went back to the 1770s, when

Congress authorized Ebenezer Hazard to open undelivered letters that might assist in the prosecution of the war. By 1828, the dead letter office had lost its connection with intelligence-gathering and had become transformed into a shrine to commerce. If a dead letter contained no bank notes or other valuable papers, it was summarily burned in a great bonfire that was one of the best known events of the national capital. If, however, it contained items of value, it was duly returned to its sender. To determine which letters were worth saving, the postmaster general empowered the staff of the dead letter office to open the mail, a unique distinction that made its work an object of special interest for journalists, writers, and other contemporaries familiar with public affairs, including Francis Lieber, who published a humorous sketch on the subject in 1831.[59]

If a lost letter could not be found, there the matter ended. In certain circumstances, postal patrons could sue postmasters or their clerks for negligence, yet under no circumstances could they institute a suit against the government to recover money or other valuables lost in the mail. McLean found this situation troubling; accordingly, in 1828 he proposed that the government insure the money that postal patrons sent through the mail.[60] Nothing came of McLean's proposal, though in 1855 the general post office did introduce a rudimentary registered mail service. Hailed as a major innovation, it proved to be of dubious value, since the service consisted merely of an additional accounting check and left the money uninsured, just as before. If anything, it gave potential thieves a convenient way to figure out which letters were worth stealing.[61] Poorly conceived, the service was also poorly advertised. It was a "singular fact," declared an editorialist in 1873, that almost two decades after the registered mail service had first been introduced, "a large majority of people have not the slightest practical knowledge of its existence."[62]

Had McLean relied on the mere force of law to monitor his staff, it is highly unlikely that the postal system could have attained the level of service that it did. The threat of mandatory prison sentences may have helped to deter theft, yet it did little to motivate the staff. How, then, was this elusive goal to be attained? A few years after McLean's resignation, distributing postmaster Woodson Wren proposed one answer. Unlike a slave, Wren laconically observed, a postmaster could not be whipped to make him "do his duty." The only effective goad, Wren concluded, was to increase his commission or guarantee him an annual salary. Only this could make him do the work: "In this business, interest

78

alone is the great controlling power that must be looked to, as physical force cannot be applied, and would not be submitted to."[63]

McLean shared Wren's suspicion that most postal officers, with the notable exception of the staff of the general post office, were badly underpaid, yet he rejected as impractical any possibility of an across-the-board increase in their pay. Given the enormous size of his staff, McLean concluded, there was simply not enough revenue to go around.[64]

As an alternative, McLean fixed his attention on improving his officers' esprit de corps and, in particular, on instilling in them the loyalty, dependability, and pride that was associated with the military, the only other institution to operate on an even remotely comparable scale. McLean freely conceded that he did not expect his staff to act with the "promptitude and decision" of a "well disciplined military corps."[65] But he remained convinced that its effectiveness could be greatly increased by adopting a number of techniques that his mentor John C. Calhoun had introduced in the Department of War. Toward this end, McLean organized the general post office into seven "divisions," a bit of military terminology almost certainly borrowed from Calhoun.[66] In addition, McLean issued a detailed code of behavior that enjoined postmasters to identify with the enterprise and to "participate in the elevation of its character." McLean may not have been the first postmaster general to prepare such a code, yet he was the first to broadcast it to the public at large. In this way, he hoped to impress upon postmasters the importance of maintaining a high standard of conduct and, if they did not, to encourage postal patrons to call them to account.[67] If all else failed, McLean always had the franking privilege, which, as he explained in 1824, was particularly important for postmasters in the smaller offices, since they were "proud of a privilege" and regarded it as a badge of honor that far outweighed any pecuniary compensation that the general post office might find it prudent to bestow.[68]

The cornerstone of McLean's appointments policy was his popularization of the doctrine that government office was a public trust. This doctrine was by no means new. As early as 1800, Postmaster General Joseph Habersham announced that it had long been a rule in his office not to dismiss a postmaster as long as he performed his duty punctually and in accordance with the law. "Were it otherwise," Habersham explained, "it would be very difficult to find reputable men to hold offices attended with as little profit as post offices generally are."[69] Yet it was not Habersham but McLean who invested this idea with the authority of a formal pledge and, even more important, who made this pledge widely known to the public. Henceforth, McLean announced in 1825, postal officers need not fear any charges that might be lodged against them without their notice: "Until they shall have been notified of the same, and had ample time for their vindication, no step to their prejudice shall be taken."[70] On the eve of the election of 1828, McLean reiterated his position once again, anxious to squelch rumors that, following the likely victory of Andrew Jackson, McLean would sanction a large-scale purge of his staff. "The postmaster general," McLean reminded his subordinates, determined to keep intact his enviable reputation as a capable administrator, "acknowledges with a high degree of satisfaction, the efficiency of many thousands who are connected with him in the discharge of arduous and responsible duties, and he confidently expects a continuance of their exertions."[71]

Just as McLean looked to the public trust doctrine to improve his public image, so too he hoped that it might improve the accountability of his staff. Should he find it necessary to dismiss a postmaster or clerk, McLean reasoned, he wanted it understood that the ex-officeholder had failed to uphold the public trust and therefore should be open to censure by the public at large. In the language of the day, this meant that dismissals would be restricted to "cause." "I have adopted a rule," McLean explained to a North Carolina congressman shortly after his appointment in 1823, "to remove no postmaster without substantial cause, and then not until he shall have had an opportunity to meet the charges made against him. This will make a removal of the highest consequence to the officer, as it will be understood that the ground on which a removal is made, is that he is not entitled to public confidence."[72] In this way, McLean sought to hold his staff hostage to public opinion and to use the threat of dismissal as a disciplinary technique.

The implications of McLean's public trust doctrine extended well beyond its role in improving the performance of his staff. A convert to Methodism following his marriage after having been raised as a Presbyterian as a boy, McLean found it abhorrent that a capable, morally upstanding postmaster might be arbitrarily dismissed. No doctrine, after all, was more fundamental to nineteenth-century Methodism than the doctrine of salvation through works and none more reprehensible than the rival Presbyterian doctrine of the inscrutability of God's grace. And few things seemed more inscrutable to nineteenth-century Americans than the politically motivated dismissal of meritorious postal officers following a change in the administration.

In addition and, from McLean's standpoint, most important of all, the public trust doctrine helped McLean consolidate his political base. By casting himself as the moral arbiter of the official performance of his staff, McLean successfully wrested control over the appointment process away from Congress, the president, and anyone else who sought to interfere with his legal right to appoint whomever he pleased. Every working day, McLean estimated, he hired between five and fifteen individuals, mostly as postmasters in small country towns.[73] By personally supervising the appointment of such an enormous number of people, McLean helped to build himself the loyal team he would need to mount a presidential campaign.

Under Monroe, McLean's control over the appointment process was constrained by Monroe's watchful gaze. Monroe had few qualms about vetoing McLean's appointments, and in certain particularly sensitive cases, such as the appointment of a postmaster in the Virginia state capital of Richmond, supervised the appointment process directly, a fact that was duly noted in the press.[74] The Richmond appointment was particularly complicated since the contenders included two former Virginia governors and a Richmond merchant who had the backing of the eighty-one-year-old Thomas Jefferson. Jefferson was particularly intent on the appointment since he owed the merchant a good deal of money and was hoping to use the appointment to help to get himself out of debt. To complicate matters still further, one of the ex-governors was Jefferson's son-in-law, who—unbeknownst to his aging father-in-law, and notwithstanding the fact that both men were living at the time on Jefferson's estate at Monticello—secretly lobbied Monroe on his own behalf.[75]

Following Adams's inauguration in 1825, McLean's autonomy appreciably increased. Though McLean routinely consulted with Adams in making his most important appointments—which, in practice, was understood to embrace those postmasterships worth more than $1,000 a year—Adams invariably deferred to McLean. McLean later confided to Monroe that Adams had refused to veto a single one of McLean's hiring decisions—a situation that was far different, McLean added, from that which had prevailed under Monroe.[76]

Adams's refusal to interfere with McLean's hiring decisions provided McLean with just the opportunity he needed to consolidate his political base. In a few celebrated cases, McLean actually went so far as to appoint men to office who publicly backed Adams's political rival Andrew Jackson in the election of 1828. Of the several Jacksonians whom

McLean appointed to office, by far the most notorious was Henry Lee, an impecunious member of the Virginia gentry whom McLean hired for a time as a postal clerk in order to provide Lee with the necessary income to contribute a steady stream of anti-Adams editorials to Duff Green's *United States Telegraph.*[77] When the New York postmastership fell vacant, McLean pursued a similar course. His initial choice for the office was the highly respected Adamsite jurist James Kent. After consulting with Calhoun, however, McLean dropped Kent in favor of Samuel L. Gouverneur, the son-in-law of ex-president Monroe and a Calhounite who backed Andrew Jackson in the election of 1828.[78] Though even McLean recognized that Gouverneur's opposition to Adams's reelection would prove to be a stumbling block to his appointment, McLean went ahead anyway, though, as a courtesy to Adams, he waited to formally make the announcement until after Adams had lost the election.[79] In Philadelphia, the story was much the same. When the postmastership fell vacant in 1828, McLean passed over several prominent Adamsites in favor of the Jacksonian legal scholar Thomas Sergeant. McLean's decision outraged several administration insiders, who urged Adams to dismiss McLean on the spot. Yet Adams kept McLean on, initially because he could not believe that McLean had adopted such a duplicitous course and eventually because he recognized that his dismissal would outrage many of McLean's myriad admirers, and in this way undercut Adams's own base of political support.[80]

McLean's success at using postal patronage to consolidate his political base troubled political insiders wary of his rapidly growing influence in American public life. As early as 1826, for example, Martin Van Buren lobbied hard to secure McLean a vacant seat on the Supreme Court, convinced that the appointment would deprive McLean of his ability to curry favor with the thousands of men who were under his charge.[81]

Even more revealing were the repeated attempts of Massachusetts congressman Edward Everett to persuade McLean to modify his public trust doctrine to suit the needs of the day. A high-minded former Unitarian minister and onetime Harvard professor, Everett was hardly the sort of man one would expect to play the part of the spoilsman. Yet McLean's patronage policy cast Everett in precisely this role. In the months preceding the election of 1828, Everett tried unsuccessfully to persuade McLean to bestow at least some of the patronage that was at his disposal on men whom Everett hoped would help boost Adams's standing at the polls. McLean indignantly rejected Everett's request and, in reply, lectured Everett about the importance of retaining in public service individuals who would enlist the "moral power" of "every good man" on the side of the existing regime.[82] "Patronage is a sacred trust," McLean somberly intoned, "committed by the people, to the hands of their agents, to be used for the public benefit." Should the principle of favoritism be introduced into the appointment process, the reputation of the "best men" in the country would inevitably be sacrificed at the "shrine of party," while the public interest would be forgotten amidst the scramble for promotion. Before long, the republic itself would be destroyed, and with it would "perish, perhaps for ever, the best hope of man."[83] McLean further declared that during his tenure in office he himself had *never* deployed the patronage at his disposal for political effect. After all, should the public ever come to believe that he had made a single appointment with the view of advancing his own interest, it would immediately denounce his conduct as corrupt: "And by what other name shall it be designated!"[84] Whether or not Everett found McLean's explanation persuasive, McLean's high-minded protestations effectively prevented the Adamsites from using the postal system to mobilize political support during the campaign, and so helped guarantee Jackson victory in the election of 1828.

NO LESS NOTABLE than the public trust doctrine in demonstrating McLean's commitment to an expansive approach to public administration was his determination to outspeed private carriers in the transmission of market information. McLean was hardly the first public figure to champion what might be called a gospel of speed. As early as 1782, Congress had declared "despatch" as well as "regularity" to be "essentially requisite" not only to the "safety" but also to the "commercial interest" of the country.[85] Yet McLean was the first postmaster general to devise a plan to transform this ideal into a reality. In effect, he sought to guarantee that the postal system would outspeed all competitors in the transmission of market information and, in this way, to eliminate the risk that had previously been borne by merchants living on the commercial periphery.

McLean's interest in the high-speed transmission of market information was the direct result of a celebrated bit of commodity trading that occurred in the spring of 1825. An enterprising group of merchants based along the Atlantic seaboard, very possibly in New York, netted several hundred thousand dollars by taking advantage of their advance knowledge of a sharp rise in cotton prices in the European markets. The key to their gambit was their ability to commandeer the horses and riders that the government used to transmit the mail and, in so doing, to greatly reduce the delay that ordinarily separated the arrival of European market information along the Atlantic seaboard from its arrival in the cotton ports of Mobile and New Orleans. According to one account, the merchants paid one mail contractor the princely sum of $300 to transmit their purchase order along one 120-mile stretch of the North-South post road and to hold back the mail until their order got through. In this way, the merchants were able to place their purchase orders long before news of the price rise became generally known, thus undermining the implicit trust that the planters in the cotton ports had come to place in the postal system as the authoritative source of information on changing market trends.[86]

McLean found the merchants' gambit outrageous and set about to prevent them from ever attempting anything like it again. Henceforth, he decreed, all mail contracts were to include a clause prohibiting the contractors from using their stock to transmit information ahead of the mail. Since mail contractors were the only regular means of conveyance in the Southwest, McLean felt sure that this would go far toward solving the problem.[87] In addition, McLean set about to eliminate the possibility that merchants might find some other way to circumvent the mail. Toward this end, he proposed the establishment of a special horse express to run between New York and New Orleans. McLean did not envision his express being run on a regular basis. Rather, he assumed it would be set in motion by Atlantic seaboard postmasters only when they learned of a sudden and unanticipated change in the European markets, an event, McLean predicted, that might occur as infrequently as three times a year.[88] But when his express did run, as McLean explained to Baltimore postmaster John Stuart Skinner, it would provide the planters of the Southwest with an "*extra* system of intelligence" that would defeat the speculation inevitably caused by the tardy arrival of the mail.[89]

McLean's proposal met with a mixed reception in the press. Hezekiah Niles praised it as a "great thing" and yet another of the "wonderful improvements" that McLean had undertaken since his appointment to office. Yet Niles wondered aloud if it would dampen speculation to the extent that McLean hoped.[90] Even more critical was Thomas Ritchie of the Richmond *Enquirer*. Though Ritchie agreed that McLean's proposal would almost certainly promote the reputation of the department, he was far from convinced that it was a good idea. "Is this minute interference with the private relations of men," Ritchie editorialized, "compatible with the general duties of government?" When would the government cease its "surveillance" over mercantile affairs?[91]

Most critical of all was Baltimore postmaster John Stuart Skinner, who responded to McLean's letter in a lengthy reply addressed to postal clerk Richard Douglass. McLean's proposal, Skinner observed, was subject to the serious objection that it depended for its success upon the cooperation of the very merchants whose speculations it was intended to thwart. How, Skinner added, could the postmaster who set the first postrider in motion be confident that he had received accurate information? "Could he, not being a practical merchant, estimate the correctness and the importance of what might be communicated to him in good faith? Could he rely on the interest which the merchants would feel in frustrating speculations, as being of sufficient strength and constancy to prompt them to communicate to him faithfully the earliest intelligence?" Might it not be possible, in short, that McLean's laudable desire to frustrate speculation would lead gullible postmasters to authorize postriders to bring highly imperfect accounts of the prevailing market conditions in Europe and, in this way, be "messengers of darkness and mischief" rather than "heralds of light and promoters of fair trade"? As an alternative, might it not be best to continue to rely in the future, as in the past, on the sacredness of the general mail, leaving all else to the "sharp-sighted rivalry of trade, and the activity of private enterprise?"[92]

McLean responded to his critics in a remarkable memorandum that he never released to the press. Terming Skinner's solicitude for private enterprise to be "most extraordinary," McLean warned that, if Skinner's ideas were taken to their logical extreme, they would transform speculators who amassed their fortunes by taking advantage of their advance information on changing market trends into the "peculiar favorites of commerce." All "honest and high-minded merchants," McLean declared, would reject this idea at once. By operating in secret—and, above all, by concealing information—the merchants had deprived the planters of their right to sell their property at the going market rate. This was clearly wrong. "On all principles of fair dealing," McLean explained, "the holder of property should be apprised of its value before he parts with it. To purchase an article at one-half or two-thirds of its value—which is known to the buyer, but carefully concealed from the seller—is in opposition both to the principles of law and sound morality."[93]

McLean's memorandum illustrated and helped to clarify his extraordinarily broad conception of the proper scope of federal power. In his dealings with merchants, as in his dealings with his staff, he sought to invest the postal system with a high moral purpose. Particularly notable in this regard was his withering contempt for private enterprise, a concept that, in this period, had a decidedly unfamiliar ring. Enterprise, of course, was a familiar enough idea, but "private enterprise" was not. On the contrary, public figures presumed that large-scale enterprises like the postal system necessarily had a public character and as such were appropriate objects of government supervision, regulation, and control.

From a present-day standpoint, it might well seem strange that the federal government could once have committed itself as a matter of principle to outspeeding private entrepreneurs in the transmission of market information. Yet in the decades following McLean's popularization of the gospel of speed, this commitment was widely shared and figured prominently in public discussions of the proper relationship of the postal system to a variety of novel technologies, including the steam railroad and the electric telegraph.

McLean's own commitment to the gospel of speed extended well beyond his projected horse express. He was particularly determined to find some way to speed the regular transmission of the mail. Toward this end, McLean commissioned South Carolina architect and engineer Robert Mills to devise a state-of-the-art high-speed postal express in 1826. Mills's proposal took the form of a horse-drawn carriage modeled on a canal packet suspended from a single overhead rail. Mills claimed that his monorail was "peculiarly adapted" to "facilitate the operations of the mail," since it could attain a cruising speed of ten miles an hour, which was considerably faster than the stagecoach and which approximated the fastest horse express.[94]

McLean also tinkered with the idea of establishing a postal telegraph. "If it were possible to communicate by telegraph all articles of intelligence to every neighborhood in the Union," he declared in 1827, it would be "proper to do so."[95] What McLean had in mind was not an electric telegraph of the kind that would later be commercialized by Samuel F. B. Morse, but an optical telegraph of the kind that had first been introduced in the 1790s by the French engineer Claude Chappe. Chappe's telegraph consisted of a series of towers, or "telegraphs," crowned by a pair of specially designed T-shaped signaling devices that could be displayed in almost two hundred different positions. Along with the guillotine, it was one of the most important technological innovations to have been spawned by the French Revolution. Originally intended to provide the French army with up-to-date military information, Chappe's telegraph quickly proved its worth and was rapidly extended throughout the country. If the towers were properly staffed, operators could transmit messages from one tower to the next at a speed of 250 miles per day, which was considerably faster than a horse express.[96]

McLean was hardly the first public figure to contemplate the commercial potential of this new technology. By 1828, optical telegraphy had become something of a popular fad. Widely hailed as one of the technological marvels of the age, optical telegraphs were in operation in the immediate vicinity of Boston and New York and had occasionally been discussed in Congress as early as 1807 as a possible solution to the otherwise challenging task of maintaining a line of communication between Washington and New Orleans.[97] Even the term itself had passed into the language of everyday speech. Like "post," "express," and "mail," it was synonymous with speed. By 1820, some forty-five American newspapers had incorporated the word into their masthead, as would Duff Green's *United States Telegraph,* the official organ of Andrew Jackson's presidential campaign in 1828.[98]

Notwithstanding McLean's best efforts, Congress never authorized the construction of either a horse-drawn monorail or a Chappe-style optical telegraph. But McLean's gospel of speed did profoundly influence the early history of the electric telegraph, which Samuel F. B. Morse successfully commercialized in 1844. Like so many religiously minded Americans of a Calvinistic cast, Morse was firmly committed to expanding the scope of the central government and, in particular, to grafting the electric telegraph onto its domain where, he hoped, it would be administered as a branch of the general post office. "The *mail system,*" as Morse explained in 1837, in justification of his position, had been founded on "the universally admitted principle" that the "greater the speed with which intelligence can be transmitted from point to point, the greater is the benefit derived to the whole community."[99] Many contemporaries shared Morse's enthusiasm for public control, including Henry Clay, the Whig presidential contender in 1844. Should the electric telegraph remain in the hands of "private individuals," Clay declared in the month before the election, "they will be able to monopolize intelligence and to perform the greatest operations in commerce and other departments of business. I think such an engine ought to be exclusively under the control of government."[100]

Support for government control of the new technology was particularly strong within the merchant community, since many merchants feared the speculative bonanza that might arise should the electric telegraph be monopolized by unscrupulous traders intent on using their inside information to manipulate the commodity markets in cotton and wheat. Many newspaper and magazine editors favored government control, convinced that the government could build the network faster than private enterprise. The supporters of government ownership briefly included the influential *American Railroad Journal,* though not *Niles's National Register,* which after "no little reflection" opted for "free trade."[101] While the rationale for government ownership varied from editor to editor, most shared the conviction of the Baltimore merchants who warned Congress in 1847 that the new technology was simply too powerful to be left under private control. "The obvious fact," the merchants declared, that control of the new technology "places in the hands of its managers to a great extent the interests of merchants, of the press, of the government itself, and indirectly of the whole people, is sufficient to show the danger of leaving it in the hands of private individuals. Its affinity to the post office, its agency in regulating commerce among the several States, and its obvious utility in directing most promptly the movements of armies and fleets, point unerringly to the government of the United States, as the authority to which this instrument ought to be entrusted."[102]

For a moment, it seemed conceivable that Morse and his supporters might get their wish. In May 1844, the first commercial telegraph in the United States, a 40-mile line between Washington and Baltimore, opened under the de facto control of the general post office.[103] And in June of that year, Congress very nearly enacted legislation to extend the line to New York. Had this legislation not been doomed by a bitter financial squabble between Morse and his business partners, the postmaster general would have had exclusive control over one of the most profitable telegraph lines in the country. In the end, however, Morse failed to secure any additional legislation, and in 1847 the general post office sold the Washington-Baltimore telegraph line to a private consortium, bringing to a close an epoch in American postal history. Never again could a postmaster general presume, as had John McLean, that the central government would have the necessary means to guarantee merchants equal access to market information. Never again could the central government presume to outspeed private enterprise in the transmission of market information.

Once it became obvious that the electric telegraph would develop independently of the postal system, public figures found themselves reconsidering the role of the postal system in American public life. For a time, it was rumored that the postal system would soon be abandoned, a rumor that greatly amused postal clerk William B. Taylor, who sagely predicted that, notwithstanding all the voices to the contrary, the postal system would survive in the end.[104] Others hoped the general post office would take this opportunity to abandon the gospel of speed altogether. Merchants "would not be satisfied," predicted special agent Cortland Stebbins in 1851, "if [for] six days their letters came by the telegraph wires, [and] on the seventh the wire was broken, and their letters have to come by mail. The great object is to satisfy the people; and I am fully satisfied that to do this most effectually, *regularity is of much more importance than speed.*"[105] Stebbins's caveat notwithstanding, postal officers retained their allegiance to the gospel of speed long after the government lost the telegraph in 1847. Even though market information could now be transmitted more quickly by wire, observed a Mobile, Alabama, editor in 1851, the mail should nonetheless always outspeed "private enterprises," since a one-day increase in the transmission of the mail between New York and Mobile would save merchants thousands of dollars every year *"in the single item of interest* on remittances."[106] Still others remained stubbornly optimistic that at some future time Congress might regain control of the new technology. When in the 1850s sculptors installed a marble frieze above the main gate of the general post office building in Washington, they took care to incorporate into its design an electric telegraph, a poignant reminder of the continuing allure of John McLean's gospel of speed.[107]

"NOTHING IS MORE easy to abuse than the post office," remarked one editorialist in 1823 shortly after McLean's appointment, "and nothing is more common."[108] In the early republic, as today, many postal patrons were convinced that the postal system had fallen far short of its potential. Yet when one makes allowance for the inevitable disgruntlement of postal patrons and the self interested vigilance of the press, it seems likely that, for the most part, the system worked remarkably well.

One measure of its effectiveness was the small percentage of items that failed to reach their intended destination. Though postal officers kept no statistics on this subject, a good deal can be gleaned from the occasional comments of editors such as Joseph Gales, Jr., and William Seaton of the *National Intelligencer* and Hezekiah Niles of *Niles's Weekly Register.* As editors of newspapers that aspired to a national readership, they were dependent on the postal system to transmit their publications to the public and so were quick to publicize any shortcomings.

Gales, Seaton, and Niles found much to praise in the level of service that the postal system had attained under McLean. Shortly after McLean's appointment in 1823, Gales and Seaton took pains to stress that postal officers had successfully delivered every properly directed and packed newspaper they had sent during the previous five years from Washington to any other office along the main North-South line.[109] Given the vicissitudes to which newspapers were often subjected, this was high praise indeed. Niles was particularly impressed by the improvements that McLean had introduced. On an average year, Niles calculated in 1823, poor mail delivery cost him between 50 and 100 of his 4,000 subscribers.[110] Thanks to McLean's improvements, Niles noted two years later, the situation had markedly improved. Not only had McLean greatly increased the level of service in the South and West, but he had also generated a large postal surplus that he could use to make further improvements.[111] During the entire period of McLean's administration, Niles reported shortly after McLean's resignation in 1829, a large percentage of Niles's subscribers (he did not say precisely how many) had not missed a single issue of his newspaper. In addition, Niles added, of the more than fifteen hundred letters he had received from north of the Susquehanna during the previous year, not more than three had failed to get through, with the exception of the occasional letter that mail robbers had purloined en route to its destination.[112] It was an impressive record, and one that the Jacksonians would find difficult to match.

No TENET OF postal policy was more fundamental than the assumption that the coordination of the communication circuit should be overseen exclusively by postal officers under the direct authority of the postmaster general. Postal officers were notoriously reluctant to grant non–postal officers access to the official portmanteau—that "sacred governmental thing," as Mark Twain wryly called it—and employed an elaborate series of locks, keys, and specially constructed sacks to protect its security.[113] In contrast, the transportation circuit, which regulated the conveyance of the official portmanteau from post office to post office, was organized on an entirely different basis. Rather than being administered by postal officers, this circuit was overseen by an army of private mail contractors, over seven hundred in 1828.[114] The decision to rely on contractors to carry the mail was by no means inevitable. At various points, McLean's predecessors had experimented with fleets of coastal mail packets and a government-owned stagecoach line.[115] In addition, they had helped to establish special military-style supply depots to facilitate the conveyance of the mail in parts of the country that were particularly thinly settled, such as the Natchez Trace in the Southwest. Occasionally they even slipped mail contractors extra allowances to keep the roads and bridges over which they traveled in proper repair. Yet by 1828 it had become well established that, with few exceptions, the general post office would rely exclusively upon contractors to carry the mail.

By present-day standards, the rate at which the contractors traveled was unbelievably slow. On the principal routes, stagecoaches rarely averaged more than four miles per hour, which, even assuming they traveled day and night, worked out to less than a hundred miles a day. Eight miles per hour was quite fast, while twelve miles per hour represented the upper limit of the existing technology and could be reliably attained only with the establishment of a special horse express. McLean's special horse express, for example, was supposed to reach an average speed of between eight and ten miles an hour and so reduce the time lag between New York and New Orleans from sixteen to seven days.[116]

The speeds the mail contractors attained may be unremarkable by today's standards, yet they were impressive indeed by the standards of 1828. No human contrivance traveled faster. Accordingly, by McLean's day it had become customary to treat the passenger stagecoach that carried the mail as the sine qua non in high-speed travel. To identify themselves with the speed and reliability for which the postal system was celebrated, stagecoach proprietors freely embellished their stagecoaches with phrases like "U.S. Mail" and "Mail Stage," since, in this way, they could identify their enterprise with the conquest of space, which was widely hailed as one of the most praiseworthy of all human endeavors. When the vehicle bearing the "magic characters" of "U.S. Mail" passed through a busy street, reported special agent James Holbrook in 1855, all of the other vehicles separated to the right and left to "do homage" to "that supreme power," the "Public Good."[117] For public men like Richard M. Johnson, the endeavor approached an obsession. During one celebrated stagecoach trip from Kentucky to Washington, Johnson so strained the capacity of his driver—to whom he had paid a handsome sum to keep up the pace—that the stagecoach twice overturned, costing Johnson a number of painful bumps on the head.

"He thought it a fair parallel," Adams sardonically reported following Johnson's triumphant arrival, "to Napoleon's passage over the Alps."[118]

Contracting arrangements varied widely, depending on the weight of the mail and the level of service. One option that McLean did not have to consider was the steam railroad, which, in 1828, remained on the horizon. Though Boston inventor Benjamin Dearborn had raised the possibility of conveying the mail by railroad as early as 1819, it was not until 1831 that a mail contractor used a railroad to carry the mail.[119]

If the railroad was primarily a technology for the future, the steamboat was a technology that, while well established, was poorly suited to the conveyance of the mail. Though the general post office had entered by 1828 into contracts with a number of steamboat firms, relatively few operated on a regular schedule, while those that did were often obliged to adjust their schedule to take into account changing river conditions. And since the general post office was committed to providing its patrons with "regular, sure, and expeditious intercourse" throughout the year and regarded a delay of even a few hours as a "fatal" objection, this meant, as McLean explained to Secretary of War James Barbour in 1825, that the general post office had little to gain from contracting with steamboat firms on the Mississippi River or its principal tributaries in the transappalachian West.[120]

Given the unavailability of the railroad and the unreliability of the steamboat, McLean's principal contracting option in 1828 involved a choice between stagecoaches and postriders. On many of the less heavily patronized routes, McLean relied on the latter, as had all of his predecessors going back to the days of Benjamin Franklin. Celebrated as the heralds of news from the wider world, postriders were important figures in their day. Though their carrying capacity was limited by the strength of their horses, they were far cheaper than stagecoaches and almost invariably on time. During the many years that postrider John Swaney carried the mail along the Natchez Trace, he was reputed to have failed only once to keep his schedule. Among the postriders' many advantages was the fact that they were easy to monitor: in keeping with a longstanding custom, they were required to announce their arrival in town by blowing loudly on a tin horn. Should a postrider fail to stick to the posted schedule, his delay would quickly become known in all the towns along his route.[121]

If the preferred mode of conveyance on the smaller routes was the postrider, the preferred mode of conveyance on the major routes was the stagecoach, which, in the early republic, referred broadly to any vehicle that carried passengers on a fixed schedule over a specified route. While most of these vehicles were little more than crudely covered wagons, a few strove to emulate the grace and elegance that seasoned travelers had come to expect from the steamboat, which remained most travelers' first choice in those parts of the country that were accessible by water. In 1828, the best known stagecoach line was operated by James Reeside on the heavily traveled Philadelphia-Boston route. Celebrated for its high speed, its bright red color, and its well-matched team of four full-blooded Virginia horses, Reeside's line boasted a novel seating arrangement that separated the driver from the passengers and that permitted the passengers to sit front to back. Even in cosmopolitan New York City, its arrival was eagerly anticipated by fashionable men and women, who sometimes journeyed up to the Bowery to catch a better view. When Reeside's stagecoach came into sight, one writer later reminisced, the driver would blow loudly on his post horn and then, laying aside this "vulgar instrument," take up his "legitimate scepter," the whip, which he would "harmlessly crack over the heads of the spirited steeds," making an impressive-sounding snap that could be heard a mile away.[122]

The close relationship between the general post office and the stagecoach industry originated long before McLean's appointment to office in 1823. The first government-sponsored stagecoach service was instituted by Congress in 1785 over the opposition of Postmaster General Ebenezer Hazard, who did everything he could to block the creation of the interlocking relationship between the postal system, the stagecoach industry, and the periodical press that would soon become a defining feature of the postconstitutional communications infrastructure. Among the individuals most committed to expanding government control was Massachusetts delegate Elbridge Gerry, who may have added the phrase "post roads" to the clause incorporating the postal system into the federal Constitution in order to increase the leverage of the central government in its dealings with the stagecoach industry, rather than to authorize it to construct roads, a power that Gerry staunchly opposed as a dangerous and unwarranted invasion upon the prerogatives of the states.[123]

Postal officers preferred stagecoaches over postriders for a variety of reasons. Stagecoach drivers were less likely than postriders to be waylaid by mail robbers, since stagecoach passengers could help the driver fend off an attack. In addition, the presence of passengers helped guarantee that the driver would stick to the posted schedule.[124] As a further advantage, the reliance on stagecoaches hastened the establishment of a rudimentary national network of stagecoach-based public transportation. The establishment of this network was actively encouraged by Congress, above all by those members who lived in districts that could not easily be reached by water. With the adjournment of Congress, reported Ohio representative Elisha Whittlesey to his wife in 1841, congressmen "filled the stages" going west.[125] More than any other circumstance, this simple fact may well explain why the industry received such a lavish measure of government support.

By 1828, the relationship between the central government and the stagecoach industry was well established. Under ordinary circumstances, the general post office awarded a given mail contract to the stagecoach proprietor, even if his bid was as much as one-third higher than a comparable bid to carry the mail by horse. This was true despite the objection of constitutional purists like Abraham Bradley, Jr., who grumbled that the federal Constitution nowhere proclaimed the conveyance of passengers to be a "constitutional or legitimate object" of public concern.[126] Though most stagecoach proprietors took great pains to conceal their dependence upon the public purse, a few were noticeably less restrained. "Having obtained the mail contract from Milledgeville to Montgomery, Alabama," announced the owners of one Alabama stagecoach firm in 1826, they would soon establish a stagecoach line between those two points.[127] Throughout most of the country, and especially in the South and West, competition between stagecoach proprietors took precisely this form. Unwilling to rely on passenger fares alone, they competed for the mail contract and, if they failed to secure it, immediately retired from the field.

The general post office awarded its mail contracts in the fall, after a competition that had been publicly announced in the press. The scale of this task was impressive. Every year, McLean considered some 6,000 separate proposals for over 400 separate contracts.[128] On a given day, he might disburse contracts totaling as much as $40,000, a considerable sum in its day, and one that McLean felt sure would impress his friends back home, since he took care to include it in an address that he delivered in Lebanon, Ohio, during one of his rare summer vacations.[129]

To consolidate his control over the bidding process, McLean introduced a number of changes in the way contracts were let. Prior to McLean's tenure, the bidding process for prospective mail contractors had been largely routine. Barring the unforeseen, existing contractors had little reason to fear that their contracts would not be renewed.

Though this presumption greatly limited the ability of postal officers to enter into new arrangements, it also reduced the risks that were inevitably associated with making a change. The old contractors, after all, could be expected to carry the mail in the future in much the same way they had in the past. New contractors were far less predictable. In addition, this presumption minimized the financial dislocations that the old contractors would inevitably suffer should they lose their contract when it came up for renewal. Should a stagecoach proprietor fail to get his contract renewed, he might well be confronted with the difficult choice of selling off his stock at a substantial loss or competing head-on with the successful contractor for the limited passenger market, an option widely regarded as a recipe for disaster for both the old line and the new.[130]

McLean altered the bidding process in two notable ways. First, he stipulated that, beginning in 1824, mail contractors could no longer expect to have their contracts automatically renewed; and, second, he added that, should the general post office make a change, the new contractors would be required to purchase the old contractors' stock. In theory, McLean hoped that this innovation would increase his ability to enter into advantageous contracting arrangements while minimizing the dislocations that would inevitably accompany a switch. In practice, it transformed the establishment of passenger service into a major new federally funded entitlement program predicated on the assumption that under ordinary circumstances the government would never discontinue passenger service on routes it had already established.[131]

McLean's innovations transformed the bidding process almost overnight. Prior to 1824, stagecoach proprietors had little reason to lobby particularly hard for their mail contracts, since it was virtually certain that they would be renewed. Now everything was up for grabs. Deciding who got what was no simple matter, since bidders had the option of proposing a wide variety of different arrangements. For a given route, McLean might find himself debating whether the mail should be carried by horse, sulky, or stagecoach and whether it should travel once, twice, or six times a week. Even in the case of identical bids for the same route, it was by no means obvious that the general post office should prefer the lowest bid, since, if the contractor found it impossible to do the work, McLean would find himself in the awkward position of having to scramble for a replacement.

Emboldened by the prospect of securing a lucrative mail contract, dozens of stagecoach proprietors, wagoners, and transportation lobbyists of all kinds flooded Washington to make their bids, transforming the once-perfunctory contracting process into an entrepreneurial free-for-all. To prevent the crush from becoming overwhelming, McLean divided the country into four sections and advertised contracts for each of these sections in a different year.[132] When the contractors were in Washington to renew their bids, they might stay at the commodious public hotel that developer John Gadsby opened in 1827. In addition, they might join the hundred-odd mail contractors who in October of that year met with the president at an official reception at the White House, curious to find out what went on behind the walls of the "Palace," as the White House was then popularly known. After shaking hands with each of the contractors, Adams served them cakes and wine and took them on a house tour, omitting only the bedrooms. It was, Adams dutifully recorded in his diary, almost certainly the first time that they had ever assembled in a body and been so entertained.[133]

McLean's innovations in the bidding process had a palpable effect on the level of service. Particularly notable were the improvements on the heavily patronized stretch of the North-South post road between Philadelphia and Boston. Frustrated by the repeated failure of the old contractor to keep to his posted schedule, McLean enlisted the celebrated James Reeside to help the government improve the level of service. Though Reeside lacked the social graces that most mail contractors had been presumed to display, he was earnest and industrious and soon put the line on a far better footing than it had been at any point in the past.

Equally notable was McLean's decision to relocate the great southern mail route between Washington and New Orleans. Prior to 1826, the Washington–New Orleans mail had followed a circuitous route that went halfway across Tennessee before finally dropping down to New Orleans by way of the Natchez Trace.[134] Though roundabout, this route had the advantage of traversing a thickly settled part of the country that was well provided with taverns, feed bins, blacksmith shops, and the other ancillary services that stagecoach drivers relied upon to service their horses and keep their passengers content.[135] The new route, in contrast, bypassed Tennessee altogether in favor of a more southerly route that traversed the more sparsely settled parts of Georgia, Alabama, and Mississippi.[136]

McLean's decision to relocate the route may have been based on sound administrative considerations, yet it had the unfortunate effect of greatly exacerbating the simmering conflict between the central government and the various Indian tribes that occupied much of the territory through which the government now carried the mail. After a series of minor clashes, this conflict came to a head in 1830, when, in a much publicized episode, the Creek warrior Tuskeneah forcibly detained a stagecoach carrying the mail along a desolate stretch of post road in Alabama.[137] Though Tuskeneah harmed neither the passengers nor the mail, his defiant gesture may well have heightened the mounting public pressure to relocate the tribes of the Old Southwest to the far side of the Mississippi River, a policy that culminated during the 1830s in the forced migration that has come to be known as the Trail of Tears.

However fateful Tuskeneah's encounter with the postal system may have been for the Indian tribes of the Southwest, it was, at best, of minor concern to McLean. Far more important were the implications of his innovations in the bidding process for his political career. By throwing the bidding process open to competition, McLean greatly increased his ability to manipulate it for partisan ends. All things being equal, he consistently awarded contracts to individuals who might frustrate the Adamsites and in this way consolidate his own political base and that of his mentor, Calhoun. To cite but one obvious example, James Reeside was not only a highly effective mail contractor, but also an anti-Adamsite political activist with great influence over the electorate in the interior of Pennsylvania, a fact that was not lost on President Adams, who privately resented the patronage that McLean had thrown his way.[138] Isaac Hill, similarly, was not only a leading mail contractor in northern New England, but also the printer of the *New Hampshire Patriot,* one of the most influential anti-Adamsite newspapers in the United States.[139]

Equally notable was McLean's willingness to bestow a lucrative mail contract on Duff Green, an ambitious Virginia-born Missouri political editor who yearned to play a part on the national stage. Early in McLean's tenure in office, Green put in a bid to carry the mail by stagecoach in Missouri and, in this way, to establish what he proudly claimed to be the first regularly scheduled passenger stagecoach line in the Trans-Mississippi West. From the start, this quixotic venture was contingent upon government support. Without the steady income from a mail contract, Green could not possibly have run the line at a profit. Even Green admitted as much. His costs, he confided to an associate, would be $6,800, of which, at best, he could expect to recover $1,000 from passenger fares. McLean initially rejected Green's bid, unconvinced of the advisability of supporting such a speculative venture in one of the most thinly settled portions of the West. Undeterred, Green lined up the support of John C. Calhoun and Richard M. Johnson, who prevailed with McLean and secured Green his contract. Pleased at his success, Green used the contract to pay off some personal debts so that he might move to Washington, D.C., where he took over a floundering political newspaper that he renamed the *United States Telegraph*.[140] Before long Green emerged as a staunch supporter of Andrew Jackson's bid for the presidency in the election of 1828 and a leading critic of government waste and mismanagement, a subject that he wrote about with particular conviction, very possibly because his own dubious financial dealings gave him special insight into the opportunities for abuse. If all went according to plan, or so Green hoped, Jackson would retire after one term in office and appoint vice president John C. Calhoun as his designated heir, who in turn would ride Jackson's coattails to the presidency in the election of 1832.

Green's success at securing a mail contract highlights one of the many ways in which the postal system shaped the stagecoach industry. With the possible exception of the newspaper press, no enterprise in the early republic was more profoundly shaped by political fiat. In New England and the Mid-Atlantic states, the demand for public transportation was sufficiently great that the stagecoach industry could almost certainly have thrived without government support. In the South and West, however, postal subsidies furnished the industry with an indispensable boost. "What is called the mail stage," British traveler Adam Hodgson casually observed as he traveled through the South Atlantic states in 1824, was the only "public conveyance" in that part of the country.[141] It was an observation that could have been repeated throughout much of the United States. According to one estimate, postal subsidies accounted for fully 33 percent of the total revenue that the stagecoach industry received.[142] For some mail contractors, such as Virginia stagecoach proprietor Jordan Woolfolk, the subsidy could be as large as 50 percent.[143] And on some routes, the subsidy could be higher still. "I think the most flagrant violation of the *rights of the quill*," wrote one Illinoisan to the postmaster general in 1843, "is maintaining lines of coaches as the expense of the Department." In this part of the country, the Illinoisan added, the coaches ran empty—meaning, presumably, that the mail subsidy approached 100 percent, doubling the cost of conveying the mail.[144]

The peculiarly close relationship between the postal system and the stagecoach industry raises basic questions about Alexis de Tocqueville's celebrated observation that in the early republic the central government played at best a marginal role in American public life. Had the government not underwritten the stagecoach industry with its postal subsidies, it would have been difficult, if not impossible, for this important industry to have attained such an impressive level of service, particularly in the thinly settled portions of the South and West. Indeed, without this subsidy, Tocqueville himself would have found it far more difficult to travel as he did through the Michigan frontier, relying as he did on the stagecoach network that the general post office had established to carry the mail.

The stagecoach subsidies lasted until 1845, when Congress, intent on cutting costs, once again changed the rules of the game. Henceforth, Congress decreed, the government would no longer require stagecoach proprietors to sell their stock to the successful bidder, ending a policy that went back to McLean. In addition, Congress created a new class of mail routes—the so-called "star routes"—that the postmaster general could secure bids for by whatever means would guarantee "celerity, certainty, and security," regardless of whether they carried passengers along with the mail. Throughout much of the transappalachian West, this regulation was the deathblow of the industry. Now that the postmaster general no longer required stagecoach service, as one mail contractor complained in 1850, he has "killed the goose that laid the golden eggs."[145]

West of the Mississippi River, however, the general post office continued to subsidize the stagecoach industry for a few decades longer. Of the many government-subsidized lines, the most ambitious was the Overland Mail, a 2,800-mile stagecoach line between St. Louis and Memphis in the East and Los Angeles and San Francisco in the West that veteran mail contractor John Butterfield established in 1858. Though Butterfield's Overland Mail is often remembered as a notable chapter in the history of private enterprise, in fact, Butterfield received 30 percent of his total revenue from the mail contract, making it more accurate to call it one of the most ambitious ventures in public transportation to have been undertaken in the United States in the nineteenth century.[146]

Just as postal policy shaped the Overland Mail, so too it shaped the brief history of the Pony Express. Begun in April 1860 by military freighter and mail contractor William Russell as a horse relay between St. Joseph, Missouri, and the West Coast, the Pony Express ran until October 1861, when it was rendered obsolete with the completion of the electric telegraph between the Atlantic and the Pacific. During much of its brief eighteen-month life, the Pony Express secured no federal funding of any kind. But this does not mean that the postal system played no role in Russell's plans. On the contrary, Russell intended from the outset to use the Pony Express as a publicity stunt to convince Congress and the postmaster general to give him the stagecoach contract for the Overland Mail. To beat out the competition, Russell later reminisced, he had tried to build himself a "world-wide reputation"; the Pony Express was a means to that end.[147] Pony Express rider J. H. Keetley put it rather more bluntly. From start to finish, Keetley later maintained, the venture was nothing more than a "put-up job" for the Overland Mail. To maximize publicity, he recalled, Russell required the first rider that left St. Joseph to wear an outlandish costume that included silver trappings, a scabbard, and jingling spurs, making him resemble a "fantastic circus rider." Once the rider reached the boat to cross the Missouri River, he quickly packed the costume away, so that it could be used by the next rider making the trip. Russell never secured the much sought-after contract, which went instead to the better connected Butterfield. His Pony Express, however, swiftly passed into American folklore as a heroic chapter in the history of the West. Here, too, publicity was the key. Intent upon keeping the memory of Russell's quixotic venture alive, William Cody, a onetime Pony Express rider turned traveling showman who went by the name of "Buffalo Bill," included a Pony Express relay in his famous Wild West shows, successfully investing Russell's venture with the iconic status that Russell had worked so hard to establish a generation before.[148]

THE HISTORY of the Overland Mail and the Pony Express illustrates some of the myriad ways in which the postal system shaped overland transportation. Particularly notable was the assumption that postal officers should retain the right to dictate the schedules that stagecoach drivers were required to maintain. By 1828, the general post office had been coordinating the scheduling of the national stagecoach network for almost forty years. Like the hub-and-spoke sorting scheme, this policy traced its origins back to the period immediately following the passage of the Post Office Act of 1792. In 1790, Postmaster General Samuel Osgood complained that every contractor was consulting his own interest as to the days and hours of his arrival and departure, without regard to the needs of the government. A "regular system of days and hours of departure," Osgood lamented, had "never been established further southward than Alexandria."[149] By 1796, the general post office had established a regular, hour-by-hour stagecoach schedule for the entire North-South post road. To broadcast this schedule to the public at large, Abraham Bradley, Jr., appended an elaborate chart to the first edition of his map of the United States.[150] Following the acquisition of Louisiana in 1803, postal officers gradually extended regular stagecoach service even to the most thinly settled regions of the Old Southwest. By the 1850s, they had extended it even to the Pacific. No feature was more characteristic of Butterfield's Overland Mail, for example, than the careful schedule that Butterfield worked out in conjunction with postal officers to regulate the movement of the stagecoaches that carried the mail. "The whole line," reminisced Atchison, Kansas, postal clerk Frank A. Root, was operated with the "precision and punctuality" of a railroad.[151]

To help keep contractors to their prearranged schedules, the general post office relied on a variety of techniques. The most basic was the collection of a vast amount of information about the contractors' routine performance. Though the general post office did not, like its British counterparts, require stagecoach drivers to carry a special clock that could be examined by postmasters along the route, it did require postmasters to report regularly on their drivers' arrival time. Further assistance was provided by stagecoach passengers who were intent upon expediting the mail.[152] Few passengers may have been as vigilant in upholding the letter of the law as Anne Royall, who in 1828 cajoled a stagecoach driver to carry herself, the driver, and the mail by stagecoach from Worcester to Springfield, Massachusetts, when the driver, along with the rest of the passengers, had hoped to finish the journey in Northampton and send the mail along to Springfield in a cart.[153] Yet it was by no means unusual for postal officers to interview stagecoach passengers about the handling of the mail after the passengers had arrived in town. Such, for example, was the settled practice of Charleston, South Carolina, postmaster Thomas W. Bacot in the second decade of the nineteenth century.[154]

Should a given mail contractor fail to keep his stagecoaches to their posted schedule, McLean had a variety of options. To begin with, he could fine the contractor for dereliction of duty. The fine itself might be a "trifle," warned one Massachusetts mail contractor in 1834, yet its effect upon the officers of the general post office might well produce consequences that were "not *very trifling* indeed," since it might predispose postal officers to switch contractors when their contract came up for renewal.[155] Should the fine fail to produce the desired improvement, McLean could require the contractor to increase his motive power. "No obstacles, which human exertions can overcome," McLean decreed in 1825, "shall excuse a failure . . . If two horses to a cart do not give sufficient force, four shall be applied."[156] Occasionally McLean might even require the contractor to abandon passenger service altogether in favor of lightweight carts.[157] And, of course, McLean always had the option of refusing to renew the contractors' contract, an important incentive, given the dependence of the industry on the government for financial support. Should the postmaster general so choose, observed one North Carolina congressman in 1832, he had the power to run out of business fully three-quarters of the entire stagecoach industry in the United States.[158]

Judging from the contemporary evidence, these stratagems worked remarkably well. Even before the passage of the Post Office Act of 1792, passengers grew accustomed to distinguishing between the mail stage, which was expected to keep to a regular schedule, and all the other stages, which were not. The Providence stage, reported one Pennsylvania traveler in 1789, was not "under the direction of the post office" and as a consequence had "no stated time for running."[159] Most passengers commonly "follow the mail," explained the proprietors of the Norfolk and Bristol Turnpike in 1818, when confronted with the possibility that the general post office might withdraw stagecoach service from their route.[160] If two stagecoach firms were engaged in head-to-head competition, predicted Abraham Bradley, Jr., in 1831, one of the firms might actually agree to carry the mail free of charge, since by so doing they would "ensure a preference by the passengers, on account of its going with regularity."[161] Given this reputation for punctuality, it should come as no surprise that when in 1831 one manager of the newly established Charleston and Hamburg Railroad wanted to impress upon his peers the importance of running trains in accordance with a regular schedule, he looked to the postal system as a model. The arrival and departure of the railroad, the manager insisted, must be regulated by a system that was "as certain and prompt as the mail arrangements."[162]

Perhaps the best testimony to the success of the general post office in regulating the stagecoach industry can be found in the travel account of Swedish traveler Carl Arfwedson, published in 1834. During the course of his journey through the United States, Arfwedson observed, he had repeatedly found himself struck by the cruel indifference that American stagecoach drivers displayed toward their passengers and horses, owing to their determination to make the fastest possible time. The explanation for this disturbing phenomenon, Arfwedson explained, lay in the utter dependence of the stagecoach firms upon their mail contracts for the necessary revenue to stay in business. Unwilling to risk a fine, the drivers customarily proceeded with the "utmost celerity," regardless of the danger of risking an accident or killing the horses through overwork. Inevitably, accidents occurred — "too often," in Arf- wedson's opinion. And when they did, the driver felt few compunctions about commandeering a cart so that he might keep to his posted sched- ule, even if this meant that he might leave the astonished passengers stranded at the accident site "in the middle of the road, in a bog, or in a forest, many miles from any habitation."[163]

IF THE CONVEYANCE of the mail from post office to post office was the most challenging task that the general post office undertook, the disbursement of postal revenue was the most time-consuming. In 1828, this task alone required the services of fully two-thirds of the staff.[164] In large measure, this was because of the enormous amount of paper- work involved. According to postal regulations, the general post office required every postmaster in the United States to prepare, in duplicate, a general financial statement (the "accounts current"); a list of every letter sent from the office (the "accounts sent"); a list of every letter received by the office (the "accounts received"); and a receipt for every packet of letters sent in the mail (the "postbill"). If postmasters followed the rules — and, judging from the care with which they prepared those accounts that have survived, it seems likely that they did — they ac- counted for every single letter that they sent through the postal system no fewer than three separate times: once on the accounts sent, a second time on the accounts received, and a third time on the postbill that they included with the mail. In addition, the general post office required local postmasters to keep comparable records for periodicals, though this task involved an even greater expenditure of energy, involving as it did the separate listing of every newspaper and magazine that was re- ceived at the office, and was routinely ignored.

The preparation of these forms remained fundamentally unchanged from the establishment of the American postal system in 1775 until the Civil War. The Post Office Act of 1792 may have transformed the re- lationship between the postal system and Congress, yet it had little impact on the way postal officers kept their accounts, which was based on principles that dated back well before the War of Independence. As late as 1825, the most recent edition of the post office laws and regulations included sample forms that dated from 1794. Had the figures been listed in pounds and shillings rather than dollars and cents, they might well have been prepared by Benjamin Franklin himself.[165] Though Congress simplified the record-keeping process somewhat in 1855 when it instituted mandatory prepayment of all letters sent through the mail, postal officers continued to follow the same basic set of procedures until 1864. The identical waybill that colonial governors had used in the seventeenth century, declared postal authority Pliny Miles in 1855, would have to be adjusted in only the most superficial respects to adapt it to the present state of postal affairs in these days of "lightning telegraphs, balloons, and locomotives."[166]

As late as McLean's tenure, these accounting procedures seem to have given the general post office a check on its officers in the field. At the very least, they reminded the far-flung army of postal officers that their day-to-day activities were being watched. Eventually, however, the staff found itself overwhelmed by the sheer volume of information with which it was deluged. As early as 1841, post office special agent George Plitt publicized what many had long suspected. Since it was impossible to examine all the postbills that the general post office received, Plitt reported, there was "no *effectual check* upon a single post office in the Union."[167] For postal officers worried about the danger of theft, this was a major concern. "Thieves learn these things," warned post office special agent Cortland Stebbins, and "take advantage of the blunders, and steal with comparative safety."[168] By the 1860s, reported British postal officer and novelist Anthony Trollope, the whole exercise had become little more than a pointless charade. Postal officers, Trollope declared with thinly concealed astonishment, routinely required local postmasters to send to postal headquarters "millions of entries" that "no one is ever expected to regard."[169] As a consequence, reported another contemporary, tons of these "worthless papers" accumulated in the general post office each year "waiting to be destroyed."[170]

Notwithstanding the manifest shortcomings of the accounting procedures, the general post office found it impossible to abandon them altogether as long as postmasters were paid by the piece. Prior to 1864, postmasters received a commission on almost every transaction they performed. Had the general post office not required the preparation of such meticulously detailed records, it would have been impossible to determine how much the various postmasters ought to be paid. Predictably, then, the abandonment of these accounting procedures followed shortly upon the establishment in 1864 of regular salaries for the staff. Henceforth, as one journalist explained, if you wished to have postal officers track the progress of your letter step by step through the postal system, you would have to pay a special fee. Otherwise, it would be treated like the rest of the regular mail, as "so many peas in a bag" with "as little trouble as possible [given to] each individual letter."[171]

The reluctance with which the general post office altered its antiquated accounting procedures highlights the institutional inertia that stymied even the most modest reforms. Not even John McLean could figure out how to simplify the process in any fundamental way. This inertia is worth noting, given the tendency of some scholars to stress the much-publicized bookkeeping innovations that Postmaster General Amos Kendall introduced in 1836. In these accounts, Kendall's innovations are credited with having revolutionized postal procedures. In fact, however, they did little to alter the basic contours of postal administration, which remained fundamentally unchanged until the Civil War. The enterprise, declared one merchant in 1845, retained all the "characteristic marks" of its British origins, having adhered with a "tenacity almost anomalous in the administration of the country" to "even the most absurd of its oldest regulations."[172]

One notable exception to this striking continuity in bookkeeping procedure involved the techniques postmasters used to keep their newspaper accounts. Since postmasters rarely filled out these accounts in the first place, McLean assumed quite naturally that it might be possible to make some improvements in the way they were kept. During the twenty years prior to his appointment, McLean dryly declared, no postal clerk had ever examined the duplicate copy of the newspaper postbills that the general post office required local postmasters to prepare. Instead, the clerks merely threw them aside as wastepaper, taking at face value whatever total the postmasters might choose to record.[173] As a consequence, McLean estimated that only half of all the newspapers that postal officers sent through the postal system were ever properly accounted for. To improve upon this situation, McLean tried to persuade printers to report to Washington the number of newspapers they sent from their office.[174] Editors, however, had other ideas. "Too Much Regulation" trumpeted one editorial in the *Pittsburgh Recorder*. Though the editorialist fully shared McLean's suspicion that something had to be done, he regarded McLean's new regulation as "troublesome and vexatious" and even went so far as to question whether McLean had the authority to make such a request.[175] Ever sensitive to public opinion,

McLean quickly backed down and shifted the enforcement burden from editors to postmasters. Henceforth, McLean stipulated, postmasters would be required to prepare, in addition to all their other forms, a special tally of all the newspapers and magazines that they sent or received.[176] Shortly after McLean's resignation in 1829, this procedure was routinized, with the general post office requiring every postmaster in the country to list by name on a special form every newspaper and magazine that passed through the office. Had this procedure not been routinely ignored, particularly in the larger offices, where it would have entailed an enormous amount of additional labor, it would have generated an enormous data bank of information on the readership of every periodical sent through the postal system in the United States.

McLean also took steps to simplify the settlement of accounts. For some years prior to his tenure, the general post office had required postmasters to remit their surplus funds to Washington. Bradley, in his capacity as chief financial officer, deposited the money in a local bank. To hasten the process, at some point prior to 1820 Bradley secured the presidency of the Union Bank of Georgetown, where he worked during those hours when his services were not required in the general post office.[177] While it might well seem highly irregular for the chief financial officer of a public agency to serve simultaneously as the president of a bank, under the circumstances this arrangement made a great deal of sense. As a postal clerk, Bradley sent out thousands of official documents under his own signature, making his name—or, more precisely, his signature—familiar to postmasters and mail contractors throughout the United States.[178] And as a bank president, he had the authority to affix this signature to every bank note that he disbursed. In an age when the central government issued no currency of its own, and when few bank notes circulated outside of the immediate vicinity in which they had been issued, this arrangement greatly simplified the payment of the widely scattered army of mail contractors. Had Bradley tried to pay these contractors in bank notes that lacked his signature, the contractors might well have found it difficult to redeem them on favorable terms.[179]

Intent upon speeding the movement of postal revenue from postal patron to contractor, McLean reorganized the procedures Bradley used to settle his accounts. Henceforth, McLean decreed, mail contractors would no longer receive their mail pay in a lump sum from the general post office, but would instead collect it directly from the postmasters who staffed the offices along their route.[180] In this way, McLean's planned decentralization of postal accounting speeded the circulation of postal revenue throughout the system and provided an additional check on his staff. McLean's policy was in certain respects a throwback to the informal disbursement procedures that the general post office had relied on in the period prior to Bradley's centralization of the accounts. But McLean was the first postmaster general to put this policy into practice as a matter of deliberate design and on a truly national scale.[181]

Even more important than McLean's planned decentralization of postal accounting was his reconceptualization of prevailing assumptions regarding how postal revenue ought to be spent. Prior to McLean's administration, it was customary for the general post office to return a portion of its postal surplus to the treasury to help service the national debt. Though the custom was rarely justified either in Congress or the press, it was consistently honored by every one of McLean's predecessors. Between 1793, when the first payment was made, and 1823, when McLean took charge of the enterprise, the general post office had transferred over $1 million to the general treasury. Though this custom was rarely alluded to in Congress, it provided postal officers with one measure of success. In 1821, for example, McLean's immediate predecessor, Return J. Meigs, Jr., publicly boasted that he had returned over $379,000, which, Meigs proudly added, was more than double the annual average of his predecessor, Gideon Granger.[182] As late as 1827, former President James Monroe paid a similar compliment to McLean.[183]

Monroe's encouragement notwithstanding, McLean had little interest in filling the coffers of the general treasury and moved swiftly to reinvest the postal surplus to improve the level of service. Acting on this principle, McLean transferred to the treasury during his tenure in office a mere $15,000, a token payment in comparison with the much larger sums that had been returned in the period prior to his appointment.[184] Though Congress took no special note of McLean's decision, it met with the full approval of President Adams and Secretary of the Treasury Richard Rush. It had *always* been the policy of the government, declared Adams in 1828, with more imagination than candor, to reinvest postal revenue in this way.[185] According to Rush—expressing sentiments with which Rush's father, Benjamin, would almost certainly have approved—the postal system best promoted national prosperity, which Rush termed the "highest purposes of revenue," not by returning its surplus to the general treasury, but by investing this surplus in improvements that contributed to "the intercourse, the trade, and the prosperity of the country."[186]

McLean's determination to apply the entire postal surplus to postal purposes owed a good deal to circumstances that were outside of his control. Meigs may have prided himself on his cumulative surplus, yet he was also the first postmaster general to run an annual deficit, having been hard hit by the economic downturn that accompanied the Panic of 1819. Though Meigs seems to have had enough reserves on hand to avoid drawing funds from the general treasury, by the end of his tenure in office the cumulative postal surplus had dropped to less than $500,000, which was considerably less than his annual disbursements.[187] Had McLean followed Meigs and returned a significant percentage of his annual revenue to the treasury, the postal system would have run out of funds.[188]

Such pragmatic considerations may help to explain why McLean was reluctant to return his surplus, but they cannot explain how he wished it to be spent. Here the critical consideration was McLean's principled determination to invest the postal surplus to improve the level of service. If McLean had had his way, the general post office would have become the administrative headquarters for a major internal improvements empire that would have built and repaired roads and bridges throughout the United States. Government-sponsored public works were popular throughout much of the country, and McLean did everything he could to link his name with the cause. In 1824 he published a notable report on a proposed 1,100-mile post road between Washington and New Orleans, and in 1827 he enlisted the celebrated French engineer Simon Bernard to prepare an elaborate series of surveys for a road project between Baltimore and Philadelphia.[189] By 1827, McLean was receiving letters directly from ordinary Americans urging him to throw his support behind various internal improvements and to build certain roads along a particular route.[190] Had Congress funded even a small fraction of the myriad road-building projects that were considered during these years, McLean might well have found himself presiding over a public agency that dwarfed even the postal system in its extent. For a time, it was even rumored that Adams might appoint McLean secretary of a new Cabinet-level "home department" to oversee the work.[191]

However much McLean may have yearned to cap his postal career as internal improvements czar, Congress had other ideas. Though Con-

gress had few qualms about spending postal revenue on postal purposes, it preferred to earmark the postal surplus for increasingly lavish
stagecoach subsidies rather than to build and repair bridges and roads.
In part, this preference can be explained by the long-standing congressional bias in favor of the hinterland: the most generous stagecoach
subsidies were earmarked for the South and West, while several of the
major road projects would have been built in the North and East. In
addition, it may well have been a response to the widespread apprehension that any augmentation in McLean's patronage would have increased his political base.

Notwithstanding McLean's failure to achieve his most ambitious
goals, there can be little doubt that he succeeded brilliantly in insulating
the general post office from the other branches of the central government. According to President Adams, McLean controlled more patronage than all the other department heads put together; according to
McLean, he controlled more patronage than President Adams himself.[192] There was "no department in the government," reported one
observer in 1827, that rested on "so independent a basis."[193] As long as
neither Congress nor the executive sought to challenge the postmaster
general's autonomy and, most important of all, as long as the postal
system remained self-supporting, it was likely to remain the freestanding entity that it had become under McLean. More than any other
circumstance, this simple fact explained how McLean was able to enjoy
such an impressive degree of administrative autonomy. His successor,
William Barry, would not be so lucky.

THE COMPLETION of the national postal network under John McLean
brought to a close an important chapter in the history of American
public life. Beginning in 1792, Congress had authorized the establishment of hundreds of separate post routes to link together virtually every
locality in the United States. By 1828, this national postal network was
complete. Even western congressmen acknowledged as much. In 1830,
for example, congressman John Bell of Tennessee opposed Richard M.
Johnson's proposal to expand the postal network on the grounds that
it was already complete and proposed as an alternative to extend the
franking privilege to the governors of the individual states.[194]

The significance of this achievement is easily overlooked. Though it
is sometimes assumed that major organizational innovations must necessarily follow the invention of novel mechanical contrivances such as

the steam engine or the electric telegraph, the history of the American postal system in the period between 1792 and 1828 suggests a different story. In 1828, as in 1792, American postal officers had at their disposal few mechanical contrivances that would have been unfamiliar to the ancients. Under McLean, the fastest, cheapest, and most reliable way to transmit information over land was by horse express, just as it had been in ancient Greece and Rome. Yet by bringing the postal system and the stagecoach industry together into a new configuration, by insisting that stagecoach service be coordinated in accordance with a regular schedule, and, most important, by establishing a network of distribution centers to coordinate the whole, the central government had created a communications infrastructure that was largely independent of the preexisting routes of maritime trade and that far outstripped anything that had existed before.

Once Congress set this process in motion, there was no turning back. Following the victory of Thomas Jefferson in the election of 1800, it was briefly rumored that the postal system might be shut down; yet, in the end, Jefferson's Republican party did little to reverse the momentous changes in postal policy that had been instituted in the 1790s by the Federalist party of George Washington and John Adams.[195] Never again would the transmission of information be utterly dependent on purely arbitrary factors such as the movement of the wind or the physical proximity of the sender and recipient to a navigable body of water. Never again would Americans lack a reliable means to transmit information from place to place. To an extent perhaps hard to imagine today, it was neither the railroad nor the telegraph nor even the commercialization of fossil fuel, but rather the stagecoach and the postrider that liberated Americans from their crippling dependence on the vagaries of geography, wind, and water.

The significance of this achievement extended well beyond its role in facilitating the transmission of information. By greatly expanding the power of the postmaster general, the completion of the postal network threatened to tilt the delicate balance between the postal system, the rest of the executive branch, and the individual states. Shortly after McLean's appointment to office, one Washington-based editorialist shrewdly predicted that the "vast patronage" under the control of the postmaster general offered "attractions" to the politically ambitious that were "not easily resisted." It was a perceptive assessment and one that would be fully borne out by the course of events.[196] McLean was not only a capable administrator but also a highly ambitious public figure who successfully used his office to catapult himself onto the national stage. For public figures troubled by the growing role of the central government in American public life, this was an ominous development, and it was one that the Jacksonians were determined to check.

· 4 ·

The Imagined Community

BY THE FINAL full year of John McLean's tenure as postmaster general in 1828, the central government had established a post office in virtually every locality of any consequence in the United States. In this chapter I consider how this achievement helped to shape the boundaries of American public life. My theme is the role of postal policy in creating an imagined community in which the government encouraged its far-flung citizenry to participate directly in the political process through an ongoing discussion of the leading events of the day. In one sense, the creation of this new kind of community was a logical extension of the inclusive national community of knowledgeable citizens that Benjamin Rush had envisioned in 1787. Yet in another sense, it marked a repudiation of Rush's universalism since, in the very process of incorporating the citizenry into American public life, postal policy marginalized a number of groups—in particular, women and blacks—and in this way identified the public sphere with free white men, the most privileged class of Americans at that time.

THE CREATION OF this imagined community owed little to the physical appearance of the republic's post offices. Congress was notoriously loath to lavish money on public buildings, and postal architecture was one extravagance that it decided the country could do without. Not until after the Civil War would Congress authorize the construction of the massive, Victorian cut-stone city post office buildings that became such a ubiquitous feature of the urban landscape of the Gilded Age.[1] In Baltimore earlier in the century, the post office was long located in the basement of a popular hotel; in Philadelphia, in a corner of the

mercantile exchange; in Boston, on the first floor of a dilapidated colonial state house.[2] Even in New York, which boasted throughout most
of the early republic the largest post office in the country, as late as 1825
the post office was located in a 12-by-20-foot room on the first floor of
the postmaster's own home.[3] In the decades to come, the New York
post office was located at one time or another in the basement of the
mercantile exchange, in a former museum, and in a former Dutch Reformed church.[4] But at no time was it located in a building that had
been designed with postal purposes specifically in mind. During its
opening months in the Dutch church, postal patrons mingled incon-
gruously with the carts transporting the coffins of long-dead New Yorkers from the church graveyard to a less congested spot. Even after Postmaster John Lorimer Graham completed the necessary renovations to
the church, much of the interior ornamentation remained, including
the pulpit.[5] "The office is not," complained veteran postal clerk William
B. Taylor in 1851, "such a one as the government should provide for
this great and growing city."[6]

Outside of the principal commercial centers, post offices were rarely
located in a freestanding building at all. Many occupied a room in a
downtown commercial building that the postmaster paid for out of the
revenue of the office, a tradition that persisted long after the Civil War.[7]
Almost none were owned by the government outright. The vast majority consisted of nothing more than a counter in the corner of a store,
tavern, law office, or apothecary shop. Many were identified merely by
a crudely lettered sign; some lacked even that. In one town, according
to special agent Cortland Stebbins, the office was kept in a house of
prostitution. Upon discovering that this particular post office was kept
by a woman, Stebbins added sarcastically that he did not stop to ask if
she was "one of the professionals."[8]

Of the few buildings in the early republic that had been built exclusively for postal purposes, by far the most notable was the general post
office in Washington, D.C., which Congress had commissioned Robert
Mills to design shortly after the fire that destroyed its predecessor in
1836.[9] Modeled after a Renaissance palace in the then-popular Italianate
style, Mills's general post office was widely praised by contemporaries
as the "choicest architectural *bijou*" in the city and had the distinction
of being the first federal office building to be built out of marble.[10] Had
Mills had his way, the building would have been grander still. In his
original plan, it was to have been crowned by an elegant tower supporting an enormous nine-foot clock whose great bell was to announce

the time at regular intervals throughout the surrounding countryside. While this imposing clock tower would have been a highly appropriate symbol for such a time-conscious enterprise, thrifty congressmen vetoed the idea, and it was never built.[11]

Outside of Washington, one of the few post office buildings that could credibly be regarded as distinguished was located in Charleston, South Carolina. Originally built in 1771 by the British government as a merchants' exchange, the Charleston post office anchored the eastern end of one of the city's main commercial thoroughfares and remains to this day a major landmark.[12] No commercial establishment in the city was more centrally located or boasted a more prestigious address. Yet even here, the post office had originally been built with some use other than a post office in mind.

Though the post office was ordinarily kept in a central location, it was often relocated from site to site, depending upon the predilections of the postmaster and the vagaries of the downtown market for real estate. So frequently was the post office in Troy, New York, shifted about the town that one wit went so far as to organize a mock epic around this notable "itinerant." As the author explained, introducing his theme:

> Not Delos, floating on the main,
> Is now the subject of my strain;
> Nor does one with on me prevail,
> To trace the course of Granger's mail:
> Another theme the muse invites,
> Who of the Troy "Post-Office" writes;
> That foundling of democracy,
> Well known for instability . . .[13]

Most post office interiors were equally plain. Almost never did they include the vaulted ceilings and elaborate grillwork that became such a common feature of public architecture in the Gilded Age. In the smaller offices, the furnishings ordinarily consisted of little more than a high wooden desk, a bit of counter space, and a single rack of pigeonholes for storing the mail until its recipient stopped by to pick it up. If the post office was also a store, patrons might be forgiven if they had trouble knowing just where the store ended and the post office began. "Kegs and barrels—nail boxes and soap boxes—customers and letter-writers—men and boys—women and dogs—the box stove and the Department letter boxes—," one contemporary reminisced, "are all mingled at the post office establishment with picturesque incongruity."[14] As late as the 1840s, the most notable pieces of furniture in the New York post office were the specially designed revolving racks, known as "alphabets," that postal clerks used to sort the mail and the banks of post office boxes that postal officers provided for those postal patrons who could afford the fee.[15] Some of these boxes had locked doors that permitted box-holders to gain access to their contents at any hour of the day or night. Others consisted of nothing more than a series of glass windows that permitted the boxholder to see if anything had arrived; if the slot was empty, the boxholder could rest assured that he had no reason to wait in line.[16]

The curious intermixture of the public and the private that was characteristic of so many post offices was nicely depicted by Thomas Waterman Wood in his painting *Village Post Office*, a rare pictorial representation of the interior of a nineteenth-century post office painted just after the Civil War.[17] Located in a country store, Wood's post office was a friendly, inviting place where men, women, and even a dog or two could come together to get their mail and catch up on the affairs of the day. Though Wood's painting did not display every bit of wall space in the store, it is worth noting that the office did not include any maps, flags, or portraits of prominent men of affairs. Here, as in so many aspects of postal affairs, parsimony prevailed. The absence of a map is particularly intriguing, since it is often assumed that maps were a ubiquitous feature of post offices throughout the country at this time. During the early years of the nineteenth century, this may have been true. As the postal system expanded, however, the general post office found it increasingly difficult to keep up with the demand. No maps could be found, reported special agent Samuel Gwin in 1837, in even the largest post offices in Mississippi.[18] The same may well have been the case throughout the rest of the United States.

POSTAL ARCHITECTURE may have been rarely imposing, yet the post-master himself was often among the leading public figures of the day. Indeed, there is good reason to suppose that the average postal officer enjoyed a social standing that was higher not only than many of the royal placemen of the eighteenth century, but also than all but the most senior government officers today. Even the most humble village post-master, writer Catherine Sedgwick observed, took pride in being "the wheel of destiny for the community" and "the oracle to announce the voice of the divinities at Washington—the herald of all news, foreign and domestic, and the medium of all the good and evil tidings."[19] In St. Louis, the office was held for a time by Wilson Price Hunt, an explorer who had taken part in the celebrated transcontinental fur-trading trek that Washington Irving immortalized in *Astoria;* in New Orleans, by George Croghan, a military hero of the War of 1812 who had gained great renown for defending a fort in Ohio against an overwhelming assault.[20] And in Richmond, Virginia, the postmasters included, at one time or another, the first mayor of the city, a former state governor, and the grandson of the celebrated eighteenth-century orator Patrick Henry. Henry's grandson resigned the office when he was elected to fill a vacancy in the United States Senate. That a postmaster might be appointed to the prestigious office of United States Senator may seem surprising enough, yet it was by no means unknown for a senator to resign his seat in Congress to become the postmaster of a major commercial center. In the opening decades of the nineteenth century, this actually happened in both Philadelphia and New York.

Many postmasters boasted a military background. The first postmaster of New York under the federal Constitution was an Austrian-trained artillery captain named Sebastian Bauman who had fought with distinction in the War of Independence. Bauman's Philadelphia counterpart was Robert Patton, a former major in the War of Independence who had been held for a time by the British as a prisoner of war. Bauman's successor, Theodorus Bailey, had also held a high office in the Continental Army, as would many other prominent postmasters in the decades to come. In Richmond, Virginia, all but two of the men to have served as postmaster of the city during the entire antebellum period had served in the military at some point during their prior careers (see Table 4.1).

Other postmasters boasted notable careers in the press. These included Baltimore, Maryland, postmaster John Stuart Skinner, the editor of the *American Farmer,* which had the distinction of being the first successful agricultural periodical in the United States; Albany, New York, postmaster Solomon Southwick, the editor of several publications, among them the first agricultural periodical published in upstate New York; and Worcester, Massachusetts, postmaster Isaiah Thomas, a leading journalistic supporter of the American cause during the War of Independence and in later life a pioneering collector of eighteenth-century pamphlets, newspapers, and magazines. Postmasters active in the political press included Richmond, Virginia, postmaster Augustine

Table 4.1 Previous occupations of postmasters in New York, Philadelphia, Boston, Baltimore, Charleston, and Richmond, 1788–1861

		Government		Professional		Business	
		Military officer	Civil officer	Lawyer	Physician	Merchant/planter	Printer/editor
New York (N = 10)							
1783–1789	William Bedlow	—	—	—	—	x	—
1789–1803	Sebastian Bauman	x	—	—	—	—	—
1804–1828	Theodorus Bailey	x	x	x	—	—	—
1828–1836	Samuel L. Gouverneur	x	—	—	—	x	—
1836–1842	Jonathan Coddington	—	x	—	—	—	—
1842–1845	John Lorimer Graham	—	—	x	—	—	—
1845–1849	Robert H. Morris	—	x	x	—	—	—
1849–1853	William V. Brady	—	x	—	—	—	—
1853–1860	Isaac V. Fowler	—	—	—	—	—	—
1860–1861	John A. Dix	x	x	x	—	—	x
Total		4	5	4	0	2	1
Philadelphia (N = 13)							
1782–1789	James Bryson	—	—	—	—	—	—
1789–1814	Robert Patton	x	—	—	—	—	—
1814–1815	Michael Leib	—	x	—	—	—	—
1815–1828	Richard Bache, Jr.	—	—	—	—	—	x
1828–1833	Thomas Sargeant	—	x	x	—	—	—
1833–1841	James Page	x	x	x	—	—	—
1841–1844	John Montgomery	—	—	—	x	—	—
1844–1845	James Hoy	—	—	—	—	—	—
1845–1849	George Lehman	—	P	—	—	x	—
1849–1853	William White	—	P	—	—	—	—
1853–1857	John Miller	—	—	—	—	—	x
1857–1859	Gideon Westcott	—	x	—	—	x	x
1859–1861	Nathaniel Browne	—	x	x	—	—	x
Total		2	7	3	1	2	4

Table 4.1 Continued

	Government		Professional		Business	
	Military officer	Civil officer	Lawyer	Physician	Merchant/planter	Printer/editor
Boston (N = 7)						
1775–1808 Jonathan Hastings	—	—	—	—	—	—
1808–1829 Aaron Hill	x	x	—	—	—	—
1829–1841 Nathaniel Greene	—	—	—	—	—	x
1841–1843 George W. Gordon	—	x	—	—	—	—
1843–1849 Nathaniel Greene	—	—	—	—	—	—
1849–1850 William Hayden	—	—	—	—	—	x
1850–1853 George W. Gordon	—	—	—	—	—	—
1853–1857 Edwin Curtis Bailey	—	P	—	—	x	x
1857–1861 Nahum Capen	—	—	—	—	—	x
Total	1	3	0	0	1	4
Baltimore (N = 11)						
1775–1789 Mary Katherine Goddard	—	—	—	—	—	x
1789–1790 John White	—	—	—	—	—	—
1790–1799 Alexander Furnival	—	P	—	—	—	—
1800–1816 Charles Burrall	—	P	—	—	—	—
1816–1839 John Stuart Skinner	x	—	x	—	x	x
1839–1841 Joshua Vansant	—	x	—	—	x	—
1841–1845 Thomas Finlay	—	x	—	—	x	—
1845–1849 James M. Buchanan	—	x	x	—	—	—
1849–1853 Charles Maddox	—	x	—	—	—	—
1853–1857 Jacob G. Davies	x	x	—	—	x	—
1857–1861 John G. Morris	—	—	—	—	—	—
Total	2	7	2	0	4	2

Charleston (N = 3)							
1783–1792	Thomas Hall	—	—	—	—	—	—
1792–1834	Thomas W. Bacot	—	x	—	—	x	—
1834–1861	Alfred Huger	—	x	—	x	x	—
	Total	0	2	0	1	2	0
Richmond (N = 8)							
1786–1802	Augustine Davis	x	—	—	—	—	x
1802–1808	Marks Vandervall	—	—	x	—	—	x
1808–1824	William Foushee	—	—	—	—	x	x
1824–1837	James P. Preston	—	—	—	—	x	x
1837	William H. Roane	—	—	—	—	—	—
1838–1841	Claiborne W. Gooch	x	—	—	—	—	x
1841–1845	Bernard Peyton	—	—	—	—	—	x
1845–1861	Thomas B. Bigger	—	—	—	—	x	—
	Total	2	0	1	0	3	6
National total (N = 52)		13	11	2	10	26	15

Source: Various biographical dictionaries and local histories.

Note: Some interim appointments are omitted.

P = postal officer.

Davis, the editor of a leading Federalist newspaper of the 1790s; Hartford, Connecticut, postmasters John Niles and Gideon Welles, both of whom had previously worked on one of the leading Jacksonian newspapers in New England—and both of whom capped their careers with Cabinet berths, Niles as postmaster general and Welles as secretary of war; and Georgetown, Kentucky, postmaster Amos Kendall, whose long and distinguished journalistic career catapulted him into the inner circles of the Jackson administration and who ably served as a frequent contributor to the semiofficial Washington *Globe* before being appointed postmaster general by President Jackson in 1835. Other postmasters with a journalistic background included Chicago postmaster John L. Scripps, the former editor of the Chicago *Tribune,* and Cleveland postmaster Joseph W. Gray, the former editor of the Cleveland *Plain Dealer.* Following the victory of Abraham Lincoln in the election of 1860, it was rumored for a time that the next postmaster general might be Horace Greeley, the editor of the influential *New York Tribune.*[21]

Printers, of course, had been closely connected with the American postal system long before the adoption of the federal Constitution in 1788.[22] Yet with the passage of the Post Office Act of 1792, the relationship of the postal system and the press was subtly transformed. Now that Congress had officially admitted newspapers into the mail, it seemed improper for postmasters to edit political newspapers during their tenure in office. Not only did postmasters have a built-in advantage when it came to securing up-to-date information on public affairs and in transmitting their publications under cover of their official frank, but they also had a clear incentive to block the opposition from transmitting their newspapers in a timely way. Accordingly, the general post office ruled that postmasters should be required during their tenure in office to give up any direct financial stake in any political newspaper with which they might be involved.[23]

One of the first postal officers to articulate this rule was Postmaster General Timothy Pickering. Postmaster-printers, Pickering explained in 1793, had such an enormous incentive to abuse their position to the detriment of their journalistic peers that he had generally avoided the appointment of printers to postmasterships where the services of other suitably qualified persons could be secured.[24] By McLean's day, this policy was well established. Following the appointment of Nathaniel Greene as Boston postmaster in 1829, Greene publicly announced his retirement as the editor of the Boston *Statesman,* a newspaper that had backed Jackson's candidacy in the preceding campaign.[25] Several years later, Postmaster General Kendall articulated his understanding of this policy in a particularly forceful way. During his tenure in office, Kendall declared in 1841, he knew of only a single instance in which he had permitted a postmaster to continue to edit a political newspaper while the postmaster remained in office, though he was aware of a second instance in which a postmaster had continued to do so without his permission. "Having been an editor myself when appointed to office," Kendall explained, in justification of his policy, "I should be among the last men in the Union to countenance their disenfranchisement. Yet it was the policy of General Jackson to require editors to relinquish their control of the press upon acceptance of office at the hands of the general government, and such has been the general policy of this department from its earliest history, enforced at different times with different degrees of severity, but never entirely abandoned. Such is now its policy."[26]

THOUGH EVERY postmastership offered the incumbent the prestige of a government office, only those in the principal commercial centers provided much in the way of a financial return. Postmasters were technically not salaried but, rather, were paid a commission on certain key tasks that they performed, up to the legal maximum of $2,000 per year. In the major commercial centers, and in some of the smaller localities as well, postmasters could supplement their commissions with various perquisites, of which the most important included the fees that they collected from renting post office boxes to merchants and other heavy users of the office. At many of the larger offices, these fees could be substantial, a major boon for the postmaster, since he was entitled to retain the entire amount. In the Boston post office, box rent came to between $4,000 and $5,000 each year, tripling the income of the postmaster and making the office one of the most lucrative in the country.[27] Even in Richmond, Virginia, box rent alone was worth $1,500, a tidy sum that, as the fortunate postal clerk whom the absentee postmaster permitted to collect it later reminisced, enabled him to entertain "as handsomely as any gentleman in Richmond."[28]

Occasionally a postmastership was so highly prized that it was actually bought and sold. Though the purchase of public office is strangely foreign to contemporary notions of how a government ought to be staffed, it remained common in Great Britain and France well into the nineteenth century and was by no means unknown in the United

States.[29] In 1815, Amos Kendall purchased the office of postmaster at Georgetown, Kentucky, from the incumbent for $180 a year. The purchase was coordinated by Kentucky congressman Richard M. Johnson, who, Kendall claimed, was well aware of the nature of the transaction. Notwithstanding Johnson's connivance, Kendall insisted that the agreement be kept secret, fearful that it had been somehow degrading for him to have secured a public office in this way.[30]

Had Kendall hoped to support himself on the proceeds of his office, he would have been sorely disappointed. Of the almost eight thousand post offices in 1829, a mere 3 percent earned the incumbent more than $300 annually, roughly what an unskilled artisan might expect to earn. Kendall himself never made more than $291 a year during his brief tenure as Georgetown postmaster, which he supplemented by using the franking privilege to help establish a printing business.[31] Not surprisingly, the vast majority of postmasters supplemented the income of their office with other sources of revenue. It was "expected" that postmasters hold down a second job, Kendall explained shortly after his appointment as postmaster general in 1836, so that lawyers, physicians, merchants, mechanics, and "men in almost every branch of human business" could hold the office while engaging in some other more lucrative pursuit.[32] While the postmaster was out of the office, he might delegate his wife, his children, or perhaps a boarder to do the work. So common was the practice that when Syracuse, New York, postmaster C. P. Richardson was asked by his superiors to explain why he had not turned in his quarterly reports, Richardson replied matter-of-factly that he was unaware they had not been filed, since he had left their preparation in charge of a subordinate so that he might go out jobbing on the Erie Canal.[33] Even in the distribution centers, it was by no means unknown for postmasters to leave the day-to-day work of the office to a clerk.[34] This was true even in New York City, where every postmaster in the early republic continued to pursue a separate business or professional career.[35]

Though the commission system was highly logical, it was not without its anomalies. Should the revenue of the office suddenly decline, a postmaster might find it necessary to dip into his own pocket to pay his staff. This actually happened to New York postmaster Robert Morris following the major drop in postal revenue that accompanied the passage of the Post Office Act of 1845.[36] Changes in contracting arrangements posed further problems. When, for example, the general post office switched the mail from the stagecoach to the railroad in upstate New York, Belvidere postmaster Andrew Hart suddenly found himself overwhelmed by the need to sort and rebag some 1,500 to 2,000 letters every day, a task that typically took him from 12 to 16 hours, all for less than $80 a year![37]

For many postmasters, the value of the office had little to do with the size of their commission. "Half the post offices in the United States," estimated Postmaster General Timothy Pickering in 1794, "would be broken up, if the postmasters were not inspired by motives other than those of a pecuniary nature."[38] This continued to be true well into the nineteenth century. As late as 1845, 85 percent of the post offices in the United States netted the postmaster less than $100 a year; 21 percent, less than $10.[39] Some took the office as a courtesy to their neighbors; others looked to the various ancillary benefits. Storekeepers prized the steady stream of potential customers that the office could be expected to bring into their store, while merchants prized the franking privilege, which permitted them to send an unlimited number of items free of charge, greatly reducing their mailing costs. Outside of the major commercial centers, with their lucrative fees for box rent, the franking privilege was often the most important ancillary benefit of the office. When the privilege was temporarily abolished in 1845, it spurred the resignation of fully one-third of the postmasters in the country during the next twenty months.[40]

The uses to which a postmaster might put his franking privilege varied widely, depending on the interests of the incumbent. Baltimore postmaster John Stuart Skinner used the privilege to transmit the many exotic varieties of seed that he had secured from naval officers who visited the city, beginning a tradition that would eventually be taken over by the Department of Agriculture.[41] Albany postmaster Solomon Van Rensselaer used it to transmit to postmasters throughout the state a tract promoting the "Post Office Temperance Society."[42] Bethany, Virginia, postmaster Alexander Campbell used it to help launch an evangelical publishing empire that broadcast the message of Campbell's Disciples of Christ to virtually every corner of the land.[43] And if Anne Royall can be believed, Presbyterian postmasters throughout the United States used it to flood their neighborhoods with all manner of religious tracts, including the *National Preacher,* a compendium of notable sermons that frequently featured the oratory of clerical luminaries such as Lyman Beecher.[44]

Postmasters also used the privilege to take advantage of opportunities that originated outside their offices. In rural North Carolina, postmasters grew accustomed to acting as agents for out-of-town merchants peddling products ranging from silk scarves to sewing machines.[45] Postmasters also sometimes participated in various lottery schemes, a practice that seems to have been particularly widespread in the 1820s, since Congress took the trouble to enact special legislation to ban it.[46] Even more important were the many links between postmasters and the press. Prior to 1847, the general post office required postmasters to use the franking privilege to cover the cost of the routine correspondence between newspaper printers and subscribers.[47] According to William Leggett of the New York *Evening Post*, the postage on fully half of his incoming correspondence from out-of-town subscribers had been paid for in this way.[48] Though this requirement did not extend to magazines, magazine editors grew accustomed to relying on postmasters to help them out as well. In return for their cooperation in signing up new subscribers, Sarah Hale of *Godey's Magazine and Lady's Book* offered postmasters elegant engravings like the *Monument to Sir Walter Scott*.[49] Editors also sometimes enlisted postmasters to perform rudimentary credit checks. In 1830, for example, Cambridge, Massachusetts, editor Thomas Whittemore sent Princeton, Massachusetts, postmaster Charles Russell a printed circular that politely asked Russell whether one of Whittemore's subscribers could be relied on to pay his bills. "What kind of a man is he in regard to the payment of his debts?" Whittemore asked. "Is he accounted an honest and temperate man?"[50]

The possession of a post office gave the incumbent an excellent vantage point from which to observe the workings of American commerce and public life. Telegraph promoter Henry O'Reilly learned a good deal about the potential market for commercial telegraphy during a stint as postmaster of Rochester, New York, while the young Abraham Lincoln obtained many insights into the electoral process during his brief tenure as postmaster of New Salem, Illinois.[51] Of all the men on the make who used the office to boost their careers, few boasted a more spectacular rise than Abelard Reynolds, one of O'Reilly's predecessors as postmaster of Rochester. When Reynolds first arrived in Rochester in 1812 to set himself up as a storekeeper, the settlement consisted of little more than a clearing in the woods. Taking advantage of his former law partner's family connections with Congressman Henry Clay, Reynolds secured the postmastership in the hope that it might increase the traffic through his store. He was not to be disappointed. By the end of his tenure in office in 1829, the Rochester post office was the fifteenth largest in the United States (see Table 4.2), and Reynolds was a wealthy

Table 4.2 The twenty largest post offices, 1794, 1822, 1829, 1835 (revenue in thousands)

1794		1822		1829		1835	
Location	Gross revenue	Location	Net revenue	Location	Net revenue	Location	Net revenue
Philadelphia	$25.3	New York	$98.9	New York	$130.0	New York	$203.1
New York	18.5	Philadelphia	77.0	Philadelphia	83.9	Philadelphia	121.2
Baltimore	11.7	Boston	49.9	Boston	51.9	Boston	78.7
Boston	10.6	Baltimore	41.4	Baltimore	45.4	Baltimore	59.5
Richmond	4.7	Charleston	27.3	Charleston	22.6	New Orleans	52.3
Norfolk	4.2	New Orleans	23.3	Richmond	15.6	Charleston	33.8
Alexandria	3.3	Richmond	16.7	New Orleans	15.1	Cincinnati	21.9
Charleston	3.0	Savannah	16.7	Savannah	11.3	Richmond	20.3
Petersburg	2.5	Augusta, Ga.	12.1	Providence	10.4	Mobile	19.2
Fredericksburg	1.8	Albany	11.0	Albany	10.3	Albany	17.6
Georgetown, Md.	1.6	Washington, D.C.	9.4	Cincinnati	9.4	Savannah	17.2
Albany	1.2	Providence	8.8	Augusta, Ga.	8.9	Pittsburgh	16.5
Portsmouth, N.H.	1.1	Petersburg	8.4	Harrisburg	8.3	Augusta, Ga.	14.6
Providence	1.0	Alexandria	7.0	Pittsburgh	7.9	Louisville	13.7
Hartford	1.0	Pittsburgh	6.7	Rochester	7.1	Harrisburg	12.8
Salem, Mass.	0.9	Norfolk	6.5	Utica	6.0	Providence	11.3
Newburyport, Mass.	0.9	New Haven	6.5	Norfolk	5.7	New Haven	10.7
Pittsburgh	0.8	Hartford	5.9	New Haven	5.4	Rochester	9.5
Wilmington, Del.	0.8	Cincinnati	5.8	Troy, N.Y.	5.0	Washington, D.C.	9.2
Savannah	0.8	Natchez	5.6	Portland, Me.	4.7	Norfolk	8.9

Source: 1794: Robert J. Stets, *Postal Operations in the United States, 1794* (Robert J. Stets, 1991); 1822: John McLean, *Amount of Postage . . . during the Year 1822*, 18th Cong., 1st sess., 1824, H. Doc. 95 (serial 97); 1829: William Barry, *Amount of Postages for One Year Prior to 31st March, 1829*, 21st Cong., 1st sess., 1830, H. Doc. 61 (serial 197); 1835: Amos Kendall, *Postage Accruing in the Year 1835*, 24th Cong., 1st sess., 1836, H. Doc. 262 (serial 291).

man. Intent upon capitalizing on his success, Reynolds underwrote the construction of Reynolds's Arcade, a major commercial venture in downtown Rochester that included, appropriately enough, an elegantly outfitted post office. Though Reynolds himself was summarily dismissed in the purge that began shortly after Jackson's inauguration in 1829 and thus never had the chance to preside over the new post office, the Rochester post office continued to be located in his arcade until well after the Civil War.[52]

POSTAL OFFICERS secured their jobs in various ways. At one time or another in the early republic, virtually everyone who had the slightest pretense to political influence seems to have tried to wrangle an office for himself or his friends, keeping alive a tradition that went back at least as far as Benjamin Franklin. Within a few years of his appointment as deputy postmaster general for British North America, Franklin managed to find offices for his son, two of his brothers, the husband of his wife's niece, his sister's son, and his brother's stepson.[53] The custom persisted long after the adoption of the federal Constitution in 1788. No fewer than six clerks in the general post office in the early republic hailed from Suffield, Connecticut, the hometown of Postmaster General Gideon Granger.[54] So frequently did postmasters appoint their sons to clerkships in their offices that when Philadelphia postmaster Robert Patton refused to do so as a matter of principle, his decision was singled out for praise as an innovation in American public life.[55]

Notwithstanding the importance of the post office to the public at large, the recruitment of postal officers remained surprisingly informal. The only relevant consideration in making a postal appointment, reported one congressman in 1822, was the "pecuniary emolument" of the office, which the postmaster general used as a rough measure of prestige. The administrative ability of the potential officer, the congressman added, was of no concern, as it would have been, for example, for a judgeship or a diplomatic post.[56] Except for periods immediately following the occasional financial scandal that plagued the larger offices, when it was customary to appoint a proven administrator to help straighten out the books, this outlook remained the norm right up to the Civil War. At no point in the early republic did postal officers institute formal job ladders of the kind that have become familiar in large-scale enterprises, public and private, throughout the United States. Of the 52 individuals to serve as postmaster of six large city post offices in the United States in the period between 1788 and 1861, only 5 had worked in the office prior to their appointment, though several others had acquired at least some familiarity with postal procedures through their work in the press (see Table 4.1). The only postmaster general in the entire pre–Civil War period who could be said to have risen up through the ranks was Horatio King, who held the office briefly, on a strictly interim basis, during the opening months of the first Lincoln administration. Given these circumstances, it was simply not realistic for an upwardly mobile young man to expect to satisfy his ambition by rising through the postal hierarchy.

Prior to Jackson's inauguration, especially during the tenure of John McLean, it looked for a time as if the government might be about to establish a merit-based civil service in which capable, career-minded public officers could advance rung by rung up the occupational ladder. During the 1820s, office seekers intent upon securing employment within the general post office vowed to "rise by merit" should they secure a berth, while a veteran clerk like Andrew Coyle took great pride in his methodical, step-by-step rise through the postal hierarchy, having started his postal career as a lowly clerk before rising to become principal bookkeeper and finally chief clerk.[57] With Jackson's victory in the election of 1828, however, all such ideas were swiftly scrapped. For Jacksonians like Amos Kendall, the very idea of such an administrative hierarchy revived disturbing memories of the bureaucratic machinery that the British had established prior to the War of Independence.

This new ethos—with its mingling of antiaristocratic, antibureaucratic, and anti-institutional themes—sought to destroy the link that had formerly existed between public preferment and social prestige. At its core was the conviction that the most important criterion to be used in determining the fitness of a given individual for public office was his conduct in the nonofficial or private realm of home or business. No one articulated this conviction with greater self assurance than Amos Kendall, whom Jackson appointed as postmaster general in 1835. Far from wishing to banish morality from public service, as is sometimes mistakenly assumed, Kendall sought to vastly expand the range of moral behavior that was deemed relevant to public service. The "first question" that should be asked of a potential candidate for public office, Kendall declared, was "is he a moral man?" After all, should the government advance immoral men to public office, this would not only imperil the public business but also, and even more important, establish a dangerous precedent that would have pernicious consequences for the rest of society. "Is it safe," Kendall asked impatiently, "to trust a man in public life who pays no regard to his moral or legal obligations in private life?"[58] For Kendall, as for so many Jacksonians, the beau ideal of a civil servant was not an upwardly mobile careerist like Andrew Coyle, but an enterprising party leader like Kendall himself, who successfully lived off the government even as he dedicated himself to trimming back its role in American public life.

Kendall's antimeritocratic outlook owed a good deal to his personal views. Like many Jacksonians, he rarely missed an opportunity to deride the pretensions of government clerks (he seems to have been particularly disturbed by their habit of throwing lavish parties) or to anticipate the day when they would be treated with no greater esteem than merchants or other men of affairs. Henceforth, Kendall insisted, public officers should be encouraged to regard their work as a "mere business matter" rather than as an esoteric profession set apart from the workaday world.[59]

Given Kendall's preoccupation with private behavior, it should come as no surprise that, when vacancies arose within the general post office, he felt few compunctions about filling them from outside of the ranks of the existing staff. "No personal claims to office or promotion are recognized in this department," Kendall declared in justifying his policy, which broke sharply with the stress on internal hiring that had prevailed under McLean. After all, Kendall sanctimoniously declared, public office was the property of the "people," while the office holders were the people's "hirelings."[60] It was a flexible doctrine, ideally suited to the needs of the emerging mass party. By making himself the final arbiter of the character of his staff, Kendall greatly increased his ability to find jobs in the postal hierarchy for the cadre men who had exerted themselves on behalf of the party during the election campaign.

If upward mobility within the postal system became increasingly rare after 1829, lateral mobility, or movement from office to office, offered somewhat greater opportunities for personal advancement. Occasionally, a clerk in a city post office might secure an appointment as a traveling inspector or even a transfer to the general post office. Opportunities were especially plentiful for those postal officers willing to move to the Far West. In the hectic early days of the California gold rush, for example, the San Francisco post office was staffed primarily by veteran postal officers recruited from the general post office in Washington, D.C.[61]

A case in point was the five-decade long postal career of William A. Davis, a Virginia native who figured prominently in the establishment of the continuous vehicle-based sorting scheme known as railway mail. Davis's long involvement with the postal system began in the 1820s when his uncle, the postmaster of Charlottesville, Virginia, secured him a clerkship in the Charlottesville office. Before long, Davis had parlayed this position into a more prestigious clerkship in Richmond, Virginia, and eventually the postmastership of St. Joseph, Missouri. Davis lost the St. Joseph postmastership in the political purge that followed Lincoln's election, though his successor did permit him to stay on as a clerk, making it possible for Davis to institute on-board mail sorting on a specially outfitted car on the Hannibal & St. Joseph Railroad, an innovation that would soon be adopted throughout the United States. Notwithstanding Davis's key role in the establishment of railway mail, he never secured a more prestigious office, very possibly because of his close ties with the by then defeated South.[62]

However important family connections and political service may have been in securing postal appointments, they were by no means the only relevant criteria. Less tangible, though hardly less important, were certain unspoken assumptions about the kind of individual who was properly qualified to hold such a responsible charge. Public figures from all of the major parties—Republicans no less than Federalists, Democrats no less than Whigs—took it for granted that the postmasters of the leading commercial centers should strive to embody the distinctive combination of moral rectitude, personal modesty, and practical benevolence that was commonly known as liberality and that was the most distinctive hallmark of the gentleman of leisure.[63] While the concept of liberality has today become so attenuated as to have become almost meaningless, in the early republic it referred to a recognizable constellation of attributes that included good breeding, financial independence, personal tact, and, very often, a certain flair for literary exposition. To secure public office, the applicant was ordinarily presumed not only to rely upon the intervention of a patron, but also to conduct himself in a manner appropriate to the conventions of the day. The income of the office, in short, was more of a reward for the mastery of a particular persona than a remuneration for the performance of a particular series of tasks. Indeed, if the official performance of public officers in the early republic is judged by the standards of a later day, they often seemed to be doing nothing at all.

These attributes were not attainable by everyone. They were confined to the small portion of the population that was commonly known as the "better sort," the "upper rank," or simply "society." In Great Britain, the persona had been artfully evoked by Henry Fielding in his sketch of Squire Allworthy in *Tom Jones*. Interestingly, Fielding based his sketch of the warm-hearted squire not on a member of the country gentry, but on royal postal officer Ralph Allen, an important figure in the annals of British postal history who is best known for his role in rationalizing the routing of the mail.[64]

If Ralph Allen exemplified the traits prized by postal administrators in Augustan England, Allen's American counterpart was surely Benjamin Franklin. Like Allen, Franklin spent much of his adult life as an officer in the royal postal system, first as postmaster of Philadelphia and eventually as deputy postmaster general for British North America, an office that he held from 1753 until his dismissal on the eve of the War of Independence in 1774. Franklin was far more industrious than many royal placemen and made a number of changes while in office, of which the most important included the appointment of New Jersey printer James Parker as his chief financial officer, an office that Parker filled with great distinction for many years.[65] Yet Franklin's heart lay not in administration but rather in science, politics, and the arts; and accordingly in 1757 he retired to London to pursue these interests and to live the life of a gentleman of leisure. Thus, Franklin was actually a resident of British North America for only seven of the twenty-one years that the postal system was ostensibly under his charge.

Franklin's conception of public office changed surprisingly little following his appointment in 1775 as first postmaster general of the soon-to-be independent United States. Convinced that his long tenure in the royal postal system had given him a right to the office, Franklin treated his postmaster generalship under the Continental Congress much as he had his deputy postmaster generalship under the Crown. Once again, he appointed a team of assistants to oversee the routine work of the office, and once again he set off to Europe as soon as he found it advantageous, though this time he was destined not for London but Paris, where for most of the next decade he represented the interests of the fledgling United States at the court of Louis XVI. To administer the postal system when he was out of the country, Franklin appointed as his surrogate his son-in-law, Richard Bache, just as he had appointed James Parker following his appointment as deputy postmaster general for British North America before the war.

Bache shared Franklin's aristocratic conception of public preferment and greatly resented his dismissal in 1782 in favor of Ebenezer Hazard, who had earned the spot through his tireless work in the New York office during the war. Convinced that he had a kind of property right to the position, Bache lobbied to get his office back as late as 1789, even though he had had no official connection with the government since his dismissal seven years before.[66] Franklin and Bache's attitude toward public office greatly disturbed William Goddard, who had worked hard to get the enterprise up and running in 1775 and who had worked even more diligently to establish his short-lived "Constitutional Post" the year before. Outraged at Franklin's temerity in passing him over in favor of Bache, Goddard bore a grudge against his onetime employer for the rest of his life and, in an extraordinary letter to printing historian Isaiah Thomas in 1811, he did everything he could to insure that posterity would share his view of events. Bache's appointment, Goddard sputtered, was "preposterous" and "iniquitous," since it enabled Franklin to monopolize all the lucrative offices "under the same roof"—including Franklin's own "sinecure"—while slighting Goddard, the "pack horse" of the American postal system who had done the bulk of the work.[67]

Franklin and Bache were by no means the last postal officers to display an aristocratic disdain toward the routine demands of the office. Well into the nineteenth century, many postal officers persisted in treating their offices as little more than a convenient source of rent, a reward for who they were, rather than a compensation for what they did. One potential postmaster, wrote Attorney General William Wirt to McLean in 1828, lived in the "first circle of society" and was "far above the crowd of applicants that swarm the offices," notwithstanding the fact that he had "experienced the vicissitudes of human affairs," by which presumably Wirt meant that he came from a good family but had run into debt.[68]

To be sure, some alluded to their qualifications for the work, or at least to their extracurricular attainments. "The remedy I have recently discovered for rheumatism pains," wrote one office seeker reassuringly to McLean in 1827, "could, I should presume, be prepared after office hours."[69] But many seem to have regarded their inability to support themselves at some other line of work as their primary qualification for a government job, lending credence to the common charge that public office was little more than a form of poor relief for the well-to-do. Little wonder that Nathaniel Hawthorne lobbied hard for the Salem, Massachusetts, postmastership before he settled for an office in the custom house. Given his genteel demeanor, his literary ambitions, and his precarious financial position, Hawthorne quite rightly presumed that he possessed some of the most important qualifications for the job.[70]

No postal officer better exemplified the persistence of this aristocratic tradition than Richard Bache, Jr., the Philadelphia postmaster between 1815 and 1828. By the standards of the day, Bache had excellent credentials for the office: he was not only the son of former Postmaster General Richard Bache, but was also the grandson of Benjamin Franklin himself. Bache was understandably proud of his lineage and remained closely involved throughout his tenure in office with a newspaper that bore Franklin's name. Yet like so many eighteenth-century placemen, Bache had little taste for the day-to-day work of the office, which he quickly delegated to his staff as he, like the aristocratic gentleman he presumed himself to be, amused himself with gambling and drink. Unfortunately, Bache lacked the levelheadedness of his famous grandfather and stooped to embezzling funds from his office to keep himself out of debt. When Bache's irregular financial dealings came to light, McLean reluctantly concluded that he had no choice but to dismiss him. To cushion the blow, McLean appointed as Bache's successor a prominent Philadelphia lawyer who, in addition to being one of Bache's closest political allies and a political supporter of the Jackson-Calhoun ticket in the election of 1828, just happened to be the husband of Benjamin Franklin's granddaughter. In this way, McLean managed to keep the Philadelphia office in the Franklin family for at least a few more years.

Throughout the rest of the country, the story was much the same. In Richmond, Virginia, the postmastership was long monopolized by absentee officeholders who only infrequently attended to the routine business of the office. "I do not use the word *office*," remarked Richmond historian Samuel Mordecai in describing the terms upon which the Richmond postmastership had been filled by two early nineteenth-century incumbents, since neither of them occupied it in *"in propria personae."* Following a fire that destroyed the Richmond post office in the opening years of the century, the incumbent postmaster had so little knowledge of its routine operations that he did not even know where it had been relocated, a circumstance that Mordecai reported with special relish, since Mordecai himself had been the first to show him the spot.[71]

Little changed even after the election of Andrew Jackson in 1828, an event that is sometimes credited with democratizing American public life. "My brother Evans," wrote one New Yorker bluntly to postal officer Charles K. Gardner in 1839, "unfortunately entered the public service too early in life, and remained just long enough to disqualify him for any independent and regular pursuit of business."[72] In Boston,

Jackson appointee Nathaniel Greene kept the aristocratic tradition alive well into the 1840s. More interested in translating literature from French and Italian than in attending to the routine work of the office—and reputedly a libertine and a drunkard—Greene moved to Concord, New Hampshire, some time after his appointment, from where he visited the Boston office a mere two days a week.[73] When Greene finally lost the office following a change in administration, he packed his bags and left for Europe, just as Franklin had almost a hundred years before. Much the same was true in Albany. As long as *someone* performed the work of his office, insisted Albany postmaster Solomon Van Rensselaer in 1837, it was no one's business whether he did any of it himself. According to family tradition, Van Rensselaer's position was sanctioned by the president of the United States as late as 1849.[74]

If some office seekers sought to emulate the aristocratic ways of Augustan England, others yearned to bring to the postal system the quasi-military esprit de corps that they identified with the Continental Army. The influence of the military on postal procedure began at the top. Of the twelve men who served as postmasters general between 1789 and 1845, six had been high-ranking army officers in the various wars of the day. Had President Jefferson had his way, the total would have been even higher, since Jefferson's first choice as postmaster general was Wade Hampton, a wealthy South Carolina cotton planter who had served with distinction during the final years of the War of Independence.[75] Many mail contractors boasted similar credentials. Seth Pease had hauled military stores during the War of Independence before emerging as a key mail contractor in New England during the 1780s; James Reeside had worked as a wagoner during the War of 1812 before McLean gave him control of the Philadelphia–New York route; and William Russell had been a highly successful army contractor during the Mormon War of 1857 before turning his attention to the Pony Express.

The military model shaped postal administration in a variety of ways. Like the army corps of engineers, the staff of the general post office quickly became a leading authority on logistics. Just as Franklin had popularized the existence of the Gulf Stream during his tenure in the royal postal system by instructing the captains of the official mail packets to take advantage of its strong currents to speed the mail between Great Britain and British North America, so Franklin's postal successors became leading authorities on the topography of the North American interior.[76] The general post office, reported travel writer William Darby in 1828, was at this time the "best authority" on geographical information in the United States.[77] Postal officers also assisted in monitoring potential subversives in the far-flung transappalachian West. During the tense months prior to the capture of freelance military adventurer Aaron Burr, for example, Postmaster General Gideon Granger maintained a special horse express that provided President Jefferson with a steady stream of information describing Burr's progress and prospects.[78]

Sometimes the links between the postal system and the military were even more direct. Like the army, the general post office frequently entered into various agreements with foreign powers. These foreign powers included the Spanish government, which tried for a time to monitor the correspondence that passed through Spanish territory en route to the American settlement at New Orleans. In addition, postal officers frequently had occasion to negotiate with the various Indian tribes of the Southwest, which continued to control large portions of territory through which postal officers sought to carry the mail.[79] During the frequent conflicts between the government and these tribes, postal officers also often enlisted army officers to keep the lines of communication open. Even in peacetime, government-Indian relations often retained a quasi-military cast, particularly in the Southwest, where postal officers often relied on Indian postriders to carry the mail. In the Creek Nation, reported one mail contractor in 1824, it was impossible to secure the services of a white rider to risk the trip.[80]

Given the affinities between the postal system and the military, it should come as no surprise that postal officers often invoked military metaphors in their official correspondence. To "elevate" the "character" of the enterprise, declared Cincinnati clerk Elam Langdon in a letter to the postmaster general in 1842, it was necessary to instill in postal officers a quasi-military esprit de corps. "This might be regarded as a small matter with many," Langdon added, "but I do not think that you will so regard it. The general, after all, has to rely upon his soldiers for the success in battle, and it is from small streams, *all running the same way and becoming united together,* that makes up the strong current and river."[81] Langdon may have been unusual in his devotion to the military model, yet he was hardly unique. Throughout the early republic, postmasters and clerks were known officially as "officers" rather than "civil servants" or "officials"; the head of the enterprise was the "postmaster general"; the enterprise was organized into "divisions"; its basic administrative units were "posts"; and the contractors the "army." James Reeside, the largest mail contractor in the 1820s, was known for a time as the "land admiral."[82] Even the operations of a city post office could be described in frankly military terms. The opening of the Philadelphia post office, declared letter carrier James Rees in 1866, resembled nothing so much as an assault upon a "besieged fort." In anticipation of the attack, the chief clerk stood at his post on an elevated platform above the fray, while the rank and file waited anxiously at the "port-holes" that doubled as the delivery windows on the main floor. When the office finally opened, the demand for "surrender" by the throng of postal patrons on one side of the battlefield was answered by a furious discharge of "*epistolary* ammunition" on the other: "Both parties retire satisfied with the result. The victory, however, is always on the side of the post-office: the effect of the fire from their port-holes is felt when all within its lines are quiet. The wheels of the department uninjured move on."[83]

However compelling the military model may have been for postal clerks like Elam Langdon, neither it nor the aristocratic tradition that it partly supplanted was the dominant influence upon officeholding in the early republic. Even more important was the egalitarian ideal, which held that every citizen had the necessary ability to hold public office and in this way to participate directly in the affairs of state. At the core of this ideal was a faith in individual enterprise that contrasted sharply with Bache's aristocratic disdain for hard work and Langdon's martial faith in esprit de corps. Here, as in so many areas of postal policy, John McLean was the innovator. Having himself risen from obscurity to public prominence on the basis of his considerable administrative ability, McLean regarded public office as a suitable reward for the enterprising man on the make. Amos Kendall, in contrast, while no less egalitarian in his outlook, gave the recruitment process a distinctly anti-meritocratic cast by downplaying administrative ability and stressing instead a constellation of extra-official attributes that included (and was often confined to) political loyalty to, and service for, the party in power.

The intuitive appeal of this egalitarian ideal owed a good deal to the paucity of alternative opportunities for public distinction in a country that had been founded on the principled rejection of aristocratic privilege. In the United States, explained Massachusetts congressman Edward Everett in a revealing letter that he wrote to McLean in 1828, public office had become, to a greater extent even than in Great Britain, "family, rank, hereditary fortune, in short everything out of the range of private life." For this reason, Everett added, its possession was linked with "innate principles of our nation," and "truly incredible" were the efforts that office seekers would make, and the "humiliations" they would endure, to secure it.[84] So great was the rush for official preferment, reported Elam Langdon in 1841, that it would be "far better for the country" if ordinary Americans gave up their quest for public office and paid more attention to the "cultivation of the soil . . . It would add vastly to our independence."[85] This pride in public service extended even to officeholders who found themselves displaced after a change in the administration. Though he was now "*out* of office, in the ordinary sense," reflected onetime postal auditor Peter G. Washington in 1851, he felt sure that he still remained "in, in a better—the best sense of the word—*in*—in the rules—organization and methods of business which we established, and which, we think, are destined to survive our natural, as they have our official, life."[86]

Perhaps the best way to grasp the growing appeal of this egalitarian ideal is to consider the changing ways in which Americans interpreted Benjamin Franklin's postal career. Prior to the War of Independence, it was by no means unknown for critics to treat Franklin's postal appointment as a sinecure and to criticize him as little more than a placeman in the pay of the Crown. In 1774, for example, Thomas Jefferson launched just such a critique in one of his very first state papers. The royal postal system, Jefferson complained, "seems to have had little connection with British convenience, except that of accommodating his majesty's ministers and favorites with the sale of a lucrative and easy office."[87] A similar critique, of course, was later launched by William Goddard.

Franklin's tenure in the postal system remained controversial long after his death in 1790. As late as 1840, neither it nor any other feature of Franklin's long and distinguished public service received more than an incidental mention in textbook accounts of American public life.[88] Isaiah Thomas, for example, devoted surprisingly little attention to the subject in his *History of Printing,* very possibly as a result of Goddard's prodding, while few postmasters general saw fit to so much as mention Franklin's name in their annual report.[89] The only tangible reminder within the general post office of Franklin's legacy, recorded postal clerk Jesse Dow in 1839, was a single portrait on the wall.[90]

With the publication of Franklin's *Life,* which was issued in many editions beginning shortly after Franklin's death, all this began to change. Franklin had always had a gift for self-promotion, and his *Life* was in many respects his greatest triumph. By highlighting his early years as a printer-postmaster and downplaying his long tenure as a placeman in the royal postal system, Franklin encouraged Americans to began the reevaluation of his public persona that would eventually transform the consummate would-be English gentleman of leisure into the archetypal American self-made man. Eventually even Franklin's postal career became reinterpreted in light of this newer, egalitarian ideal. "Like Franklin," declared Jesse Dow in 1839, Amos Kendall had "worked in detail in season and out of season . . . he divided responsibility, and worked the true magic of division of labor."[91] While Dow was right to praise Kendall's industry, his implicit assumption that Franklin had been equally industrious during his postal career owed more to the Franklin of legend than the Franklin of fact. Far more historically accurate was the invocation of Franklin's name by postal officers to *oppose* the anticipated reduction in postal rates that would culminate with the Post Office Act of 1845.[92] Franklin's primitive "system of postage," sniffed postal reformer Joshua Leavitt indignantly in 1849, would prove to be of no greater relevance to contemporary policymakers than Franklin's primitive experiments with electricity had been for inventor Samuel F. B. Morse.[93]

But Leavitt was in the minority. When Morse visited Europe in 1845, one American journalist declared matter-of-factly that the famous inventor was treading in the footsteps of his "illustrious predecessor," Benjamin Franklin.[94] Franklin and Morse, added Maine congressman Francis O. J. Smith at about the same time, would "glide down the declivity of time . . . the equals in the renown of inventive achievements, until the hand of History shall become palsied, and whatever pertains to humanity shall be lost in the general dissolution of matter."[95] It was a "singular coincidence," added another journalist a few years later, that Franklin, the very individual who had "cradled our postal system in its infancy," had paved the way with his electrical experiments for Morse's electric telegraph, the "other great medium for transmitting intelligence."[96]

The transmogrification of Franklin's public image gained a powerful boost in 1847 with the inclusion of his portrait on the first postage stamp. From this time onward, it became customary to hail Franklin as the founder of the American postal system and to credit him with innovations (such as, for example, the admission of newspapers into the mail) that he could not possibly have introduced, as they did not occur until after his death. Indeed, in retrospect, by far the most notable feature of Franklin's postal career is the extent to which it failed to anticipate the revolutionary changes in postal policy that would be set in motion with the passage of the Post Office Act of 1792.

WHILE THE egalitarian ideal greatly expanded opportunities for the aspiring Benjamin Franklins of the day, it worked to exclude many others who might otherwise have expected to secure employment in the enterprise. In particular, it excluded women and blacks. When nineteenth-century Americans championed the egalitarian ideal, they sought to create opportunities for *citizens,* which in practice ordinarily meant white men. Although the exclusion of women and blacks from employment in the postal system may not seem particularly surprising, there was nothing inevitable about this particular course of events. During the War of Independence, Mary Goddard had served with distinction as the postmaster of Baltimore, and well into the nineteenth century blacks had worked as stagecoach drivers and postriders, especially in the South Atlantic states. It was "generally allowed," declared Postmaster General Joseph Habersham in 1801, to employ blacks in this capacity, since they had proved to be more trustworthy than "that class of white men who will perform such services . . . The stages on Colonel Hoomes's route . . . are driven by slaves and most of the contractors employ them as mail carriers in the southern states."[97] Similar arrangements could have persisted in the following decades. Yet they did not, in large measure because of the emergence of the egalitarian ideal, which worked to the advantage of the white men who dominated the electorate and to the disadvantage of everyone else.[98]

The exclusion of women from employment in the postal system was often rationalized on the grounds of certain implicit metaphors of manhood. It was a serious mistake, explained Postmaster General Amos Kendall in 1835, as he opposed the appointment of a woman to a medium-sized postmastership in Virginia, to permit the appointment of "ladies" to offices that required the "most masculine energies."[99] Should a postmaster be so daring as to appoint a woman as a clerk, it was by no means unheard of for his decision to be cited as a cause for his dismissal.[100] Occasionally, contemporaries raised questions about the appointment of a widow to an office that had formerly been held by her husband. Though this practice was common in government offices in other parts of the world, it could not be taken for granted in the United States.[101] "Ought a female to be appointed to *office?*" one Virginia editorialist wondered aloud, following the appointment of a widow to succeed her late husband as the postmaster of Trenton.[102]

Similar considerations doomed the appointment of Elizabeth Linn as postmaster of St. Louis in 1845. Linn was the widow of a popular Missouri congressman and for this reason had a solid base of political support. But in the end, though it took a formal Cabinet meeting to settle the point, Linn's opponents prevailed. The reason, explained one of Linn's female friends in Washington, was simple. The Cabinet had concluded that the administration of such an important office would not be consistent with her "delicacy of character . . . The *difficult* management of the post office for a lady is the only reason why we are all disappointed."[103]

To be sure, female postal officers were by no means unknown. In the February 1850 issue of Sarah Hale's popular *Godey's Magazine and Lady's Book,* for example, subscribers would have found an elaborate engraving of a "village postmistress" that illustrated a story about a woman's postal career.[104] Most women postmasters ran small post offices in the North, particularly in Pennsylvania, where Quaker notions of relative gender equality may well have eased their way. In many offices, the employment of women was strictly a family affair. In one village post office, declared a traveler in the mid 1830s, the staff included a seventy-five-year-old man, an equally ancient woman "with spectacles on nose," a "great, fat, ruddy-faced damsel of twenty-five," and a "half-dozen barefooted urchins," all "down upon their knees on the floor, overhauling the huge pile before them, flinging those letters which were for their office into a distant corner of the room, amongst sundry wet mops, brushes, molasses barrels etc."[105] Often women worked in the postal system without ever having their names entered on the books. During an unannounced visit to a Michigan post office, for example, special agent Stebbins reported with evident surprise that there did not seem to be anyone of the "male gender" at work.[106]

Yet the number of female postal officers was never large. According to one estimate, women held eighty-one postmasterships in the entire United States in 1852.[107] Though this total was regarded as newsworthy, it was considerably less than 1 percent of the national total, a far smaller percentage than those for Great Britain and France, where as many as 20 percent of the total postmasterships were held by women at any point. This was largely because these offices were regarded as the possession of particular families, in which women often played a prominent role, rather than as a reward for political service, from which women were ordinarily excluded.[108]

Though women were barred from clerkships in the general post office until the Civil War, women did occasionally clerk in local offices, particularly when the postmastership itself was held by a male relation. In Seneca Falls, New York, for example, women's rights activist Amelia Bloomer worked for a short time alongside her postmaster husband in this capacity in the 1840s. Bloomer acknowledged that it was novel for her to work in the office in this way, adding that many doubtless thought that such an occupation was "out of woman's sphere."[109] Similarly, in the Albany post office, Postmaster Solomon Van Rensselaer long employed his daughter in copying his post office accounts. When political antagonists challenged the propriety of the practice, Van Rensselaer justified it by pointing to his daughter's disability—she was deaf, and thus entitled to special consideration—adding for good measure that she did the copying not in the office but in his own house.[110] Women sometimes also carried the mail. Eager to help her sick husband, a woman briefly carried the mails to Rochester, New York, in the second decade of the nineteenth century. Still, this situation was regarded as such a novelty that local wags grew accustomed to asking if the *"fe-male"* had arrived.[111]

The position of blacks within the postal system was even more circumscribed. While the exclusion of women had no legal standing, the exclusion of blacks had been officially codified in 1802, when Congress decreed that henceforth no one besides a "free white person" would be permitted to carry the mail.[112] This prohibition, explained Postmaster General McLean in 1828 in a widely publicized letter to a postmaster in Connecticut, extended not only to blacks living in the slaveholding states but also to any "colored person" living in a nonslaveholding state. He conceded that blacks might be permitted to unload the mail portmanteau from a stagecoach that had stopped in front of a post office. But they were strictly prohibited from carrying the portmanteau from the tavern where the stagecoach driver had stopped for dinner to the post office to which the mail had been sent.[113]

The exclusion of blacks from the postal system was partly spurred by the presumption that their involvement in the conveyance of the mail could spark a slave insurrection. Slave mail carriers were known to have carried news of a Virginia slave rebellion throughout the countryside in 1800, and public figures were determined to prevent them from ever doing so again.[114] Above all, Americans feared a slave rebellion similar to the notorious uprisings in the West Indies island of Santo Domingo, which had culminated in the establishment of the republic of Haiti. Postmaster General Gideon Granger explained the rationale for the policy in a remarkable letter that he wrote to Georgia congressman James Jackson in 1802. Should the government permit a mail contractor to employ blacks in the carriage of the mail, Granger lectured Jackson, the blacks would quickly come to learn that "a man's rights do not depend on his color." Granger took special care to extend the prohibition to free blacks, since they were the "most active and intelligent." If these men were permitted to carry the mail, they might discover the value of the postal system as a "machine." And once they did, Granger added, it would not be long before they took advantage of this knowledge to use this "machine" to coordinate the movements of the slaves living along the route. "The hazard may be small," Granger concluded, and the "prospect remote, but it does not follow that at some day the event will not be certain."[115]

Fear of a slave rebellion, of course, can hardly explain the exclusion of blacks from the postal system in the nonslaveholding states. Here the key consideration was the deeply etched presumption that blacks were socially inferior to whites and the determination to perpetuate this inferiority though the establishment of a public policy that was uniform throughout the country. This was particularly true for postal officers like McLean, who, though not a slaveholder himself and nominally opposed to the institution, sought to curry favor with the politically powerful slaveholding South.

The exclusion of blacks from employment in the postal system was not entirely successful. In 1806, a "person of color" drove the mail stage in New Jersey on the heavily traveled post road between Philadelphia and New York.[116] And in 1817, a "skillful black driver" carried the mail in Virginia. To "save the law," reminisced one contemporary, the driver was accompanied by a white boy who was no more than ten.[117] Similarly, as late as the 1830s, it was by no means unknown for contractors to employ blacks to carry the mail, as we know from the fines that the contractors were routinely assessed for the infraction.[118]

Blacks also occasionally worked in a variety of subordinate positions within post offices in the major commercial centers. For a time during the 1820s a slave worked in the Richmond post office, a circumstance that came to light when he was implicated in a complicated scheme to rob the mail.[119] And for several years during the 1830s, free black Nathaniel Herbert worked as a messenger in the general post office, having secured his office through the personal intervention of mail contractor William Bradley, Phineas Bradley's son. Not everyone approved of Herbert's appointment. For example, the journalist Anne Royall viciously ridiculed Herbert as "NATT the NIGGER" in several of the editorials on the postal system that she penned during these years.[120] But by all accounts Herbert was a conscientious public officer who labored diligently and well. Particularly notable was Herbert's long-standing interest in the slavery issue, which he followed closely by reading the antislavery press. Every summer, he left his office for a few days so that he might travel to Philadelphia to attend a free black political convention as the Washington delegate.[121] Herbert was so closely identified with the cause of black freedom that, when Washington was rocked by antiabolitionist riots during the summer of 1835, he briefly fled the city, fearful that he might be a victim of mob attack.[122] Yet however suggestive Herbert's career may have been of the opportunities that the central government could provide free blacks, it was the exception rather than the rule. Not until after the Civil War would blacks secure employment in the postal system in large numbers, and when they did it was less likely to be in big-city post offices than in such recently established branches of the service as railway mail.

The highly circumscribed postal careers of free blacks such as Nathaniel Herbert or women such as Amelia Bloomer help to illustrate how official norms helped to shape public attitudes regarding the boundaries of American public life. Had women been permitted to hold public office in large numbers, it would almost certainly have been harder to exclude them from other privileges of citizenship, including, perhaps, even the right to vote. But as matters stood, even the terminology that postal officers used subtly excluded women from the public sphere. Consider the term "postmaster." Throughout the early republic, it was sometimes doubted that this honorific could be applied to a woman, probably in large measure because of the widespread assumption that public office ought to be confined exclusively to men. For this reason, female postal officers were popularly known as "postmistresses," even though this term had no legal standing and was explicitly rejected by postal officers as inappropriate in official address.[123]

The outright ban on the employment of blacks was, if anything, even more detrimental to their full integration into American public life. However sporadically the ban may have been enforced, it further sharpened the psychological distinction between the free and the unfree and robbed blacks of the opportunity to participate on an equal basis in the new informational environment that the government had done so much to promote. By excluding blacks from the civil service in this way, complained free black antislavery activist Frederick Douglass in 1849, the central government had increased the hatred of whites toward blacks even as it stigmatized blacks with a sense of their own inferiority. It was nothing short of outrageous, Douglass fumed, for the government to tax free blacks as if they were whites, but to regard blacks as so "mean and degraded" that, by "State enactment" they were "not trusted even to carry a mail bag twenty yards across the street, or even to lift it off from the top of a stagecoach." Even an Irishman, Douglass added indignantly, might be employed at this task, though, as a recent immigrant, the Irishman might be "totally unacquainted with our institutions."[124]

THE PUBLIC AT LARGE, lamented postal journalist Peter G. Washington in 1851, may have been intimately acquainted with the interior of a post office, yet it had little understanding of the process by which its "stupendous and multiform machinery" was maintained in "harmonious and benignant operation."[125] This, Washington felt, was most unfortunate, for it was in precisely those parts of the post office that were hidden from public view that the bulk of the routine work of the institution was performed.

Every post office in the United States was responsible for three basic tasks: accounting for postal revenue; sorting the mail; and serving the public. The core of the accounting process was the preparation of an enormous number of forms, a task that in most offices occupied fully half the time of the staff.[126] Under postal regulations, the general post office required its officers to include a separate receipt known as the postbill with every packet of letters that they sent out of their office. In fact, the mail was technically defined as a packet of letters accompanied with the postbill and tied together with twine. The sheer volume of paperwork could be enormous. In the Albany post office alone, one clerk annually filled out some six thousand pages of forms.[127] No less burdensome was the complexity of the task, which had quickly become the subject of innumerable jokes. "Yes, gentlemen," one street juggler was said to have remarked, "I can balance anything you please, but a post office account."[128] Predictably, the preparation of this paperwork quickly became a monopoly of the most senior clerks, who actually preferred it to the less esoteric, though hardly less essential, business of waiting on patrons and sorting the mail. For reformers such as Samuel Gridley Howe, this was little short of outrageous. The "non-laboring" clerks who prepared the paperwork, Howe complained in 1848, made high salaries, while the "simple, honest, laboring men" who actually sorted the mail earned a mere $1 a day. Were the postmaster general to abandon the "*credit* system" and require that all letters be prepaid, Howe added, "the occupation of most of these gentlemen would be gone; their ledgers, their journals, their blotters, their way-bills, and most of their trumpery accounts would be done away with" so that, in short order, they would have no choice but to "wipe their pens, and pack off to spoil paper elsewhere."[129] As matters stood, however, few forms of employment were more secure. Within the New York post office, the average tenure of the twelve most highly paid clerks in 1839, all of whom earned more than $1,000, was sixteen years; by 1851, it had increased to twenty-two years. Even after changes in the administration, these clerks were not likely to be displaced. Three years after Jackson's victory in the election of 1828, for example, all four of the highest paid clerks in the New York office still retained their positions, while three years after the victory of the Whig party's William Henry Harrison in 1840, all but two of the twelve remained on the job.[130]

Less prestigious than the preparation of the various accounts, though no less important to the work of the office, was the sorting of the mail. In most of the larger offices, as well as in the distribution centers, this task customarily demanded the uninterrupted attention of at least a portion of the staff throughout the year, morning, noon, and night. In the New York post office, a typical workday might begin at 5:00 A.M. and end at 7:00 P.M., by which time the night shift had arrived.[131] To facilitate the work of the second shift, many city post offices included specially designated sleeping areas, complete with cots.[132] In the Montgomery, Alabama, post office, clerk Neil Blue was required to work even on Christmas. "Christmas—indeed," recorded Blue in his diary, but "not for post office clerks—today was an exceedingly busy one."[133]

The sorting process involved three principal stages. In the first stage, postal officers sorted the incoming mail; in the second, they routed it through the system; and in the third, they readied it for its final distribution to the public. Following the establishment of the hub-and-spoke sorting scheme in 1800, the bulk of the second and most critical stage was performed in specially designated distribution centers. Often located outside of the major commercial centers—in such places as Cumberland Gap, Tennessee, Gallipolis, Ohio, and Washington, Pennsylvania—distribution centers were among the busiest post offices in the country, often requiring their staff to work many hours on Sunday, a rare occurrence for other post offices at this time.[134]

Few offices processed a larger volume of mail than the distribution center at Wheeling, Virginia, where, the Wheeling Board of Trade proudly announced in 1846, postal officers routinely sorted as much as one-quarter of the mail for the entire United States.[135] The greatest challenge that the Wheeling staff faced, however, had less to do with the volume of the mail that it sorted than with the physical location of the office. Situated on the east bank of the Ohio River, the distribution center was hard-pressed to maintain an uninterrupted line of communication with the West. It was not uncommon, reported Wheeling postmaster George W. Thompson in 1838, for a contractor to load as many as forty-five bags into a canoe that he then forced through the river's "grinding cakes of ice at great peril and loss of life." Little had changed, Thompson added, from the early days of the office, when contractors had no alternative than to pitch the mailbags from one cake of floating ice to another.[136] Not until 1849, with the completion of a bridge over the Ohio, would this problem finally be satisfactorily resolved.

While there is good reason to suspect that, on balance, the sorting scheme worked reasonably well, it was not without its problems. Try as they might, postal officers found it impossible to centralize all of the sorting at the distribution centers, and this was an invitation for trouble, since the postmasters at the branch depots rarely possessed the necessary geographical information to avoid mistakes. "It is my opinion," declared special agent Cortland Stebbins in a letter to the postmaster general in 1850, "that the ignorance of postmasters, as to the location of offices, is one of the greatest evils in the working of the postal system." In part, this problem could be explained by the general shortage of maps, a problem that seems to have increased as the enterprise expanded.[137] No less exasperating was what can only be termed the stubborn reluctance of certain postal officers to master the fine points of American geography. In certain cases, this could lead to a comedy of errors, as inexperienced postal officers rerouted packages around the country in an effort to figure out in which direction a given package ought to be sent. "Where is it?" scribbled one perplexed postal officer on a package whose address he failed to recognize. "Try it in Illinois," wrote back another. "Let it go North," added a third. "Don't send it this way again," responded a fourth.[138] "Ye who know where this is directed to forward," wrote one particularly exasperated postal officer, "I know not where it is, and I'll be damned to do it."[139]

Often, changes in postal procedures only made matters worse. Theoretically, postal officers could expedite the delivery of the mail if they rerouted letters to take advantage of routine changes in contracting arrangements, such as the seasonal shift from steamboats to stage-coaches in Michigan during the winter when the Great Lakes were frozen. Postmasters, however, did not always make the necessary adjustments, to the constant frustration of special agents like Cortland Stebbins. After having struggled to teach the new routings to Michigan postmasters, Stebbins found to his chagrin that all his efforts had come to naught: "By the time they get the winter arrangement learned summer comes, and it takes all season to *learn them back again*. So they send wrong the whole year."[140]

Further problems occurred at the post offices at which the mail was received. Since letters from abroad were often written in languages other than English, postal officers sometimes found it expedient to hire a special foreign language clerk. This was true not only in cosmopolitan New York, but also in Fayetteville, North Carolina, where the postmaster retained a clerk who understood Gaelic to read the large volume of letters that the recently arrived Scottish Highlanders exchanged with their families and friends back home.[141] Poorly written addresses posed a further problem, particularly when the letter writer had little familiarity with the appropriate conventions. While in Washington, D.C., reported one British visitor in a travel book published in 1853, he received a letter that had been traveling "half over the Union, and had been sent back from twenty-three other Washingtons, scrawled all over: 'not known here,' 'try t'other,' 'no such person,' and so on," and that would have been properly delivered in twelve hours, had the correspondent only put the letters "D.C." under the word "Washington" on the address.[142] One particularly enigmatic address, written in Ireland to a family member in the United States, read in its entirety: "To Mike Donovan or to his cousin Eliza MacFarrelly. Postman will find him by findin Betsy Brennen who was engaged to Mike before they left Ireland and may be married."[143] To puzzle out problem addresses such as this, the New York postmaster established a special deciphering office, whose staff grew accustomed, as one journalist reported, to fathoming the meaning of handwriting that resembled the "footprints of a gigantic spider" that, after "wading knee deep in ink, retreated hastily across the paper."[144] The disposition of a properly addressed letter posed still further problems. Did it belong to a boxholder? Should it to be sent out to the addressee? Or should it be held at the office to be picked up at general delivery? Answers to questions such as these might require clerks to be familiar with as many as twenty thousand different names.[145]

To help keep this complicated system working smoothly, postmasters counted on the general post office to supply them with a steady stream of printed circulars, personal letters, and bulletins in widely circulated periodicals such as *Niles's Weekly Register*. Additional information could be secured from the distributing postmasters, who oversaw the performance of the offices in their immediate vicinity. And for particularly challenging problems, there was always the most recent edition of the *Post-Office Laws, Instructions, and Forms,* an encyclopedic compendium of all manner of information about postal affairs. Frequently, however, the manual was in short supply. Lacking as he did the necessary funding to publish a new edition, complained Postmaster General Charles Wickliffe in 1842, "a large number of post offices" were "without any definite guide in the performance of their duty."[146] When *Niles's* ceased publication in 1849, postmasters also briefly had their own trade journal, the *United States Postal Guide and Official Advertiser,* which was ostensibly intended to serve the entire civil government, but was primarily aimed, as its title implied, at the thousands of postmasters who were scattered throughout the United States.[147]

The *Postal Guide* was a genuine innovation in American public life. Established to show public officers "what is done, and what should be done, in office," it has the distinction of being the first periodical in the United States to focus exclusively on the ongoing administration of the civil government.[148] Explaining why he had undertaken to publish the *Postal Guide,* editor Peter G. Washington declared in 1852 that the postal system had grown entirely too large to be administered solely by means of occasional written letters between the general post office and postmasters in the field.[149] "The fact is," wrote one grateful Tennessee postmaster to Washington, in praise of his publication, "the small fry of postmasters like myself" could not do without the *Postal Guide,* if they wanted to do what "ought to be done in office," since their instructions were "very limited"; in fact, the writer continued, he himself had not received "one-third of the instructions to postmasters contained in your columns."[150] Few postmasters may have been quite so conscientious as the North Carolina prodigy who, upon receiving the latest thirty-odd page installment of the *Postal Guide* at 10:00 P.M. one Saturday evening, read it through before going to bed.[151] Yet during its brief two-year existence, the *Postal Guide* provided postmasters with a wealth of information about sorting procedures, as well as a host of other topics that they might not have received in any other way.

*   *   *

THROUGHOUT the United States, in both the thousands of villages scattered throughout the interior and the major commercial centers along the Atlantic seaboard, the arrival of the mail was, as one writer put it, "the great event of the day."[152] For merchants, it furnished the most up-to-date information about changing market trends. For the political cognoscenti, it provided news about late-breaking developments in public affairs. And for everyone else, it brought tidings of family and friends from afar.

Not even the commercialization of the electric telegraph in 1844 could diminish in any fundamental way the significance of the mail. Political reporters, reminisced one veteran Washington insider in 1902, looking back on the history of news coverage in the antebellum period, continued to rely on the postal system to transmit their dispatches for almost two decades after the electric telegraph had linked Washington to the rest of the country.[153] Even merchants, contended telegraph promoter Ezra Cornell, were slow to recognize the commercial potential of the new technology, since they had long grown accustomed to relying on the postal system, which already "served every purpose of ordinary intercourse."[154] As late as 1866, according to Philadelphia letter carrier James Rees, the receipt of a single letter could "convulse the market" and create a "commotion" at the commercial exchange.[155]

Nowhere was the arrival of the mail more eagerly awaited than in San Francisco during the opening months of the California gold rush. For the thousands of men who had traveled across the continent to make their fortunes in the gold fields, the postal system provided the only link to their families and friends back East. And at no time was the mail greeted with greater interest than during the fall of 1849, when, due to an unprecedented series of administrative foul-ups, the steamer *Panama* finally deposited at the post office no fewer than thirty-seven mailbags containing countless newspapers and 45,000 letters, or fully one-quarter of all the mail for California for the entire year.[156]

For San Francisco postmaster Jacob Bailey Moore and his staff of eight clerks, the arrival of such an enormous volume of mail posed a major administrative challenge. How could they possibly insure that it would be distributed in a timely manner? Rising to the task, Moore immediately closed the office and barred the entryways, well aware that, had he not done so, the office might well have been stormed. Next Moore turned himself to the task of sorting the mail. Among his assistants was Bayard Taylor, a popular travel writer who felt it only fair that he should offer his services as a "clerk-extraordinary," since he was staying at the time as Moore's guest in the post office garret.[157]

For the better part of the next two days, Moore and his staff worked doggedly to get the office in order, oblivious to the steadily growing crowd of miners that had gathered outside the office to pick up their mail. "Where the source that governs business, satisfies affection and supplies intelligence had been shut off from a whole community for three months," Taylor explained, "the rush from all sides to supply the void, was irresistible."[158] By the middle of the first day, the impatience of the crowd had reached a "most annoying pitch": "They knocked; they tried shouts and then whispers, and then shouts again."[159] Some postal patrons resorted to ingenious stratagems to get their mail in advance of the crowd. The well-to-do offered hefty bribes for special favors, while the ministers and naval officers tried to trade on their rank. To all of these appeals, Postmaster Moore turned a deaf ear. And so the clerks worked on, undaunted by the constant din of the besiegers.

On the second day, Moore and his staff were finally ready to open for business. In accordance with postal procedure, Moore first opened the office to those patrons fortunate enough to have rented special glass post office boxes. To minimize the crush, a clerk tried to form the box holders into a single line. As soon as the key to the post office was turned, however, this stratagem failed. Intent upon forcing their way into the office, the box holders broke through the glass faces of the post office boxes and very nearly pushed through the wooden partition that divided the public lobby from the rest of the office.

The following noon—almost three full days after the mail had arrived—Moore's staff finally opened the post office to the public at large. For the miners or their agents, there was simply no alternative to waiting in line. And they were in for a long wait, since there were only two windows for the entire population of the city: one window for the army and navy, the clergy, women, and the French, Spanish, and Chinese inhabitants of the city, and the other window for everyone else.[160] Miners unfortunate enough to find themselves at the end of the second line might have to wait for as long as six hours to get their mail. A few enterprising Californians intentionally arrived early so that they might sell their places in line, with a single spot often going for as high as $25, a considerable sum even given the boomtown economy. The rest waited patiently while roving vendors did a brisk business selling pies, cakes, and coffee.[161]

* * *

THE COMMOTION that surrounded the arrival of the mail in gold-rush San Francisco was unusual, perhaps unique. But it illustrates an important point. Throughout the early republic, the vast majority of postal patrons had no choice but to visit the post office in person to pick up their mail or to send someone to pick it up on their behalf. It was for this reason that social scientist Henry C. Carey could declare in 1858 that, though the postal system might be an admirable "machine" for communication at a distance, it was "totally useless" for individuals who lived near each other.[162]

The problems postal patrons confronted were largely an artifact of postal policy. Notwithstanding the enormous geographical expansion in the enterprise that had taken place since the adoption of the federal Constitution, postal officers had failed to establish comparable facilities for the local distribution of letters.

There was nothing inevitable about this shortcoming. Between the passage of the Post Office Act of 1792 and the resignation of Joseph Habersham in 1801, it looked for a time as if city postmasters might establish a system of "penny posts" that would soon come to match the well established city delivery systems in Great Britain or France. The penny posts had the enthusiastic support of Postmaster General Habersham, and during his tenure in office he did everything he could to discourage the renting of post office boxes, which he regarded as a second-best solution to the perennial problem of getting postal patrons their mail.[163] For a small fee, usually one or two cents, the penny posts transmitted letters and other mailable items between the post office and the recipients' office or home, with the carriers (or penny posts) keeping their accounts in their head.[164] In 1793, one postal officer estimated that in Philadelphia the penny posts delivered as much as nine-tenths of the incoming mail, a circumstance that probably owed something to the proximity of Congress, whose members were quick to complain about lapses in service.[165] In New York, the service seems to have been more limited. "Almost every man" was "his own letter carrier" during these years, reported one New Yorker in his memoirs.[166]

However important the penny posts may have been for certain fortunate classes of Americans, such as the members of Congress, they quickly lost out to the box system, which remained the keystone of postal distribution from 1801 until the Civil War. Though the box system was inconvenient for postal patrons, it proved to be a godsend for postmasters at the major commercial centers, since it provided them with a much-coveted additional source of income. As long as it remained in place, large numbers of postal patrons had little choice but to check their post office boxes or, if they were not so fortunate to have their own, wait in line. In Great Britain, such a situation would have been inconceivable. In all the major cities, observed postal reformer Pliny Miles in 1856, the British government had long before established a "vast machinery, which picks up a hundred thousand letters and brings back a hundred thousand answers, more swiftly, more surely, and more cheaply than we send a single thousand."[167] The same was true in France. But in the United States, office delivery remained the norm right up to the Civil War. "With all due deference to those who had the framing of our postal laws," Miles concluded, "there has not been a single step made in advance of that system, which gives a single post office in every town, city, and village, and which obliges everyone to go after his letters, no matter how dense the population, or how dense the place."[168]

Whether or not a given postal patron visited the post office in person depended on a variety of considerations. Merchants, for example, might send a clerk to pick up their mail for them, while the well-to-do might send a servant. And for those who could afford the cost, there were always the penny posts or the private city delivery firms that entrepreneurs established beginning around 1840. Everyone else, however, had to visit the post office in person. Shortly after the introduction of postage stamps in 1847, postal reformer Joshua Leavitt explained just how the process worked in New York. To pick up your letters, you had to step up to one window; to get your newspapers, you had to step up to another. If you wanted to purchase postage stamps, you "must go round by a back way, through an obscure door, up a narrow, winding stairway, into a lobby having several doors, and when you find the one leading into the cashier's room, you may enter there, and be allowed to purchase stamps!" When a steamer arrived, or at the close of the day, it was taken for granted that you were in for a long wait. As late as 1850, Leavitt noted in disgust, the New York office provided a mere fifteen delivery windows for the entire population of the city. This posed a particular problem for common laborers, since they were rarely able to leave work during the morning or early afternoon, when the post office was least likely to be crowded. Should a laborer wish to pick up his mail, Leavitt observed, he had no choice but to go in the late afternoon, after work, when he could count on a long wait.[169] This could be an ordeal. "It not infrequently happens," explained Miles, that long lines of these "unfortunate victims of routine, red tape, incompetency and folly" could be found slowly wending their ways in rows to the appropriate delivery window to ask if there were any letters for them, only to be told, in "six cases out of seven, that there are none."[170] An analogous problem confronted the young women who worked in the burgeoning textile mills in Lowell, Massachusetts. "There is for them a room with one little aperture" through which the mail was transferred, lamented one mill worker in 1849, "much as food is passed to a wild beast in his cage." Was it not possible, the mill worker added, for postal officers to make it possible for the mill girls to do their business at the post office "without feeling it to be a death-struggle"?[171]

To simplify the delivery process, postal officers introduced a variety of expedients. These included improving the facilities for office delivery, increasing the number of post office boxes, and relocating offices to a more centralized location. In addition, they made perfunctory efforts to expand the penny posts. Compared to London or Paris, however, these efforts never amounted to much. As late as 1846, the Boston penny post employed a mere five individuals as mail carriers, an entirely inadequate number given the size and commercial importance of the city.[172] As a consequence, postal patrons might have to wait two, three, or even four days to receive a letter sent in this way.[173] Not surprisingly, the penny posts remained confined to the downtown business district, performed a limited range of services that often did not include reasonably priced delivery *within* the city, and were patronized primarily by merchants and other men of affairs. Even many businessmen, reported one citizen in 1852, were "ignorant of the existence of a governmental city express for letters."[174]

To help fill this gap in service, entrepreneurs established nongovernmental or private city delivery firms in most of the major commercial centers. The first of these was the short-lived Penny Post Association, established in New York City in 1838.[175] By the 1840s, private city delivery firms were well established in several cities, including New York and Philadelphia, though not in Boston or Baltimore.[176] In cities where the private city delivery firms competed head-to-head with the government-supervised penny posts, the city delivery firms generally prevailed. Indeed, when antebellum Americans referred to the "city post," it was ordinarily these private city delivery firms, not the penny posts, that they had in mind: Boyd's or Swart's in New York, Blood's in Philadelphia. The two most successful of these private firms, Boyd's and Swart's in New York, delivered 20,000 letters a day in the 1850s, or 9.1 million letters a year, nine times the volume of letters transmitted by the government-run penny posts.[177] During their heyday in the three decades before the Civil War, these firms introduced many of the innovations associated with the modern postal system, including mailboxes and postage stamps.

Even the city delivery firms, however, were not without their problems. Rarely did they serve more than a fraction of the public. This was particularly true in Boston where, as reformer Samuel Gridley Howe observed, it took more time, more labor, and therefore more money to send a note from the North End to the South End of the city than it did to send it from Boston to New York or even to New Orleans: "We must hire a messenger, who must run two miles and spend some time, perhaps, in finding the place; he must then run back again; and our friend, when he has got his answer ready, must employ not only another pair of legs, but the body, arms, and head, all the powers, in short, of a human being, for the safe conduct of a little bit of paper."[178] In addition, none of the delivery firms used uniformed carriers, a serious shortcoming, since uniforms made the carriers appear more professional and reduced the incidence of tardiness and theft. And, of course, none had any legal relationship to the government. As a result, they were an object of scorn to reformers who, like Miles, sought to emulate the uniformed carrier services of London and Paris. "We are not required by courtesy, truth, or the circumstances of the case," Miles huffed, "to speak of the few irresponsible persons who go about our cities delivering letters and papers, for a fee, to those who choose to employ them, as a part of our postal system."[179] Notwithstanding Miles's complaint, the city delivery firms remained a key element in the distribution system until the Civil War, when Congress formally established a salaried, uniformed corps of letter carriers and, with it, the modern postman.

The limitations of the penny posts and the persistence of the box system provide further proof of the enormous influence over American postal policy that was exerted by congressmen in the South and West. As long as the congressional committees on the post office and post roads were dominated by congressmen from the rural hinterland, it was virtually impossible to press for meaningful reform. Though these congressmen saw nothing untoward in lavishing enormous sums of money on highly questionable mail contracting ventures for their own constituents, they had little interest in alleviating the problems that postal patrons in other parts of the country confronted in picking up their mail. In the South and the West, Miles estimated in 1862, the inhabitants of an entire county might receive fewer letters than the inhabitants of a single city ward in the major commercial centers of New York, Philadelphia, Baltimore, and Boston.[180] It was primarily due to these narrowly political considerations that delivery services in these cities remained extremely limited even though as late as 1829 they generated 28 percent of the total postal revenue in the country, with the New York City post office alone generating almost half of the postage in the state of New York, and 12 percent of the postage in the United States.[181]

ON A GIVEN DAY, the average post office was fairly bursting with various kinds of reading matter. Government documents, periodicals, and religious tracts were routinely transmitted through the mail, often free of charge. Throughout the early republic, earnest evangelicals like Joshua V. Hines routinely addressed stacks of religious tracts to postmasters, who would oblige them by putting the tracts out where they could be freely sampled by whoever happened to stop by.[182] For a time, backcountry radicals like William Manning had hoped that magazines might emerge as the great democratic medium. By 1800, however, it was clear that newspapers had won the title, partly because they were cheaper to send, and partly because they were the most flexible medium for transmitting up-to-date information about commerce and public affairs.[183] Outside of those post offices located in the major commercial centers, newspapers made up the vast bulk of the mail. Letters might be useful to perhaps one man in a thousand, noted one editorialist in 1813, yet newspapers were the "*pabulum* which sustains the government itself."[184] Most village post offices, reported mail contractor Isaac Hill in 1832, received little else.[185] This remained true, declared one village postmaster, as late as 1852.[186] To be sure, not everyone took a newspaper. According to Amos Kendall, as late as 1817 not more than 3 percent of the population of Kentucky subscribed to one.[187] Even in Massachusetts, the total was probably no greater than one in ten.[188] Yet if a postal patron living outside of the major commercial centers received anything in the mail, it was far more likely to be a newspaper than a letter or magazine.[189]

Once newspapers arrived at the post office, they were regarded, by what seems to have been an almost universal convention, as less the private property of the subscriber than a kind of public resource to be made available to anyone who wished to catch up on the latest news. "There is scarcely a village or country post office in the United States, particularly if it be kept in a tavern or store," declared one contemporary in 1822, "in which the newspapers are not as free to all comers, as to the persons to whom they rightfully belong."[190] Intent upon giving the custom the sanction of law, Newburgh, New York, postmaster Aaron Belknap went so far as to formally secure the permission of newspaper subscribers so that nonsubscribers might have the opportunity to catch up on the latest news when they stopped by to pick up their mail.[191] Before long, enterprising postal clerks like Elam Langdon began to establish reading rooms in the immediate vicinity of the post office where, for a fee, subscribers could be reasonably certain to find the leading periodicals of the day.[192]

While the transmission of reading matter was for most Americans the most important public service that the postal system provided, it was by no means the only task that it performed. A case in point was the brief experiment that Congress instituted in the second decade of the nineteenth century to use the postal system to transmit smallpox vaccine through the mail. This curious experiment in public health began in 1813 when Congress granted Dr. James Smith of Maryland the right to transmit his smallpox vaccine free of charge to post offices throughout the United States. Smith was a protégé of Benjamin Rush and shared his mentor's abiding faith in the postal system as an agent of change. During the next nine years, Smith and his army of postmasters used its facilities to arrange for the vaccination of as many as 100,000 people against the disease.[193]

The postal system boosted Smith's experiment in a variety of ways. Most obviously, it reduced the cost of obtaining the vaccine, an important consideration in an age in which the cost of transmission could be a major constraint. In addition, it helped to guarantee that the vaccine would reach its destination in a timely fashion (the vaccine was only valuable if it was received within a certain period of time). Finally, having the vaccine handled by the postal system invested the experiment with the imprimatur of the central government and so encouraged many to take it who might otherwise have doubted its value. Should Congress permit Smith to distribute the "inestimable matter" through the postal system free of any expense, explained one group of supporters, this implicit government sanction would "induce many to use it, who have yet no confidence in its efficacy."[194]

Unfortunately, Smith's experiment came to a tragic end in 1822 when, in a bizarre episode, ten inhabitants of Tarboro, North Carolina, mysteriously died of smallpox after having been treated with his vaccine. When Smith investigated what had gone wrong, he discovered to his amazement that the Tarboro victims had been accidentally exposed not to his vaccine, but rather to the live smallpox virus. When this incident came to the attention of Congress, it promptly rescinded the law and, notwithstanding Smith's determined efforts, never repeated the experiment, much to his chagrin. "If this law had not been repealed," Smith declared bitterly in 1826, "the smallpox would have been extirpated from among us long ago."[195] Just how the tragic mix-up occurred remains a mystery to this day. To the end of his life, Smith remained convinced that some ill-disposed individual, possibly a rival, had switched his vaccine with the smallpox virus at some point in the course of its transmission through the mail. Though the historian of this episode terms Smith's claim "incredible," it is conceivable that the inhabitants of Tarboro fell victim to one of the first major product-tampering schemes in American history.[196]

WHILE NEWSPAPERS constituted the vast bulk of the mail, letters were far more rare. Prior to the passage of the Post Office Acts of 1845 and 1851, each of which reduced the basic letter rate, few Americans ever sent or received a letter through the mail. Even after 1851, the arrival of a letter remained for many rural families an "unusual thing."[197] So rare was this event that, as late as 1830, Tennessee congressman John Bell could term the high letter fees "popular," since they helped to prevent the postal system from running into debt.[198] In a similar spirit, three years later New York congressman C. C. Camberleng publicly opposed the reduction in the basic letter rate on the grounds that this would throw the expense of the postal system on the many who did not write letters while providing relief for the few who did.[199]

Even postal reformers were slow to turn their attention to the need for a reduction in the basic letter rate, convinced that it was more important to press for still further reductions in the already low rates on newspapers and magazines on the grounds that the latter reform would benefit a far larger percentage of the public. For example, when Campbell's Station, Tennessee, postmaster Samuel Martin began a one-man campaign in the 1820s to lower the existing postal rates to meet the needs of the day, he focused initially not on the basic letter rate, but on the nominal postage on newspapers and on the postage that editors paid on the letters that they exchanged with each other to improve their ability to report on the news.[200] Not until the 1830s would a few progressive congressmen begin to contemplate the possibility that the existing rates of letter postage might pose a hardship for the public at large. Among the first congressmen to reach this conclusion was Edward Everett, whose interest had no doubt been spurred by his personal knowledge of the many New England families who had migrated to the transappalachian West and who wished to keep up a correspondence with their friends and relatives back East.[201] Prior to this time, public figures seem to have assumed that sending letters through the postal system was confined to merchants, who could treat the postage as a business expense; the well-to-do, who could afford it; and public figures active in the central government, most of whom had the privilege of sending their correspondence free of charge.[202]

Precisely who did send letters through the postal system is a difficult question to answer. American postal officers kept no official statistics on the subject—much to the surprise of British counterparts, such as Anthony Trollope—while the best contemporary estimates remain incomplete.[203] A good deal, however, can be gleaned from the retrospective data that postal reformer Pliny Miles compiled in the 1850s with the assistance of the staff of the general post office.

Perhaps the most obvious conclusion to be drawn from Miles's data is that letter writing became increasingly common as the nineteenth century progressed. In 1790, the postal system transmitted just under 300,000 letters, or roughly one letter per year for every ten inhabitants of the United States, excluding Indians and slaves. By 1830, the total had increased to 14 million, which was roughly one letter per free person per year (see Table 1.2). By 1856, the comparable total had increased to around 130 million, or 5.3 letters per free person per year.[204] No less notable was the regional variation. In 1856, in North Carolina, the average inhabitant sent 1.5 letters per year; in Indiana, 3; in Louisiana, 5.5; in Massachusetts, 10.[205] Within the major commercial centers, the totals could be higher still: in New York, the average inhabitant sent 30 letters per year; in Boston, 41.[206] Since the urban population included large numbers of transients who could not be expected to post many letters, Miles concluded that, on average, urban Americans wrote between five and twenty times as many letters as rural Americans, while in the major commercial centers, the average adult man engaged in business wrote from 100 to 1,000 letters per year.[207]

Though Miles compiled no data on letter writing by social group, a few tentative conclusions can be drawn from the various other sources that have survived. In 1845, as in 1765, the vast majority of letter writers were merchants engaged in long-distance trade. No longer, however, did the vast majority of letters travel across the Atlantic. In 1761, Franklin had declared matter-of-factly that a particular post office could be expected to generate little revenue since its inhabitants were involved in "little or no foreign trade."[208] By the 1820s, this was no longer true. Particularly notable was the increase in the volume of mail that was sent comparatively short distances within the immediate vicinity of the major commercial centers. In 1840, for example, one journalist observed that three-quarters of the letters sent out of the New York post office traveled no farther than Boston, Albany, Philadelphia, or Baltimore.[209] Prior to the 1790s, a far greater percentage would almost certainly have gone overseas.

Though the vast majority of all letters were written by men, women wrote many letters too. How many is impossible to say. If we take the percentage of male and female addressees on a list of undelivered, or "dead," letters as a rough measure of the relative percentage of letters written by these two groups, women may have written as many as 20 percent of all the letters in the country.[210] Some of these letters were written by mothers to their grown-up children who had moved far from home. "We have no excuse for being strangers," declared one mother in 1831, in a magazine article in which she urged her fellow mothers to stay in touch with their distant kin.[211] Others were written to female friends. So important was this female-female correspondence that one historian has gone so far as to use the surviving letters as evidence for the existence of a distinctive "female world of love and ritual."[212] Had these women not been able to take advantage of the facilities for communication that the postal system provided, and had they not had the means to make the considerable financial outlay to cover the cost, such intense long-distance relationships would have proved virtually impossible to sustain. And without the surviving correspondence, the existence of this forgotten world would necessarily be a matter of speculation.

Free blacks used the postal system as well. Free black barber William Johnson did so much business at the Natchez, Mississippi, post office that he rented his own post office box, though he bitterly complained in his diary about the various indignities he suffered in picking up his mail.[213] Free black women also wrote many letters, in some cases relying upon white women to help them put their thoughts into writing.[214] Even slaves sometimes used the postal system to maintain a correspondence with their absent masters. Slave carpenter John Hemings, for example, maintained a correspondence with his master, Thomas

Jefferson, as did the household slave Lucy Skipwith with her master, John Hartwell Cocke.[215]

However widespread letter writing may have been among various social groups, it is important to remember that, prior to the passage of the Post Office Act of 1845, it was expensive to post a letter. Prior to 1845, postage was computed using a complicated formula based not only on the distance that a given letter was to travel, but also on the number of sheets it contained. No matter how small or lightweight a bank note, receipt, or other enclosure, postal officers charged each with the full letter rate.[216] To send a single sheet of paper from New York to Buffalo, a distance that postal officers reckoned at over three hundred miles, cost 25 cents. Should the letter contain two enclosures, the expense would be tripled, to 75 cents. For this reason, envelopes were rarely used; instead, postal patrons would simply fold up their letter and write the address on the back.

In an age in which few common laborers made more than $1.00 a day, letter writing was an expensive proposition. The cost of a single letter from a friend or relative in the East or South to a loved one in the Northwest, calculated one Rhode Island congressman in 1845, was the equivalent of a bushel of wheat, or a day's labor for a man.[217] Even to send a letter a relatively short distance, reported the citizens of Huntington County, Pennsylvania, might cost a poor man the equivalent of half a day's labor.[218] In some instances, poor women had to pawn their possessions in order to raise money to pay for a letter from a beloved husband or child.[219] Even subordinate postal officers, who, unlike postmasters, did not enjoy the franking privilege, avoided charges if they could. Postal clerk James M. Campbell always used a "private conveyance," since it prevented a "small tax" and he was scarce of money.[220] Particularly hard hit were the many Americans who lacked access to currency redeemable in gold, the only legal tender for the payment of postage. To help alleviate the problem, one North Carolina postmaster publicly defied Jacksonian postmaster general Amos Kendall, who, like most Jacksonians, insisted that the government conduct its business on a strictly hard-money basis, and broadcast his willingness to accept for letters rated, respectively, at 5, 12½, and 25 cents, a half-grown chicken, a full-blooded rooster, and two laying hens.[221]

However onerous letter postage may have been, many Americans found it worthwhile to foot the bill. This could be expensive indeed. During one three-month stretch, estimated Andrew Jackson in 1822, he paid out as much in postage as he took in from his cotton crop.[222] Ministers were particularly hard-hit, since they were expected to maintain a correspondence with parishioners who had moved out of the area. In 1828, Unitarian minister Orville Dewey spent $70 a year on postage, while Albany merchants spent between $5 and $60. In Elbridge, New York, in contrast, most inhabitants paid between $1 and $5 annually, with one machine builder paying $15, one minister $20, and one farmer $45.[223]

A further reason for a writer's reluctance to mail a letter was that the recipient might be saddled with the cost of the postage. Though postal patrons had the option of prepaying the postage, few did, since they were unwilling to pay for a service until they could be sure that it had been properly performed. Consequently, frequent correspondents often found themselves paying large sums for letters that they would never have bothered with had they known their contents in advance. "Unnecessary postage," stormed Francis Lieber in 1831, more than a decade before the first major rate reductions went into effect, "puts me in a rage; it is hard to pay for the stupidity of your correspondents, and how can you evade it?" In an effort to improve postal etiquette, Lieber proposed three rules for letter writers, which he urged them to always keep in mind. The first rule to consider was whether the letter was worth writing; the second, whether it was worth receiving; and the third, the most important rule of all, whether it was "worth the postage."[224] "For my part," wrote Henry David Thoreau a bit peevishly in 1854, "I could easily do without the post office," adding that in the period before the recent rate reductions, he had never received more than one or two letters that were worth more than he had paid to pick them up.[225]

The Post Office Acts of 1845 and 1851 went far toward eliminating these problems. In addition to tightening the postal monopoly—and, in this way, effectively driving private firms out of the field on the heavily traveled routes in the North and the East—the acts dramatically reduced and simplified the basic letter rate; eliminated most (but not all) of the distance-based rate differentials; and substituted weight for the number of sheets as the basic unit of measure. Beginning in 1851— and with a few notable exceptions, such as mail sent from the Atlantic seaboard to the West Coast—domestic correspondence was charged at a flat rate, 3 cents, per half-ounce. It would remain at this basic rate, with minor changes, for the next hundred years. No less important, the acts facilitated prepayment of postage through the use of postage stamps, which the government first introduced on a national basis in 1847, and which became common after 1851.[226] Taking advantage of this innovation, postal patrons quickly grew accustomed to prepaying the postage, rather than sending their letters "postage due," as the once-standard practice then came to be known. Prepayment became mandatory in 1855.

Most important of all, the rate reductions brought about by the acts of 1845 and 1851 made it possible for virtually anyone, regardless of financial circumstances, to carry on a correspondence with distant family and friends. Predictably, this precipitated an explosion in letter writing and, with it, a burgeoning market for how-to manuals to teach ordinary Americans the once-arcane custom of maintaining a correspondence with distant friends and family.[227] To meet this need, publishers issued a spate of guides aimed at the "middle and lower ranks of society."[228] Now that postal rates had declined, one manual explained, it was important to assist the many thousands of individuals who could now afford to carry on a correspondence, but who might still need assistance in some of the "minor, but still important, formalities."[229]

To be sure, even after 1851, some reformers continued to press for improvements. Particularly objectionable to some was the half-ounce weight requirement, which proved burdensome to those who had trouble confining their handwriting to a relatively small space. The present policy, charged petitioner John Junius Flourney of Georgia in 1852, amounted to a tax against those who had not "seven coppers in their pocket" or whose "poor penmanship and large scrawls" required lots of room.[230] But for almost everyone else, the cost of postage ceased to be a serious constraint. This was true not only for letter writers, but also for merchants. Now, for the first time, they too had the opportunity to take advantage of the low rates that had long been enjoyed by the editors of newspapers and magazines. Predictably enough, soon the mails were flooded with enormous quantities of handbills, advertising circulars, and unsolicited business mail—what is known today as junk mail. "Hundreds of thousands, and, perhaps, millions of circulars, &c.," one journalist predicted, immediately after the passage of the Post Office Act of 1845, "will now be sent through the post-office, in consequence of this uniform and cheap rate of postage."[231]

THROUGHOUT the United States, the local post office was far more than the place where you went to pick up your mail. It was a favorite gathering place for merchants, tradesmen, and other men of affairs, making its interior, as the English traveler Basil Hall observed, the "most picturesque object in every travelers' landscape."[232] In rural localities like Concord, Massachusetts, it was one of the "vitals of the village," as Thoreau observed.[233] In state capitals, it was invariably the best place to feel the political pulse of the country. "The post office was thronged for an hour" before the arrival of the mail, reported one New York public figure in 1820, and "everyone stood on tip toe" to hear the latest news.[234] And in the major commercial centers, it was the place where, as one postal clerk aptly put it, the leading men of the day "most do congregate."[235]

So popular was the custom of visiting at the post office that even in bustling commercial centers such as Rochester, New York, the "village method" of delivering letters persisted long after the town had become large enough to support its own carrier service. According to longtime inhabitant Frederick A. Whittlesey, it was "mainly" for this reason that Rochester remained "so homogeneous and family-like."[236] Even in New York City, the post office retained a decidedly familial cast well into the 1820s, which may not be surprising, since it was still kept on the first floor of Postmaster Theodorus Bailey's own home. Every morning, Bailey would descend the stairs, still clad in his bathrobe and slippers, to greet his clerks before returning to his family for breakfast.[237] In the afternoon, several of the city's leading newspaper editors gathered in the sorting room, where they helped sort the incoming newspapers themselves. And in the evening, a constellation of distinguished public figures such as George Clinton, De Witt Clinton, and Samuel Osgood—the first postmaster general under the federal Constitution— could be found in Bailey's back parlor enjoying wine and cigars.[238]

The post office may have been "family-like," as Whittlesey suggested, yet its clientele was hardly a representative cross section of the public. On the contrary, the post office quickly became, like the city saloon or the Masonic lodge, a bastion of white male solidarity and an adjunct to the racially and sexually stratified world of politics and commerce. Few settings more pointedly revealed the enormous problems that women and blacks encountered when they sought to challenge the boundaries that limited their participation in American public life. None more graphically illustrated the distinctive set of assumptions that have come to be known as herrenvolk democracy.[239]

Two paintings reveal just what these assumptions entailed. In *Village Tavern,* which was probably completed during the darkest days of the War of 1812, genre painter John Lewis Krimmel explored the tension that could arise when a mother enters the local post office, with her daughter in tow, to confront her husband, who is idling the hours away with his male friends in conversation and drink.[240] At the very moment the mother is imploring her husband to return home, a mail carrier arrives at the office with news from the front. By juxtaposing these two very different events, Krimmel dramatizes how the local post office was helping to define the boundaries between the male-dominated public realm of politics and world affairs and the female-dominated private realm of family and home. Genre painter Richard Caton Woodville touched on a similar theme in his *War News from Mexico* of 1848, which he set on the front porch of a village post office during the Mexican-American War shortly after the arrival of the mail.[241] In the middle of Woodville's painting is a crowd of boisterous men reading a newspaper detailing the latest news from the front. As citizens and potential soldiers they are obviously intent upon exercising their right to be well informed. On the margins of the scene hover a woman and a free black man. Though both are within earshot, they are silent and subdued, little more than bit players in the highly animated drama that is being staged by the white men who dominate the scene.

On no day of the week was the fraternal character of the local post office more pronounced than on Sunday. As soon as the planters heard the sound of the steamboat whistle that signaled the arrival of the mail, recounted Mississippi planter William Alexander Percy in his memoirs, the leading planters routinely repaired to the post office. This was true even if the whistle blew during the middle of church services. When the planters heard the whistle they would rise as a body and, oblivious to the choir's smirks and their wives' indignant glares, calmly and deliberately file down the main aisle out of church, only to reconvene at the post office, where, after having checked their mail and the latest news, they would settle down for a lazy afternoon of drinking, card playing, and male camaraderie.[242]

A similar situation prevailed in the North. In Rochester, New York, for example, it was customary for the men of the town to spend a good portion of every Sunday in the post office, an event captured in a rare interior view of a post office photographed shortly after the Civil War. In the picture, the men of Rochester are fraternizing in the post office lobby while waiting for their mail. "It was an established hour of friendly greetings and of gossip," recounted one local historian, at which women were "tabu." Allowing for the vagaries of fashion (such as the sea of bowler hats in the Rochester picture), this scene could have been repeated in the early republic in thousands of post offices through-out the United States.[243]

The post office may have been a fraternal setting for white men, but the fellow feeling rarely extended to free blacks. Though postal regu-lations prohibited postal officers from tampering with anyone's mail, free blacks frequently had trouble receiving newspapers or magazines and occasionally suffered the humiliation of having their letters opened as well.[244] For black abolitionists such as Frederick Douglass, this was yet another sign of the deeply etched antiblack sentiment that was such a prominent feature of the age. Should Abraham Lincoln and the Re-publican party triumph in the election of 1860, Douglass defiantly pro-claimed, perhaps Republican postal appointees in the slaveholding states would no longer "burn every newspaper and letter supposed to contain antislavery matter" and "refuse to hand a black man a letter from the post office because he is of the hated color."[245]

Women intent upon using the facilities of the post office confronted a similar series of obstacles. Few could have relished a visit to an office that was often overrun, as one postal officer described it, with "scores of blackguard boys" who frequented the windows and stoops, creating much noise and confusion.[246] For this reason, respectable women were well advised to secure their postage stamps and pick up their mail by "sending to the post-office"—that is, by employing a servant or male friend to make the trip on their behalf.[247] This was true even of Lucy Skipwith, the Alabama house slave who maintained an extensive cor-respondence with her master in Virginia.[248] So infrequently did women venture into the New York post office that in 1851 postal clerk William B. Taylor observed that, from the standpoint of the staff, women might well be inhabitants of "another sphere."[249] And should a woman have the misfortune to step inside, she could expect to confront verbal ha-rassment and even imputations about her moral character. For this rea-son, declared Virginia Penny, the author of the plainspoken, proto-feminist advice manual *How Women Make Money, Married or Single,* a trip to the post office was one adventure that respectable women would do their best to avoid. The majority of regular female postal patrons, Penny added, were either prostitutes or other loose women who re-ceived their letters under fictitious names.[250]

Though women obliged to visit the post office in person encountered the most serious difficulties in the major commercial centers, even in the rural hinterland problems were by no means unknown. Connecticut schoolgirl Mary Wilbor provided a revealing commentary on the obstacles she confronted in 1822. Were she to visit the post office, Wilbor recorded in her diary, she could be reasonably certain that it would be "very much crowded with gentlemen" and therefore a morally questionable journey for her to undertake. Notwithstanding her hesitation, she went anyway; though, to be safe, she enlisted a fellow schoolgirl to accompany her. "I do not think it is quite proper for us to go to the post-office so often," Wilbor confessed, "but still continue going!"[251]

Writer Catherine Sedgwick left an even more detailed account of the tribulations women encountered in getting their mail in a short story that she published in 1843. Sedgwick's story recounts the various indignities that Rosy, a young girl in Clifton, Illinois, endures in order to keep up a correspondence with a young man who had left the village. Journeying to the post office alone, Rosy arrives just after the mail has come in. The "chief dignitaries" receive their mail promptly; the less prominent face the indignity of having their letters scrutinized by the postmaster, who might hold them up to the light or offer some guesses as to what they might contain. Little wonder, then, that when poor Rosy enters the office, her "heart beat quick with fear and hope," for "the 'store' was already full of people, all men," while "our chary womankind do not reckon it a feminine service to go to the post office, being afraid, as one of their witty punsters once said, of seeming to 'run after the *males!*' "[252]

Some women fought back. Anne Royall, always quick to avenge a slight, publicly criticized Washington, D.C., postmaster Thomas Munroe for permitting his clerks to harass her when she picked up her mail. "My business obliges me often to enter the office," Royall fumed, so "is my person to be put in jeopardy when engaged in my lawful business?"[253] Other women lobbied to increase employment opportunities for women. "Let there be women, instead of men, to wait upon this department," urged an editorialist in the Lowell, Massachusetts, textile workers' magazine. "We know of girls who have served long and faithfully as mill operatives . . . whose promptness, probity, and efficiency in every requisite, would render them the most suitable persons in the world to wait upon the sisterhood."[254]

Even male reformers eventually took up the cause. Should a "female in humble condition" wish to carry on a correspondence through the postal system, observed Massachusetts congressman James Gorham Palfrey in 1849, she would be compelled to go to a public place and wait her turn amidst the "annoyance of a crowd."[255] Under existing conditions, reported reformer Samuel Gridley Howe in 1848, "timid females" were prevented from writing by the "difficulties attendant upon the delivery of letters," since they had no alternative to visiting the post office, the "most public place" in the city, to pick up their mail. Before a woman might secure an anticipated letter, Howe explained, she might have to visit the office "half-a-dozen times" and be "liable to detention, to rudeness, and to a thousand vexations."[256]

Postal officers responded to the difficulties women encountered in getting their mail in a variety of ways. In many cities, they established gender-segregated facilities to provide women with separate-but-equal access to the office. The most common of these facilities were the special ladies' windows at which women could pick up their mail unmolested by a crowd of men. By the 1830s, ladies' windows had become a standard feature in the post offices of the major commercial centers. In Cincinnati, the post office boasted a special ladies' lobby, which, one journalist contended in 1855, displayed a "commendable concern" for "women's rights."[257] In at least one instance, postal officers took the unusual step of ordering the dismissal of a male postal clerk whom a female clerk had accused of harassing her on the job.[258] San Francisco's post office included, in addition to a window for ladies, a window for men getting letters on behalf of ladies who did not choose to visit the post office themselves.[259] Even the lists of undelivered letters that newspapers routinely ran were divided into two columns: one for the men and one for the "ladies."[260] These reforms were justified on the grounds that it made it easier for women to use the post office, though of course they did little to alter its aggressively masculine character. The "proverbial gallantry of Americans," observed one journalist in 1853, mingling thinly veiled condescension and genuine concern, could not permit ladies to be "jostled in a crowd of men."[261]

The special needs of women also figured prominently in the sporadic public debates that took place in New York, Boston, and several other commercial centers over the relocation of the offices to less congested sites. As long as the New York post office remained on Wall Street, editorialized one journalist in 1835, women would remain "virtually excluded" from the premises.[262] In Boston, the story was much the same. Women "pay a large part of the postal revenue," estimated one contemporary in 1858, and thus "have a right to be considered" in the public discussions over the possible future location of the office.[263] Toward this end, postmaster Nahum Capen took special care to consult persons of "both sexes" in soliciting public opinion regarding the anticipated move.[264]

One further, less draconian expedient involved the installation of special letter-delivery boxes at convenient locations. Though this innovation did nothing to simplify the task of receiving one's mail, it did make it easier for women to mail a letter. Yet even here there were problems. Prior to the 1850s, few delivery boxes were located out-of-doors, since postal officers feared that this would make them susceptible to theft. Instead, the vast majority were located in the lobbies of bars and hotels, where, as one etiquette-book author observed, a woman "cannot properly go alone."[265] Though these boxes had supposedly been located in "public places," as an editorialist in *Scientific American* explained in 1859 in an article describing the new innovation, in practice neither the "gentler sex" nor the aged and the infirm could "avail themselves of these advantages."[266]

To solve this problem, city postmasters designed durable, all-weather "pillar boxes" that could be attached to lampposts and other outdoor objects easily reached from the street. Henceforth, or so implied an illustration that the *Scientific American* ran to accompany its article on the new innovation, even an elegantly dressed woman could mail a letter on her own, without having to rely on her servants, husband, or male friends to mail it on her behalf.[267] The early pillar boxes were not without their problems: they were awkwardly designed and hard to use. "Had some mortal in the pay of the genius of inconvenience and stupidity engaged to make a post-office box embodying every possible source of annoyance and trouble," postal reformer Pliny Miles huffed indignantly in 1862, "and had he then bribed our city postmaster to pass it and give him absolution, I should suppose he could not possibly have arrived at greater perfection than did the unfortunate simpleton who designed and fabricated these."[268] Still, their installation throughout the central business district of the leading cities did make it possible for postal patrons to mail a letter without having to pay a visit to the post office in person and, in this way, made it easier for women to use its facilities, though of course they remained excluded from the fraternal world of the post office interior, which continued to be overwhelmingly dominated by men.

NOTWITHSTANDING the difficulties that women and blacks encountered in getting their mail, it would be a mistake to overlook the magnitude of the changes that the expansion of the postal system set in motion for the public at large. To an extent that the Founding Fathers could not possibly have imagined, the expansion of the postal network had created by 1828 an imagined community that incorporated a far-flung citizenry into the political process. For millions of Americans, reading a newspaper became, rather like attending a political rally or a religious revival, a great collective ritual in which the faithful joined together to affirm their fundamental beliefs. And of these beliefs, none was more important than the assumption that the citizenry had an important role to play in public affairs. No longer did ordinary Americans defer to their betters, as they had during the colonial period; no longer did they stand against the government, as they had in the years immediately preceding the War of Independence. Now, for the first time in American history, a politics of vigilance supplanted a politics of trust, and participation became a valued ideal.[269]

The creation of this imagined community was a complicated drama of inclusion and exclusion in which certain groups won while others lost. The principal winners were the white men who constituted the core of the citizenry; the major losers were women and blacks. Still, at no point in the early republic was it possible to exclude women and blacks entirely from American public life. In myriad ways, they participated in the new informational environment and sometimes even challenged the ways in which its boundaries were defined. But to an extent that would be inconceivable today, they lived on the margins of American public life. Through a combination of customs, laws, and social conventions, the central government and ordinary Americans had together constructed a new social type—the citizen as free, white, and male—and a new kind of social space—an imagined community that was more or less congruent with the territorial confines of the United States. Ordinary Americans experienced these new social forms every time they visited a post office to pick up their mail and every time they read a newspaper to catch up on the latest news. Together, they were at least as important in shaping the boundaries of public life as the occasional elections, political rallies, and other major political events of the day. Much has changed in the intervening century and a half. But even today this nineteenth-century world has not entirely vanished from the scene, a legacy of cultural and institutional practices deeply rooted in the past.

· 5 ·

The Invasion of the Sacred

TWICE IN THE EARLY REPUBLIC—once between 1810 and 1817 and again between 1826 and 1831—thousands of ordinary Americans joined with a galaxy of distinguished public figures to protest the transmission of the mail and the opening of the post office on the Sabbath. The cause had broad public support within most of the leading Protestant denominations and brought together such famous clerical antagonists as the crusading Presbyterian preacher Lyman Beecher and the genteel Unitarian moralist William Ellery Channing. The nub of the protest, Beecher grandly proclaimed at the height of the second phase of the protest in March 1829—that is, whether the central government should continue to require eight thousand postmasters and "several thousand other agents" to "violate the Lord's Day"—was "perhaps the most important that ever was, or ever will be submitted for national consideration."[1] In opposition to the cause, thousands of counterprotesters banded together to defend the status quo. They too boasted a solid base of public support that brought together an equally diverse coalition, ranging from the backwoods evangelical Alexander Campbell to the Wall Street merchant Preserved Fish. Though the Sabbatarian controversy is largely forgotten today, at the height of its second phase it was widely regarded as one of the leading public events of the age and was recognized as a key test case of the effectiveness of the voluntary association as an organizational form.[2] In this chapter I reconstruct the history of this notable yet overlooked episode in the annals of American reform and consider its role in shaping the boundaries of American public life.

*   *   *

LIKE SO MANY antebellum reform movements, the Sabbatarian controversy grew out of the remarkable surge of popular religiosity that has come to be known as the Second Great Awakening. Though the cause was of obvious concern to the clergy and had a particular resonance in the Puritan strongholds of Connecticut and Massachusetts, its origins lay neither in New England nor in the protestations of ministers such as Beecher and Channing. Instead, the controversy began in a postal distribution center in western Pennsylvania when, in 1808, the postmaster chose to honor the regulations of his official superiors over those of his church. The postmaster was Hugh Wylie, and the town was Washington, a bustling county seat in the far western corner of the state.[3]

Wylie's involvement in the Sabbatarian protest began as a classic confrontation between church and state. As an elder in his local Presbyterian church, Wylie had an obligation to his congregation to honor the fourth commandment by refraining from any unnecessary labor on the Sabbath; yet, as a postmaster, he was required by Postmaster General Gideon Granger to sort the mail every day that it arrived. Since the mail arrived in Washington on the Sabbath, this meant that Wylie had no choice but to sort the mail on this day so that it might be sent along without delay to its final destination.[4] Wylie, after all, was a middle manager, and the Washington office was a major distribution point for the transmission of the mail between the Atlantic seaboard and the West. As a courtesy to the townspeople, Wylie had, by 1808, grown accustomed to opening the office on that day to the public at large as well.[5] When one of the townspeople complained to Granger about this practice, Granger stood firm. "I cannot think," Granger replied, that the work that the general post office required Wylie to perform was "immoral or will be offensive to Heaven." Granger did concede that if Washington's postal patrons did not mind the delay, the Pittsburgh postmaster could hold their mail until the next post day, "in which case the Washington post office need not be opened."[6] But Granger strongly advised against such a course. Given the imminent prospects of a second war with Great Britain, he reminded Wylie, "it becomes the duty of all of us to rally and stand at our posts."[7] Begrudgingly, Wylie complied with Granger's directive, determined to assist his country in its moment of peril, eager to please the many postal patrons who came to town on the Sabbath to attend church, and unwilling to risk an income that may well have totaled as much as $1,000 a year.[8]

Before long, the propriety of Wylie's conduct raised questions among his fellow townspeople. Was it compatible, some wondered, with his "profession" as a Presbyterian?—or, for that matter, with his position as an elder in the church? By 1808, the issue seems to have come to a head, with some church members supporting Wylie's decision to keep the office open as a courtesy to out-of-town churchgoers and others calling on him to resign. To settle the issue, local church leaders turned the question over to the Presbyterians' juridical hierarchy, where it eventually found its way to the Pittsburgh synod. In October 1809, the synod rendered its verdict. After "maturely considering" Wylie's case, the synod decreed that, under "existing circumstances," Wylie should be excluded from the "special privileges of the church," by which, presumably, it meant at the very least that until Wylie closed his post office on the Sabbath to the public at large, he would be barred from communion.[9] Outraged by his censure, Wylie appealed his case to the Presbyterian General Assembly, which backed the synod and expelled Wylie from the church. The general assembly wished "to render unto Caesar the things which are Caesar's," the church leaders decreed, "but must at every hazard, render unto God the things which are God's."[10]

Wylie's tribulations probably troubled few non-Presbyterians, yet they did highlight the considerable discretion that the general post office permitted postmasters in setting their office hours. Prior to Wylie's run-in with the Presbyterians, Congress had never specified the hours that it expected postmasters to maintain.[11] To rectify this situation—and, very possibly, to invest Wylie's conduct with the authority of law—Congress decreed in April 1810 that henceforth postmasters would be required to deliver on demand any item that they received at their office on every single day of the week, including the Sabbath, and to open their offices to the public on every day of the week that the mail arrived.[12]

Opposition to this new law was swift and by no means confined to western Pennsylvania. In New York, Boston, and Philadelphia, a broad-based coalition of ministers, church leaders, and laymen quickly emerged to petition Congress to bring about its repeal. In New York, the petitioners included former postmaster general Samuel Osgood; in Boston, William Ellery Channing, who was well on his way to becoming one of the most widely respected religious liberals in the United States; and in Philadelphia, James P. Wilson, the influential minister of Philadelphia's First Presbyterian Church and a close friend of Benjamin Rush. Joining Wilson was an impressive array of church officers from

various denominations, including the German Reformed Congregationalists, the Lutherans, the Methodists, the Episcopalians, and the
Baptists.[13]

Other Sabbatarians worked more quietly behind the scenes. In Connecticut, Lyman Beecher joined a fellow minister to draft a letter of
protest to the state governor, beginning an involvement with the issue
that was to last for over twenty years.[14] In Philadelphia, postmaster
Robert Patton persuaded his good friend Samuel Carswell to write a
letter to Carswell's friend President Madison in which Carswell warned
the president that Patton, a devout Presbyterian, would assuredly resign
if the law were not repealed.[15] And in Washington, D.C., Postmaster
General Granger urged Congress to reconsider its decision. Having
closely monitored the impact of the new law, Granger concluded that
it posed a hardship for postmasters and tended to bring into "disuse
and disrespect the institutions of this holy day." In addition, Granger
explained, it confronted him with a major administrative challenge,
given the enormous religious diversity that prevailed at this time in the
United States. Intent upon minimizing the impact of the new law,
Granger interpreted it in the narrowest possible way. The new law,
Granger insisted, applied only to offices at which the mail actually arrived. At these offices, Granger further stipulated, postmasters would
be required to open their office to the public for no more than one
hour after the mail had been sorted. Should this hour coincide with the
hours of public worship, Granger gave postmasters his official permission to remain closed to the public until after the usual time the services
had ended. As a final precaution, Granger reiterated the long-standing
ban on the "sounding of horns or trumpets" on the Sabbath by the
postriders and stagecoach drivers when they arrived in town.[16]

Had the Sabbatarians confined themselves to the repeal of the new
law, the issue might soon have been forgotten. But they quickly expanded their grievance to oppose not only the Sabbath-day opening of
the post office to the public at large, but also the transmission of the
mail on this day by the hundreds of contractors on whom the general
post office relied to carry the mail. The latter issue significantly broadened the grounds of complaint. Postal officers had always taken for
granted that the regularly scheduled transmission of the mail on the
Sabbath served the public good. Now, for the first time, the Sabbatarians challenged this presumption, bringing a central pillar of American
postal policy under attack.

The first organization to articulate this new, broadened formulation

of the Sabbatarians' grievance was the Pittsburgh synod, the same clerical body that had previously found Wylie's conduct open to rebuke.
Intent upon eliminating all possible grounds of conflict between church
and state, the synod petitioned Congress in 1810 to suspend not only
the opening of the post office on the Sabbath to the public at large, but
also all postal regulations that required postal officers or agents to work
on this day. To require *anyone* to labor on the Sabbath, the synod explained, violated not only the "rules of conscience" but also the "laws
of God." For the Pittsburgh synod, this was no mere theological con-
ceit. After all, had the synod limited its grievance to the repeal of the
new law, it would have done nothing to resolve Wylie's predicament,
which antedated the enactment of the new law. In fact, the committee
that drafted the Pittsburgh petition included Matthew Brown, the minister of Wylie's own church.[17]

The Pittsburgh synod's broader, more comprehensive indictment of
the status quo was soon seconded by a number of influential religious
bodies. Among the first to follow the synod's lead was the Presbyterian
General Assembly, which formally adopted the synod's position in 1812.
As the "rulers in the Church," the general assembly declared, in a report
inspired by an appeal from several of Wylie's fellow townsmen to reconsider his expulsion, they felt "constrained" to discipline any church
member who had profaned the Sabbath by laboring in any capacity for
the postal system on this day. Two years later, the general assembly
organized a national petition effort to bring the issue to the attention
of every Presbyterian congregation in the country. To publicize the
cause, the general assembly printed up 2,000 petitions and appointed
a special committee of thirty-nine ministers to oversee their distribution.[18] In addition, it enlisted the support of the Congregationalist clerical establishments in Massachusetts and Connecticut, which soon organized petition efforts of their own, almost certainly at the prodding
of Lyman Beecher.[19] By the end of 1814, this unprecedented Presbyte-
rian-Congregationalist joint effort had flooded Congress with 150 petitions from sixteen different states and territories.[20] By 1817, the total
number of petitions had risen to over 300.[21] Though most petitioners
identified themselves merely as inhabitants of a certain town or county,
or as "members of the several Christian denominations," they were ordinarily the members of individual Presbyterian or Congregationalist
congregations under the supervision of their local minister. To clarify
this point, Monson, Massachusetts, Congregationalist minister Alfred
Ely crossed out the word "inhabitants" on the printed petition that he

circulated throughout the town and substituted in its place "members of the Congregational church."[22]

This outpouring of concern owed a good deal of its impetus to circumstances that were only indirectly related to the Sabbath mails. Some petitioners may well have been motivated by the staunch opposition of many Presbyterians and Congregationalists to the War of 1812. Who knew how many petitioners opposed the Sabbath mails as an indirect critique of a foreign policy they deemed ill advised, inept, or immoral? Some made the connection explicit. As one petitioner declared, the war furnished irrefutable proof that God had a "controversy with this nation" on account of "our profanation of His Holy Sabbath."[23]

Others used the Sabbath mails issue as an occasion to publicize their opposition to the commercial penetration of the interior that postal policy had done so much to bring about. Why, brooded one Sabbatarian activist, did the government require that the post offices be open to the public at large on the Sabbath and the mails be kept constantly in motion? To ask the question was to answer it: "It is to accommodate the merchants, and other men of business, who have agents and correspondents in different parts of the country."[24]

Still others linked seven-day mail delivery to the growing chasm between rich and poor by stressing its role in preventing ordinary people from securing the temporal benefits that the Sabbath could bring. Only the proper observance of the Sabbath, explained one group of New York petitioners, could prevent the spread of the "ignorance and profligacy" that tended to reduce the body of the people to "poverty and slavery" by "throwing the property and power of the nation into the hands of the few."[25]

While examples of the Sabbatarians' anticommercial animus could easily be multiplied, it would be a mistake to exaggerate its import. Strict Sabbath observance was, after all, perfectly compatible with the energetic pursuit of commerce the rest of the week. Indeed, to the extent that Sabbath observance soothed the conscience of guilt-ridden merchants, it may even have helped to give market transactions an aura of legitimacy. At the very least it reinforced the emerging notion that time was money and that even God had his price. The Sabbath, one Sabbatarian observed in a revealing turn of phrase, was God's "peculiar property." The rest of the week presumably belonged to whoever could foot the bill.[26]

No less pressing than commercial considerations were religious considerations rooted in the notorious rivalries between the various Protestant denominations. In Salem, Massachusetts, according to the anti-Sabbatarian Unitarian minister William Bentley, the Sabbatarians hoped to eliminate all travel on this day and, in this way, to lure dissenters back into the established church by making it impossible for them to attend services that were located outside the center of town.[27] And in western Pennsylvania, the Sabbatarians found themselves embroiled in a complicated controversy among rival groups of Presbyterians that was soon to lead breakaway Presbyterian preachers Thomas Campbell and his son Alexander to establish the Disciples of Christ. It was probably not coincidental that during the same months the Pittsburgh synod debated Hugh Wylie's fate, it found itself embroiled in an extended controversy with Thomas Campbell over the merits of infant baptism, which the synod supported and Campbell opposed; or that Alexander Campbell would emerge during the second phase of the petition effort as one of the Sabbatarians' most inveterate foes. In some complicated way, the proper observance of the Sabbath may have become, like the merits of infant baptism, a litmus test in the synod's attempt to define the permissible bounds of dissent.[28]

However important such military, economic, and religious considerations may have been in shaping the contours of the protest, none explains why this particular issue proved so compelling. Why did the protesters fix their sights on the postal system?

The answer to this question hinges on the unique position that the postal system in the early republic enjoyed in American public life. In this period, the transmission of the mail and the opening of the post office to the public were two of the only activities that state and local public officers routinely exempted from the welter of state and local laws that restricted the kind of work that could be performed on the Sabbath. In Connecticut, the state government specifically exempted the mail coach and its driver, but not any passengers, from the laws banning travel on this day. No other vehicle, reported one startled foreign traveler in 1818, could escape the "Argus eye of the civil officers."[29] Should a passenger try to sneak along for the ride, reminisced showman P. T. Barnum in his memoirs, both the driver and the passenger would be immediately subject to arrest.[30] Few states were as strict as Connecticut. Yet throughout the United States, state and local Sabbatarian laws were well established, widely respected, and routinely enforced.[31] For this reason, the opening of the post office to the public on the Sabbath did cause a good deal of disruption, particularly in the rural hinterland. With the passage of the Post Office Act of 1810, the local post office became in hundreds of localities the only institution that was impervious to local control. Before long, a trip to the post office on the Sabbath became no less obligatory for many of the men of the town than attendance at church was for their wives. In Boston, one Sabbatarian fumed, "hundreds" of men went there immediately after church services ended.[32] Even the passage of a mail coach through a country village on the Sabbath could prove disruptive, explained another Sabbatarian, since it unavoidably diverted public attention from the "sacred design and employments of that holy day."[33]

For many Sabbatarians, the single most disturbing feature of this desecration of their sacred day was the violation of what one might term the moral geography of the Sabbath. In the early republic, Sabbath observance for thousands if not millions of Americans was a cherished custom that provided them with a regular opportunity to put aside their work, to dedicate themselves to contemplation and prayer, and to cultivate the ties of family and kin that were so vital to the emerging middle class.[34] It was, in short, not the boring, gloomy ordeal that many historians have assumed it to be. The custom further shaped the pattern of everyday life by furnishing a constant reminder of both the cyclical nature of the religious calendar and the ongoing role of the church in public affairs. With the Post Office Act of 1810, Congress threatened this heritage. Requiring a small but highly visible segment of the public to work on the Sabbath not only posed a hardship for pious postmasters like Hugh Wylie, but also robbed the day of some of its sanctity by subordinating the cyclical rhythm of the religious calendar to the linear logic of the mechanical clock, and by supplanting the church as the final arbiter of morality. Now that the central government had invaded the Sabbath, warned one worried petitioner, the day that the church had consecrated to the "Oracles of Divine Truth" was fast becoming no different from the rest of the week.[35]

Most disturbing of all were the theological implications of this government-sanctioned invasion of a sacred realm. At the core of the Sabbatarian argument was the Calvinistic belief that Christians had an obligation to uphold a covenant with God that extended beyond the conduct of the individual and the local congregation to embrace the administration of the state. Because of this covenant, the community of believers had an obligation to participate in public life and in particular to hold their rulers morally accountable for their actions. But here was a crucial ambiguity: Was the central government like the individual states that made up the Union—that is, was it a true state invested with a moral character that possessed the authority to oversee the well-being of everyone living within its domain? Or was it merely a league of friendship whose jurisdiction was confined primarily to the regulation of commerce and foreign affairs? Prior to 1810, few Sabbatarians had assumed that the central government could be a true state, since its authority seemed so far removed from their day-to-day affairs that they could not imagine how it might shape the pattern of everyday life. As a consequence, most Sabbatarians assumed that their covenant with God extended no farther than the boundaries of the states and localities within which they lived. With the passage of the Post Office Act of 1810, this assumption came under close scrutiny for the first time in the history of the republic.[36] Now that the central government had invaded the sacred realm of the Sabbath, the Sabbatarians concluded that it, too, like the governments of the individual states, should be held morally accountable to God. Accordingly, they expanded their understanding of their covenant with God to embrace the central government, thus hastening the gradual transformation of the United States from a loose confederation of autonomous states into a unified nation. Not until the 1830s, with the emergence of the abolitionist movement, would a group of Americans articulate a more expansive understanding of the moral obligation of the American state.

The Presbyterian General Assembly articulated this broadened understanding of the moral obligations of the central government in the petition to Congress that it prepared in 1812. Now that Congress had invaded this sacred realm, the General Assembly declared, it had an obligation to abide by those "principles of truth and equity" that were revealed in the Scriptures. The General Assembly was quite explicit on this point. Proclaiming to derive its authority from the "special Providence of God," and freely citing the Bible in support of its position, it saw nothing incongruous in holding Congress accountable to the fourth commandment, with its injunction to remember the Sabbath. "God honors those who honor him," the general assembly warned, "and casts down those who forget him." Even the horses that the government contractors relied on to carry the mail became an object of concern to the petitioners. Ought not the righteous man be merciful to his beast? The very form of the petition reinforced the basic theme. Modeled after a Biblical jeremiad, it portentously warned that, should the rulers of the nation fail to mend their ways, they would "draw down upon our nation" the "divine displeasure."[37]

As long as the United States remained at war with Great Britain, the

Sabbatarians were not likely to gain much of a hearing. Preoccupied as the government was with maintaining communication with its armies in the field, it was not about to take any steps that might impede the steady flow of information.[38] Once the war ended, however, the petitioners redoubled their efforts, and public figures found themselves obliged to articulate a peacetime rationale for upholding the status quo. This task fell primarily to Postmaster General Return J. Meigs, Jr., who defended Sabbath mail delivery in a report he delivered in 1817. Should Congress suspend the transmission of the mail on every seventh day, Meigs warned, this would inevitably disrupt the mail arrangements on more than seven hundred routes and enable foreign agents to out-speed the government in transmitting information vital to national security. Meigs also warned about the possible impact of these changes on postal finance. Should Congress require stagecoach firms that carried the mail to suspend service on the Sabbath, Meigs explained, this would work to the advantage of competitors who would continue to carry passengers on this day. As a consequence, mail contractors would find it necessary to increase the fees that they charged the government to carry the mail, significantly increasing costs. Meigs also warned that Sabbath-breaking passengers would get into the habit of carrying letters outside of the system, further decreasing postal revenue. To buttress his point, Meigs reminded Congress of the large volume of letters that stagecoach passengers carried outside of the system during the War of 1812, when Congress increased postal rates 50 percent to help finance the war.[39]

Within Congress, the Sabbatarians' most vocal champion was New York congressman James Tallmadge, who called for the suspension of all mail service on the Sabbath in an impassioned harangue in March 1816. Tallmadge conceded that his proposed change ran afoul of the selfishness and greed that were among the "predominant passions of the human heart," yet he stood his ground. The Biblical injunction "Thus saith the Lord," he somberly intoned, should "silence every objection" and "lay the whole race of Adam at his footstool." Tallmadge even brought the issue to a congressional vote; he lost, 100 to 35. Among Tallmadge's supporters was Robert Wright of Maryland, who tried to revive the issue as late as 1822. Among his opponents was John McLean, who as postmaster general would confront the question of Sabbath-day mail delivery again in 1828.[40]

Tallmadge's speech may not have had an immediate impact upon postal policy, yet his belief in the moral obligations of the central government was destined to cast a long shadow on American public life. Three years later, Tallmadge introduced an even more controversial motion: to prohibit the continuance of slavery in the soon-to-be established state of Missouri. Once again, Tallmadge failed to carry the day. This time, however, he triggered a fierce congressional debate over the slavery question that became a landmark in the crisis between the slaveholding and the nonslaveholding states. Historians have long puzzled over why Tallmadge introduced his celebrated amendment at this particular time.[41] His prior support for the Sabbatarians suggests one possible explanation. Having endorsed the Sabbatarians' extension of God's covenant with humanity to embrace the central government, it was but a short step for Tallmadge to apply an analogous principle to the institution of slavery.

Less strident than Tallmadge, and more conciliatory than Meigs, was Elijah Hunt Mills, a congressman from the Congregationalist stronghold of Northampton, Massachusetts, and a keen student of constitutional law. Like Tallmadge, Mills refused to rest his case on mere "considerations of economy"; yet, like Meigs, he too ultimately defended the status quo. Should the Sabbatarians prevail, Mills explained in 1817, merchants would soon establish their own network of private carriers, thus causing far more noise and commotion on the Sabbath than existed at present. Only if every state banned all forms of public conveyance on the Sabbath, Mills concluded, would Congress be justified in prohibiting the transmission of mail on this day. And until every state took this step, Mills was convinced that the uninterrupted transmission of the mail was not only "sound and enlightened policy" but also "consistent" with the "requirements of the *moral law*."[42]

MILLS'S REPORT brought the first phase of the Sabbatarian protest to a close. After seven years of agitation, the mail coaches still ran on the Sabbath and the post offices remained open to the public at large. For the next nine years, the issue lay dormant. Not one petition seems to have found its way to Congress; and only Congressman Robert Wright of Maryland devoted to the Sabbatarians' grievance so much as a single speech. Beginning in 1826, however, all this would change. Spurred by a new combination of circumstances, the Presbyterians once again took up the issue, sparking an even larger popular protest and, for the first time, an organized anti-Sabbatarian response.[43]

The catalyst for the second phase of the protest was not a specific event like Hugh Wylie's confrontation with his church but rather the general determination of the Presbyterian General Assembly to limit the desecration of the Sabbath, which it felt had been greatly hastened by the completion of public works projects such as the National Road between Cumberland, Maryland, and Wheeling, Virginia, and the Erie Canal in upstate New York. Toward this end, in May 1826 the General Assembly urged Presbyterians throughout the United States to boycott every transportation company that ran a stagecoach, steamboat, or canal packet on the Sabbath. The following month, in a pattern reminiscent of the earlier Sabbatarian protest, a similar, albeit more moderate, appeal was launched by the general association of Congregationalist ministers in Connecticut.[44]

Among the individuals who responded to the Presbyterians' call was Josiah Bissell, Jr., an enterprising and warmhearted merchant from Rochester, New York, and an elder in his local Presbyterian church.[45] Though Bissell had no aversion to money-making, he was staunchly Sabbatarian and in January 1827 petitioned Congress to shut down post offices on the Sabbath to the public at large, convinced that the pursuit of commerce could be squared with the Ten Commandments.[46] Significantly, Bissell said nothing about the transmission of the mail on this day, well aware that the expansion of commerce in the past decade had made its outright suspension increasingly unrealistic. Still, he remained optimistic that even this utopian goal could eventually be attained and, to help bring it about, organized the General Union for Promoting the Observance of the Christian Sabbath the following year.[47]

The General Union marked a new departure in the annals of American reform. Like the American Temperance Society, upon which it was closely modeled, the General Union was intended to unite like-minded individuals from throughout the United States in a single cause.[48] According to Massachusetts reformer William Lloyd Garrison, this egalitarian approach to reform was destined to make the General Union the "most efficient instrument in the cause of religion and public morality ever put into practice in any age and country."[49]

Lyman Beecher explained the rationale for the new organization in an address that he delivered at the introductory meeting of the General Union in May 1828.[50] Though the General Union had been founded to promote the better observance of the Sabbath, Beecher explained, it had not been established primarily to lobby either the individual states or the central government to enact new Sabbatarian legislation or to improve the enforcement of Sabbatarian legislation that was already on the books. "We have not the madness," Beecher intoned, "to think of coercion merely." On the contrary, the General Union was a voluntary association that sought to instill in its members the necessary self-discipline to mold public opinion.[51] The "pivot" of the protest, Beecher explained to Sabbatarian merchant Lewis Tappan in justification of his position, must be not the enactment of legislation, but rather the recruitment of Sabbatarians throughout the United States to boycott every transportation company that refused to suspend its service on the Sabbath and, in this way, to supplant the coercive authority of church and state with the moral authority of individual choice.[52]

The linchpin of the General Union strategy was the Sabbatarian pledge, a device that Bissell borrowed directly from the temperance movement. Just as the American Temperance Society promoted complete abstinence from the evils of drink, so the General Union would promote complete abstinence from the evils of Sabbath-breaking. By taking the Sabbatarian pledge, General Union members bound themselves not only to abstain from all work, travel, and recreation on the Sabbath, but also to boycott all transportation companies that operated on this day. In this way, Bissell hoped to act directly on the hearts and minds of the public. In short, it was an exercise in what today might be called consciousness-raising.[53]

Lyman Beecher was well aware that some Americans might regard the General Union pledge as coercive, and he did his best to meet this objection head-on. After all, though the General Union had no interest in enacting a particular piece of legislation, it did seek to change public opinion by redefining the increasingly common practice of Sabbath travel as the very epitome of evil. Should individuals refuse to heed the Sabbatarians' call, they would presumably be open to censure and rebuke. Eager to take the moral high ground, Beecher responded that it was not the Sabbatarians but their critics who were the real party of force, since, by challenging the Sabbatarians' right to mount a consumer boycott, their critics sought to coerce them into sanctioning the "perpetration of evil." "This is a land of slavery," Beecher declared, in which a citizen could not choose to spend his money as he saw fit.[54] Taking the offensive, Sabbatarian activist Matthias Bruen went so far as to equate a traveler's willingness to patronize a Sabbath-breaking stagecoach firm with a merchant's willingness to treat a slave ship as a "common passage vessel."[55]

Had Bissell done nothing more than establish a new kind of lobbying technique, the Sabbath mails issue might have soon been forgotten.

But he took the additional, and far more controversial, step of establishing a new kind of transportation company to demonstrate the viability of Sabbatarian principles. His company, the Pioneer Line, was to operate on the Albany-Buffalo route in upstate New York. Had Bissell succeeded in demonstrating the viability of six-day passenger service on this route, he would have solid warrant for contending that seven-day travel could be abolished throughout the United States, since the Albany-Buffalo route was at this time one of the most heavily traveled passenger routes in the country.

The Pioneer Line was something new in American public life. Particularly notable was Bissell's determination to cater to the special needs of the rapidly growing evangelical middle class. By requiring his drivers to be polite and well mannered and to patronize rest stations at which coffee and other nonalcoholic beverages were freely dispensed, Bissell hoped to expand travel opportunities not only for fastidious men, but also for women and even children, who had formerly been largely barred from long-distance travel by its close identification with the aggressively masculine rules of the road.[56] Most important of all, Bissell insisted that his stagecoaches rest on the Sabbath, and so give the traveling public a practical way to honor the consumer boycott that the Presbyterian General Assembly and the General Union had tried to enforce. Though Bissell was committed to suspending service for one day out of seven, he remained convinced that he could still outspeed the competition by employing a fast team of horses and the latest stagecoach technology. If all went according to plan, even the most time-conscious and enterprising man on the make would come to agree that a scrupulous regard for the fourth commandment was neither anachronistic nor visionary but perfectly compatible with the needs of the day.[57]

The success of Bissell's venture depended on his ability to lure to the Pioneer Line a portion of the traveling public that had formerly relied upon the Old Line Mail, the transportation company that until then had dominated the Albany-Buffalo route. And here the trouble began. Having long enjoyed a monopoly of the passenger traffic on this route, the proprietors of the Old Line Mail had no intention of surrendering without a fight. Under the leadership of Jason Parker and John Sherwood, the company had grown accustomed to charging high prices for a low level of service and relying on a series of generous mail contracts to help them cover their costs.[58] Bissell was determined to break up the monopoly, convinced that he could provide a superior level of service to the public at a comparable price. According to George Sill, the editor of the pro-Bissell *Rochester Observer,* Bissell would triumph in the end just as the "feeble Jews" had ultimately triumphed over the "sons of Anak," the legendary giants of the Bible.[59] Bissell was particularly indignant when Parker and Sherwood tried to brand him and his company an improper "opposition," thus implying that he had no right to compete in this lucrative market. "You certainly have not the exclusive privilege of running carriages between Albany and Buffalo," Bissell exploded, in an open letter to Parker and Sherwood in May 1828, shortly before he ran his first stagecoach.[60] Bissell's supporters were equally outraged at Parker and Sherwood's claim that Bissell sought to interfere with the public's "liberty of conscience" by coercing them to adopt sectarian views. "The people will judge," Sill charged, whether a "real regard for liberty of conscience" had prompted Bissell's critics to "oppose 'coercion,' " which was "so much talked about." From Sill's standpoint, the answer was plain. It was not "liberty of conscience," but rather the financial interests of the Old Line Mail that lay at the root of this "opposition to obedience to the commands of God."[61] It was a perceptive assessment, and one with which many contemporaries readily concurred.[62]

To secure a significant percentage of the passenger market was of course only part of Bissell's challenge. After all, if his stagecoaches rested on the Sabbath while others remained in operation, the evil would remain. For Bissell, as one supporter took pains to stress, the Sabbath mails were a "national measure," while the "people," who "*might* order it otherwise," were "involved in the guilt."[63] Accordingly, Bissell took the further and even more controversial step of entering a bid for the mail contract on the Albany-Buffalo route. Not only would the mail contract increase Bissell's ability to run his line at a profit, but also—and even more important—it would enable him to save the country from its complicity in its profanation of the Sabbath. The *"one great and insuperable objection to stopping the running of the stages on the Sabbath,"* Sill explained, *"has been* that the proprietors were under *contract* to carry the mail on that day."[64] By proposing a different contracting arrangement, Bissell would help to bring the United States government into accordance with the will of God.

Postmaster General McLean considered Bissell's bid but found it unacceptable, convinced that public opinion in upstate New York would not sanction such a radical change.[65] McLean did agree, however, to suspend Sabbath-day mail service on the Albany-Buffalo route temporarily, giving Sabbatarians and anti-Sabbatarians alike the opportunity to rally support. As McLean explained to Parker, upon renewing Parker's mail contract without the customary provision for Sabbath service on the Albany-Buffalo route, he had decided to leave the future of Sabbath mail service open for "discussion and decision" until Congress should reach a decision as to the advisability of discontinuing the Sabbath mails "throughout the United States."[66] Whether McLean sincerely believed the Sabbatarians could prevail is an open question. He well understood, however, that by assuming the mantle of impartial arbiter, he could only buttress his already enviable reputation as a public-spirited statesman sensitive to the changing currents of public opinion.

McLean's decision prodded Bissell to escalate the protest still further. If the Sabbatarians could demonstrate that a large portion of the public at large opposed the current policy, Bissell assumed, the postmaster general himself, a pious man and a friend of evangelical reform, might well throw his support behind the suspension of Sabbath mail service throughout the United States. But how were the Sabbatarians to rally support? The answer, concluded Bissell and his fellow Sabbatarians, was to mount a publicity blitz that would take full advantage of the facilities for communication provided by the postal system, the very institution they hoped to reform. By using the organizational capabilities of the General Union to deluge the public with petitions, pamphlets, and printed appeals of all kinds—and, most important of all, by reviving the petition effort they had suspended in 1817—the Sabbatarians could demonstrate the genuine popularity of their cause and bring about the desired change. The "main cause" for the success of the General Union, observed William Ellery Channing (and for the success of other voluntary associations that adopted a similar approach to reform) was the ability of its leaders to take advantage of the "immense facility" that recent improvements in transportation and communication, including the postal system and the periodical press, had given to "intercourse" of all kinds. "Through these means, men of one mind, through a whole country, easily understand one another, and easily act together," Channing explained. Like Napoleon, Channing added, the Sabbatarians had discovered how to take full advantage of these "facilities" to concentrate all of their energies on a single issue, to "find one another out through a vast extent of country," and to join together with "the uniformity of a disciplined army . . . So extensive have coalitions become, through the facilities now described, and so various and rapid are the means of communication, that when a few leaders have agreed on an object, an impulse may be given in a month to the whole country. Whole States may be deluged with tracts and other publications, and a voice like that of many waters, be called forth from immense and widely separated multitudes. Here is a great new power brought to bear on society, and it is a great moral question, how it ought to be viewed, and what duties it imposes."[67]

The voluntaristic premise that undergirded the General Union strategy had a subtle yet far-reaching impact on the physical act of signing a petition. Prior to 1828, Sabbatarian petitioners had ordinarily regarded themselves as members of a particular church, town, or other corporate body, and the vast majority of petitions had been prepared by church leaders who had carefully supervised their distribution. When an individual added his name to a petition, he did so less as an expression of individual choice than as an endorsement of the authority of the corporate bodies that had organized the appeal. This was why, for example, Monson, Massachusetts, minister Alfred Ely had taken such pains to identify the petitioners who signed the Sabbatarian petition in his town as members of the local Congregational church. From Ely's standpoint, this identification enhanced the petitioners' credibility, since it demonstrated that they were part of a legally constituted corporate body and not merely a random collection of individuals. Following the popularization of the General Union pledge, however, Sabbatarian activists inverted the priorities of the previous petition effort. Now, spurred by the organizational innovations that Bissell had helped to perfect, thousands of ordinary Americans came for the first time to regard the signing of a petition—rather like the taking of a temperance pledge—as a consummate expression of individual choice.[68] In 1815, one Sabbatarian publicist felt obliged to consider whether it might be "disrespectful" to Congress to petition it directly. By 1828, few Sabbatarians felt so constrained. "We will let Congress know," declared the Maine association of Congregational churches, "that our rulers shall obey us; that *WE are their MASTERS!!*"[69] No longer, another Sabbatarian explained, should the process be confined to the well-to-do. On the contrary, "persons *of all sorts and class*" had the "right" to "petition their rulers." After all, there was no subject on which a "plain farmer or mechanic" was in a better position to express his opinion.[70]

To highlight the voluntaristic cast of the petition effort, neither the Presbyterian General Assembly nor the general associations of ministers in Connecticut and Massachusetts petitioned Congress in their corporate capacity. Indeed, even the General Union itself refrained from petitioning Congress in its own name. Should the "great body of our fellow citizens" earnestly desire the anticipated reform, Matthias Bruen explained, success would be guaranteed, regardless of whether the General Union itself had lent its name to the cause.[71]

No Sabbatarian better exemplified this new approach to soliciting public support than Jeremiah Evarts, the Boston lawyer who is best known today as an eloquent critic of the forced removal of the Indian tribes of the Old Southwest to west of the Mississippi River.[72] Intent upon reaching Americans not likely to be impressed by the fine points of covenant theology, Evarts downplayed the Calvinistic preoccupation with God's divine plan for humankind in favor of less sectarian, yet still resolutely Protestant, considerations of morality and law.[73] In New England, Evarts went so far as to prepare a blandly worded petition that was addressed, simply, to the "Postmaster at [blank]."[74] Evarts also encouraged laymen to prepare the texts of their own petitions and to supervise their printing and circulation, a circumstance that would have been inconceivable during the earlier phase of the protest.

Evarts's innovative methods helped guarantee that the petition effort cut across denominational and class lines to unite thousands of Americans in a common cause. By May 1829, the Sabbatarians had sent 467 petitions to Congress, over three times as many as in 1814. By the end of the second phase of the protest in May 1831, the total had increased to 935, over three times as many as their predecessors had sent in the previous phase.[75] While 75 percent of the petitioners came from the Mid-Atlantic and New England, the strongholds of Presbyterian and Congregationalist orthodoxy, 11 percent came from the South Atlantic, 9 percent from the Northwest, and 5 percent from the Southwest. Evarts was hardly impartial, yet he was not far off the mark when he declared that Sabbatarians could be found from Vermont to Alabama and from Maine to the banks of the Mississippi.[76] Even anti-Sabbatarians conceded that the Sabbatarians' novel strategy had proved highly effective. The Sabbatarians had brought forth such a "deluge" of "religious clamor," one anxious anti-Sabbatarian warned, that congressional candidates might come to regard the issue as a "stalking horse to popularity." Many Americans, the critic added, knew far less of the federal Constitution than they did of what they understood to be the "law of God." And should this tyrannical majority be permitted to prevail, "the *few* may tremble for their safety."[77]

Most petitions contained between 20 and 50 signatures, suggesting that, as in the earlier period, each may have been primarily the work of an individual church or denomination. A few, however, represented the voice of a far larger, more heterogeneous constituency. One Boston petition contained 2,000 signatures; one New York petition, 7,000.[78] "God's blessing will rest upon the effort," wrote Lewis Tappan in his diary in December 1828, after duly noting that he himself had personally collected 5,600 signatures in support of this "all-important" cause on the streets of New York.[79] Even the most stridently anti-Sabbatarian activist could hardly claim that the individuals who signed these "monster petitions" (as they were commonly called) all belonged to some tiny clerical cabal. Fully 40 percent of the signers of Tappan's New York petition, for example, were artisans, a notable index of the Sabbatarians' solid base of support among a group of Americans often assumed to be highly ambivalent about evangelical reform.[80]

Petitioners hailed from all the major Protestant denominations. In addition to Presbyterians and Congregationalists, they included large numbers of Dutch Reformed, Methodists, Episcopalians, and Baptists.[81] One petition from New Brunswick, New Jersey, included the signatures of a Dutch Reformed theologian and college president, a local Methodist minister, a local Baptist minister, and the Episcopal bishop of New Jersey. In Boston, William Ellery Channing once again lent his name to the cause, notwithstanding his well-known misgivings about evangelical reform.[82] So did Alexander H. Everett, the editor of the Unitarian-tinged *North American Review*, a magazine that was often praised for its wide ranging interests and cosmopolitan tone.[83] Particularly notable was the Sabbatarians' popularity among the Baptist rank-and-file, given the outspoken opposition of Baptist leaders such as John Leland to evangelical reform.[84]

Among the most intriguing features of the Sabbatarian petition effort was its organizers' ability to secure a solid base of merchant support. Merchants, after all, might ordinarily be expected to *oppose* any initiatives that would impede the transmission of market information. A small but significant number of merchants, however, chose to throw their support to the cause. In Boston, Sabbatarian merchants included shipping magnate Thomas Handasyd Perkins, textile manufacturers Amos and Abbott Lawrence, and banker Peter Chardon Brooks; in New York, they included investment banker James Brown and silk merchant Arthur Tappan. Little wonder, then, that in surveying the scene, the chairman of the House Committee on the Post Office and Post Roads was moved to declare that there had never been a time when the

American people had made a "stronger expression" of their views on a public issue, if one took into account the petitioners' intelligence, their wealth, or their numerical strength.[85]

The support of such a distinguished array of merchants is a tribute to the Sabbatarians' organizational sophistication.[86] Evarts believed that it was particularly important to enlist the support of merchants, lawyers, and other professional men because, as the principal postage payers, they were "competent, both on account of their practical knowledge, and their large acquaintance with human affairs, to form a correct judgment of the subject."[87] Indeed, protest organizers often confined their petition-signing campaign to these individuals, convinced that their support would help to convince Congress of the practicality of the anticipated reform. It would have been "easy," declared one Maine Sabbatarian, to obtain many more signatures of individuals friendly to stopping the seven-day mails, yet he had not thought it necessary since, having obtained the signatures of a "large proportion of our men of business, merchants, lawyers, &c.," it was thought of "less importance" to secure the signatures of those individuals who were less likely to be directly affected by the proposed suspension.[88]

Merchant support for Sabbatarianism was by no means exclusively a product of the energetic efforts of reformers such as Evarts. Leading merchants regarded themselves as pillars of their community and as such were predisposed to oversee the well-being of the public. But, as mentioned earlier, the willingness of merchants to lend their names to the cause was highly surprising for at least one reason: Why would merchants support a cause that, if successful, would inevitably slow the transmission of commercial information on which they relied? One possible answer is suggested by their location. Living, as so many Sabbatarian merchants did, along the Atlantic seaboard, they secured the bulk of their information on the state of the European commodity markets directly from incoming ships, and thus were less likely to be directly affected by the anticipated suspension than merchants living on the far-flung commercial periphery that stretched from Rochester to New Orleans.

If merchants had the most to lose from the proposed suspension, postal officers had the most to gain. Though only ninety-one post-masters are known to have signed Sabbatarian petitions, many more doubtless aided the cause behind the scene.[89] Postmasters, explained McLean, had been "constantly" directing his attention to this "great grievance" ever since he took office.[90] For Matthew M. Campbell, a clerk in the Lexington, Kentucky, office and an ardent Presbyterian, the issue posed a genuine dilemma. Should he jeopardize his future career by resigning his clerkship, or should he work on the Sabbath and risk the wrath of his church?[91] So resentful was Connecticut senator Calvin Willey of the fact that he had been forced to violate the Sabbath when he had been postmaster of Tolland, Connecticut, during the second decade of the nineteenth century, that when he secured a seat in Congress he vowed to press for the repeal of the offensive section of the Post Office Act of 1810.[92]

Further support for the Sabbatarian cause came from the many wives and mothers intent upon forging a collective identity as members of the evangelical middle class. Determined to strengthen the female-dominated realms of home and church—and, in particular, to limit the recreational opportunities of their husbands on the one day of the week when they could not claim to be at work—women lobbied diligently behind the scenes to circulate petitions and rally support. Direct evidence of female involvement in the Sabbatarian protest is surprisingly hard to come by. Yet there are a number of hints that it may have been substantial. "I blush for my sex," fumed anti-Sabbatarian Anne Royall, in recounting the key role women had played in building support for the cause.[93] A similar note was struck by James Akin in a savage anti-Sabbatarian engraving published around 1829. In the foreground of his scene, Akin depicts a church congregation of moralistic women singing hymns and enlisting Sunday school children to sign Sabbatarian petitions, while in the middle of scene their male allies block the passage of a mail coach through the town.[94]

If Royall and Akin can be taken as reliable guides to the world in which they lived, it may well be that Sabbatarianism, like anti-Masonry and temperance, should be remembered as an important intermediate step between the church-based women's activism of the 1820s and the emergence after 1835 of an organized women's movement. But it would be a mistake to exaggerate the role of women in building support for Sabbatarianism. Of the hundreds of petitions that found their way to Congress, every one was headed by a man. Indeed, no woman seems to have proved so bold as even to add her name to a list. Lacking more direct evidence of female participation in the cause, then, it may make more sense to treat the role of women in the petition effort less as a harbinger of things to come than as a reminder of the powerful constraints that continued to hinder female involvement in the public sphere.[95]

Notwithstanding the obvious appeal of Sabbatarianism among postal officers and women, it would be misleading to treat the petition effort as nothing more than the predictable response of a loose alliance of self-interested groups. Far more important was the Sabbatarians' principled determination to bring the central government into conformity with what they took to be the will of God. Though the Sabbatarians had not opposed the initial extension of the postal system into the hinterland, they were among the first to question its steadily growing influence in shaping the pattern of everyday life.

To understand the Sabbatarians' grievance, it is important to recognize the magnitude of the evil that they sought to redress. And there can be little doubt that, from their standpoint, this evil was large and growing worse every year. By 1828, after forty years of rapid expansion, the central government had finally fulfilled Benjamin Rush's bold vision of providing a basic level of mail service to every city, village, and town in the United States. Since 1810, the number of post offices had more than tripled, increasing from 2,300 to 7,651, while the mileage of the postal network had expanded in parallel fashion, increasing from 36,406 to 114,536. From 1826 to 1828 alone, the size of the postal network expanded by some 20,000 miles.[96] Though the Sabbatarians were not opposed on principle to the expansion of the postal network, they well understood that its rapid penetration into the hinterland greatly increased the likelihood of a clash between the central government and the individual states. Further exacerbating the potential for conflict was Postmaster General McLean's almost fanatical determination to outspeed private enterprise in the transmission of market information by eliminating bottlenecks that had previously kept the mails idle on the Sabbath. On dozens of routes the government was now transmitting the mail seven days a week where no such service had existed in 1810. "We deeply regret," remarked a group of Sabbatarians from Sackett's Harbor, New York, that the postmaster general has contracted for the "future transportation" of the mails between Utica and Sackett's Harbor on the Sabbath. "Hitherto," they added, the mails had been carried on this route "but six times a week."[97] For the past six months, complained Ohio missionary Joseph Badger, the mail between Warren and Ashtabula, Ohio, had been carried on the Sabbath. "This appears to me to be a most unreasonable encroachment on our Christian privileges," he wrote.[98]

Often the Sabbatarian argument assumed a decidedly anticommercial cast. No consideration of commercial expediency could justify the profanation, declared New Jersey senator Theodore Frelinghuysen in an eloquent speech in May 1830. "I wait for the evidence," he declaimed, "that any earlier information thus obtained ever contributes to the welfare of the merchants or manufacturer. No, sir, I believe it to be blighted with a curse on its way, which, whether seen or not, actually and certainly attends it." And even if it could be proved that the Sabbath mails were conducive to temporal prosperity, Frelinghuysen refused to back down. "I trust, sir," he defiantly declared, that "we shall never graduate public worth by dollars and cents. Let us, by arresting this national profanation, reject the miserable pelf that is amassed by labor pursued on a violated Sabbath."[99]

However important such an anticommercial animus may have been for individual Sabbatarians such as Frelinghuysen, it fails to explain why seven-day mail delivery aroused such enormous concern. Even more important to the Sabbatarians was their determination to prevent the central government from actively encouraging the profanation of this sacred day.

Once it is understood that the core of the Sabbatarian controversy was a struggle over the proper role of the central government in American public life and not, as is often presumed, merely a struggle between competing social groups, it becomes possible to understand its true place in the annals of American reform. More than any other issue to come before the American public in the period between the adoption of the federal Constitution and the election of Andrew Jackson, the Sabbath mails issue challenged ordinary Americans to stretch their perceptual horizons well beyond the boundaries of the individual states.[100] By 1828, this perceptual revolution was well under way. Even though the general post office did not transmit any mails on the Sabbath in Vermont—which meant, of course, that the local post offices could legally remain closed—this did nothing to prevent Vermonters from petitioning Congress to oppose the profanation of the Sabbath.[101] In short, the critical issue was not whether a particular class of Americans had actually been harmed by the Sabbath mails, but whether the central government had acquired the capacity to shape the pattern of everyday life. By 1828, it was plain to Sabbatarians that it had. This was a discovery that was destined to shape American public life long after the issue itself had faded from view. It was impossible to conceive of a situation, observed Sabbatarian Alexander H. Everett in 1830, "either in public or private life," in which it was not the "duty" of "every member of the community" to act under the influence of "religious motives."[102] The

Sabbatarian petition effort gave thousands of Americans the opportunity to apply this insight to the administration of the government of the United States.

Most petitioners, like their predecessors in 1814, continued to rely on the Bible as the ultimate authority. No text was more authoritative than the Ten Commandments, no argument more compelling than the Biblical injunction "Thus saith the Lord." But it would be a mistake to treat the petitioners' grievance as purely theological. To a far greater extent than their predecessors, the Sabbatarians proved willing to supplement Biblical appeals with arguments derived from more secular sources, such as political theory, jurisprudence, and constitutional law.

Many stressed the necessary relationship between the proposed suspension in mail delivery and the future of republican government. The Sabbath mails, declared one group of petitioners from Perry, Ohio, had a "direct tendency" to destroy the "piety and morality" that was "so necessary to be cherished by a REPUBLICAN PEOPLE."[103] Others stressed the privileged status of the Sabbath in common law and, to buttress their position, cited the stirring defense of the Sabbath that English jurist William Blackstone included in his well-known *Commentaries on the Laws of England*.[104] Still others questioned whether seven-day mail delivery was necessary to national security in times of peace. This presumption, claimed one group of petitioners from Sullivan County, Tennessee, was nothing short of "antirepublican" and was analogous to the patently outrageous claim that the central government had the right to maintain a standing army in peacetime merely because it might be necessary to recruit such an army in time of war.[105]

Nowhere was the petitioners' preoccupation with law and morality more evident than in their reconceptualization of the predicament of the pious postmaster. In addition to berating the central government for its violation of the strictures of the church—the major Sabbatarian contention in the first phase of the protest—Sabbatarians now placed even greater stress on the impact of existing legislation upon the ability of the central government to recruit the best possible men for the job. Paradoxically, petitioners contended, Congress had proscribed from office precisely those men who, as professing Christians, were most worthy of the public trust. Public officers, declared one group of petitioners, ought to possess the "highest degree of moral feeling" and the "strictest integrity." But at present, warned another, postal regulations had a "direct tendency" to consign the "very responsible charge" of the mail to men who paid no regard to moral obligation.[106] Some went so far as to deride the Post Office Act of 1810 as an *"American test act,"* that, by requiring postmasters to work on the Sabbath, was no different from English legislation that excluded from public office anyone who was not a member of the Church of England.[107] Others invoked the free exercise clause of the First Amendment to champion the rights of postmasters who refused to work on the Sabbath, investing the Bill of Rights with the moral authority of the Ten Commandments.[108]

NO FEATURE of the second phase of the Sabbatarian movement had a greater influence on its outcome than the emergence of an organized anti-Sabbatarian opposition. Like the Sabbatarians, their opponents were determined to identify their cause with the public at large. And while many anti-Sabbatarians seem to have honestly feared that the Sabbatarians had the necessary public support to succeed, in the end, the anti-Sabbatarians prevailed and Congress upheld the status quo.

The anti-Sabbatarian campaign took a variety of forms. One particularly ingenious ruse involved hiding mailbags in carts in order to embarrass Sabbatarian local authorities. One well-publicized episode of this kind occurred in the Presbyterian stronghold of Princeton, New Jersey, in the spring of 1829. Having carefully hidden a mailbag filled with post office forms and dead letters in a wooden box that was nailed shut so that it could not be inspected, a wily anti-Sabbatarian wagoner arrived in town on the Sabbath, well aware that he would be stopped by the alderman and ordered to remain in town until sundown, in keeping with local Sabbatarian laws that prohibited unnecessary travel on the Sabbath. True to form, the alderman spotted the wagoner and ordered him to remain in town until the end of the day. Had the alderman known what was in the wagoner's box, he would have permitted him to continue on his way, since the mail was exempt from the local strictures and the Princeton authorities had no wish to challenge the federal law that prohibited any governmental body from impeding its uninterrupted transmission. But as matters stood, the alderman saw no reason why the wagoner should not be stopped.

This was precisely what the wagoner had counted on. Intent upon embarrassing the town authorities, the wagoner waited until sundown, at which time he triumphantly produced the mailbag and accused the alderman of having intentionally conspired to block the transmission of the mail, in plain violation of federal law. Outraged at the wagoner's deception, the local authorities immediately ordered him to leave town and promptly wrote a letter to the postmaster general explaining how they had been duped.[109] But the damage to the Sabbatarians' reputation had been done. For the next two years, the periodical press was filled with accounts of Presbyterian attempts to block the transmission of the mail.[110] So widespread was this allegation that, in 1831, General Union organizers felt it prudent to formally deny that they had played any part in the various attempts to stop the mail in violation of federal law.[111]

Isolated episodes like the one in Princeton hurt the Sabbatarians' cause in the press, but did little to undermine the Sabbatarians' oft-voiced contention that they represented the considered judgment of the public at large. To meet this contention directly, anti-Sabbatarians organized a counterpetition effort in December 1828. McLean had solicited the views of the public with regard to the advisability of the proposed suspension of Sabbath-day service, and the anti-Sabbatarians were quick to respond. The anti-Sabbatarians might lack a *"great central body"* like the Presbyterian General Assembly, one supporter lamented shortly after the counterpetition effort began, yet they soon found a ready substitute in Tammany Hall, a New York political club whose leadership was notoriously unsympathetic to evangelical reform.[112] Prominent leaders in the anti-Sabbatarian petition effort included Robert Bogardus, a real estate mogul who would soon emerge as a leading antiabolitionist; Barnabas Bates, a Baptist minister and a leader of the nascent Workingman's Party; and Preserved Fish, a wealthy merchant and shipowner whom the Sabbatarians slyly dubbed "Pickled Herring."[113] Though the anti-Sabbatarian petition effort never matched either the size or the sophistication of its Sabbatarian counterpart, by December 1831 Bogardus, Bates, Fish, and their allies had sent off to Congress some 240 petitions, or 20 percent of the total number of petitions on this issue that Congress had received since the second phase of the petition effort had begun in 1828.[114]

Anti-Sabbatarian petitioners placed great stress on their wealth, social standing, and the amount of postage that they paid during the course of a year. Anxious to rebut the Sabbatarian charge that merchants supported the proposed suspension, they went to great lengths to demonstrate that this was simply not true. McLean had sought an "expression of opinion" with regard to the advisability of the proposed change of policy, declared Canandaigua, New York, postmaster Lewis Jenkins, in a cover letter that he enclosed with an anti-Sabbatarian petition from the merchants of the town, and the merchants of Canandaigua were happy to oblige. The postal patrons who accounted for 56 percent of all the postage that was received at the Canandaigua post office, Jenkins certified, opposed any reduction in the level of service.[115]

By framing the issue in this way, Jenkins provided compelling testimony for the fundamentally conservative cast of the anti-Sabbatarian appeal. To a far greater extent than the Sabbatarians, the anti-Sabbatarians were determined to restrict the petition effort to merchants and other men of affairs who had traditionally dominated American public life. Most Sabbatarians, explained Massachusetts anti-Sabbatarian George Savary in a letter to a congressman in which Savary described the protest at the local level, did not pay "one cent of postage in a year" and thus had "nothing at stake to win or lose" from the proposed suspension. "I bet," Savary added, that many signed the petition just to "let people know that they can write their names."[116]

Anti-Sabbatarian organizers proved particularly successful in rallying merchant support in such commercial centers as Canandaigua, Rochester, and New Orleans, which were located at the extreme periphery of the international commodities market that linked American wheat and cotton planters with the European market. Given the location of these merchants, this should come as no surprise. Should the government suspend the transmission of the mail on the Sabbath, they would be the most severely affected. The anticipated suspension, Rochester merchant William B. Rochester explained in an open letter to Postmaster General McLean in December 1828, would occasion "immense loss and inconvenience" throughout the United States, but would be particularly devastating in commercial centers that were located, as Rochester was, far from the Atlantic seaboard. Rochester was particularly worried that McLean might follow Bissell's lead and authorize a permanent suspension in seven-day mail service on the Albany-Buffalo route—a development, Rochester warned, that would cause "incalculable injury" to local merchants by placing them "constantly" at a one-day disadvantage in the struggle for up-to-date market information.[117]

McLean treated arguments such as Rochester's with great respect and considered them at length in a major report on the subject that he issued in January 1829. Were the government to suspend seven-day mail delivery, McLean warned, merchants in New Orleans might have to wait as many as three additional days to receive up-to-date information on sudden fluctuations in European demand. In contrast, the opening of the post office on the Sabbath to the public at large posed less disruption to the workings of the international commodity markets. Adopting a compromise position that he hoped would mollify both camps,

McLean strongly hinted that he favored a return to the practice that had prevailed prior to 1810, when it had been up to the discretion of the postmaster general to determine which post offices should be open to the public on this day.[118]

Joining the merchants in opposition to the proposed reform were the members of various religious denominations who were opposed for one reason or another to evangelical reform. Among the most prominent religious bodies that officially backed the anti-Sabbatarian cause was the Alabama Baptist Association, which was joined by various congregations that treated Saturday as the Sabbath, including one Jewish synagogue.[119] Further support was provided by a host of distinguished writers, including social critic Orestes Brownson, feminist freethinker Frances Wright, labor organizer Eli Moore, and utopian socialist Robert Dale Owen.[120]

Anti-Sabbatarians attacked the proposed suspension in the transmission of the mail on a variety of grounds. Some feared that if Congress shut down the post office to the public at large, favored insiders would prevail upon the postmaster to receive market information in advance of everyone else.[121] Others opposed any move that would slow the transmission of information on commerce and public affairs. For Americans living in the hinterland, the possibility that Congress might enact legislation interrupting the flow of information seemed like a step in the wrong direction. "Everything has been done," declared one group of petitioners from Trumansburg, New York, to speed the transmission of the mail so that merchants living in different parts of the United States might have "equal advantages" as nearly as "space will permit." What was needed was greater expedition, not less. "In this section of the country," reported another group of petitioners from Pulaski, Tennessee, the mail traveled so slowly that "we should rather be induced" to petition Congress for their "more speedy conveyance" than to support any measures that would occasion a greater delay.[122] "Republican principles require that the less should yield to the greater—individual convenience to public good," explained postal special agent James Holbrook. "And an excellent illustration of the practical application of these principles by the wisdom of Congress, is found in the provisions which that body has made to secure the uninterrupted transmission of the mails."[123]

Occasionally the anti-Sabbatarians took the high ground and challenged their opponents with having violated the rights of "conscience," neatly inverting the very same arguments that Sabbatarians like Lyman

Beecher had already deployed. "Is it not necessary," declared Barnabas Bates in 1829, "that something should be done to guard the equal rights of all, whether Jews or Christians, believers or unbelievers, whether they belong to any sect, or to no sect at all? Are not the equal rights of conscience the privilege of every man and guaranteed to us by the federal Constitution? For myself, I do not believe that it is true in religion, any more than in politics, to use the language of the venerated Jefferson, 'that the mass of mankind has been born with saddles on their backs, and the favored few, booted and spurred, ready to ride them legitimately by the grace of God.' "[124]

No feature of the Sabbatarian petition effort proved more disturbing to anti-Sabbatarians than the Sabbatarians' success at using the postal system and the press to consolidate their political support. For many anti-Sabbatarians, the Sabbatarian petition effort was but the "entering wedge" of a "grand system" that, if it were left unchecked, would speedily bring to the United States an *"ecclesiastical hierarchy"* as "oppressive and dangerous" as any that existed in Papal Rome. Should the present combination of "professedly religious individuals" achieve its goal, one anti-Sabbatarian charged, it would produce "discord and disunion among the people," lead to a bloody "civil war," and "finally overthrow our republican institutions."[125] Capitalizing on this concern, engraver James Akin compared the Sabbatarians to the antirepublican, pro-Catholic "Holy Alliance" that dominated Europe after the fall of Napoleon. Freely mingling anti-Catholic and anti-Calvinistic themes, Akin portrayed the Sabbatarians as a club-wielding mob of fanatic vigilantes spurred on by a vengeful Calvinist clergy still gloating over the execution of Michael Servetus, a Spanish heretic burned to death by John Calvin in 1553. Though the immediate target of the mob's wrath was a stagecoach carrying the public mails, their ultimate goals were far more insidious. "Look after your Liberties, my Boys!" exclaims one onlooker to a group of immigrant working men. "That's just the way they wanted to shackle us in Ireland!!!"[126]

Few commentators viewed these developments with more concern than Anne Royall. Crisscrossing the country to assemble material for her travel books, Royall rarely missed a chance to expose what she was firmly convinced had become a vast Sabbatarian conspiracy against popular liberty. Not content to denounce the Sabbatarians in print, Royall dumped overboard the tracts that Sabbatarians had deposited on steamboats for the edification of passengers and even threatened postmasters who sent their tracts through the mails postage-free that she would report them to Washington and see to it that they were heavily fined. Anti-Sabbatarian mail contractors opposed to any reduction in the level of service were grateful for her support and gave her free passage throughout the country. Royall, for her part, filled her books with lurid hints of the secret conspiracy that Presbyterian postmasters throughout the South had masterminded to end the separation of church and state.[127]

Even Sabbatarians found cause for concern. Though William Ellery Channing had twice supported the proposed suspension on principle, he remained deeply troubled by the Sabbatarians' use of the voluntary association as a club to force minorities to accept majoritarian views. In the United States, Channing warned, few things were more to be dreaded than the creation of organizations by which "public opinion may be brought to bear tyrannically against individuals or sects." Taking his position to its logical conclusion, Channing proclaimed his princi-pled opposition to any attempt to manipulate the new facilities of com-munication to rally public support. "All associations," Channing de-clared, "aiming or tending to establish sway by numbers" ought to be opposed, regardless of "whether the opinion which they intend to put down be true or false."[128]

The high point of the anti-Sabbatarian counteroffensive came in 1829 with the publication by Kentucky congressman Richard M. Johnson of the first of a notable pair of anti-Sabbatarian reports. In 1817, Elijah Hunt Mills had angrily rejected all considerations of commercial ex-pediency as a legitimate basis for resolving the controversy. In 1829 and again in 1830, Johnson neatly inverted Mills's position by declaring commercial expediency to be the only plausible grounds upon which the issue could be judged.

Central to Johnson's argument was his artful elaboration of the stock anti-Sabbatarian claim that Congress had no business suspending the mail on the Sabbath since this suspension would necessarily involve it in a religious dispute. Never before, Johnson declared, had a consid-erable body of citizens presumed Congress to be a "proper tribunal" to determine the laws of God. Should the Sabbatarians prevail, Congress would find it necessary to determine on which day of the week the Sabbath properly fell, and, in this way, arrogate to itself the power to settle a religious controversy through legislative means. Such power, Johnson stressed, had never before been vested in the central govern-ment, a mere "civil institution, wholly destitute of religious authority."[129] And should the central government ever acquire such power, the "catastrophe of other nations" furnished "an awful warning of the consequence." Freely impugning the Sabbatarians' motives, Johnson went so far as to compare them with Benedict Arnold, traitor to the republic, and Judas Iscariot, traitor to Christ.[130]

Though Washington insiders knew perfectly well that Johnson lacked the necessary education to produce such a learned exposition of theology and law, the actual authorship of Johnson's two reports was long a subject of debate.[131] Many assumed that they were the work of a clergyman, with the leading candidates including the anti-Sabbatarian evangelicals Alexander Campbell and John Leland.[132] It was a "most excellent sermon," remarked one skeptical congressman shortly after Johnson issued his first report, if "it had only had a suitable text."[133] Only many years later would it become generally known that both reports had been ghostwritten by postal clerk Obadiah Brown.[134]

Brown's hand was evident in several features of Johnson's reports. As a postal clerk, Brown was highly sensitive to the potentially disruptive impact of the proposed suspension upon the commercial periphery, lending special force to his charge that such a change in policy would sink the postal system into a "state of pusillanimity incompatible with the dignity of the government of which it is a department."[135] And, as a Baptist minister, Brown was familiar with the evangelical anticlericalism that was the Baptists' stock-in-trade and well equipped to prepare a vigorous, brief, and effective harangue that was sure to be reprinted in newspapers throughout the United States.[136]

Brown's authorship of Johnson's reports highlights a feature of the anti-Sabbatarian counteroffensive that is often overlooked. While anti-Sabbatarians were often stridently anticlerical, only rarely did they express any overt hostility toward organized religion. And puzzling as this might seem today, this was fully compatible with their larger aims. Anticlerical rhetoric, as a number of recent historians have stressed, was often a hallmark of populistic Christian sects, such as Campbell's Disciples of Christ, that notwithstanding their strident opposition to evangelical reform were themselves resolutely evangelical in their internal affairs. From this standpoint, the anti-Sabbatarian counterprotest may have been less of a secular challenge to religious authority than an evangelical assault on allegedly anachronistic vestiges of ecclesiastical control, and the controversy itself less of a debate pitting liberals against conservatives, evangelicals against anti-evangelicals, or promoters against opponents of social control, than a family quarrel among evangelicals over the proper relationship between church and state.

If the Sabbatarians are to be judged on the basis of their ability to bring about the enactment of specific legislation, then there can be little question that they failed. In 1831, as in 1817, the government transmitted the mail on the Sabbath and opened many post offices to the public at large. Yet it would be a mistake to conclude that their protest had been wholly unsuccessful. In the short term, they prevailed upon Postmaster General McLean to temporarily suspend Sabbath mail service on the Albany-Buffalo route and to instruct a number of postmasters to shut the post office on this day to the public at large.[137] And in the long term, they came surprisingly close to achieving their goals.

Among the changes in the wider society that worked to the Sabbatarians' advantage was the coming of the steam railroad. Though postal officers initially tried to run mail cars on the Sabbath, they soon discovered it to be prohibitively expensive, given the light demand for passenger service on this day. Taking advantage of the situation, Sabbatarians pressed once again to persuade the government to shut down mail service on the Sabbath. This time they had considerably more success. Beginning in 1841, Sabbatarians prevailed upon postal officers to curtail Sunday service on some 80,000 miles of routes, a fact that the organizers of the American and Foreign Sabbath Union proudly included in their annual report for 1845.[138] "To a greater extent than is commonly supposed," added the directors of one New Jersey railroad company the following year, "the post-office authorities and the railroad companies have found it alike for their interest to suspend Sunday mail trains." The report went on to say that the directors were "perfectly satisfied with the result, regarding its omission as conducive to the true interest of the company, in the increased efficiency of their operatives and equipment, and the diminished liability to accidents, by not overworking the men, machinery, and road, but giving to all one day of rest."[139] The commercialization of the electric telegraph in 1844 further reduced pressure for the Sabbath mails, since merchants quickly came to rely on the new technology as their major source of up-to-date market information on changing market trends.

With the end of the Civil War in 1865, Sabbatarians returned to the subject once again. Now that the country was back on a peacetime footing, seven-day mail delivery no longer seemed like such a pressing concern. Many railroad managers agreed. Swayed by Sabbatarian appeals, in 1866 one convention of railroad managers urged the postmaster general to eliminate all unnecessary Sunday mail trains so that their employees could keep the day "in accordance with the moral sentiment of the community." Now that the war was over, they reasoned, military exigency no longer required that this service be maintained. Finally, in 1912, an alliance of ministers and postal clerks convinced Congress to close down all of the post offices that were still open to the public on the Sabbath for good, bringing to fruition in the Progressive era a reform that dated back a hundred years. Among the leaders of the 1912 protest were the ministerial association in the old Presbyterian bulwark of Newark, New Jersey, and the National Association of Letter Carriers, whose membership resented being forced to work Sunday and who provided a key element of support to bring about this long-sought reform.[140]

Just as the Sabbatarian controversy shaped American postal policy, so too it shaped the political careers of a number of leading public men. John McLean's willingness to submit the question to the judgment of public opinion boosted his already glowing reputation, while his judicious report on the subject earned him the plaudits of Sabbatarians and anti-Sabbatarians alike. Sabbatarians hailed McLean as "friendly to all practicable reform," while anti-Sabbatarians took comfort from the fact that in the end he had refused to challenge the status quo.[141] Another beneficiary of the controversy was Richard M. Johnson, whose landmark reports on the Sunday mails proved a major boon to his political career. Prior to the publication of these reports, Johnson lacked stature as a statesman, and was probably best known as the Indian fighter who had supposedly killed Tecumseh during the War of 1812. Following their publication he rapidly emerged as a champion of religious liberty and garnered enough political support to secure the vice presidency in the election of 1836, notwithstanding his irregular family arrangements (though Johnson never married, he lived openly for many years with a mulatto woman) and his highly questionable dealings with the stagecoach industry.

It would be hard to exaggerate the intensity of the public interest that was generated by Johnson's reports. Widely reprinted, they made him a household name throughout the United States. According to one Pennsylvania congressman, there was "scarcely a country paper" in the land that had not reprinted Johnson's first report in full. No man who read anything, added a congressman from New York, had not seen Johnson's report in the newspaper.[142] In Philadelphia and Baltimore, printers issued cheap pamphlet editions that quite literally capitalized on the reports' flamboyant tone: key passages were set off in special type to heighten the effect. A few even went so far as to prepare special silk editions to be proudly mounted as a "new Declaration of Independence" and a "supplement to our Bill of Rights."[143]

To be sure, not everyone was impressed. Among Sabbatarians, Johnson's reports remained notorious until well into the twentieth century.[144] "Satan never accomplished a greater temporary victory" over the Sabbath, Harmon Kingsbury declared, "through any agency, in any country, unless the infidelity of France be an exception."[145] It was nothing short of outrageous, fumed Sabbatarian jurist Thomas Baird, that Johnson should term the Sabbatarians a "dangerous combination." "Never," Baird exploded, "has the right of the people to 'petition for redress of grievances,' been so set at naught: never have their wishes been so slighted—their feelings so mocked—and their delegated authority so perverted."[146]

The significance of the Sabbatarian controversy extended far beyond its role in boosting particular individuals like Johnson and McLean. More broadly, it demonstrated how easily a small group of activists could take advantage of the communications revolution that had been wrought by the postal system, the stagecoach industry, and the press to mobilize public support throughout the United States. It is a commonplace of American history that at some point between the victory of Andrew Jackson in the election of 1828 and the victory of William Henry Harrison in the celebrated "Log Cabin" campaign of 1840, the Democratic and Whig parties completed the transformation of the gentry-based political order of the Founding Fathers into the mass-based political order that has endured to the present day. Yet it is often overlooked that this transformation had been made possible by the prior expansion of the communications infrastructure and in particular by the sudden injection into national politics in the 1820s of highly charged religious issues such as Sabbatarianism, which neatly polarized the electorate into mutually antagonistic camps.

Both the Sabbatarians and the anti-Sabbatarians proved innovative in this regard. The Sabbatarian petition effort demonstrated how reformers could take advantage of the communications infrastructure to mobilize support for their cause throughout the United States. No less innovative were such anti-Sabbatarians as Richard M. Johnson. By appealing directly to a national audience, Johnson signaled the emergence of a new relationship between Congress and the electorate. When the Founding Fathers drafted the federal Constitution in 1787, they had assumed that Congress would be insulated from the public by its geographical isolation. This was particularly true of the Senate, which was intended to be an intermediary between the federal executive and the governments of the individual states. By 1828, however, it had become technically feasible—and, as Johnson demonstrated, highly effective—for a senator to appeal directly to the public. By taking advantage of his office in this way, as one skeptic sardonically observed, Johnson had gone far toward transforming Congress from a body that received the reflected "light" from the "people" into a "college of political wisdom" that broadcast its edicts to the public at large.[147]

Just as the form of the controversy was innovative, so too was its content. Unlike most of the questions that had come before the Founding Fathers, the Sabbatarian issue was explicitly religious and, like so many religious issues, not easily susceptible to compromise. It should therefore come as no surprise that Sabbatarians such as Lyman Beecher found it highly disturbing that the issue could ever become subordinated to the "collisions incident to popular elections"; that anti-Sabbatarians like Johnson felt few qualms about savaging the Sabbatarians' motives; or that, of the hundreds of petitions sent to Congress between 1828 and 1831, not one so much as mentioned the signers' party affiliation or alluded to the recent presidential campaign.[148] One might suppose that the Sabbatarians would have backed John Quincy Adams, given Adams's personal piety and his intensely moralistic approach to public life. Yet Adams was a Unitarian, making him suspect in the eyes of many evangelicals, while Andrew Jackson was a Presbyterian, a circumstance that filled at least some Sabbatarians with the hope that Jackson might back their cause. Shortly before Jackson's inauguration, one Virginia Sabbatarian went so far as to declare the present moment to be an "auspicious time" for the petition effort, since the country was about to have a "*Presbyterian* president."[149] In addition, several prominent Jacksonians were outspoken Sabbatarians, including Tennessee congressman Felix Grundy and Presbyterian minister Ezra Stiles Ely, whose call for a "Christian Party in Politics" had greatly disturbed anti-Sabbatarians troubled by the growing role of evangelical religion in American public life.[150]

By the election of 1840, however, the Sabbatarian issue had been largely absorbed into the routine give-and-take of two party politics.

Democratic leaders courted the anti-Sabbatarians, a plausible alliance, since, like the Democrats, most anti-Sabbatarians supported the commercial expansion of the periphery and were wary of evangelical activism. Whig leaders, in contrast, courted the Sabbatarians, an equally plausible alliance, since, like the Whigs, the Sabbatarians supported the improvement of core institutions like the Sabbath and were generally sympathetic to organized moral reform. Under the leadership of Harmon Kingsbury, a Cleveland merchant who had helped purchase horses for Josiah Bissell, Jr., in 1828, the Sabbatarians helped to elect William Henry Harrison president; in 1844, they helped nominate Sabbatarian Theodore Frelinghuysen as Henry Clay's running mate in the veteran Whig's final, ill-fated bid for the presidency. Following Harrison's election, Sabbatarian ministers such as Thomas Robbins held out high hopes that Harrison's postmaster general, Francis Granger, might lend his support to the cause, particularly since Francis's father, Gideon, had proved so sympathetic toward the Sabbatarians thirty years before.[151]

Kingsbury found particularly impressive Harrison's opposition to the continuing expansion of the central government, since he remained convinced that state governments should retain wide discretion over the moral well-being of the public at large, while he could not believe that the states had ever granted to the central government the "power to require labor on Sunday." And if they had, Kingsbury added with true Calvinistic certitude, such a grant ought to be contested, since "no human authority, contravening the law of God, can be of any validity whatever."[152] Harrison's sudden death and Granger's resignation doomed the Sabbatarians' hopes. Still, when Granger's successor, Charles Wickliffe, agreed to discontinue the Sabbath mails on thousands of post routes, Sabbatarians such as New Jersey chief justice Joseph C. Hornblower treated the move as a vindication of party principle and wrote Wickliffe personally to thank him for his "deep interest" in the cause.[153]

Just as the Sabbatarian controversy highlighted the cultural conflicts that would undergird the emerging party system, so too it helped to transform prevailing expectations with regard to the proper role of the central government in American public life. After 1831, it became increasingly difficult to share the conviction of anti-Sabbatarians such as Richard M. Johnson that the central government had no role to play in shaping the moral character of American institutions. It was hardly coincidental that several leading Sabbatarians—including William Lloyd Garrison, Lewis Tappan, and William Jay—would soon expand their perceptual horizons to implicate the central government in the perpetuation of the institution of slavery. Now that the central government had invaded civil society, it had also become morally accountable to God. This was a momentous realization, and one that was destined to shape American public life profoundly in the decades to come.

· 6 ·

The Wellspring of Democracy

IN THE EIGHT-YEAR PERIOD between the inauguration of Andrew Jackson in March 1829 and the inauguration of Jackson's successor, Martin Van Buren, in March 1837, the Jacksonians transformed the American postal system from the central administrative apparatus of the American state into a wellspring of the mass party, a new institution that the Jacksonians had created to defeat John Quincy Adams in the election of 1828. Most accounts of this notable chapter in the history of American public life treat it as a morality play in which the Jacksonians are either praised as champions of democracy or condemned as apologists for political corruption. I take a different approach. In order to probe beneath the surface of the overwrought, and often fantastic, rhetoric with which this transformation is so often described, I shift the angle of vision to focus less on the morality of the Jacksonians' conduct and more on its broader historical significance as a response to the expansion of the postal system in the period following the passage of the Post Office Act of 1792.

APPREHENSION regarding the expansion of the central government was hardly confined to the Jacksonians. Alexis de Tocqueville, in reflecting back on his trip to the United States in 1831 and 1832, observed that anxiety on this score was the "one great fear" shared by virtually every public figure he had met.[1] Yet the Jacksonians were far more committed to defending the prerogatives of the individual states than Adams, Clay, and the loose coalition of development-minded "national republicans" who had defeated Jackson in the election of 1824.[2] Skeptical of the Adamsites' support for the "American System" and, in particular, of the federally funded national program of internal improvements that the Adamsites had hoped to establish, the Jacksonians strove to check the expansion of the central government that had taken place since the end of the Madison administration in 1817. The recent expansion of the central government, warned Jacksonian congressman Thomas Hart Benton in 1826—and, in particular, the expansion of executive patronage in the form of lucrative contracts and jobs—"completely overthrew" Madison's celebrated contention in his *Federalist* essays of 1787 and 1788 that the central government would never acquire the capacity to challenge the prerogatives of the individual states. Should Congress fail to take specific steps to check its further expansion, Benton added, the central government would soon dominate the states as effectively as if they were "so many provinces in one vast empire."[3]

No government programs were more threatening to the Jacksonians, or more integral to the Adamsites' domestic agenda, than the construction of a national program of internal improvements. In the period between the passage of the Post Office Act of 1792 and the inauguration of John Quincy Adams in 1825, ordinary Americans had grown accustomed to petitioning Congress to designate the routes over which the government was to carry the mail. It was but a short step for them to begin to petition Congress to build the roads as well. This they began to do in anticipation of Adams's inauguration, confident that the incoming president would throw his support behind the cause.[4] According to Martin Van Buren, the total cost of the various projects that Congress considered during these years amounted to a staggering $100 million, more than ten times the cost of the Erie Canal, the most ambitious public works project completed up to then.[5] Among the various projects that Congress considered was a proposed 1,100 mile "National Southern Post Road" between Washington and New Orleans that was sometimes linked with a similar northern post road between Washington and Buffalo.[6] Prior to the Monroe administration, the possibility that the central government might embark upon such an ambitious national program was held in check by a variety of constitutional objections. Under Monroe, however, as McLean would later reminisce, outside of Virginia there came to be a "general acquiescence" in the constitutionality of such a program throughout the United States.[7]

Few Jacksonians warned more eloquently against the dangers of this new federal program than Congressman John Bell of Tennessee. Should the central government build the Buffalo–Washington–New Orleans road, Bell warned gloomily on the eve of Jackson's inauguration in

February 1829, this would bring to the national capital an unprecedented influx of lobbyists intent on securing for their clients a part of the "national spoil." And once these lobbyists arrived, Washington would soon be transformed from an institution of strictly limited jurisdiction into a "great central power" far more formidable than anything that the Founding Fathers could have possibly imagined. To make his point, Bell reminded his colleagues of the army of lobbyists who had flooded Washington during the Adams administration to help determine the course of a far more modest federally funded road project to be built on a thinly settled stretch of the main North-South post road between Baltimore and Philadelphia. Though the projected Baltimore-Philadelphia road was to be less than one hundred miles long, its precise location proved extraordinarily controversial, with at least eight different groups vying for the prize. How much more contentious would the debate become, Bell wondered, should Congress undertake to build a road all the way from Buffalo to New Orleans?[8]

It would be easy to conclude that Bell had small cause for concern. The Adamsites failed to enact their domestic agenda, neither the Buffalo–Washington–New Orleans road nor the Baltimore–Philadelphia road was ever built, and Jackson won the election of 1828. As a consequence, historians have long dismissed the antistatist thrust of the Jacksonian campaign as partisan claptrap or, at best, a covert expression of hostility toward the market economy.[9] But at the time, the future seemed far less clear. By the middle of the Adams administration in 1826, it was widely presumed that the Adamsites were about to prevail.[10] And should the Adamsites secure the necessary funding to get even a few of these projects under way, the additional patronage that they would bring the administration in the form of contracts and jobs might well enable it to enlist the services of the necessary army of campaign workers to defeat Jackson in 1828 just as they had defeated him in 1824. Given these circumstances, the Jacksonians had solid cause for concern.[11]

To popularize their opposition to the recent expansion of the central government, the Jacksonians enlisted an unprecedented cadre of publicists that included Duff Green, Amos Kendall, and Isaac Hill, making Jackson's election campaign by far the most expensive to have been waged until then.[12] Never before had party leaders established such a far-flung network of political newspapers to rally support. The medium that the Jacksonians adopted to publicize their cause may have been novel, but their message was not. To a far greater extent than the Adamsites, the Jacksonians fixed their sights on the past. Far from being progressive heralds of the nineteenth-century liberal tradition—with its faith in commercial expansion, its skepticism toward the wisdom of the ancients, and its solicitude for the well-being of the individual—the Jacksonians cast themselves as the conservative heirs of the classical republican tradition that the eighteenth-century American colonists had deployed against the Crown. Obsessed with executive patronage, repulsed by the seemingly unstoppable expansion of the central government, and preoccupied with Greek and Roman antiquity as the best possible model for American public life, they strove to restore the American republic to the better days of its youth.[13] Week in and week out, Jacksonian publicists filled the periodical press with lurid accounts of the evils that had supposedly plagued the central government during the administrations of Adams and Monroe. "Executive patronage" was their bogeyman, "retrenchment and reform" their rallying cry. Even the bow of the barge that bore Jackson up the Ohio River en route to his inauguration furnished a commentary on this theme. Graced with a pair of hickory brooms, it dramatized the determination of "Old Hickory" to clean out the Augean stables that Jackson's predecessors had permitted to fester in the twelve years since the end of the Madison administration in 1817.[14]

No Jacksonian publicist proved more adept at manipulating the classical republican creed than Duff Green. Tall, thin, handsome, and supremely self-confident, Green arrived in Washington early in Adams's administration with a single pair of pants after having rescued himself from bankruptcy by securing a lucrative mail contract for a stagecoach line in Missouri.[15] Taking charge of a floundering political newspaper that he promptly renamed the *United States Telegraph,* Green championed Jackson's candidacy, and that of Jackson's running mate, John C. Calhoun, in a stream of hard-hitting editorials that quickly earned him a reputation as one of the most effective partisan publicists of the day. Rarely before had a journalist done more to shape the course of an election campaign. Never before had a partisan publicist emerged as such a pivotal figure on the national stage. Green really seems to think, observed Amos Kendall on the eve of the inauguration, that he is the "ruler of the nation."[16]

Green's revival of the classical republican creed shaped virtually every editorial that he wrote. Profoundly influenced by the eighteenth-century English radical James Burgh, Green was firmly convinced that the election of 1828 posed a challenge for the Americans of his day that was fully analogous to the challenge that Britain's American colonists had confronted in the period immediately preceding the War of Independence. Just as the expansion of the British state under George III had spurred Britain's American colonists to rebel against the Crown, so the expansion of the central government under the Adamsites had threatened to block the ascendancy of the "REPUBLICAN TICKET" of Jackson and Calhoun.[17] In the language of the day, this was corruption: the systematic manipulation of executive patronage to perpetuate the power of the existing regime.

Green's strident rhetoric could not have been expected to make much of an impression on the public at large. Neither the *United States Telegraph* nor the affiliated party papers circulated in numbers large enough to reach more than a tiny fraction of the electorate. But Green's editorials *were* eagerly read by the audience for whom they were doubtless intended: the growing cadre of party workers who had organized Jackson's election campaign.[18] For this audience, their meaning was plain. By charging the Adamsites with corruption, Green had virtually guaranteed that should the Jacksonians win the election, the incoming administration would dismiss hundreds of officeholders. After all, a conspiracy so immense could hardly go unpunished. In this way, Green deployed the familiar antistatist rhetoric of the classical republican creed to create the necessary financial incentives to rally support for the cause during the election campaign. Who could be better suited to fill the myriad openings in the public offices that the incoming administration was about to create than the very men who had invested their energy, time, and money on the Jacksonians' behalf? So important was this financial incentive for the Jacksonians' success that Adamsite congressman Edward Everett laconically observed that should Jackson publicly proclaim his opposition to the dismissal of public officers on partisan grounds, it would "cost him every vote out of Tennessee."[19]

To build public support for the anticipated purge, Green ran an increasingly brazen series of editorials during the final frenzied weeks of the campaign. Once Jackson's victory was assured, Green threw caution to the wind. He boldly predicted that beginning shortly after Jackson's inauguration in March, the incoming president would "reward his friends and punish his enemies." When an Adamsite publicist prodded Green to explain how this policy would affect the political press, heavily dependent as it was on the government for financial support, Green responded with a single word: "PROSCRIPTION," leaving little doubt that, at the very least, the printing contracts of Adamsite editors would not be renewed. When Green was urged to clarify whether major

changes would be made in the staffing of the public offices, Green repeated his threat, this time in bold capital letters: "REWARD HIS
FRIENDS AND PUNISH HIS ENEMIES."[20] For Washington insiders, the
point was plain. Once in office, the Jacksonians intended to undertake
an unprecedented purge of the governing class. Not even the Jacksonians' most inveterate foes could have conjured up a more vivid portrait
of the changes that the incoming administration intended to make.

For the men who staffed the general post office, Green's editorials
were an ominous sign. Few doubted that the incoming administration
fully intended to undertake the large-scale purge of officeholders that
Green had so luridly described. Even before the inauguration, Jacksonian stalwarts had begun to compose secret lists of the political alle-
giances of the staff.[21] Equally apprehensive were the postmasters in the
field. According to Massachusetts congressman Edward Everett, many
had become so fearful about the prospect of Jackson's victory that they
switched their allegiance from Adams to Jackson, convinced that if
Adams won and they had supported Jackson, they might retain their
office, while if Jackson won and they had backed Adams, they would
surely be dismissed. In this way, Everett informed McLean, Adams's
very reputation for impartiality and fair dealing had inspired a "most
furious opposition" that encouraged the open or secret hostility of
three-quarters of the officeholders in the United States. Everett probably exaggerated this figure. Shortly after Jackson's inauguration, one
journalist estimated that a third to a half of all the postmasters in the
country remained loyal to Adams.[22] But there is little reason to doubt
that Green's strategy had the desired effect. In Boston, Everett added,
with mingled amusement and contempt, Jackson supporters had even
broken into a quarrel over vacancies *"yet to be."*[23]

Green's anticipated purge, of course, would require the cooperation
of the postmaster general. And as long as John McLean remained in
office, this would not be easy. Though McLean had secretly backed
Jackson in the election of 1828, he had no intention of permitting a
mere party publicist like Green to subordinate the administration of the
postal system to petty considerations of partisan gain. For this reason,
Everett felt sure that as long as McLean remained in office there could
be no "general turn out" of post office staff.[24]

McLean's principled opposition to Green's scheme may have calmed
Everett's fears, but it provided scant comfort for the dozens of Jacksonian publicists who had journeyed to Washington to get their little
piece of the promised reward. On the day after Jackson arrived in the

city for his inauguration, these publicists visited him "in a body," reported Amos Kendall to a political associate back in Kentucky.[25] Having paid, often at considerable expense, for the various newspapers, pamphlets, and handbills that the Jacksonians had relied on during the campaign, these "money-martyrs," as Nathaniel Greene aptly described himself and his journalistic peers, had come to Jackson's inauguration for the express purpose of recouping their investment.[26] "I am disposed to think," Kendall reflected after surveying the scene, "that but few of those who have shouted Reform really desire anything else" than "the privilege of availing themselves of the very abuses with which we charge our adversaries."[27]

The arrival of such an enormous number of office seekers in the national capital had a profound influence on the character of Jackson's inauguration. Today Jackson's inauguration is often hailed as a defining moment in the rise of political democracy, when ordinary Americans from all parts of the country and all walks of life joined together to celebrate the victory of a man of the people. "Thousands and thousands of people," wrote one eyewitness, "without distinction of rank, collected in an immense mass round the Capitol, silent, orderly, and tranquil . . . It was grand—it was sublime!"[28] But not everyone at the time saw the event in such a flattering light. For many discerning observers—Southerners as well as Northerners, Jacksonians as well as anti-Jacksonians—the assembled throng was less a triumph of democracy than a classical republican nightmare, a humiliating display of the political clout of campaign workers intent upon securing their reward. Of course, not everyone at Jackson's inauguration was an expectant postmaster-to-be. Yet if contemporary accounts of the inauguration are to be believed, it was this army of Jacksonian cadre men—not, as many historians have romantically assumed, a disinterested crowd of well-wishers—who muddied the carpets, mobbed the punch bowl, and smashed the furniture at the White House reception that followed Jackson's inaugural address, transforming what Jackson had hoped would be a genteel celebration into a near-riot. For a moment, it looked as if the office seekers had actually stormed the capital and taken the government hostage. The scene prompted Martin Van Buren to warn that before Jackson turned his attention to the business of dismissals, he would be well advised to first clear the streets.[29]

Contemporary accounts of Jackson's inauguration testify to the revulsion with which it was greeted by political insiders familiar with the motives of the crowd. So mercenary were the participants' motives,

Everett observed, that the congressional delegations from Virginia and South Carolina had become thoroughly disgusted with the new administration two weeks before the inauguration.[30] Many Jacksonians agreed. One spoke for many when he thanked God that he had not been present at an event that, when called to mind, covered "every American cheek with a blush." He added that the "throng that pressed on the president before he was fairly in office, soliciting rewards in a manner so destitute of decency, and of respect for his character and office," was "among the most disgraceful reproaches to the character of our countrymen." Another Jacksonian declared that before he would again behold a similar event, he would rather see the "whole district of Columbia blown to heaven, with all that it contained."[31]

Even more revealing were the sentiments that Massachusetts senator Daniel Webster included in a letter to his brother's wife on the day of the inauguration. "Today we have had the Inauguration," Webster duly reported. "A monstrous crowd of people is in the city . . . and they really seem to think that the country is rescued from some dreadful danger." Had Webster's relation stopped reading his letter with that sentence, she might have assumed that the Jacksonians' victory represented a genuine triumph of democracy. But as the rest of Webster's letter made plain, this was not how Webster understood the course of events. For, as Webster took pains to add, it was not the "people" who had attended Jackson's inauguration, but rather the "thousand expectants for office who throng the city."[32]

If the Jackson inauguration can be said to symbolize anything, it was the triumph neither of the common man nor of the "people," but rather of the political workers who had staffed Jackson's campaign and, more broadly, of a novel method of campaign finance.[33] Given the high cost of travel and the exorbitant cost of Washington's hotels, few other Americans had the incentive to make the trip.[34] Office seekers might plead poverty in seeking official preferment, yet they somehow managed to find the necessary money to travel to Washington to secure their anticipated reward.

No feature of the incoming administration was of greater interest to the office seekers than the criteria that would be used in making appointments. And here, at least for the moment, they were gravely disappointed. Though Jackson did stress the need for *"reform"* in his inaugural address, he made no allusion to the principle of rotation in office or even to the possibility that his administration might find it expedient to make major changes in the staffing of public offices. On the contrary, Jackson decreed that the incoming administration would dismiss only those public officers who had proved unworthy of their trust, echoing almost word for word the high-minded personnel policy that McLean had popularized prior to 1829.[35] In the language of the day, this meant that the Jacksonians would limit their dismissals to "cause." Had the Jacksonians followed through on this pledge, many, if not most, of the office seekers at Jackson's inauguration would have gone home without having secured their anticipated reward.

Within three days of the inauguration, however, the new president found himself obliged to pursue a more realistic course. Besieged by office seekers and assailed by Green, Jackson found it impossible to forestall the long-anticipated purge. But before he could proceed, Jackson had to find some way to get rid of McLean, who as postmaster general presided over the largest and most politically influential source of federal patronage, and who was adamantly opposed to abandoning the public trust doctrine that he had done so much to promote. Jackson hoped to avoid a head-on confrontation with his popular postmaster general by offering McLean the secretaryship of the navy or of war. When this proved impossible, Jackson offered McLean a vacant seat on the Supreme Court. McLean accepted the position, thus bringing his distinguished six-year tenure as postmaster general to an unexpected close.

Precisely why Jackson took this step was a subject of intense discussion among contemporaries and remains something of a mystery even today. Jacksonians insisted that McLean fully approved of the switch. According to Amos Kendall, McLean agreed with the staff changes that the Jacksonians intended to make, yet found it impossible to "do his duty" to oversee the necessary dismissals without "losing a portion of the popularity he had acquired."[36] "He goes out," Kendall insisted, "of his own choice; for in truth he might have had the War or Navy Department or the Post Office."[37] Green concurred and, in a private letter to Treasury Secretary Samuel Ingham in May, went so far as to contend that McLean had secretly agreed to give Green control over the dismissals even before the inauguration.[38]

Administration critics, in contrast, attributed McLean's resignation to his difference of opinion with Jacksonians like Green. Though the Supreme Court berth might seem like a promotion, they understood perfectly well that, by depriving McLean of the formidable patronage that he had formerly controlled, it threatened to derail his political career. According to Supreme Court justice Joseph Story, McLean's resignation had been forced upon the president by the "governing ultras," while, to "make the matter fair," Jackson had agreed to appoint McLean, "not much to his will," a judge.[39] Ex-president Adams was blunter still. McLean declined to be "the broom to sweep the post offices," Adams sardonically declared, having refused to be the "instrument of that sweeping proscription of postmasters which is to be one of the samples of the promised reform."[40]

Edward Everett provided the most elaborate account of McLean's resignation in a letter to Everett's brother. He contended that the event had been spurred by McLean's refusal to permit Green to dismiss Aaron Hill as postmaster of Boston. When McLean learned that Green sought Hill's dismissal and that Jackson supported Green, McLean was said to have immediately requested a private interview with the president. McLean would cheerfully dismiss political partisans like Hill, McLean allegedly told Jackson, but he would do so impartially, by ordering the dismissal of *all* postmasters who had actively participated in the election campaign, not only those who had worked on Adams's behalf. In addition, Everett added, McLean requested Jackson's official permission to prepare a signed testimonial in which McLean would declare his intention to administer the postal system under the Jacksonians in accordance with the same principles that he had administered it under the Adamsites.[41] Jackson was said to be somewhat taken aback by McLean's determination to frustrate the incoming administration in this way and paced up and down the room several times before finally reaching his decision. How would you like, Jackson asked McLean, to take the vacant seat on the Supreme Court? McLean promptly accepted, convinced that he could do nothing to block either Hill's dismissal or the purge to come.[42] Back in Boston, Hill's successor, Nathaniel Greene, was said to have boasted to his friends that "*he* turned out the postmaster general."[43]

McLean himself always maintained that the Jacksonians had forced him out of office, and he missed few chances to publicize this fact in the years to come.[44] Though he had secretly backed Jackson during the election campaign, he despised the Jacksonians' manipulation of public office for partisan gain, and retained the Adamsites' faith in the career civil service that he himself had done so much to promote. Indeed, there is good reason to suppose that McLean manipulated the circumstances of his retirement to portray himself as the first victim of the new regime, just as McLean had manipulated the Sabbatarian controversy to cast himself as an impartial judge of public opinion. After all, few events could display more advantageously his unswerving commitment to the public good or his keen solicitude for the men whom the Jacksonians had dismissed on purely partisan grounds. As one admiring anti-Jacksonian explained, by refusing to sanction the partisan dismissals McLean preserved his "Roman virtue" and signaled his determination to prevent the incoming administration from transforming the postal system into a political "machine" to "execute a system which he abhorred."[45] McLean himself could hardly have put it better.

As McLEAN's SUCCESSOR, Jackson appointed William Barry, a Kentucky judge, a close personal friend of the president, and a chronic spendthrift who was badly in need of a job, having gone deeply into debt in the course of an unsuccessful gubernatorial race in Kentucky. Popularly known as the "Demosthenes of Kentucky," Barry was widely praised as a spellbinding public speaker who combined the erudition of a classical scholar with the wry humor of a frontier wit, and was said to bear a striking resemblance to Patrick Henry, the legendary eighteenth-century Virginia orator who had declaimed so eloquently against the tyranny of the Crown. At less than 100 pounds and by all accounts far from handsome, Barry was hardly an imposing presence. But he did his best to emulate the genteel refinement of the old planter families whose sons he had mingled with at the College of William of Mary. Like Duff Green, he was well versed in the highly stylized lexicon of the classical republican creed and frequently drew upon its stark opposition between monarchical and republican forms of government to explain the course of events.[46]

Barry may have been a gifted public speaker and a conscientious student, but he lacked administrative experience and proved utterly incapable of running the postal system, setting in motion a sequence of events that would drive the system into debt and lead to Barry's forced resignation in 1835. The contrast with McLean was impossible to overlook. Under McLean, the postal system attained a level of service that won it the praise of contemporaries throughout the United States. Under Barry, it very nearly collapsed as a consequence of the staggering ineptitude of its chief executive officer and of the disastrous policies over which he was obliged to preside. To assume, as so many Jacksonian publicists tried, that nothing had changed—in short, to pretend that the general post office under Barry was being administered much as it had been under McLean—was, as the Jacksonian journalist Anne Royall sardonically declared in 1834, to perpetuate one of the "greatest insults that had ever been offered human understanding."[47]

Barry's limitations as an administrator were no mystery to insiders familiar with his previous career. One political insider warned Jackson several months before his inauguration that Barry was totally unfit for any public office requiring "great intellectual force or moral firmness."[48] Though Jackson had originally intended to heed his friends' warning by appointing Barry to fill the relatively undemanding vacancy on the Supreme Court—where presumably Barry's lack of "intellectual force" would prove to be less of a liability—Jackson changed his mind when it became plain that he had to find some way to get rid of McLean. Initially, Barry's appointment seemed sensible enough. Since Barry lacked the political ambition to emulate McLean's example and build himself an independent political base, his appointment helped to neutralize the postal system as a spawning ground for rival presidential contenders. Jackson well understood how effectively McLean had used his control of postal patronage to frustrate the Adamsites in the election of 1828, and Jackson had no intention of falling victim to a similar ploy. In addition, and no less important, Jackson could rely on Barry to authorize whatever staffing changes party leaders like Green might consider necessary. Barry could not be expected, as Joseph Story perceptively observed, to "stickle" at the dismissal of meritorious postmasters whose offices the Jacksonians needed to pay off the debts they had incurred in the preceding campaign.[49]

No one was more disgusted with Barry's appointment than McLean. To manipulate postal patronage behind the scenes by making occasional partisan appointments, as McLean himself had done, was one thing. But to institute a large-scale purge of the existing staff, to the inevitable detriment of the public, was quite another. "The history of the present administration is already in view," McLean wrote Monroe within a month of Jackson's inauguration. "In its progress and termination I shall be no more disappointed than I am in that of the late administration." Jackson, McLean added, was "lamentably deficient in requirement and capacity . . . Never before have I apprehended serious danger to our institutions. I now fear their moral force will be impaired. Political gladiators will, for a time, gain the ascendancy . . . until the good sense and sober judgment of the people shall apply the corrective."[50] McLean found particularly outrageous the blatant partisanship of the Jacksonian press, which consistently misrepresented the changes that were taking place. "If General Jackson should call out a regiment, and drive the Senate and perhaps the House of Representatives into the Potomac," McLean sarcastically observed, "the act would be eulogized by the great mass of his editors, as one evidencing great firmness, and by which the liberties of the country were preserved."[51]

Taking the offensive, McLean prepared dozens of public testimonials for postmasters whom he believed the Jacksonians had improperly dismissed. In addition, McLean issued a steady stream of private letters to public figures to explain his position. McLean had not found "one individual, of high standing," he assured New York politician John Taylor in the summer of 1829, who did not share his revulsion at the "proscriptive policy" that the Jacksonians had undertaken, adding that his views were fully shared by the "most intelligent friends" of the Jacksonians in the West.[52] McLean's conduct so infuriated the Jacksonians that Obadiah Brown prepared a circular letter (over Barry's signature) that attempted to blacken McLean's reputation by insinuating that McLean had left the postal system in such a disorderly state that the Jacksonians had found it necessary to institute a number of administrative reforms in order to balance the books.[53] McLean promptly issued a public rejoinder that effectively rebutted Brown's unsubstantiated charges; but the damage was done. Thirty years later, postal insiders continued to hint that McLean himself had set the stage for the humiliating postal finance scandal that led to the forced resignation of Barry and Brown in 1835.[54]

McLean was hardly the only public figure to be disturbed by Barry's appointment. Equally troubled was the staff of the general post office, who feared, quite understandably, that Barry's arrival might threaten their jobs. "Oh how dreadfully must a parent feel," observed veteran Washington insider Margaret Bayard Smith in describing the clerks' predicament, "when he looks on his children gathered round him, and knows that one word spoken by a stranger, may reduce them to beggary. Such is the situation of hundreds at the present moment—and of men too far advanced in life to be able to enter on new paths of industry."[55] One postal clerk was said to have gone mad and died in anticipation of the changes to come.[56] "There are," reported postal clerk Michael Simpson shortly after the inauguration, "many palpitating hearts." His eye squarely on the main chance, Simpson added resignedly, "It is a period of great interest—and agitation. But in all of which I am not likely to receive promotion."[57] Unfortunately for Simpson, his prediction turned out to be correct. Though he had risen to a position of considerable responsibility under McLean, his salary never rose above the $1,200 he had received on the eve of Jackson's inauguration in 1829.[58]

By the middle of March, the tension had become almost unbearable. Now that McLean had been displaced, wrote Adams in a letter to one of his sons, it was only a matter of time before the much-heralded "reform" would begin. And when it did, Adams grimly predicted, there would inevitably be a purge in "the whole swarm of post offices throughout the Union." The "next step" for the postal system, he added sarcastically, "will be to turn it into a police department" and, in brazen defiance of the cherished principle of postal inviolability, to give the executive the power of "fingering . . . all the letters."[59] According to Henry Clay, the clerks' predicament was comparable to that of the inhabitants of a city that had been ravaged by plague: "No one knows who is next to encounter the stroke of death . . . or, which with many of them is the same thing, to be dismissed from office."[60]

Further exacerbating the tension was the considerable uncertainty about just who was in charge. Though Barry was ostensibly the chief presiding officer, the partisan dismissals were coordinated neither by Barry nor by any members of his staff but rather by a tiny band of Jacksonian publicists that included Amos Kendall, Samuel Ingham, and Isaac Hill, led, at least in the opening months of the administration, by Duff Green. Green quickly fell out with the Jacksonians and, still hopeful that Calhoun might someday win the presidency, used the *Telegraph* to lambaste them for the very appointment policy that he had done so much to inspire. Yet during the crucial opening months of the Jackson administration, no one exercised a greater influence over the allocation of jobs. It was a curious position for an individual who in the period prior to the election of 1828 had so savagely criticized the supposedly corrupt manipulation of political patronage under Adams and Monroe.

The Jacksonians' delegation of authority to Green, Kendall, Ingham, and Hill marked something of an innovation in American public life. When Thomas Jefferson brought a new party to power following his inauguration in 1801, he issued a number of frank, believable public statements explaining the rationale for the staff changes that his administration intended to make. When the Jacksonians came to power in 1829, Jackson did nothing of the kind. Rather than taking charge of the appointments policy himself, he permitted party leaders such as Green to run the postal appointments office as a covert operation. At no point during his administration did Jackson issue a public statement explaining in straightforward terms the criteria for the changes that he was overseeing. Equally novel was the delegation of authority to individuals outside the official chain of command. Though Green, Kendall, Ingham, and Hill all had at least a modicum of familiarity with postal procedures, none had ever held a regular appointment in the general post office. Far more important was the extensive network of political contacts that each had cultivated as a party leader during the course of the election campaign. Before long, office seekers got into the habit of writing them directly.

All this backroom maneuvering sparked a good deal of gossip in the political press. Just who, it was asked, was running the government? Should the Jacksonians fail to move decisively to stop the "reckless career of whoever controls the post office," warned the editors of the *National Intelligencer* in September, in an obvious reference to Green, "the total derangement of that department is INEVITABLE."[61] By 1832, opposition publicists began to speak openly of the various party leaders who oversaw the partisan dismissals as the "kitchen cabinet," a phrase that nicely suggested the essential ambiguity of their role. Like the kitchen staff, these men worked primarily behind the scenes, yet like the official Cabinet, they had assumed control of an important branch of executive power. Never before had an incoming administration bestowed so much power in the hands of men unaccustomed to addressing a crowd or even to appearing in public.[62]

Green, Kendall, Ingham, and Hill supported the partisan dismissals for a variety of reasons. For all four, purely personal considerations provided an obvious goad. All but Hill had run up large debts during the course of the campaign: Green's debts ran to some $20,000, Kendall's to $10,000, Ingham's to a large sum that was probably somewhere in between.[63] And Hill was bent on revenge, harboring as he did a burning resentment against the Adamsites for their alleged manipulation of postal patronage in New Hampshire during the election campaign.[64] Thus, all four had an obvious incentive to find places for men upon whom they could rely for financial or moral support. This, in large measure, they did, particularly in the larger and more lucrative post offices in the North and the East.

Even more important than personal considerations was their principled determination to staff the postal system with individuals committed to blocking the further expansion of the central government. Here, too, they were eminently successful. By checking the momentum that the postal system had acquired under McLean, the Jacksonian party leaders sought to restore the republic to the supposedly better days of its youth. In a phrase, theirs was a dismantling operation.[65] Though the Jacksonian party leaders had no intention of reducing the level of postal service, they did doom any possibility that the general post office might soon become the headquarters for a national program of internal improvements. Symptomatic of this narrowing in the ambit of the central government was the subtle transformation in the meaning of the phrase "spoils system." Prior to Jackson's inauguration, when contemporaries spoke of the "spoils system" they ordinarily were referring to the potential *benefits* that the government might confer upon the public at large as, for example, had Tennessee congressman John Bell in his 1829 speech in opposition to the Buffalo–Washington–New Orleans road. Following Jackson's inauguration, however, the meaning of the phrase gradually narrowed to refer merely to the *contracts* and *jobs* that party leaders had the power to bestow upon their supporters. Before long, virtually everyone would forget that it had ever meant anything else.

The Jacksonians' dismantling operation was not without a certain irony. Green, Kendall, and their associates may have been committed to reducing the role of the central government in American public life, yet they themselves had worked much of their lives in the newspaper and stagecoach industries, two of the most heavily subsidized sectors of the American economy. No less ironic was their success as party publicists in creating the familiar image of the archetypal Jacksonian Democrat as a moralistic, egalitarian, and independent-minded foe of government privilege, an image that continues to inform our understanding of this period. While this image closely resembled the kind of individual that Jacksonian party leaders assumed themselves to be, there were in fact few Americans who were less justified in making such a claim.

THE PURGE of the general post office staff got under way by the middle of the summer. In July, Barry dismissed chief clerk Andrew Coyle on the grounds that the postmaster general had a right to employ as his personal assistant an individual who shared his political views. As Coyle's successor, Barry appointed Obadiah Brown, in gratitude, or so Abraham Bradley, Jr., claimed, for Brown's role in writing the official circular that had savaged McLean.[66] By the end of September, the Bradley brothers were dismissed as well, completing the clean sweep of the senior staff that had begun with McLean's resignation the previous

March. As the successor to Abraham Bradley, Jr., Barry chose Charles K. Gardner, a postal clerk who had worked closely with McLean in appointing postal officers loyal to Calhoun. In place of Phineas Bradley, Barry brought in from outside the office Selah Hobbie, a former congressman from New York and the son-in-law of prominent Jacksonian Erastus Root.

The dismissal of the Bradley brothers came at the end of a long summer of political maneuvering. The catalyst was the partisan dismissal of James W. Hawkins of Frankfort, Kentucky, a postmaster who had backed the Adamsites in the election of 1828. "Prepare the public mind," Amos Kendall instructed his political associate Francis P. Blair shortly after the inauguration, for a "revolution" in the government offices that would "strike out of Clay's hands many of his favorite weapons." The dismissal of Hawkins was a means toward this end.[67]

To justify the dismissal to Hawkins's many friends in Kentucky, Kendall set about to blacken Hawkins's reputation. Though the dismissal had clearly been made on partisan grounds, Kendall felt it imprudent to say so outright. Intent upon putting the best possible face on his decision, Kendall secured a mass of financial information from the general post office that purported to demonstrate that Hawkins had failed to keep his accounts in accordance with the law, and contended that his dismissal was therefore justified on the basis of cause, just as it would have been under McLean. To Kendall's embarrassment, however, he soon discovered that the information he had secured failed to sustain his charge; he had either been intentionally misinformed by the general post office staff or, just as likely, had misinterpreted the information he had been given. Kendall's assault upon Hawkins's reputation outraged Abraham Bradley, Jr., who took the extraordinary step of issuing a public letter that cleared Hawkins from any imputation of wrongdoing. During his entire thirty-five-year career, Bradley had never before issued such a blatant challenge to the authority of his official superiors. Infuriated by Bradley's audacity, Kendall responded by issuing a public letter of his own in which he accused Bradley of having conspired to deceive him, an accusation that Bradley indignantly denied.[68] The following day, using Bradley's insubordination as an excuse, Barry dismissed him, at the instigation, according to Phineas Bradley, of "Duff Green & Co." When Phineas protested his brother's dismissal, Barry dismissed him, too.[69]

The dismissal of the Bradleys brought to a close an epoch in the history of the postal system. In the six months following Jackson's inauguration, the Jacksonians had replaced the four most senior postal officers: the postmaster general, the chief clerk, and the first and second assistant postmasters general. Though these men constituted but a small fraction of the total staff, they had traditionally exercised a major influence over the appointment of postmasters, the awarding of mail contracts, and the allocation of funds. Now that the Jacksonians had filled these slots with their own appointees, they could administer the enterprise pretty much as they pleased. No longer would office seekers find themselves frustrated by McLean's well-known refusal to authorize dismissals on partisan grounds. No longer would contractors find themselves stymied by Andrew Coyle's command of postal protocol or the Bradleys' passion for fiscal propriety. "The whole department," lamented Phineas Bradley in October, "is now political."[70] To the relief of the rest of the staff, however, the purge stopped with these four. Kendall might have wished, as he confided to a friend, to "turn adrift at one blow about half of the establishment," but he never got the chance.[71] Having guaranteed that the senior staffers would back the party in power, the Jacksonians had no need to interfere with the rank and file. Two years after Jackson's inauguration, almost 90 percent of the men who had worked in the general post office under McLean remained at their posts, even though over half had backed Adams in the election of 1828.[72]

Far more extensive were the dismissals in the field. In the year following Jackson's inauguration, Barry oversaw the dismissal of over 400 postmasters. By the end of Jackson's administration in 1837, the number of dismissals had risen to at least 973, or 13 percent of all the postmasters in the United States.[73] Though numerically a small percentage of the possible total, the dismissals were highly concentrated in the lucrative offices in New England, the Mid-Atlantic, and the Northwest. Fully 87 percent of the 423 postmasters that the Jacksonians dismissed during their first year in office were from these three sections (see Table 6.1). Breaking down the dismissals by state makes the sectional pattern even more apparent. In Indiana, the Jacksonians dismissed 10 percent of all the postmasters in the state; in New Hampshire, 23 percent; in Delaware, a staggering 46 percent. The comparable totals in the South Atlantic and Southwest never exceeded 8 percent. In Virginia, North Carolina, Georgia, and Alabama, the Jacksonians dismissed just over 1 percent of each state's postmasters; in South Carolina, the home state of Jackson's vice president, John C. Calhoun, they dismissed no one at all.[74]

Table 6.1 The dismissal of postmasters during the first year of the Jackson administration, by section and level of compensation

	Postmasters	Dismissals	Percentage
New England			
$300–	50	19	38.0
$0–299	1,408	91	6.5
Not available	76	0	0.0
Total	1,534	110	7.2
Mid-Atlantic			
$300–	74	28	37.8
$0–299	2,461	147	6.0
Not available	180	9	0.5
Total	2,715	184	6.8
Northwest			
$300–	9	3	33.3
$0–299	870	63	7.2
Not available	115	4	2.6
Total	1,000	72	7.2
South Atlantic			
$300–	44	1	2.3
$0–299	1,438	15	1.0
Not available	143	1	0.1
Total	1,625	17	1.1
Southwest			
$300–	37	11	29.7
$0–299	818	24	2.9
Not available	170	5	2.9
Total	1,025	40	3.9
National			
$300–	220	64	29.1
$0–299	6,995	340	4.9
Not available	684	19	2.8
Total	7,899	423	5.4

Source: postmasters: Register of Officers and Agents (1829); *dismissals:* Charles A. Wickliffe, *Post Office Department—Persons Employed,* 27th Cong., 2nd sess., 1842, H. Rpt. 170 (serial 404).

Note: Dismissals are for the period between March 4, 1829, and March 24, 1830; post office totals are for the year ending March 31, 1829. Compensation is annual. The sections are defined as follows: *New England:* Maine, New Hampshire, Vermont, Massachusetts, Connecticut, Rhode Island; *Mid-Atlantic:* New York, New Jersey, Pennsylvania, Delaware, Maryland, District of Columbia; *Northwest:* Ohio, Indiana, Illinois, Michigan Territory, Wisconsin Territory, Iowa Territory; *South Atlantic:* Virginia, North Carolina, South Carolina, Georgia, Florida Territory; *Southwest:* Missouri, Kentucky, Tennessee, Alabama, Mississippi, Louisiana, Arkansas Territory.

The sectional pattern is even more striking when the postmasterships are broken down by compensation. The Jacksonians dismissed 33 percent of the postmasters making more than $300 in the Northwest, 38 percent in New England, and 38 percent in the Mid-Atlantic. In contrast, in the South Atlantic they dismissed a mere 2 percent of the possible total. The only section that failed to fit the sectional pattern was the Southwest, where the Jacksonians dismissed a substantial 30 percent of all the postmasters earning over $300. Of these dismissals, over 80 percent came from the single state of Kentucky, the political base of Jacksonian party leader Amos Kendall and of the Jacksonians' most formidable political rival, Henry Clay.

The sectional character of the partisan dismissals owed a good deal to the sectional character of the Jacksonian party. Jackson was not only the first president to hail from the Southwest; he was also the first to boast a running mate who came from the same side of the Potomac. Never before had a major party run a presidential campaign in which both the presidential and vice presidential candidates were from the South. Given the Jacksonians' sectional base in the South and West, it should hardly come as a surprise that the Jacksonians used postal patronage to consolidate their political base in those parts of the country where they were relatively weak—New England, the Mid-Atlantic, and the Northwest—while leaving undisturbed the incumbents in those parts of the country in which they were relatively strong—the South Atlantic and, with the exception of Kentucky, the Southwest.

Green laid out the sectional logic that lay behind the Jacksonian strategy in the myriad personal letters that he wrote to his friends and associates in the months preceding Jackson's inauguration. Deeply disturbed by the prospect of a North–West political alliance headed by Adams and Clay, Green was determined to deploy the patronage at his disposal to unite the South and the West in opposition to New England. In this way, Green hoped, the incoming administration would strengthen the Jackson-Calhoun coalition, cripple the opposition, and build a powerful new party that would guarantee Calhoun the presidency in 1832. "Power and patronage," Green assured an associate soon after Jackson's election, "are now in the hands of the Republican party, and you may rest assured that they will remain there for the next twenty years."[75] Though Green himself lost control over postal patronage by the middle of the summer and went into the opposition when Jackson broke with Calhoun, the sectional strategy that he set in motion continued to shape American public life for decades to come. The South perpetuated its control of the central government, observed one contemporary matter-of-factly in 1849, by bestowing postmasterships upon its northern supporters.[76]

Green's hostility toward Adams and Clay stemmed from a variety of considerations. Though Green had few qualms about taking advantage of the public largesse—he had, after all, rescued himself from near-bankruptcy by securing a lucrative mail contract in Missouri—he staunchly opposed all efforts to expand the scope of the central government, convinced that this expansion would threaten the future of the Union. Green found particularly disturbing the prospect that Adams or Clay might take up the banner of antislavery as a rallying cry to create a sectionally based political party in the nonslaveholding states, setting in motion a chain of events that would ultimately put the institution of slavery at risk.[77] Though Green devoted little attention to the slavery question in the *Telegraph,* it was never far from his mind. Green was extraordinarily sensitive to the merest hint that a public figure might seek to raise the issue and took great pride in his role in keeping it off the public agenda. It was part of his "business," Green explained to a friend in 1828, to "prevent the agitation of that question."[78] Having lived for many years in the border state of Missouri, where the institution of slavery was particularly insecure, Green well understood the vulnerability of the peculiar institution to outside assault. To forestall such a frightening eventuality, Green was determined to "carry the war into the enemies' camp" through the "influence of our principles" and, not incidentally, the appointment of postmasters loyal to Jackson and Calhoun.[79]

While such strategic considerations can hardly account entirely for the sectional character of the partisan dismissals, they do help to explain why public figures in different sections of the country, as well as the historians who have followed their lead, have differed so markedly in their assessment of the implications. If, like Congressman Felix Grundy, you hailed from the Jacksonian stronghold of Tennessee, it made a good deal of sense to conclude that the incoming administration had confined its dismissals to "unworthy" postmasters who had committed offenses ranging from drunkenness and dishonesty to "insulting or unaccommodating deportment."[80] For Delaware senator John Clayton, however, Grundy's interpretation was plainly wide of the mark. Hailing as he did from a state that saw almost half of its postmasters dismissed in less than a year, Clayton considered it nothing short of outrageous to contend that the Jacksonians had confined their dismissals to postmasters guilty of some palpable violation of their public trust. This might well be the case south of the Potomac, Clayton conceded. But those who lived north of the Potomac knew hundreds of "worthy citizens" who had been dismissed for no other cause than their opposition to Andrew Jackson in the election of 1828.[81]

HISTORIANS have long explained the partisan dismissals that the Jacksonians oversaw as the inevitable consequence of the triumph of a new political party. Just as President Jefferson dismissed a sizable portion of his political opponents following his election in 1800, so did President Jackson in 1828. Since Jefferson's party remained in power during the intervening twenty-eight years, none of Jefferson's successors felt impelled to make a corresponding change.

But this was not how the dismissals were explained at the time. Had Jackson candidly proclaimed, following Green, that the incoming administration fully intended to reward its friends and punish its enemies, he would have chalked up a minor victory for candor, but at a potentially disastrous cost. To dismiss meritorious public officers to make room for loyal supporters was widely regarded by Jacksonians and anti-Jacksonians alike as a serious abuse of power and even grounds for impeachment. Few were as forthright as New York Jacksonian William L. Marcy, who, echoing Green, boldly announced in 1832 that regardless of how public figures might choose to justify their conduct, in practice they operated on the premise that "to the victor belongs the spoils of the enemy."[82] On the contrary, public figures from across the political spectrum attacked the partisan dismissal of otherwise meritorious public officers as a dangerous precedent that, unless speedily checked, might well put the republic at risk. In the first federal Congress, no less an authority than James Madison had publicly declared that the partisan dismissal of an otherwise meritorious public officer would properly subject the president to impeachment. Forty years later, few saw reason to question Madison's conclusion, which was much cited not only in the anti-Jacksonian press, but also in widely respected treatises on constitutional law such as Story's *Commentaries on the Constitution*.[83] Jackson himself had come close to acknowledging as much in a celebrated letter that he wrote in the months preceding the election of 1824. At the "very moment" that he dismissed an individual from office "on account of his political opinion," Jackson declared, he himself would become a "despot" and, as such, unworthy of the public trust.[84]

Opposition to the partisan dismissals was by no means confined to sticklers for the fine points of constitutional law. To some, the dismissal of postmasters without cause seemed remarkably analogous to the proscription of religious dissenters on account of their unorthodox beliefs, an issue that greatly disturbed those many Americans whose outlook on public life was deeply colored by their knowledge of religious persecution in Europe. Intent upon linking the Jacksonians with bigotry, intolerance, and sectarian squabbling, Delaware senator Clayton filled his attack on the partisan dismissals with highly charged religious terms, such as "sins," "expiation," "ex cathedra," and "heresy." Clayton was particularly disturbed by Tennessee congressman Grundy's contention that the dismissals had been confined to individuals who had failed to uphold their public trust, and he went to great lengths to set Grundy straight. Grundy had fallen into error on this point, Clayton explained, because he hailed from a section of the country whose "political sins" had not yet demanded such an "expiation." "But we," Clayton exploded, "who live north of the Potomac, know . . . hundreds of our worthy citizens who have been removed without any other transgression than that which, according to the orthodox creed emanating *ex cathedra* here, is denominated political heresy."[85] Bolder still was Maine senator John Holmes, who compared the partisan dismissals with the mass murder of 500 senators in ancient Rome that had been engineered by the infamous triumvirate of Lepidus, Octavius, and Mark Anthony. "Proscription *here*," Holmes reminded his Senate colleagues, is "not yet so bloody," yet "in looking round us . . . it would not, I think, require a very fertile fancy to find an analogy to this triumvirate to which I have referred."[86] Not to be outdone was Abelard Reynolds, the ex-postmaster of Rochester, New York, who angrily proclaimed himself to be a victim of the "political pestilence" of the "proscription system" by which the incoming administration had replaced the incumbents at all the important offices who "did not fall down and worship *Baal*."[87]

To dramatize their cause, the Jacksonians' critics portrayed the ex-officeholders as innocent victims of a vengeful party cabal. In every instance in which the incoming administration had singled out a "victim" for "proscription," charged Senator Clayton, its effect had been to destroy his reputation.[88] Particularly outrageous to the Jacksonians' critics was the refusal of Congress to permit ex-officeholders to testify before Congress as to the circumstances of their dismissal. The Jacksonians even blocked Abraham Bradley, Jr., from testifying on his own behalf, a circumstance that turned the dour old clerk overnight into such a cause célèbre that anti-Jacksonian party leaders found it advantageous to mention it as a grievance at the National Republican convention preceding the election of 1832.[89]

The Jacksonians may have successfully blocked the ex-officeholders from testifying before Congress, but they could do nothing to stop them from taking their case to the public. Shortly after his dismissal, Abraham Bradley, Jr., issued a series of stinging public letters in which he ridiculed Barry's notorious ignorance of American geography (Bradley's strong suit), warned that Barry's poor memory seriously unfitted him for the work of his office, and publicly urged him to resign.[90] Even bolder was Andrew Coyle, McLean's former chief clerk, who, shortly after his dismissal, lambasted Barry for "prostituting the department to *party purposes*" and wondered aloud whether Barry had authorized Green to take charge of its affairs. "Has *he* too been advanced to the station of an official confidant?" Coyle asked. "Is he charged with the well-being of the national government? Does *he* direct your movements? and is he, alone, to be held responsible for your official acts? These points, permit me to assure you, are of some importance to the public. They desire to know who in reality is the person upon whom the powers of the national government have devolved."[91]

So notorious were the partisan dismissals that the officeholders' plight even found its way into imaginative fiction. In 1837, Catherine Sedgwick recounted the trials and tribulations of a postal clerk whose principled opposition to President Jackson threatened to prevent him from securing a much-deserved appointment as postmaster of a thriving Massachusetts town.[92] Fifteen years later, Herman Melville touched on a similar theme in "Bartleby the Scrivener," the classic tale of the plight of a clerk in the Washington dead letter office who had been "suddenly removed" by a change in the administration.[93]

Opposition to the partisan dismissal of public officers was so widespread that the Jacksonians found it necessary to devise a variety of stratagems to conceal the true nature of the changes over which they presided. Intent upon blocking a potentially embarrassing Senate investigation, the noted Jacksonian jurist Edward Livingston flatly declared in 1831 that could it be proved that Jackson had dismissed a single public officer on partisan grounds, this would be cause for Jackson's impeachment, and that the investigation should therefore be shifted to the House of Representatives. This was because, under the provisions of the federal Constitution, it was the House that had the responsibility to oversee the prosecution of such a serious offense.[94] John McLean struck a similar note in a letter to a friend. Were he a member of Congress, McLean declared, he would vote for impeachment for such an abuse of power.[95]

Though Livingston's ruse had the desired effect of quashing the potential investigation, it outraged anti-Jacksonians like John Holmes of Maine, who accused him of invoking the "high responsibility" of Jackson's name to mask his true intentions. "Every petty tyrant," Holmes fumed, "is to cover his crimes by this *aegis*. No, sir, the truth must be that neither the president nor his minions can give any good reason for these corrupt and corrupting measures, and they therefore have to resort to silence as their only defense against an indignant and insulted people. They know, and everyone here knows, that the removals have been chiefly made to provide for partisans, and they are ashamed to acknowledge it."[96]

Equally evasive were the Jacksonians in the House. In 1832, for example, one administration critic angrily declared that he had recently read that the Jacksonians had settled on the policy of appointing postmasters "for the purpose of sustaining particular newspapers," by which presumably he meant that they were bestowing public office upon editors who had gone into debt to help finance Jackson's election campaign. It was an allegation that a fair-minded observer of the Jacksonians' appointment policy would have found impossible to deny. Jacksonian stalwart Richard M. Johnson did, however, flatly deny it, adding that the administration had magnanimously decided against prosecuting the newspaper responsible for publishing such a deliberate falsehood, since it was "better that the press should be a little licentious than that it should be put under any restraint."[97]

Precisely how much Jackson knew personally about the partisan dismissals remains an open question. Surprisingly little direct evidence has survived to implicate him in particular dismissals, while the evidence that has survived has tended to exonerate him from any direct involvement in the kinds of changes that Green oversaw. Jackson probably knew a good deal more than he let on, but intentionally concealed his knowledge in order to shield himself from congressional scrutiny. On occasion, he was perfectly capable of blocking an anticipated dismissal, even if the dismissal was earnestly desired by his trusted advisors.

A case in point was Jackson's celebrated endorsement of Solomon Van Rensselaer as postmaster of Albany. Van Rensselaer had initially secured the Albany postmastership in 1822, following a bitter political battle in which his appointment had been vigorously contested by Martin Van Buren, then a United States senator. With Jackson's election, it was widely assumed that Van Buren, now Jackson's secretary of state, would secure his revenge. To frustrate Van Buren's designs, Van Rensselaer joined the horde of expectants who traveled to Washington for Jackson's inauguration, where he secured a personal introduction to Jackson through the intervention of Edward Livingston, an old friend and, like Van Rensselaer, a patrician from a prominent New York family. To impress the old general with his valor, Van Rensselaer was said to have bared his breast in Jackson's presence to reveal the wounds that he had suffered in the War of 1812.[98] Clearly impressed, Jackson assured Van Rensselaer that "your office is sacred." Back in Albany, Van Rensselaer confided to his son that his "little recreation" had proved worthwhile, which indeed it had. Van Rensselaer remained postmaster until 1839, when he was finally dismissed by Van Buren, only to be reappointed by the Whigs in 1841.[99] All in all, it was a suggestive reminder of the extent to which, even after Jackson's election, the gentry-based political order of the Founding Fathers remained intact.

Notwithstanding Jackson's intervention on Van Rensselaer's behalf, his supporters remained adamant in their determination to shield him from the negative publicity that would inevitably accompany the disclosure that he understood the full magnitude of the changes that were taking place. This should come as no surprise, given the unpopularity of the policy with the anti-Jacksonian press, not to mention its highly questionable legal standing. Had Jackson himself been directly implicated in the partisan dismissal of meritorious postal officers in order to make room for party supporters, political opponents might well have pressed for his impeachment. Plainly troubled by the implications of such a disclosure—and, more important, determined to avoid the appearance of partisanship—the editors of the anti-Jacksonian *National Intelligencer* went so far as to declare that they had no idea if the president had been personally consulted with regard to the appointment of *any* postmasters in the United States.[100] Had Jackson had a free hand to run the government as he pleased, the editors added, he would never have sanctioned the policy of "proscription for opinion's sake." The problem, rather, was the "malignant influence" of party insiders. Had Jackson been left to his "own convictions," they felt sure that the course he would have pursued would have been "directly the reverse."[101]

Jackson himself did a good deal to reinforce this impression. Though he almost certainly knew far more about the partisan maneuverings than his supporters let on, he continued to uphold the pretense that nothing had changed. Three years after his inauguration, Jackson saw nothing amiss in challenging his Tennessee friend William Lewis to name a single instance in which his subordinates had dismissed a public officer who had been neither a swindler nor a defaulter.[102] Before long, Jackson's professed ignorance of the changes taking place became a subject of public discussion. What might his ignorance suggest, it was wondered aloud, about his command of the routine operations of the government over which he ostensibly presided? How, wondered one irate Floridian in 1830, could Jackson possibly persist in contending that public officers had been dismissed exclusively on account of their "oppression or defalcation"? The answer, Van Buren innocently explained, was simple. Jackson had simply forgotten that, in all matters pertaining to appointments and dismissals, his administration had long since refused, as a matter of policy, to give *any* explanation for the changes it found necessary to make.[103]

Even after Jackson left office, the issue would not go away. When Jackson was on his deathbed, he was supposed to have asked a trusted minister what posterity would blame him for most. Of all the questionable acts in Jackson's life, the minister replied, the single act that posterity would find most reprehensible was Jackson's policy of "proscription for opinion's sake." Jackson was astonished. During his entire administration, the dying man insisted, he had only turned out a single subordinate—a postmaster—on his direct personal authority. Though Jackson's principal nineteenth-century biographer, James Parton, duly reported this anecdote in his 1861 biography of Jackson's public career, even he was unconvinced. The partisan dismissals, Parton declared, were "an evil so great and so difficult to remedy, that if all his other public acts had been perfectly wise and right, this single feature of his administration would suffice to render it deplorable."[104] Jackson was never impeached, yet his apparent complicity in the partisan dismissals shaped the outlook of many historians toward his presidency for almost a century after his death. Not until the middle of the twentieth century would historians finally absolve him of responsibility for his complicity in the introduction of the "spoils system" and, in this way, for significantly weakening the role of the central government in American public life.

No PUBLIC OFFICER was more directly affected by the political unpopularity of the partisan dismissals than Postmaster General Barry. As the head of the largest and most geographically extended branch of the central government, Barry was entrusted with the difficult task of justifying the changes that the party leaders wished to make. This did not prove to be easy. Few of the dismissals that the party leaders had sought could be justified according to the strict criteria that McLean had established, and which, in his inaugural address, Jackson had taken pains to defend. Thus, in order to comply with the party leaders' demands, Barry had two choices. Either he could accuse his subordinates of offenses that they had not committed, or he could admit that he had found it necessary to change the rules of the game. Initially, Barry chose to play it safe. He lodged—or, as the phrase went, "preferred"—trumped-up charges against each postmaster whom the party leaders wished to replace. Typically, Barry charged the postmaster with having circulated Adamsite campaign literature or, better still, with having fiddled the books, a charge that, given the byzantine complexity of postal accounting, was almost impossible to refute. Next, Barry leaked the charge to the Jacksonian press, which, in turn, hailed the dismissal as a vindication of Jackson's assault on executive tyranny. The Jacksonians had *not* embarked on an indiscriminate policy of partisan dismissals, Barry reassured his daughter three months after his appointment, notwithstanding what she might have read in the press. Dismissals had been confined to those postmasters who had practiced "abuses"; they were "not done in other cases."[105]

Insiders knew better. "It appears to us not a little singular," editorialized Baltimore editor Hezekiah Niles in July, that "nineteen-twentieths" of the dismissals that had taken place since Jackson's inauguration had occurred in precisely those sections of the country that boasted the "greatest safety and promptitude in the mails."[106] Particularly notorious was the dismissal of Hartford postmaster Benjamin Norton a mere one day after he had officially secured his appointment.[107] Since Norton had not yet taken office, he could hardly be accused of having done anything wrong. Picking up on this point, political satirists coined the phrase "to Nortonize" to refer to the politically expedient dismissal of an officeholder who had somehow run afoul of the party in power.[108] In his *Political Reminiscences,* one-time Jacksonian activist John Barton Derby prepared a satirical how-to guide on how the process worked. To secure a postmastership, Derby observed, the office seeker must first prepare a petition to the postmaster general containing the signatures of "half a dozen Jacksonmen" declaring himself to be an "original Jacksonian" and the incumbent an opponent of the "glorious Administration" of the "immortal Jackson," the "father of his country." Having prepared the petition, the office seeker must next enlist some noted Jacksonian to take it to the general post office, taking care to give his personal assurance that the signatures were genuine and that the change would be "beneficial to the *'cause.'*" After glancing briefly at the petition, Barry would jot the word *"change"* on its back and "in a trice, the head of the postmaster . . . flies from his shoulders."[109]

By June 1829, Barry found it impossible to maintain the pretense any longer that the partisan dismissals were justified according to the strict criteria that had been laid down under McLean. After all, not even the most ingenious of Barry's subordinates could invent plausible reasons for dismissing postmasters whose meritorious public service was a matter of public record. Even more embarrassingly, Barry repeatedly found himself in the awkward position of impugning the reputation of postmasters whom for one reason or another he did not wish to offend.

The most celebrated case of this kind involved James Platt, the postmaster of Utica, New York. In June, Barry agreed to dismiss Platt in order to make room for a deserving Jacksonian, even though, as it turned out, Platt himself had backed Jackson in the preceding campaign.[110] To cushion the blow, Barry issued a testimonial declaring that his decision had not been occasioned by any charges affecting Platt's "moral character" and that, at least as far as he was concerned, Platt's "personal standing" remained "unimpeached." Barry's testimonial was quickly seconded by McLean, who issued a testimonial of his own on Platt's behalf, upholding the reputation of a trustworthy public officer even as he advertised his revulsion at the partisan dismissals that the Jacksonians had set in motion following his resignation the previous March.[111]

Barry's public statement may have mollified Platt, but it provided scant comfort to administration critics in the press. When the editors of the *National Intelligencer* learned that Barry had dismissed a public officer without having preferred any charges against him, they could hardly suppress their indignation. Such a flagrant abuse of power, the editors fumed, was no different than the partisan manipulation of public office under the Crown. Like George III, Barry was a *"single individual"* who had arrogated to himself the power of "farming out all the offices in the country" as "rewards to his personal adherents." Was it not to prevent such a thing, the *Intelligencer* railed, that the Founding Fathers had "laid the foundation of a Republic?"[112]

To prevent these embarrassments from recurring, Barry found it necessary to modify the position that Jackson had sketched out in his inaugural address. Three days after he exonerated Platt, Barry outlined his new position in another letter to his daughter. Echoing Green's preinauguration *Telegraph* editorials almost word for word, Barry now explained that, while it was doubtless important to exercise restraint in "punishing enemies," it was equally important for him to "reward" his "friends." Henceforth, "public employments" must "necessarily" be based upon the principle of "rotation in office." No longer would Barry pretend that every dismissal had been called forth by an antecedent "abuse."[113]

Barry's invocation of the principle of rotation in office owed a good deal to the classical republican revival that Green had done so much to promote. The principle itself was familiar to all students of political thought, having been championed by the celebrated seventeenth-century English political theorist James Harrington as an antidote to the abuses of an entrenched officeholding elite and an alternative to the indirect participation of the citizenry in the affairs of state through the election of representatives.[114] Harrington's ideas were well known to the Founding Fathers and continued to find their way into college curricula in the early republic, often at second or third hand. Barry himself had almost certainly encountered Harrington's ideas as a student at the College of William and Mary and took great satisfaction in his ability to invest the policy with the best Harringtonian gloss. Rotation in office, Barry explained to his daughter, was necessary to prevent the incumbents from assuming that their offices were their personal property and, in this way, from transforming the United States into a "monarchy," a prospect that Barry seems greatly to have feared was fast approaching under Adams. Postmasters might "cry out robbery" when they were dismissed, but it would not "suit a republic" to take them at their word: "Republics are necessarily agitated and excited; when they cease to be so, the calm ends in monarchy and despotism."[115]

Party leaders clarified this new policy by including a justification of rotation in office in Jackson's first annual message in December 1829. Flatly rejecting McLean's presumption that public officers should be permitted to remain in office for as long as they remained faithful to their trust, Jackson declared that "no man" had any more "intrinsic right" to public office than another. Should public officers be permitted to remain in office indefinitely, Jackson explained, this would tend to convert public office into a "species of property" that offered few concrete benefits for the public at large, however convenient it may have been for the officeholder himself. "I cannot but believe," Jackson added, "that more is lost by the long continuance of men in office than is generally to be gained by their experience." Even if public officers *had* managed to acquire valuable expertise while in office, Jackson insisted, this was cause for concern. Public offices ought to be made so "plain and simple" that all "men of intelligence" could "readily qualify themselves" for the work. In certain instances, Jackson conceded, the dismissal of a meritorious public officer might produce "individual distress." Yet he contended that it should not be understood to be a personal affront, as it had been under McLean. On the contrary, public officers should regard their dismissal with satisfaction, since, by encouraging rotation in office—a "leading principle" in the "republican creed"—it would give "healthful action to the system."[116]

Jacksonian publicists took Jackson's justification for the new policy more or less at face value and praised rotation in office as a notable contribution to democratic theory. Administration critics knew better. Rotation in office, charged Edward Everett's brother Alexander H. Everett in 1832, was nothing but a "stale sophistry" that the Jacksonians invoked when they became "ashamed" of the need to fabricate charges against the postmasters that they wished to dismiss on partisan grounds.[117]

THE CHANGES in the appointment process that Jackson had codified in his first annual address had far reaching implications for American public life. By creating a mechanism for the periodic replacement of a large portion of the lucrative offices in the postal system, the largest and most geographically dispersed source of federal employment, the Jacksonians established the technical preconditions for the mass party, a fundamentally new institution that, along with the voluntary association, was one of the most notable organizational innovations of the day. So enduring was the Jacksonians' achievement that the organization they created, the Democratic party, has figured prominently in national politics ever since. No less important, the Jacksonians' critics quickly established a similar organization, the Whig party, which competed for national office with the Democrats for twenty years before falling victim in the 1850s to the looming sectional crisis between North and South.

Party competition, of course, was hardly new. During the preceding forty years, Federalists and Republicans had competed for Congress and the presidency, while a bewildering variety of parties had competed for public office in the individual states. The Jacksonians' achievement lay in their creation of the party as a permanent organization with a life of its own. Though this new institution bore a certain resemblance to the older, gentry-based parties that had loomed so large in American public life in the period between 1788 and 1828, its organizers quickly abandoned the deferential style of electioneering that the Founding Fathers had taken for granted in favor of an avowedly participatory approach to the recruitment of electoral support. For this reason, it has become customary to term the party that the Jacksonians created a *mass* party and to term these older parties *gentry* parties, or *parties of notables*. Though the "mass" to whom party leaders appealed remained tightly restricted to the white men who made up the bulk of the electorate, this group was far larger than the tiny circle of local notables to whom party leaders had appealed in the past. Like the voluntary associations, whose methods party leaders were quick to emulate, the mass party became a key element in the democratization of American public life.[118]

The genuine novelty of the Jacksonians' patronage policy is worth stressing, given the fascination of historians with the percentage of men whom they dismissed. This preoccupation dates back to the 1830s and was fully shared by the leading public men of the day. In the first edition of his *Democracy,* for example, Tocqueville mistakenly observed that he was "not aware" of a single instance in which Jackson had allowed a public officer to "retain his place beyond the first year which succeeded his election."[119] Twenty years later, the veteran Jacksonian Thomas Hart Benton quite rightly took Tocqueville to task for exaggerating the magnitude of the change. Loyal Democrat to the end, he did take pains to add that had Tocqueville visited the United States following the Whigs' victory in the election of 1840, he would have been closer to the mark.[120]

If Tocqueville greatly exaggerated the magnitude of the partisan dismissals, twentieth-century historians have gone to the opposite extreme. There was, observed the eminent Jacksonian scholar Robert V. Remini in a recent summary of this point of view, "nothing new" in the Jacksonians' appointments policy: "Every intelligent man knew this . . . There never was a purge, never a bloodletting, never a reign of terror . . . For the entire eight years of his presidency a little more than ten percent of all officeholders were replaced. When these figures are considered in light of normal replacements due to death and resignation or those whose contracts had expired, plus people dismissed for incompetence and dishonesty, they constitute a very credible record."[121]

Remini's summary is a valuable corrective to the older view, which exaggerated the magnitude of the staff changes that the Jacksonians introduced. But in his determination to exonerate the Jacksonians, he subtly reinforces the older tradition by describing these changes in frankly moralistic terms: Had the Jacksonians dismissed a higher percentage of officeholders, Remini seems to imply, their record would presumably have been less "credible" and therefore open to censure. In fact, as noted earlier, in the most lucrative offices the percentage was considerably higher, averaging over 30 percent in New England, the Mid-Atlantic, and the Northwest. Even more important was the criteria the Jacksonians used to justify the dismissals. The partisan dismissal of postmasters helped Jackson's party leaders pay off their campaign debts; rotation in office changed the rules of the game.

THE POSTAL SYSTEM buttressed the emerging mass parties in a variety of ways. Most obviously, it provided the Jacksonians, and later the Whigs, with the necessary financial incentives to reward the army of campaign workers that party leaders relied upon to rally support for their cause among the public at large. The *"mass"* of the party, as Congressman Everett reminded McLean in the summer preceding the election of 1828, was bound together not by common principles, but rather by the "hope of office, and its honors and emoluments."[122] Once it became plain that the incoming Jackson administration intended to make good on Green's threat to purge a large portion of the existing staff, the office seekers redoubled their efforts to get the long-anticipated purge under way. "There seems not to be a poor devil of a Jackson man in Kentucky," Amos Kendall wrote a political associate in July, who was not in Washington "gaping for an office."[123] Before long, even high-minded critics of the Jacksonians' appointment policy found themselves forced to admit that the opposition had no choice but to emulate the Jacksonians' example. To defeat the Jacksonians at the polls, Delaware congressman John Clayton told McLean in 1833, the opposition had no choice but to adopt rotation in office as a rallying cry. "Without it," Clayton warned, the new party would be "crushed by the officeholders, against whom there can be brought no sufficiently powerful countervailing force."[124]

Pressure for the partisan dismissals came primarily from below. It was not the party leaders, but the cadre men who set the process in motion. Intent upon securing their anticipated reward, they left party leaders with no choice but to include more and more offices in the expanding web. When the Whigs won their first presidential election in 1840, they proved equally adept at rewarding friends and punishing enemies. In the first five months following William Henry Harrison's inauguration in March 1841, the incoming administration dismissed almost twice as many postmasters as Barry had in four years (see Table 6.2). Following the surprise victory of James K. Polk in the election of 1844, one Democratic cadre man provided an unusually frank assessment of his views on this score. Furious with Polk for hinting that the incoming administration might pursue a cautious "milk and water course" with respect to dismissals, he reminded the deputy postmaster general of all the sacrifices that he and his fellow cadre men had endured during the course of the campaign. "We are not disposed," he warned, "to fight and toil, spend our time, our strength, and our substance, year

Table 6.2 The dismissal of postmasters, 1829–1841, by section and presidential administration

	Postmasters	Dismissals	Percentage
1829–1833 (Jackson)			
New England	1,534	162	10.6
Mid-Atlantic	2,715	284	10.5
Northwest	1,000	108	10.8
South Atlantic	1,625	39	2.4
Southwest	1,025	69	6.7
Total	7,898	662	8.4
1837–1841 (Van Buren)			
New England	1,967	193	9.8
Mid-Atlantic	3,666	255	7.0
Northwest	2,123	243	11.4
South Atlantic	2,297	50	2.2
Southwest	1,777	97	5.5
Total	11,830	838	7.1
1841 (Harrison-Tyler)			
New England	2,032	291	14.3
Mid-Atlantic	3,663	544	14.9
Northwest	2,953	189	6.4
South Atlantic	2,397	28	1.2
Southwest	2,364	33	1.3
Total	13,409	1,085	8.1

Source: postmasters: *Register of Officers and Agents* (1829–1841); *dismissals:* Wickliffe, *Post Office Department—Persons Employed.*

Note: For a definition of the sections, see Table 6.1. The totals cover the periods, respectively, between March 4, 1829, and March 3, 1833; between March 4, 1837, and March 3, 1841; and between March 4 and July 16, 1841.

after year, to keep a set of sycophantic, crawling, and rascally Whigs in office." Should the Democrats fail to make the anticipated dismissals, he would never again support a presidential candidate who did not "assure his friends beforehand, that he will do them and his party justice in this particular."[125]

The services that political appointees provided the party in power extended well beyond their support in the election campaign. Once in office, they helped to consolidate the political base of their party through the skillful deployment of artfully crafted public appeals, their vigorous use of the franking privilege, their assistance at party-sponsored functions, and, most important, their daily contact with the public. "A village postmaster with the franking privilege and only ten dollars per annum income," explained one Jacksonian publicist in defending the mass dismissals, "has more influence than a city postmaster with $5,000; and when we take into account how many thousand postmasters there are throughout the Union, we can readily estimate their combined influence" in shaping the course of events.[126]

None of this was entirely new with the Jacksonians. Ever since the adoption of the federal Constitution, public figures had recognized the political value of local postmasterships. And ever since 1820, when Martin Van Buren engineered the dismissal of two postmasters in upstate New York, the partisan dismissal of postmasters could be a subject of national public concern.[127] But rarely before had party leaders marshaled their resources in such a systematic way. And never before had they deployed postal patronage so deliberately to shape the attitudes of the public at large, rather than to cultivate the support of the tiny circle of gentry leaders who had long dominated American public life.

This newer, more systematic approach to the recruitment of electoral support was not without a certain ambiguity. To reach this larger and more heterogeneous audience, party leaders came to rely on cadre men to perform tasks ranging from the publication of party literature to the organization of party conventions and other party-sponsored events. Rarely before had party leaders tried so determinedly to bypass local notables in their efforts to reach the public. Rarely before had they held the independent judgment of ordinary voters in such high esteem. And never before had they invested more time, money, and energy in shaping the opinions of the very electorate whose independence they so enthusiastically proclaimed.

*   *   *

JUST AS THE Jacksonians' patronage policy helped to shape the electoral process, so too it had a major effect on postal administration. In the absence of systematic data on delivery times, error rates, and the incidence of theft, there is no easy way to determine whether the partisan dismissals reduced the level of service from the impressive heights it had attained under McLean. But many informed contemporaries certainly thought they had. Beginning in the summer of 1829, a significant portion of the press, led by the generally reliable *National Intelligencer* and *Niles's Weekly Register,* dramatically increased its coverage of postal mishaps of all kinds. Not since the winter of 1787, when opposition printers in Philadelphia and New York had accused postal officers of holding back periodicals hostile to the federal Constitution, had the press subjected the postal system to such an enormous torrent of editorial abuse.

None of the editors treated these failings as part of a deliberate design. It was simply inconceivable that public officers might intentionally reduce the level of postal service. Yet neither did they blame them on bad weather, poor roads, or other circumstances that were obviously outside of the Jacksonians' control. Rather, they charged the Jacksonians with having gutted an effective, highly skilled civil service solely to provide employment for a cadre of party hacks.

Initially, the editors confined their critique of the Jacksonians' appointments policy to the dismissal of such a large number of talented men. Barry's financial embarrassments, the *National Intelligencer* explained in 1830, were "justly imputable" not to the supposed shortcomings of Barry's appointees, but rather to the dismissal of the Bradley brothers.[128] Soon, however, the editors broadened their critique. In June 1830, *Niles's* featured a story about the conviction for mail robbery of Christian Weirich, the postmaster of Claysville, Pennsylvania, and, as editor Hezekiah Niles took pains to add, a Jackson appointee.[129] Seven months later, it featured a similar story about Mortimer Cunningham, the "newly-made" postmaster of Abington, Maryland.[130] The following May, Niles duly noted that he himself had recently been a victim of theft, having received through the postal system a letter from which someone had pilfered a $5 bank note, payment for a year's subscription to *Niles's Weekly Register.* The following October, Niles had still further cause for alarm. "AGAIN!" his headline screamed. Weirich's successor as Claysville postmaster, Green Van Sickle, had himself been convicted of robbing the mail.[131] The conclusion seemed unmistakable. The postal system was in an "awful state," Niles editorialized: "There are *many* Weirichs and Van Sickles, who, not 'rewarded' to the extent of their wishes, are in the habit of robbing the mails. A week hardly elapses without an incident of this kind." And there could be no doubt, he added, that the "alarming progress" of the institution was directly traceable to the dismissal of "faithful officers" to make room for *"politicians."*[132]

Press coverage of crooked postmasters was nothing new. What was new was the connection that Niles made between this misconduct and the partisan dismissals. He had no doubt that the two were related. Like the partisan dismissals, Niles observed, the thefts were "depredations": the latter against "private property," the former against "political rights." And since Jackson's inauguration, both kinds of depredations had greatly increased and indeed were inextricably linked, the inevitable product of the subordination of postal administration to the needs of the mass party. "The 'monster party,' " Niles moralized, "should never have entered into the post office department."[133] Should Barry resign, Niles added, he would willingly contribute $200 for his pension, "provided a competent man was put in his place, politics being kicked out of the department—into which they ought never to have entered."[134]

WHETHER OR NOT the Jacksonians' appointment policy reduced the level of service for the public at large, as the Washington editors charged, there can be little doubt that the Jacksonians' contracting policy quickly ran the enterprise into debt. This unprecedented event prompted Congress in 1834 and 1835 to undertake an extensive investigation of Jacksonian postal policy that culminated with the passage of the Post Office Act of 1836. "No department of the government," Martin Van Buren later reminisced, "had ever before been subject to so severe an ordeal."[135]

The crux of the problem was Barry's inability to prevent his subordinates from awarding lavish mail contracts to stagecoach proprietors with little regard to cost, a circumstance that was exacerbated by an unusually generous route bill that Congress enacted in 1832. The consequences were predictable. In 1823, the general post office paid the ten largest mail contractors in the country $118,000 a year for carrying the mail; by 1833, this total had increased to $439,000, an increase of over 300 percent.[136] No improvement in level of service could possibly have justified such an enormous increase. In fact, the price rise was largely due to an enormous increase in new stagecoach service in the South and the West, along with a comparable increase of existing stagecoach service in the North and the East. "Stage mania" was how Abraham Bradley, Jr., described the result, and he was very nearly right.[137]

Even Jacksonians found these excesses disturbing, notwithstanding the obvious embarrassment that the criticisms posed. In an 1835 report, North Carolina Jacksonian Henry W. Connor exposed the myriad shortcomings of Barry's administration of the postal system. Since Jackson's inauguration in 1829, Connor concluded, the postal system had been administered "without frugality, system, intelligence, or adequate public utility," while the payments that Barry had lavished on the mail contractors had "run into wild excesses."[138] Nowhere was the over-payment of mail contractors more notorious than in Kentucky, where, as Martin Van Buren candidly admitted in his *Autobiography*, Congressman Richard M. Johnson found it impossible to "check the cupidity of his friends."[139] Particularly outrageous was the practice of awarding certain mail contractors "extra allowances" for improvements in service that the general post office negotiated *after* having entered into the basic agreement to carry the mail. Virginia stagecoach proprietor William Smith proved so successful at this ruse that pundits quickly dubbed him "Extra Billy" Smith, a nickname he retained for the rest of his life. Equally successful was Phineas Bradley who, following his dismissal, traded on his extensive knowledge of postal procedure to net himself a fortune as a stagecoach lobbyist. "All's well that end's well," Bradley later remarked to a friend, reflecting on the money he had made in his second career.[140]

Given Barry's inability to maintain even a modicum of control over the contracting process, it was inevitable that he would soon find it impossible to cover his costs. After all, the postal surplus had been dwindling for years, leaving the postmaster general with little margin for error. For a time, Barry did his best to conceal his financial condition by privately borrowing money from banks. He knew that such conduct was highly suspect, since under the federal Constitution Congress was the only government body empowered to raise revenue on the credit of the general treasury. But he justified it by claiming that he was borrowing against the credit not of the general treasury but of the general post office. Among the bankers who lent Barry money was Wall Street trader James Hamilton, who, though a devoted Jacksonian, was prudent enough to secure Jackson's personal guarantee that the arrangement had the sanction of the party in power.[141]

As Barry's position worsened, so did the level of service. Unable to cover his costs, Barry resorted to the expedient of delaying the payment of mail contractors for work they had already performed. Some contractors went unpaid for as long as eight months. In response, a few stopped carrying the mail altogether. Before long, the situation became desperate. By January 1834, according to one Mississippian, Barry's policy had led to the "utter breaking up" of the postal system in his state: "There never was anything like it before."[142] By March, Barry's financial standing had become so compromised that mail contractors began to openly lobby Congress to make an appropriation to bail him out.[143] Without a congressional appropriation, warned Gales and Seaton of the *National Intelligencer*, it would be impossible to prevent the "whole machine" from "running down," while forcing in certain parts of the country the outright suspension of the transmission of the mails.[144] Significantly, the editors flatly denied the widely circulating rumor that the Jacksonians had deliberately held back the transmission of newspapers hostile to the party in power. There might be a few "slaves to party," the editors conceded, but the real problem was not the partisan behavior of Jackson's appointees; it was Barry's inability to pay the contractors who carried the mail.[145]

Even more troubling was the notorious fact that contracting procedures soon acquired a decidedly partisan cast. Before long, it became taken for granted that if you wished to secure a lucrative mail contract it would be advantageous to make a contribution to the party in power. Sometimes contractors made a cash award to a party newspaper; occasionally they emerged as party leaders themselves. In Pennsylvania and New York, according to Anne Royall, the Jacksonians expected mail contractors James Reeside and Isaac Avery to deliver the "republican" vote.[146] One humorist described how the process worked. Under the Jacksonians, postal officers got in the habit of awarding two separate contracts, a low contract to please Congress, and a much larger contract to give the Jacksonians "plenty of pocket money as extra wages tu make 'em be active all over the country in hoorain, and making speeches and resolutions, 'cause they work for 'emselves as they work for me."[147] In reviewing this policy in 1840, Democratic Postmaster General John Niles summarized its effects. Mail contractors, Niles confided to a political associate back home, had by this time become the "most noisy and abusive partisans in the whole country, and they will all come on here to be paid in good jobs and contracts. This was the case, to some extent, when General Jackson came in, and was the ruin of poor Barry."[148]

By November 1833, Barry's indebtedness became impossible to conceal. In that month, Anne Royall helped to break the story that Washington insiders like Congressman John Floyd of Virginia had "long expected." Notwithstanding Barry's repeated assurances to the contrary, the postal system was as much as $800,000 in debt, fully 30 percent of its total annual revenue.[149] "Some animated proceedings," Hezekiah Niles predicted, "will probably grow out of these transactions of the postmaster general."[150] He was not to be disappointed.

In June 1834, the Senate committee on the post office and post roads issued the first of a series of increasingly critical congressional reports. Speaking for the majority was Thomas Ewing of Ohio; speaking for the minority was Felix Grundy of Tennessee. Though Ewing and Grundy differed on many particulars, both agreed that the postal system was deeply in debt and that Barry had intentionally concealed his indebtedness by secretly borrowing large sums from banks.[151]

Ewing's report consisted of a searing indictment of the Jacksonians' administration of the postal system. Under the federal Constitution, Ewing declared, Congress reserved to itself the power to borrow money on the credit of the government. Thus, Barry's bank loans were plainly illegal. In addition, Ewing exposed a number of irregular contracting procedures, including a complicated price-fixing scheme in which two leading mail contractors paid postal clerk Obadiah Brown a financial gratuity in return for Brown's assistance in negotiating an agreement to fix the cost of passenger fares on the National Road in Pennsylvania, which was at this time one of the most heavily traveled routes in the country.[152]

Ewing had mostly refrained from editorializing in his report, content to let the facts speak for themselves. His Senate colleague and fellow committee member Samuel Southard of New Jersey was noticeably less restrained. In a major speech on the Jacksonians' administration of the postal system that he delivered shortly after the publication of Ewing's report, Southard declared that Ewing's investigation had revealed evidence of "more misconduct and maladministration" than was "ever known to exist in any department of any government."[153] While Ewing had scrupulously refrained from implicating President Jackson in the rapidly growing scandal, Southard felt no such constraint. "Did the president know the facts?" Southard asked rhetorically. "Or was he intentionally imposed on? Did he mean to deceive Congress and the country? Or was he himself deceived? In either case, how has he discharged his duty? . . . Did he not know that the money had been borrowed? And was it right, was it fit, in his high office, to conceal that knowledge from Congress, until a committee of investigation exposed it?"[154]

Speaking for the administration was Felix Grundy, who did his best to explain away the financial irregularities that Ewing had exposed. This did not prove to be easy. Though Grundy freely conceded that Barry had borrowed money from banks, Grundy refused to term Barry's conduct "illegal," preferring instead to term it "extra-legal," since Barry had relied on the credit of the postal system and not the general treasury. Had Barry refused to secure the loans, Grundy added, the postal system would have "gone down," and given its importance to the public at large, it would have been better for Barry to have "done almost anything" than to permit this to happen.[155]

Grundy did his best to defend the administration, but few other Jacksonians saw fit to take up the cause. Not even Amos Kendall seems to have had the stomach for the fight, freely conceding in retrospect that Barry had been but "feebly defended."[156] Of the few who did speak in the administration's defense, the most notable was Isaac Hill, now a New Hampshire senator. Taking the offensive, Hill attributed the postal deficit not to Barry's mismanagement but rather to Congress's insatiable appetite for more post routes. And since it was Congress and not the postmaster general who had put these new routes in service, it was Congress and not Barry who should be held accountable for Barry's inability to cover his costs.[157]

Notwithstanding the best efforts of Grundy and Hill, their Senate colleagues remained unimpressed. On June 27, 1834, Daniel Webster of Massachusetts introduced a resolution flatly declaring Barry's bank loans to be "illegal and void." Bowing to the judgment of their peers, even Grundy and Hill gave the resolution their support, which passed without dissent, making it, as Hezekiah Niles duly observed, "one of the most decisive and remarkable things on the journal of that body."[158]

EWING'S INVESTIGATION was but the first in a series of hostile congressional probings that dragged on for almost a year. Particularly devastating for the Jacksonians was the publication of Henry W. Connor's highly critical report in February 1835. Everyone expected the Whigs to lambaste the Jacksonians, but when fellow Jacksonians joined their voice to the chorus, it was obvious that something was seriously wrong. Immediately after its publication, Obadiah Brown resigned, unable to refute the charge that he personally profited from an agreement with a mail contractor. "This is the age of novelties," commented Hezekiah

Niles sarcastically, upon hearing the news: "Since the 'beginning,' perhaps, no *chief clerk* ever made such a resignation!"[159] By the end of the spring, Jackson found it necessary to order Barry's dismissal as well. After all, as one Virginia senator explained, "It is not Obadiah that has tied all these knots . . . All the curses of the anathema ought not to be denounced against him alone."[160] To cushion the blow, Jackson appointed Barry minister to Spain, ostensibly to improve his health. En route to his new assignment, Barry died at sea, a broken man. "Poor little fellow," remarked his former postal colleague Phineas Bradley, with mingled pity and contempt.[161]

Intent upon restoring a modicum of order to the enterprise, Jackson appointed Amos Kendall as Barry's successor. It proved to be an excellent choice. A capable administrator, Kendall restored the postal system to financial solvency within less than two years, effectively eliminating postal finance as a political issue. Diligent and well organized, he brought to the general post office the same kind of administrative energy that it had enjoyed under McLean. But, though he deserves much credit, it would be a mistake to attribute this turnaround to Kendall alone. No less important was the commercial boom that coincided with Kendall's appointment, which in three years increased annual postal revenue by almost 50 percent. This briefly generated a large surplus, which Kendall promptly spent on an express mail service that was far grander than anything McLean had ever overseen.[162] Not surprisingly, Jacksonian publicists overlooked the boom and credited the turnaround to Kendall. Postal insiders knew better. The recent upsurge in postal revenue, explained Phineas Bradley to Ohio congressman Elisha Whittlesey in the fall of 1835, was attributable not to Kendall's "wisdom and justice &c. &c." but to "business causes."[163]

Kendall's appointment was but one of the changes that the Barry scandals set in motion. Another was the passage of the Post Office Act of 1836, which reorganized the general post office and introduced a number of accounting checks that were intended to prevent a recurrence of the abuses that had prevailed under Barry.[164] It was the "concurrent opinion" of Democrats as well as Whigs, explained Whig congressman Hiland Hall, in the most detailed account of the circumstances surrounding its enactment, that the mismanagement of the postal system had been largely due to the want of a legal check on its disbursements.[165] The Post Office Act of 1836 was a means to this end. Though Amos Kendall, as postmaster general, assisted in the drafting of the bill and made a number of detailed suggestions as to how it might be improved, he was neither its chief inspiration nor its principal architect.[166] Rather, it was the product of a bipartisan congressional effort that was led by the Whigs Hiland Hall of Vermont and George N. Briggs of Massachusetts, and the Democrat Abijah Mann of New York.[167] Indeed, for a time Jacksonian party leaders actually opposed the bill, fearful that it would embarrass the administration by exposing its shortcomings to public view and convinced that it was a mere "electioneering device" to help defeat Van Buren in the election of 1836. After all, the Washington *Globe* added, the postal system could not be "revolutionized" overnight. But in the end, even the Jacksonians eventually swung around to its support, convinced, like their Whig critics, that the reputation of the postal system could be salvaged in no other way.[168]

THE IMPACT of the Barry scandals extended well beyond its role in shaping postal administration. For a brief interval between the publication of Ewing's majority report in 1834 and the election of 1836, it seemed as if the issue might well come to rival Jackson's assault on the Bank of the United States as a defining issue in American public life. "The post office establishment," warned jurist Joseph Story in 1833, "is susceptible of abuse to such an alarming degree . . . that if ever the people are to be corrupted, or their liberties are to be prostrated, this establishment will furnish the most facile means, and be the earliest employed to accomplish such a purpose."[169] By 1835, it looked to many as if Story's nightmare vision had come true. For South Carolina senator John C. Calhoun, the investigations had revealed nothing less than a grand conspiratorial design against popular liberty. "We see here," he moralized, after surveying the various congressional reports, something of the "rotten system" that was "spreading corruption through the whole country" and which was "more dangerous and more disgraceful" than any of the abuses that had existed in the "most corrupt ages of the Roman republic." During his twenty-two year tenure as a public officer, Calhoun added, he had witnessed nothing that had been "half so much calculated to impair the public confidence."[170] For Calhoun's South Carolina colleague William Preston, the issue was far too important to be treated as merely a question of partisan gain. The corruption in the postal system, Preston declared, had become "so manifest to the public eye" that no one could be found to defend it. "Why should we stir up party feeling now?" Preston asked imploringly, discouraging any further Jacksonian attempts to excuse Barry's failings. "What object can we hope to obtain? We have been beaten."[171]

Few contemporaries viewed the Barry scandals with greater concern than the crusading Jacksonian journalist Anne Royall. Between the initial disclosure of Barry's indebtedness in November 1833 and his resignation in 1835, no issue—not the tariff, not Indian removal, not even President Jackson's refusal to recharter the Bank of the United States and his subsequent decision to deposit the federal revenue in other, non–federally chartered banks—took up more space in Royall's hardhitting political newspaper, *Paul Pry*. "No one knew the secrets and corruption of the party from A. to Z. better than I," Royall confided to a North Carolina congressman shortly after the scandals broke, adding that, unless there was a "radical change" in the general post office, the postal system would "completely control the presidential election."[172] Indeed, Royall soon became convinced that it posed an even greater threat to popular liberty than the Bank of the United States, which, like the good Jacksonian she was, Royall soundly denounced as well. The postal system, Royall charged, shortly after Barry's bank loans came to light, had by this time become "an irresistible and gigantic enemy, in the shape of an electioneering machine, as much so as the BANK."[173] Even after Kendall had restored the enterprise to financial solvency, Royall remained convinced that the maladministration of the postal system was a far more important political issue. Indeed, at one point she went so far as to speculate that Jackson's advisors may have deliberately fixed the president's attention upon the Bank in order to divert his gaze from the even greater enormities that were unfolding in the postal system.[174] Everyone agreed, Royall added in 1840, that the control of the postal system must be the first goal of anyone intent upon gaining control of national politics since, given the enormous influence of the patronage that was under its control, it had the power to elect "any man to any office it may decide upon in the United States."[175]

No group was more determined to take advantage of the Jacksonians' misfortunes than the founders of the Whig party, who used the issue to give their fledgling party a principled rationale. Just as the eighteenth-century Anglo-American Whigs had attacked George III for his corrupt manipulation of Parliament in the years immediately preceding the War of Independence, so their nineteenth-century American counterparts would challenge the Jacksonians' efforts to manipulate the electorate through their control over the postal system, the stagecoach industry, and the press. Many Whig leaders, including Thomas Ewing and Elisha Whittlesey of Ohio and Hiland Hall of Vermont, were genuinely indignant at the abuses that had occurred. Others, like Henry Clay, seem to have regarded the issue primarily as a convenient way to draw public attention to the specter of corruption that haunted the mass party and so hasten Van Buren's defeat in the election of 1836.[176] Clay was particularly sensitive to the magnitude of the contracting irregularities that had occurred, Van Buren later reminisced, since, as a Kentuckian, he knew firsthand how closely the mail contractors had "clung to the skirts" of his fellow Kentuckian Richard M. Johnson.[177] At the very least, the issue gave the Whigs a monster of their own to exploit just as the Jacksonians had exploited the "monster bank." "The last anchor of the crazy, dismasted and rudderless ship of the piratic crew of officeholders and expectants," warned one sympathetic editorialist, "is the cry of 'Bank! Bank!! Bank!!' Tell them of the unprecedented corruptions, and unparalleled defalcations of the post office department, and they cry out 'the Bank'!"[178]

Few Whig publicists proved more determined to expose the evils of the Jacksonians' postal policy than David Crockett, the celebrated Tennessee backwoodsman who would be immortalized as a folk hero following his death at the Alamo in 1836. In a campaign booklet that Crockett prepared with the assistance of Whig strategist Matthew St. Clair Clarke to boost the Whig cause in the upcoming election, Crockett described how the general post office had become under the Jacksonians the "general hospital, the poor-house, the lazaretto" for incompetent political appointees whom the Jacksonians had promoted to prestigious positions "over the heads" of the "honest old fellows" who had worked "day by day for twenty years."[179] Prior to the election of 1832, Crockett observed, the Jacksonians had established four-horse mail coaches throughout his home district in the backwoods of Tennessee, even though the mail they carried "would not fill a pocket-handkerchief." Yet when these imprudent expenditures ran the enterprise into debt, Barry concealed his financial situation by secretly channeling postal revenue from mail contractors such as "Extra Billy" Smith to Jacksonian publicists, who dutifully obscured the "true situation" until after Jackson had won the election. The problem, Crockett insisted, lay not in the rapacity of individual mail contractors, but rather in the "system" itself. "Give the contractors their due," Crockett declared, "if *the system* required favoritism, who would turn his back? . . . The fact is, the system did require it; and they began by shoving John McLean overboard. Postmasters were to be kicked out, new post-offices established, new routes opened, contractors to be encouraged in supporting newspapers to huzza for Jackson and reform; and, in fact, the whole . . . business of the department was put at scramblings." The conclusion seemed inescapable: "If this kind of Jacksonism is what they call *democracy* and republicanism, God deliver me from it as soon as possible."[180]

Intent upon doing everything they could to publicize the Barry scandals, Whig leaders had Congress print Ewing's Senate report in an edition of 30,000 copies, an unusually high total for its day.[181] Sympathetic printers further boosted the cause. In Baltimore, Hezekiah Niles reprinted Ewing's report in its entirety on eighteen consecutive pages of *Niles's Weekly Register*. In Philadelphia, one printer appended it to the most recent edition of the official directory of the central government. In New York, another printed it in a pamphlet that included an introductory essay sharply critical of the Jacksonians' manipulation of the stagecoach industry and the press. "Extravagant compensations have been allowed," the editor complained, "to the printers who sustained a profligate administration, and to the mail contractors who disseminated their poison throughout the land," which, when exposed to public view, revealed a "scene of monstrous abuse" that was without parallel in the history of the American republic, and for which there was "scarcely a precedent" in the entire "annals of European corruption."[182]

For a time, it looked as though the Barry scandals might figure prominently as a major issue in the election of 1836. This is the "best document for the *People* we have yet seen," wrote one Whig cadre man upon receiving from Ewing a copy of his report, predicting that it would become the *"textbook"* for stump speakers in the upcoming campaign.[183] For the past several years, reported Massachusetts congressman George N. Briggs, no issue—including, presumably, Jackson's war on the Bank—had generated a greater measure of public concern.[184] Particularly vulnerable to the Whig assault, given his notoriously close ties to the postal system and Obadiah Brown, was Richard M. Johnson. To capitalize on this point, one printer published a cartoon depicting Johnson being hailed by a number of politically unpopular individuals, including (in addition to a black man and the abolitionist William Lloyd Garrison) a stout postmaster who promised to back Johnson's bid for the vice presidency if he would pledge to keep them in office following the election.[185]

By the time the election campaign actually got under way, however, the Barry scandals were all but forgotten, preempted by the furor over the abolitionist mails and, more generally, by the slavery issue, which came to dominate the national political agenda. Sadly, lamented one Ohio Whig, the Barry scandals had failed to strike a responsive chord with the public at large, since the "eyes of the people" remained shut to the full import of the disclosures that Ewing had brought to light. The only way to prevent the Jacksonians' crimes from fading from view, the Whig added, was to publicize them in the press, so that at the very least they might "meet the eye of other times and of the historian."[186] North Carolina congressman Willie P. Mangum reached a similar conclusion in the spring preceding the election. Two years before, Mangum observed, the postal system lay under a "load of guilt, corruption, and disgusting rottenness." Two years later, what had happened? "It scarcely produced a sensation, it hardly produced an impression."[187] Had Van Buren lost the election of 1836, the Barry scandals would probably have figured prominently in subsequent explanations of his defeat. Since he won, they were promptly forgotten by contemporaries and historians alike. When Whig historian John Pendleton Kennedy published his 130-page history of the origins of the Whig party in 1843, he did not mention them at all.[188]

WHILE the Barry scandals may not have had much of an enduring impact on the political imagination of nineteenth-century Americans, they did help to redefine the role of the postal system in American public life. Prior to Jackson's inauguration, few Americans imagined that the postal system could be administered as a private enterprise since, by virtue of its size, complexity, and importance, it was assumed that it must necessarily be administered by the central government. Indeed, for McLean, the very phrase "private enterprise" had a somewhat exotic ring. Following the Barry scandals, however, a small number of thoughtful Americans, intent on preventing the recurrence of the kind of abuses that Congress had exposed, began to contemplate the possibility that the postal system might be privatized.

Few Americans devoted more attention to the privatization of the postal system than William Leggett, a Jacksonian journalist and an editor of the New York *Evening Post*. Hoping to scale back the influence of the central government in American public life, Leggett urged Congress to establish a "free trade post office" that would abandon all pretensions to monopolize the regular transmission of information and permit private parties to enter freely into the business of carrying the mail.[189]

Leggett justified his proposal partly on economic grounds. Troubled by the various postal cross-subsidies that Congress had authorized, Leggett declared that the "plain principles of justice" and "equal rights" demanded that the "tax on postage" ought to fall "equally on the community," rather than being borne disproportionately by merchants living along the Atlantic seaboard. "We would withdraw all government *stimulants*," Leggett declared—including the postal subsidies that the government provided Leggett's own *Evening Post*—"for they are bad things at best." Leggett found particularly outrageous the rapid expansion of postal routes into the hinterland in advance of demand. Should Congress abandon these "stimulants," Leggett added, the "solitary squatter" in the transappalachian West might no longer "hear the forest echoes daily awakened by the postman's horn" and might even find it necessary to pay a higher fee on his "annual letter." But from a purely economic standpoint, this was all to the good. The current "forcing system," Leggett explained, was at once unjust, since it obliged some Americans to pay for others' postage; unfair, since its principal beneficiaries were those speculators who had arrived first on the scene; and environmentally unsound since, by promoting settlement in parts of the country that could not otherwise be self-sustaining, it encouraged "sickly and immature productions" that exhausted the soil.[190]

Notwithstanding Leggett's concern over the economic costs of the status quo, he reserved his greatest scorn for the threat to the American polity that was posed by the rapidly emerging alliance of the postal system, the central government, and the party in power. All government monopolies were vulnerable to partisan manipulation, Leggett proclaimed.[191] But none could be more dangerous than the postal system, given the enormous influence that its army of postmasters exercised over public opinion. The influence that the postmaster general wielded over his "dependents," Leggett moralized, was nothing short of "monstrous." In particular, the postmaster general had the capacity to deploy the "facilities" of the postal system to encourage the rapid and simultaneous transmission of favorable "political intelligence," to obstruct that of a "contrary tenor," and to monitor the results.[192] Since Leggett was himself a Jacksonian, he found it particularly disturbing that this "sickening scene" had unfolded during the administration of a president whose integrity "no arts can corrupt, whose firmness no difficulties can appall, and whose vigilance no toils can exhaust." Clearly, no mere legislative solution could solve the problems that the expansion of the postal system had posed.[193] What the situation demanded was nothing less than the privatization of the postal system; only it could restore the republic to the better days of its youth.

Leggett was a highly idiosyncratic thinker, making it easy for contemporaries to dismiss his support for the privatization of the postal system as nothing more than the eccentric musings of a crank. Far harder to ignore was John Bell of Tennessee, who in his capacity as Speaker of the House, urged the privatization of the postal system on a number of occasions between 1836 and 1839. Bell freely conceded that in the early years of the republic it may have made some sense for Congress to maintain a postal monopoly on the plausible yet still highly "questionable grounds" that postal revenue would help fill the public coffers. Now that the central government had almost paid off the national debt, however, this rationale no longer applied. Accordingly, Bell urged Congress to throw open the letter-carrying business to the "enjoyment" of all citizens of the United States. Not only would the resulting "free competition" of "private capital and enterprise" increase the level of service for the public at large, but also, and even more important, it would check the rise of the mass party—and, though Bell did not say so explicitly, weaken the political base of public figures such as Martin Van Buren, who had come to rely on this new organizational form to consolidate their political power.[194]

Congress never did abolish the postal monopoly—indeed, it chose instead to greatly strengthen it with the Post Office Act of 1845. But the arguments that Leggett and Bell had introduced would soon inspire a host of private entrepreneurs to compete directly with the government on many of the most lucrative East Coast routes. Beginning with William Harnden, who in 1839 began to carry packages, money, and letters on a regular schedule between Boston and New York, a host of entrepreneurs emerged to compete head-on with the postal system in the lucrative East Coast market, offering in many cases a significantly better level of service at a lower cost. By 1845, according to Maryland senator William D. Merrick, these private mail delivery firms, in conjunction with other, more informal means of conveyance, were transmitting two-thirds of all the mail in the United States.[195]

Among the most successful of these entrepreneurs was James W. Hale, the founder of Hale & Co., a far-flung private mail delivery firm that during its brief heyday in the mid-1840s proved to be such a formidable competitor for the government that Hale soon became known as the "Father of Cheap Postage."[196] By demonstrating the practicality of a major reduction in the basic letter rate, declared Vice President George M. Dallas during a celebrated court case in which the government sought to prosecute Hale for his violation of the postal monopoly (and notwithstanding the illegality of his challenge to the postal monopoly), Hale had done more to improve the lot of the ordinary citizen of the United States than all the postmasters general since the adoption of the federal Constitution.[197]

In the end, however, all such efforts were doomed by precisely the evil that political insiders like Leggett and Bell had sought to redress: the intimate relationship between the postal system and the mass party. Such was the discovery of Henry Wells, who prior to making his fortune as the eponymous founder of the freighting firm of Wells, Fargo, & Company, had briefly entered the mail delivery business in upstate New York. During the 1840s, Wells briefly contemplated the possibility of purchasing the postal monopoly from the government and administering the postal system as a private enterprise, convinced that he could provide a higher level of service for the public at a lower cost. Postal officers had other ideas. *"Zounds, sir!"*—assistant postmaster general Selah Hobbie was purported to have declared in response to Wells's proposal—*"It would throw 16,000 postmasters out of office."* For the nineteenth-century express industry historian who recounted this anecdote, the explanation for Hobbie's remark seemed perfectly obvious. "That was so," the historian added, "and what would the administration do without its 16,000 postmasters? They constituted too important an element of party strength to be set aside by any postage reform movement."[198] Notwithstanding the determination of Wells and his fellow entrepreneurs, the government retained its postal monopoly, and the mass party remained a key element in American public life.

ALTHOUGH the private mail delivery boom ultimately failed, the very fact that it had occurred served as a pointed reminder of the changes in American postal policy that the Jacksonians had set in motion. Troubled by the recent expansion of the central government—and in particular by the growing political influence of Postmaster General McLean and the possibility that the government might soon establish a national program of internal improvements, the Jacksonians strove to restore the balance of power between the central government and the individual states that had existed prior to the administrations of Adams and Monroe. In the process, they created the mass party, a new institution that dated from the months immediately preceding the election of 1828.

It is impossible to know what might have happened had the Jacksonians not checked the momentum that the postal system had acquired under McLean. One possibility is suggested by a comparison of the

American postal system and the postal systems in Great Britain and France. At precisely the moment when the American postal system was being displaced from its central role in American public life, the British and French postal systems were expanding their scope to embrace a variety of new tasks, including commercial telegraphy and railway mail. Indeed, what is perhaps most notable about American postal policy in the decades between the inauguration of Andrew Jackson and the Civil War is how little it changed. Thirty years after the coming of the railroad, the American postal system continued to be administered in accordance with principles that had been devised prior to the election of 1828. Had the enterprise retained the degree of administrative autonomy that it had enjoyed under McLean, it is hard to believe that railway mail and city delivery would have been so long delayed, or that the government would not have played a more prominent role in the history of electric telegraphy, as had been the earnest hope of Samuel F. B. Morse.

Even more intriguing issues are raised by the Jacksonians' rejection of the Adamsites' commitment to a national program of internal improvements. How might the completion under federal auspices of this public works empire have shaped the boundaries of American public life? In certain regions, such as the western counties of Virginia, the construction by the central government of a major post road could have strengthened the political power of interest groups opposed to the institution of slavery as an impediment to trade. And had these interest groups emerged, it is conceivable that the Virginia legislature might have approved the gradual abolition of slavery within its borders, instead of narrowly rejecting it, as it did in 1832.[199] And further, it is possible that such a decision could have blunted the increasingly polarized sectional politics that followed the abolitionist mails controversy in 1835 and hurtled the country toward civil war. At any rate, such was the hope of John Quincy Adams, who, though resolutely opposed to the partisan manipulation of public contracts and jobs that has come to be known as the "spoils system," was determined to use the resources that were at his disposal—including the public contracts and jobs that would have been generated by his proposed national program of internal improvements—to perpetuate the Union. Tragically, however, with Adams's defeat in 1828 the Jacksonians abandoned the Adamsites' broad-minded vision of a developmental state in favor of the mass party, thus evading the most pressing political challenge of the age.

· 7 ·

The Interdiction
of Dissent

ON WEDNESDAY, July 29, 1835, at some point between 10:00 and 11:00 P.M., a small group of men broke into the post office in Charleston, South Carolina, by forcing open a window with a crowbar. Had the men been ordinary mail robbers, they could easily have netted themselves a small fortune by rifling the merchants' letters, which on any given day were sure to contain thousands of dollars in cash. Yet this was no ordinary robbery, and these were no ordinary thieves. The intruders belonged to a Charleston vigilante society known as the "Lynch Men," and the purpose of their assault was to destroy the bundle of several thousand abolitionist periodicals that the steamboat *Columbia* had brought to the Charleston post office earlier that day.[1] The periodicals, as virtually everyone in Charleston knew by this time, were part of an enormous mass mailing that the New York–based American Anti-Slavery Society had sent into the slaveholding states in an unprecedented attempt to convert the South to the immediate, uncompensated emancipation of slavery. Though the transmission within South Carolina of publications containing such potentially incendiary discussions of the slavery issue was clearly prohibited under state law, the abolitionists had hoped that postal officers would help them circumvent this ban. The Lynch Men foiled their plans. Intent upon enforcing the laws of the state of South Carolina, committed to preventing the abolitionists from transforming the postal system into an instrument of agitation, and skeptical of the loyalty of Charleston postmaster Alfred Huger, a Unionist well known as a champion of strong central government, the men had broken into the post office in deliberate defiance of federal law.

The abolitionist periodicals proved surprisingly easy to find. Though the men had entered the building after dark, Huger had taken care to separate the periodicals from the rest of the mail and to isolate them in a special sack, as if in anticipation of just such an assault. Once the men located the sack, they spirited it out of the post office, leaving everything else undisturbed.

The following night, the Lynch Men burned the periodicals, along with effigies of three of the leading abolitionists, in a spectacular bonfire that was watched by a loud and enthusiastic crowd of 2,000, roughly one-seventh of the entire white population of the city.[2] To underscore the symbolic character of this event, the Lynch Men staged the bonfire on the Parade Grounds, a training field immediately adjacent to the Citadel, a military academy that the South Carolina legislature had established to protect the citizenry from a slave rebellion. For con-temporaries familiar with the highly stylized protests that eighteenth-century Charlestonians had organized to publicize their opposition to British tyranny, the public burning was sure to bring to mind the hal-lowed exploits of the earlier Anglo-American mob. Like the patriots of 1776, the Lynch Men chose their target with care, displayed a gift for the theatrical, and demonstrated considerable ingenuity in identifying their cause with the public good.

The identity of the men who led the break-in can be pieced together from the scattered evidence that has survived. The perpetrators, Huger confided to Postmaster General Amos Kendall shortly after the event, were no "ignorant or infuriated rabble."[3] On the contrary, they were prominent Charlestonians who had the backing and very possibly the active assistance of ex-governor John Lyde Wilson, a low-country planter, an authority on the etiquette of the duel, and a militant de-fender of the rights of the state. Wilson was almost certainly in Charles-ton on the night of the break-in and publicly defended its perpetrators at a heated public meeting shortly after the event.[4] Long a champion of extralegal acts of civil disobedience, Wilson was known to have joined with the Lynch Men later that month in a widely publicized ritual humiliation of a white barber accused of having stolen cotton from slaves.[5] Had Wilson led the break-in as well, it would have been per-fectly consistent with his long-standing opposition to the encroachment of the central government on the rights of the states and his own long history of participation in extralegal acts of civil disobedience. Shortly after the humiliation of the barber, one Charleston editorialist acknowl-edged as much. Like the shaming of the barber, the editorialist observed, the break-in was a "parallel case of proceeding in opposition to law" that was grounded in a plea of "extreme necessity."[6] Whether Wilson was in fact one of the perpetrators must, however, remain a matter of speculation. Though insiders like Huger recognized the hand of the Lynch Men in the event, no one saw fit to leak their names to the press. After all, mail robbery was a federal crime, and no Charleston editor wanted to give the hated federal prosecutors any leads should they wish to bring the guilty parties to trial.

Whether or not Wilson led the assault, it seems almost certain that the break-in was the work of a small number of men, making it more like a burglary than a mob assault. Earlier that evening, the post office had been surrounded by an angry crowd of several hundred, intent, several of its members boasted, upon storming not only the post office but also the Catholic church, a Catholic-run school for free blacks, and the official residence of the Reverend John England, the Catholic bishop of Charleston. According to the local Catholic newspaper, the cry had gone out that "Charleston should become a Charlestown," by which it meant that Charleston was about to be swept by anti-Catholic riots comparable to the notorious mob assault that had led to the destruction of the Ursuline Convent in Charlestown, Massachusetts, the previous year.[7] However, as the most detailed newspaper account of the break-in took care to stress, it was not until after the crowd had been dispersed by the city guard that a "few gentlemen" entered the post office, unaware that Huger and the "leading citizens" had already agreed to detain the abolitionist periodicals in Huger's office.[8] To be sure, not everyone agreed on this point. Had the "mob" waited to enter the post office until the following day, observed one crowd member in a letter to a friend, it would have had little trouble securing the periodicals from Huger. But as matters stood, the "excitement was so great that they could not wait," so they broke into the post office instead.[9] Still, there is good reason to suppose that the attack was premeditated and that the size of the crowd was small. Had a large number of men been involved, they would almost certainly have once again roused the city guard. And had the break-in been spontaneous, it is hard to believe that the perpetrators would have had the necessary self discipline to leave the merchants' letters untouched. In fact, the break-in proceeded in an orderly manner and went undetected until the following morning.

THE CHARLESTON post office break-in and the public burning of the abolitionist periodicals have long been familiar to historians. Few textbook accounts of the period fail to mention these events, if only in a cursory way. Ordinarily, historians interpret them either as an outrage against civil liberties or as a prelude to civil war. In this chapter, I take a different approach. I contend that the events in Charleston and the national controversy that they inspired are best understood as the response of Southern slaveholders and their Northern antiabolitionist allies to the challenge that the prior expansion of the postal system posed to conventional assumptions regarding the boundaries of American public life. The abolitionists had tried to expand these boundaries to embrace the slavery issue, and the antiabolitionists frustrated their designs. More broadly still, the controversy can be seen as the tragic epilogue to the communications revolution that Congress had set in motion with the passage of the Post Office Act of 1792. Between 1792 and 1835, the expansion of the facilities of communication had worked to strengthen the bonds of Union. Between 1835 and 1861, however, the same facilities worked no less inexorably to drive the Union apart.

FROM TODAY'S STANDPOINT, the abolitionists' mass mailing may not seem like an unusual event. These days, the unsolicited mass mailing of reform literature of one kind or another has become so commonplace that it is routinely dismissed as junk mail. In 1835, however, the technique was far more rare.

Much of the novelty of the abolitionists' mass mailing lay in the content of the appeal. Rejecting as immoral the various institutional solutions to the slavery issue, including the government-funded compensation of slaveholders and the resettlement of former slaves outside the United States, the organizers of the mass mailing sought instead to stigmatize slaveholding as a sin and to convert the slaveholding class to the cause of abolition. Far more than a publicity campaign to focus public attention on the slavery issue in the nonslaveholding states, this mass mailing was nothing less than a moral crusade to shape the hearts and minds of the men who dominated public life in the South. During the 1820s, Lyman Beecher had demonstrated the effectiveness of the voluntary association as a technique for combating a wide variety of social evils, from intemperance to Sabbath-breaking. In 1835, the abolitionists applied the same technique to the cause of the slave. Though in retrospect it is plain that the abolitionists seriously underestimated the setbacks they would encounter, it was hardly evident that they would fail. Prior to 1835, few Southerners openly proclaimed slavery to be a positive good, while many slaveholders treated the institution as, at best, a necessary evil that at some point in the future should be terminated. By flooding the slaveholding states with abolitionist appeals, the organizers of the mass mailing hoped to hasten this eagerly awaited moral reform.

The abolitionists may have rejected an institutional approach to the slavery issue, yet the success of their mailing hinged on their ability to take advantage of several of the leading institutions of the day. To raise the revenue that they needed to mount such an ambitious appeal, the abolitionists drew on the financial resources of a number of like-minded New York businessmen, including Arthur Tappan, a wealthy silk merchant and a tireless supporter of moral reform.[10] To publicize their cause, they relied on a variety of recent improvements in paper-making technology as well as the newly perfected steam-powered printing press. And to get their message into the slaveholding states, they took advantage of the postal system, the largest and most administratively sophisticated enterprise of its day. The organizers of the mass mailing were by no means the first group of reformers to rely on the postal system in this way; a variety of single-issue lobbyists, including lottery promoters, temperance advocates, and Sabbatarians, had preceded them. But these organizers were the first reformers to use the postal system to promote the immediate, uncompensated abolition of slavery within the slaveholding states.

The postal system boosted the abolitionists' cause in a variety of ways. Most obviously, it facilitated the transmission of an enormous volume of information to a target audience over a geographically vast expanse. During the height of the mass mailing in the summer of 1835, the abolitionists sent into the slaveholding states no fewer than 175,000 separate pieces, or roughly half of the total number of items that the entire New York City periodical press ordinarily sent through the mail in a comparable period of time.[11] According to one account, this informational blitz was roughly equivalent to the entire output of the periodical press of the South.[12] In certain rural districts that lacked a vigorous local press, this meant that the abolitionists originated nearly all the printed information that postal patrons were sent through the mail.[13]

Even more important, the postal system provided the abolitionists with an ingenious way to circumvent the formidable constraints that would otherwise have prevented them from agitating the slavery issue in the slaveholding states. Consider the alternatives. Had the abolitionists deposited their publications on the floor of steamboats, stage-coaches, and the other common carriers that traveled between the

North and the South, they could easily have been ignored, confiscated, or simply dumped overboard. And had they relied instead on a network of lecturers and colporteurs, these agents would swiftly have run afoul of the welter of state and local laws that prohibited the transmission of information that could be construed as inciting slaves to rebel. Shortly after the Charleston post office break-in, for example, the local authorities in Nashville, Tennessee, arrested, convicted, and publicly whipped a recent seminary graduate named Amos Dresser for the crime of carrying in his luggage a copy of an Anti-Slavery Society publication. Had Dresser been confronted by a vigilante society instead, he might well have been lynched.[14]

The abolitionists well understood the indispensability of the postal system to the success of their moral crusade and took great pains to package their appeals in a format that minimized the likelihood that postal officers would exclude them from the mail. Under postal regulations, postal officers were required to transmit without discrimination *every* newspaper that had been issued in the proper format, while retaining wide discretion over the transmission of tracts, pamphlets, and oversized non-newspaper periodicals such as magazines. Well aware of this distinction, the abolitionists took care to issue two of their four major publications, the *Emancipator* and the *Anti-Slavery Record,* in a newspaper format, and to issue their two other principal publications, *Human Rights* and the *Slave's Friend,* in a magazine format that was indistinguishable in format from many magazines that postal officers routinely admitted into the mail. As a further precaution, the abolitionists deliberately refrained from prepaying the postage. Though it might seem odd that the abolitionists would require their potential converts to cover the cost of material that they had never requested, the abolitionists well knew that prepaying the postage on the periodicals would eliminate a major incentive for their proper delivery by depriving postmasters of their accustomed commission on every item that they received.

As a final precaution, the abolitionists aimed their mass mailing at a preselected target audience of 20,000 Southerners whose names they cobbled together from city directories, the proceedings of religious bodies, and other compendia of prominent men of affairs. This boosted their cause in a variety of ways. First, it greatly increased the likelihood that postal officers would treat their publications with respect, since, as preaddressed periodicals, they were technically the property of the recipient, making their detention a federal crime. Second, it anticipated the potentially devastating objection that, by flooding the slaveholding states with such an enormous volume of abolitionist literature, the abolitionists had virtually guaranteed that at least some of their publications would find their way into the hands of slaves, free blacks, or other potentially dangerous elements. Southerners warned constantly that the abolitionist mass mailing might spark a slave rebellion and in the months following the Charleston break-in freely compared the abolitionists to the Amis des Noirs, the French antislavery society that was widely believed to have helped incite the slave rebellions in Santo Domingo in the 1790s that led to the establishment of the slave-backed republic of Haiti.[15] By preselecting their audience, the abolitionists did their best to prevent such a disaster from befalling the United States. As Anti-Slavery Society organizer William Jay sarcastically retorted when confronted with the charge that the abolitionist mass mailing was likely to incite a slave rebellion within the South, "Are the southern slaves, sir, accustomed to receive periodicals by mail?"

Symptomatic of the abolitionists' determination to avoid misunderstanding on this point was Jay's insistence that the abolitionists refrain, as a matter of policy, from sending a single periodical to a single free black. Jay's position greatly troubled fellow abolitionist Elizur Wright, Jr., who could not understand why the abolitionists should have to make such a concession. After all, free blacks were among the abolitionists' most stalwart allies, and had an obvious interest in the proposed reform. But Jay stood firm. The purpose of the mass mailing, Jay lectured Wright, was to reach that class of Southerners who had the power to set the institution of slavery on its way to ultimate extinction, and this class, Jay felt sure, did not include free blacks. Not surprisingly, Jay was particularly indignant when he learned that the Norfolk, Virginia, postmaster had accused the Anti-Slavery Society of transmitting abolitionist publications to a group of between thirty and forty free blacks in the vicinity of Norfolk. Having taken great pains to prevent just such an eventuality, Jay testily replied that if the accusation were true, the periodicals had been sent not by the Anti-Slavery Society but rather by saboteurs.[16]

THE ABOLITIONISTS' mass mailing posed a major challenge for the postal officers it most directly involved, namely Charleston postmaster Alfred Huger, New York City postmaster Samuel L. Gouverneur, and Postmaster General Amos Kendall. From the outset, neither they nor any other high-ranking member of the Jackson administration had the slightest intention of permitting the abolitionists to use the postal system as an instrument of agitation. Accordingly, they moved swiftly in the days immediately following the break-in to establish an informational *cordon sanitaire* between the slaveholding and the nonslaveholding states, which effectively blocked groups like the American Anti-Slavery Society from using the postal system to establish a national discussion on the slavery issue. For the next quarter century, this *cordon sanitaire* remained in place, only to be swept away along with the institution of slavery during the Civil War.

Huger's response to the post office break-in was shaped by his overlapping obligations as a federal public officer and a citizen of the state of South Carolina. As a federal public officer, Huger had taken an oath to transmit promptly and without discrimination all mailable items that arrived at his office. Yet as a citizen of the state of South Carolina, Huger was obliged under state law to hand over to the appropriate state authorities any publication whose transmission might incite a slave rebellion. In 1835, no public figure in Charleston doubted that the Anti-Slavery Society periodicals fell into this category. Thus, Huger was torn between his obligations as a federal officer and as a citizen of his state. Should he transmit the periodicals and risk a confrontation with the government of South Carolina? Or should he delay their transmission and risk the censure of the government of the United States?

Huger's response was further complicated by his position within South Carolina society. As a Unionist who championed the superiority of federal law and opposed the states' rights radicalism of public figures like Senator John C. Calhoun, Huger was determined to prevent any nonfederal body—whether it be the Lynch Men, the Charleston city guard, or even the city intendant—from gaining access to the mail. But as a well-to-do rice planter who owned over seventy slaves, Huger had little sympathy with the abolitionists' cause.[17] If the abolitionists were right and slavery was indeed a sin, Huger mused, this would convict "his own soul and his own ancestors for five generations," a possibility so abhorrent that he dismissed it at once.[18] Huger was particularly disturbed by the possibility that the mass mailing might spark an antiblack backlash by the city's poor whites, whom Huger despised. After all, he reasoned, if by some fluke the mass mailing should spark a slave rebellion, the slaves would stand "no earthly chance of success."[19] Far more likely would be a bloody white reprisal in which hundreds of innocent slaves would perish, victims of the misplaced altruism of abolitionist zeal.[20]

Prior to the break-in, Huger felt confident that he could resolve the conflict between the central government and his state with a minimum of disruption. To mollify the state authorities, immediately after the arrival of the first shipment of abolitionist periodicals Huger met with representatives of the South Carolina Association, a vigilante society that, while more moderate than the Lynch Men, was equally determined to uphold the rights of the state. Though the South Carolina Association had hoped to persuade Huger to give up the abolitionist periodicals voluntarily, Huger persuaded it to accept a compromise. To meet his obligation as a federal public officer, Huger would deliver the periodicals that had already arrived, while to uphold his obligation as a citizen of South Carolina, he would urge Postmaster General Kendall to prevent future shipments of abolitionist publications from reaching his office.

For the moment, this compromise seemed to settle the issue to everyone's satisfaction. Once the Charlestonians discovered the nature of the publications that the American Anti-Slavery Society had sent, they quickly returned them to the post office, unwilling to pay the postage and outraged at the audacity of the abolitionists for having mounted such an appeal.[21] To prevent any possible misunderstanding on this score, the Catholic bishop of Charleston, John England, took the extraordinary step of issuing a public disclaimer in the principal Charleston newspapers in which he declared categorically that Charleston's Catholics joined with the rest of the white population to deplore the mass mailing; that none of the offensive periodicals had been addressed to any of the students at the recently established Catholic Church-run school for free blacks; and that he himself had neither solicited nor retained the abolitionist periodicals that he had been sent.[22]

Had the break-in not disturbed Huger's plans, a similar fate would probably have befallen the many abolitionist periodicals that had arrived at the Charleston office for distribution to post offices in the South and West. Here, too, Huger and the South Carolina Association agreed to compromise. Though Huger refused to permit the Association to impound the periodicals, he did agree to place them in a separate sack and attach to each packet a warning label informing postal officers of the nature of its contents. As a further concession, Huger agreed to temporarily hold this sack in his office until he could receive official instructions from Washington as to how best to proceed.[23] It was this sack, with the abolitionist periodicals carefully separated from the rest of the mail, that the Lynch Men spirited out of the post office later that night.

With the break-in, Huger's compromise collapsed. Now that the post office had been burglarized, Huger became convinced that the mail might be stolen in the street as well and for this reason categorically refused to send any future abolitionist periodicals out of his office, even if he should be specifically required to do so by the postmaster general. "If I am directed to forward them," Huger reported to New York postmaster Samuel L. Gouverneur, "they will unquestionably be arrested in the streets by the civil authority of the state and destroyed—this is inevitable—nor do I believe that any military force not strong enough to subdue South Carolina, can prevent it."[24] Huger recognized that his decision was at variance with the strict letter of the federal law, but remained convinced that it was fully in accord with its spirit. "Very early in this business," Huger explained to Gouverneur, "I saw plainly that the mail could not pass thro' the streets with those pamphlets contained in it; I *therefore,* to *save the mail* took them out and told the citizens I had done so . . . Where then has been the compromise? I have made none, and should think myself dishonored if I had."[25]

Huger's nightmare was that a roving band of poor whites might emulate the example of the Lynch Men and use the presence of abolitionist periodicals in the mail as an excuse to pilfer the enormous sums of money that merchants routinely transmitted from the Atlantic seaports to the Southern interior. "The commercial intercourse between the two cities must cease, if this is persisted in," Huger warned. "Every boat will become an object of suspicion and search, and if the mob once lay its hands upon the mail in the streets, it is easy to determine what will become of the letters, money, &c. which it contains." This was an eventuality that, as a Unionist, Huger was determined to prevent since, as he repeatedly taunted his critics, the Unionists were the wealthiest South Carolinians and accordingly had the most to lose should the mail fall victim to mob attack.[26]

Shotgun in hand, Huger felt confident he could protect the mail when it was under his direct control. But he lacked the resources to insure the safety of the mail during its transfer from the steamboat landing to the post office and from the post office to the railroad station. To help protect the mail when it was in transit within the city, Huger persuaded the civil authorities to establish an honor guard of prominent Charlestonians to escort the incoming mail from the steamboat landing to the post office and the outgoing mail from the post office to the railroad station. In addition, Huger repeated his plea that Postmaster General Kendall declare the transmission of the abolitionist periodicals illegal and, as a further safeguard, implored New York postmaster Gouverneur to separate any future shipment of abolitionist periodicals from commercial correspondence and mark the latter "Nothing but Letters" and the former "Suspicious." In this way, Huger explained, it would be less likely that a crowd intent upon destroying the abolitionist periodicals might somehow gain access to the merchants' letters by mistake.[27]

If Huger found himself struggling to protect the mail from the wrath of the mob, Gouverneur found himself challenged to devise some principled basis upon which he could accommodate Huger and exclude the abolitionist publications altogether. Few northerners were less inclined to take any steps that might embarrass the South. Though Gouverneur was a native New Yorker, he had married a daughter of the Virginia planter-president James Monroe and had been a frequent visitor of his father-in-law's slave plantation during the final years of the ex-president's life. But how was Gouverneur to proceed? No New York state law barred the abolitionists from entering their publications in the mail, and as a federal postal officer Gouverneur was required to transmit all publications that had been issued in the proper format, regardless of their content. Once Gouverneur learned of the Charleston post office break-in, however, he ignored this requirement and decided to block the abolitionists from using postal facilities, regardless of his obligation under federal law. In justification of his position, Gouverneur explained, he considered himself bound not only by federal law, but also by the laws of South Carolina, even though he himself continued to live in New York. If it was illegal for the Charleston post office to receive abolitionist publications, Gouverneur reasoned, then he considered himself legally obliged to detain these publications in New York. This doctrine, which would soon become known as the federal reinforcement of state law, provided Gouverneur with a legal cover for a decision that could otherwise be plausibly derided as arbitrary and capricious. Well aware of the precariousness of his position, Gouverneur defended it nonetheless. "The laws which secure to you the rights you claim," Gouverneur taunted abolitionist Elizur Wright, Jr., when Wright challenged Gouverneur to square his conduct with the letter of the law, "also impose the penalties on those who infringe them. I shall assume the responsibility in the case you have made with me, and to the law and my superiors will hold myself accountable."[28]

Gouverneur was so confident in the fundamental justice of his position that he freely elaborated upon it in a public meeting that was organized shortly after the break-in to demonstrate the sympathy of New Yorkers for the slaveholding South. By honoring the laws of South Carolina over those of the United States, Gouverneur explained to the crowd, he had upheld the "great principles of the revolution" and in particular the hallowed principles of individual responsibility, self government, and states' rights as they had been championed by the Founding Fathers. Had he permitted the abolitionists to pervert the postal system to their nefarious ends, this precious heritage might well be lost. "They must all see," Gouverneur told the crowd, "that the great principles of liberty throughout the world, were at stake on the issue of this question, and that it involved the essence of the problem whether man can govern himself, or is to be governed by somebody or nobody."[29] Though Gouverneur's position outraged the abolitionists and was greeted with skepticism even by many Northerners who had no special sympathy for the abolitionists' cause, it was widely hailed in the South as magnanimous, judicious, and politically astute. Later that summer, one group of Virginians wrote him a formal letter of commendation thanking him for his refusal to permit the abolitionists to transmit into the slaveholding states any information that might encourage an "insubordinate or insurrectionary spirit among the slaves of the South."[30]

Gouverneur's refusal to permit the abolitionists to enter their publications into the postal system brought the first phase of the abolitionist mails controversy to a close. The abolitionists may have hoped to expand the boundaries of the public sphere, but when it became plain that their venture might threaten the routine operations of the national market and, in particular, the security of the large sums of money that merchants sent in the mail, two middle managers in the postal system had banded together to frustrate their designs. From an administrative point of view, this settled the issue. Not until after the Civil War would the government dismantle the *cordon sanitaire* that Huger and Gouverneur had established in 1835 to block the transmission of abolitionist literature into the slaveholding states. Yet many Southerners remained profoundly suspicious of the central government, and for them, the issues the abolitionists had raised were hardly resolved. How could it be guaranteed that the government would not reverse its policy at some future date? How could the South prevent the abolitionists from shaping public opinion in nonslaveholding states? To help answer these questions, the antiabolitionists mounted a counteroffensive that quickly dwarfed the abolitionist mass mailing in its scale and intensity and that, ironically enough, given its organizers' determination to stifle debate, soon thrust the slavery issue onto the national political agenda, where it would remain more or less continuously from 1835 until the Civil War.

The opening phase of the antiabolitionist counteroffensive began within the inner circle of the Jackson administration less than one week after the break-in. "All parties unite to write Postmaster Huger," reported Secretary of State John Forsyth in a letter to Vice President Van Buren on August 5, "in fixed resolve to prevent the circulation of those papers, the laws of the United States to the contrary notwithstanding."[31] Two days later, Amos Kendall reached a similar verdict. The abolitionist publications, Kendall duly informed President Jackson, were "most flagitious," adding that he was fully committed to stopping their transmission with "as little noise and difficulty as possible" and in general toward doing whatever might prove to be necessary to "pacify the South."[32]

Kendall's determination to block the transmission of abolitionist publications may have posed few questions within the Jackson administration, yet its implementation posed problems analogous to those that Gouverneur had confronted in New York. The abolitionists, after all, had broken no federal law, and Kendall, as postmaster general, was required to insure the uninterrupted transmission of every item that had been properly entered into the mail. How then could he stop a practice that he was legally required to uphold?

Jackson responded to Kendall's predicament with characteristic bravado. If there were no laws barring the transmission of abolitionist publications, Jackson reasoned, then Congress should take action to prevent the abolitionists from taking advantage of this unfortunate omission. Accordingly, Jackson urged Congress at its next session to enact legislation barring the transmission of abolitionist periodicals in the mail. In the interim, Jackson urged Kendall to take advantage of the existing laws to bring the guilty parties to trial—who, Jackson felt, included not only the abolitionists but also the Lynch Men. Jackson found the abolitionists' conduct particularly outrageous since it so obviously implicated his administration in a policy that he himself strenuously deplored. "Could [the abolitionists] be reached," Jackson thundered, frustrated at the legal obstacles that seemed destined to block the Southern states from bringing the abolitionists to trial under state law, they "ought to be made to atone for this wicked attempt with their lives." Jackson extended his scorn even to those who voluntarily subscribed to abolitionist publications through the mail. To impress these individuals with the enormity of their crimes, Jackson instructed Kendall to require the Washington, D.C., postmaster to publish their names in the local newspaper. Doing this throughout the United States, Jackson predicted, would speedily destroy the abolitionist press, since few Americans could be "so hardened in villainy" that they would successfully "withstand the frowns of all good men."[33]

Kendall has left no record of his response to Jackson's recommendations. In the end, however, he chose to pursue the more cautious course of sanctioning the suppression of the abolitionist periodicals without declaring their suppression to be mandated under federal law. Perhaps it was to be expected that Kendall would react in this highly equivocal way. Not yet confirmed as postmaster general, Kendall well knew that his future would be decided primarily by the powerful bloc of Southern senators who were loyal to Calhoun and he understood perfectly well their hostility toward any action that hinted at a deliberate arrogation of power. Kendall surely remembered that Calhoun had cast the tiebreaking vote that guaranteed Kendall his previous appointment as a treasury department auditor in 1829, and in 1835 he was in no position to antagonize the South.[34] Kendall had "truckled to the domineering pretensions of the slaveholders" in order to guarantee his confirmation, reported a thoroughly disgusted William Leggett, a formerly loyal Jacksonian who broke with the party over its handling of the abolitionist mails. In the process, Kendall had permitted the South to establish a *"censorship of the press."*[35]

However important personal considerations may have been in shaping Kendall's course, his position was perfectly compatible with his own long-standing opposition to the growing role of the central government in American public life. As a veteran newspaper editor, Kendall understood how dramatically the communications revolution being wrought by the postal system, the stagecoach industry, and the press were collapsing the distance between the various sections of the United States, and he was determined to slow this trend. "Our nation is not one in relation to many subjects discussed in newspapers," Kendall observed to a congressman a few years later. "In many respects, we are twenty-six independent nations. Each of these has its separate interests, systems of jurisprudence, and police."[36] Kendall was by no means alone in this view. Indeed, his opposition to the growing influence of the urban press in American public life was shared by many rural abolitionists, including the Ohio Whig Joshua Giddings. Still, few public figures could match Kendall's conviction that the very possibility of a national discussion on such a controversial topic as the morality of slavery would inevitably put the Union at risk.[37]

Kendall articulated his position in a pair of open letters to Post-masters Huger and Gouverneur in the weeks immediately after the break-in. When Kendall was asked by a Louisiana postmaster the following September if he might be prosecuted in federal court for refusing to transmit an Anti-Slavery Society periodical that had found its way to his office, Kendall directed him to consult these open letters, adding that they furnished the "only practicable remedy" for the "evil of which you complain."[38]

Kendall's open letter to Huger, dated August 5, 1835, laid out his position emphatically. Central to Kendall's approach was his implicit rejection of the superiority of federal law. Though he freely conceded that under ordinary circumstances federal public officers had an "obligation" to obey the laws of the United States, he took pains to add that under extraordinary circumstances they had an even "higher" obligation to the "communities" in which they lived, while "if the *former* be perverted to destroy the *latter,* it was patriotism to disregard them." Kendall left little doubt that he regarded the abolitionist mass mailing as such an extraordinary event. He struck a similar note in his open letter to Gouverneur, dated August 22. Gouverneur's refusal to permit the abolitionists to transmit their periodicals from the New York post office, Kendall declared, was "best for the country" and fully in agreement with Kendall's personal views—even if it was not, strictly speaking, in accord with the laws of the United States. "I have no hesitation in saying," Kendall added with a flourish, "that if I were situated as you are, I would do as you have done."[39]

Kendall expanded on his position in his annual report for 1835. Here, too, he championed the suppression of the abolitionist periodicals without invoking the authority of federal law. Few documents better illustrate the integral relationship that the Jacksonians assumed to exist between slavery, states' rights, and the perpetuation of the Union. Following an ingenious line of argument that had been popularized the previous summer by Charleston Unionist Richard Yeadon, Kendall explained that the mass mailing constituted a violation on the abolitionists' part of international law, with the "nations" in this instance being the individual states. After all, at no point had the inhabitants of the slaveholding and the nonslaveholding states formally ratified a "compact or treaty" giving the abolitionists the "right" to transmit their publications to the "nations" of the South. Under the circumstances, for the abolitionists to pretend that they had a right to carry on from a distance "discussions" in the slaveholding states for which they could have been prosecuted had they done so in person would be precisely analogous to the patently outrageous claim that English labor radicals had the right to transmit subversive information to the "laboring population" of the United States. To clinch his point, Kendall turned briefly to history. The adoption of the federal Constitution, he explained, had been acceptable to the slaveholding states precisely because it enabled them to gain "more perfect control" over their slave population, over which, a half century later, they still retained their "sovereign will." For the central government to interfere with this arrangement would therefore be tantamount to repudiating one of the pivotal compromises upon which the Union had been forged.[40]

KENDALL'S REPORT helped win him confirmation in the Senate the following spring. More important, it constituted a major victory for the states' rights radicals in the South. Rarely before had a public figure linked the future of the Union so closely to the perpetuation of the institution of slavery. Never before had a federal public officer so obsequiously deferred to the superior authority of the individual states. But few Southerners were content to permit Kendall, or any federal public officer, to dictate their response. Within days of the post office break-in, a small yet determined group of Southern antiabolitionists launched a counteroffensive that soon came to dwarf the abolitionists' mass mailing in its scale and scope. The antiabolitionists took action on three fronts: first, they hailed slavery as a positive good; second, they urged the enactment of antiabolitionist legislation in the federal Congress and the nonslaveholding states; and third, they exported to the nonslaveholding states the same extralegal vigilante techniques that the Lynch Men had already deployed so effectively in Charleston.

The defense of slavery as a positive good was the predictable response to the abolitionists' attempt to begin a national discussion of the issue. Once the abolitionists had tried to persuade Southerners that slaveholding was a sin, it was only a matter of time before antiabolitionists would undertake to convince them that it was a positive good. While this proslavery argument was by no means entirely new in 1835, it had rarely before been urged upon the public with such evangelical zeal. Prominent spokesman for this view included Calhounite publicist Duff Green, who championed the moral virtues of the institution in the *United States Telegraph* in late 1835, and South Carolina governor

George McDuffie, who did the same in his annual address to the South Carolina legislature in November of that year. Both had been moved to speak out as a reaction to the mass mailing of abolitionist periodicals that had begun to flood the South the previous July.

McDuffie's address was particularly notable for its flamboyant rhetoric and vigorous tone. Not since Richard M. Johnson had assailed the Sabbatarians in his celebrated reports on the Sunday mails had such a prominent public figure issued such an intemperate screed. Slavery, McDuffie confidently proclaimed, was at once a noble institution sanctified by God and the "cornerstone" of our "republican edifice." But McDuffie did not stop here. Deriding the abolitionists as "wicked monsters" and "deluded fanatics," McDuffie assailed them for having embarked on a "fiend-like errand" to destroy the South. "Under the influence of this species of voluntary madness," McDuffie railed, "nothing is sacred that stands in the way of its purposes. Like all other religious impostures, it has power to consecrate every act, however atrocious, and every person, however covered with 'multiplying villanies,' that may promote its diabolical ends, or worship at its infernal altars."[41]

Once the antiabolitionists had proclaimed slavery to be a positive good it was but a short step to press for federal legislation to ban outright the transmission of abolitionist literature in the mail. Here, however, the antiabolitionists met with a resounding defeat. Notwithstanding the support of many of prominent public figures, including President Jackson, Vice President Martin Van Buren, and Senator John C. Calhoun, Congress refused to take any concrete steps to restrict the freedom of the press. The Jacksonians might seek federal legislation declaring the transmission of abolitionist publications illegal under federal law, while the Calhounites might seek legislation reinforcing the laws of the individual states, yet in the end Congress chose to reaffirm its traditional commitment to the inviolability of the mails.[42] This surprising turn of events, which Congress codified as section 32 of the Post Office Act of 1836, was the product of a complicated series of backroom congressional compromises engineered by the members of the House Committee on the Post Office and Post Roads under the leadership of Hiland Hall of Vermont.[43]

Hall explained his support for the principle of postal inviolability in a major report in March 1836. The American people, Hall proclaimed, had never granted the central government the power to limit the freedom of the press, and therefore neither the Jacksonians nor the Calhounites had the right to propose legislation that would interfere in any way with the transmission of abolitionist publications in the mail. "The prohibition of 'incendiary publications' from mail circulation," Hall declared, "is not within the legitimate scope of the post office power; the power of proscribing them not being at all necessary to the safe, convenient, or expedient transportation of the mail." Should Congress enact either bill, Hall added, this would be both unfair, since it would rob the proscribed publication of its market, and dangerous, since it would involve Congress in an essentially religious controversy over fine points of abolitionist doctrine. How, after all, was the central government to determine precisely which ideas should properly fall under the ban? And how would this be different, Hall added provocatively, from permitting the Sabbatarians to ban the transmission through the postal system of publications that *they* deemed to be hostile to their cause?[44]

Hall was well aware that if his position were taken to its extreme, the central government would be precluded from banning the transmission of *anything* sent through the mail. This was precisely his intention. Should a particular publication contain information illegal under state law, Hall added, this was all the more reason to prohibit Congress from interfering with its transmission: "If it be said that the publications which we are now called upon to suppress are *really* and *truly* dangerous, seditious, and incendiary, then the minority say they are *really* and *truly* some of the precise publications against which it was designed by the Constitution that Congress should have no power to legislate. The People of the United States never intended that the government of the Union should exercise over the press the power of discriminating between true and erroneous opinions, of determining that this sentiment was patriotic, that seditious and incendiary, and therefore wisely prohibited Congress all power over the subject."[45]

Hall's report has a familiar ring, anticipating as it does the main lines of the modern libertarian defense of the free press guarantee in the First Amendment. Yet it had surprisingly little influence at the time. Never published as a congressional document, it was soon forgotten by contemporaries and has been almost entirely overlooked by twentieth-century legal scholars, notwithstanding their preoccupation with tracing the origins of our contemporary understanding of the Bill of Rights.

Section 32 fared little better. Narrowly construed both by postal officers and the courts, it was never successfully invoked to expand the permissible boundaries of dissent. On the contrary, in the quarter century between 1835 and the Civil War, Southern postmasters routinely delivered up abolitionist literature to local authorities to be destroyed in accordance with state law.[46] Should a postmaster refuse to cooperate with the local authorities, he could face prosecution and even imprisonment. In 1849, for example, Spartanburg, South Carolina, postmaster George H. Legg was jailed by state authorities for his refusal to hand over to a local vigilance society a letter that the society claimed it had the right to inspect.[47]

As long as the slaveholding states continued to dominate the central government, Southern public figures had little reason to fear. With the triumph of the Republican party in the election of 1860, however, the future suddenly looked far less certain. The Republicans, after all, were an exclusively northern party with virtually no support in the slaveholding states. Now that they had gained control of the central government, it suddenly became conceivable that the incoming administration might encourage the national discussion of the slavery issue that the abolitionists had sought, or at the very least appoint individuals sympathetic to the abolitionist cause to key postmasterships within the South. For many, this was a frightening specter that helped to stiffen the resolve of the secessionists when in 1861 they chose to reject the Union and cast their lot with the South.

IN FEBRUARY 1836, John C. Calhoun made a striking observation. The greatest danger of the abolitionist mass mailing, Calhoun declared, lay not in those states in which abolitionist publications were prohibited by law, but rather in those states in which they were not. "The incessant action of hundreds of societies, and a vast printing establishment," he warned, "throwing out, daily, thousands of artful and inflammatory publications, must make, in time, a deep impression on the section of the Union where they freely circulate, and are mainly designed to have effect."[48] Calhoun was mistaken when he claimed that the abolitionists sought "mainly" to reach an audience in the nonslaveholding states. From the outset, the abolitionist mass mailing was far more than a mere publicity campaign. But Calhoun's observation did raise a major issue. How would the antiabolitionists prevent the abolitionists from using the postal system and the press to shape public opinion in the nonslaveholding states?

Antiabolitionists answered Calhoun's question in a variety of ways. Some urged the enactment of legislation in the nonslaveholding states that would deny the abolitionists the protection of the laws, outlaw the formation of abolition societies, and ban the publication of information advocating the abolitionists' cause. "We trust," wrote Charleston editor Richard Yeadon, in reference to the events surrounding the Charleston post office break-in, "that this proceeding will tend to open the eyes of our northern friends to the necessity of some energetic step to prevent the unwarrantable and criminal interference of northern fanaticism with southern interests."[49] South Carolina planter James Henry Hammond, in a private letter to a friend in New York, agreed. "These men can be silenced in but one way," he wrote. "*Terror—death*. The nonslaveholding States must pass laws denying protection to them and yielding them up on demand to those whose laws and whose rights they have violated, and whose lives they have endangered and in some times destroyed. This is the *only remedy*. *This alone can save the Union*."[50] The South Carolina legislature was more expansive still. In an extensive report issued in January 1836, it declared that the nonslaveholding states had an obligation to "promptly and effectually suppress" all those "associations" within their borders that purported to be "abolition societies" and to make it "highly penal to print, publish, and distribute newspapers, pamphlets, tracts, and pictorial representations, calculated and having an obvious tendency to excite the slaves of the southern states to insurrection and revolt." Only in this way could the slaveholding states avoid the moral ostracism that was sure to follow should the abolitionists be permitted to proceed unchecked. "Are we to wait," the report went on, "until our enemies have built up, by the grossest misrepresentations and falsehoods, a body of public opinion against us, which would be almost impossible to resist without separating ourselves from the social system of the rest of the civilized world"?[51]

Notwithstanding this steady stream of southern appeals, no northern legislature answered the call. Far more effective was the antiabolitionist-led vigilante campaign, which exported to the nonslaveholding states the same extralegal techniques that the Lynch Men had deployed so effectively in Charleston. Once again, it was Secretary of State John Forsyth who set the tone. Outraged at Gouverneur's "tolerance" toward the abolitionists in permitting the first shipment of abolitionist periodicals to leave the New York post office for the South, Forsyth urged Vice President Van Buren to move swiftly to gain control of the situation. "Instead of mobbing the poor blacks," Forsyth urged, in an apparent reference to recent antiblack riots in New York, "a little more mob discipline of the white incendiaries would be wholesome at home and abroad. A portion of the magician's skill is required in this matter, be assured, and the sooner you set the imps to work the better."[52]

Van Buren's "imps" proved fully equal to the task. By the end of the summer, Jacksonian party leaders had organized well-attended antiabolitionist public meetings throughout the North at which speaker after speaker reviled the abolitionists and praised the suppression of the abolitionist periodicals by Gouverneur and Huger. Sometimes the message was even more direct: in some instances, antiabolitionist mobs destroyed abolitionist presses and threatened the abolitionists with physical violence should they refuse to desist.[53] Southerners found these antiabolitionist efforts highly satisfying and occasionally boasted that they had been directed from the South.[54] Others warned that perhaps things were going a bit too far. It was highly gratifying, wrote South Carolina lawyer Hugh Swinton Legaré to Postmaster Huger, to learn of the "very kind demonstrations" that the antiabolitionists had organized in the North. But, Legaré added, it was high time that Southerners gave up their attachment to "*Lynch law,*—a good thing only in the absence of all other good things, and in the midst of all evil ones."[55] Not everyone was so understanding. Terming the antiabolitionists' determination to secure legislation to restrict the freedom of the press "monstrous" and Kendall's open letters to Huger and Gouverneur "more monstrous," New York congressman William Seward warned that, unless checked, the "Van Buren men" would secure "potent legal restraints" to block the transmission of abolitionist periodicals within the North.[56]

THE ABOLITIONISTS responded to the antiabolitionist counteroffensive with a mixture of surprise and dismay. Initially, they did their best to discount its import. The great majority of Southern whites, William Jay insisted, would have eagerly embraced the abolitionists' appeals had only they not been blocked by a tiny proslavery cabal. "Inquiry," Jay explained, was what the "advocates of perpetual bondage" feared. And in order to prevent this inquiry the Southerners "affected to believe" that the abolitionist periodicals might somehow spark a slave rebellion.[57] Renegade Jacksonian editor William Leggett agreed. "There is no other topick but slavery," he shrewdly observed, "in relation to which the propriety of free discussion is not universally acknowledged in this country."[58] One abolitionist engraving made this point well. Entitled *New Method of Assorting the Mail, as Practiced by Southern Slaveholders, or Attack on the Post Office, Charleston, S.C.,* it portrayed a lawless mob of Southerners indiscriminately rifling the mail—merchants' letters included—in its search for abolitionist periodicals to destroy.[59] From the engraver's standpoint, the Lynch Men were an anomaly in American public life, with their criminal behavior threatening not only cherished values like the freedom of the press but also the routine workings of commerce and trade.

Before long, however, it became plain that the antiabolitionists were not so easily dismissed. The abolitionists' reliance upon the "common system of agitation," reported William Ellery Channing in a judicious survey of the slavery issue published in 1836, had proved to be "signally unsuccessful." Though the abolitionists may have "made converts of a few individuals," they had "alienated multitudes" while inadvertently strengthening the position of the slaveholder in American public life. Most distressing of all, they had goaded public figures such as George McDuffie into launching "deliberate defenses of slavery" that were reminiscent of the Dark Ages.[60] Channing's assessment, while unflattering, was one with which the abolitionists themselves gradually came to agree. Even the mobbing of abolitionists failed to elicit much in the way of public support. Abolitionist historian William Goodell, looking back in 1852 on the aftermath of the post office break-in, conceded that, "except by the intended victims of this proscription, few, feeble, and hated as they were, no voice of remonstrance was uttered, no symptoms of alarm were exhibited."[61]

Far more significant in shaping the public response to these events was the widespread revulsion at Postmaster General Kendall's refusal to take responsibility for the conduct of his staff. Abolitionists understandably found Kendall's conduct outrageous. "Had the people been disposed," fumed William Jay, to delegate to the central government the "censorship of the press," they certainly would not have vested so "formidable a power" in "the 10,000 deputies of the postmaster general."[62] On this point the abolitionists were not alone. For renegade Jacksonians such as William Leggett, Kendall's policy was "monstrous" and "imperial," even as it was "nullifying" and "anarchical." "A less evil than this," Leggett gasped, "drew forth Milton's *Areopagitica*."[63] For British visitor Harriet Martineau, Kendall's continuance in office was "one of the deepest wounds which has been inflicted on the liberties of the nation."[64] And for postal clerk Phineas Bradley, Kendall's approach to postal administration was a humiliating rejection of everything he had accomplished under McLean. Now that Kendall had ceded authority over the mails to his subordinates, Bradley fumed, every "Tom,

Dick, and Harry" in the country would be free to suppress the transmission of any periodical they happened to consider offensive, undermining in this way the "shield of the palladium of public liberty—the great mail establishment of our country."[65]

Most telling of all was the response of John Quincy Adams who, following his defeat in the election of 1828, had returned to Washington as a Massachusetts congressman. Adams had little patience with the abolitionists, whose mass mailing he derided as "inflammatory" and which he freely conceded might well "kindle the flame of insurrection" among the slaves.[66] Kendall's conduct, however, was something else altogether. Seven years after the event, Adams could still not contain his outrage. "Here is an officer of the United States government," Adams exploded in 1842, reviewing Kendall's open letter to Gouverneur, "who unequivocally admits that retaining papers in the post office without distribution is contrary to law, who expressly says that he does not and will not authorize it, and yet tells the postmaster who has applied to him for directions in the case, that he must act in the matter upon his own discretion. I denounce it as a violation of the freedom of the press, as a violation of the sacred character of the post office, and of the rights and liberties of all the free people of the United States."[67]

It is hard to know whether Kendall's conduct was generally unpopular with the public at large. There is reason to suppose that it did raise concerns among many who were unlikely to be swayed by the abolitionists' solicitude for the lot of the slave. "Men of very ordinary understanding," reported journalist Nathan Sargent, in looking back on this period, "could not fail to see that if the officers of the government could, under any pretense whatever, exercise such a power over the mails as to withhold or deliver any publication sent therein at their option, the freedom of the press would henceforth be nothing but a name, a mere shadow without substance. Mr. Kendall's letter struck the public mind at the North with a force that stirred thousands to action who had never sympathized with the abolitionists and who were even opposed to their movements."[68]

In this way, Kendall's handling of the abolitionist mails controversy came to symbolize the emerging alliance between the slaveholding South, the mass party, and the central government that would soon lead even sober-minded Northerners like Abraham Lincoln to conclude that proslavery conspirators had captured the central government in order to consolidate the control of the Southern-backed "slave power" over American public life. And in certain respects it marked a turning point in the history of American public policy as well. By linking as he did the future of the Union with the perpetuation of slavery, Kendall's conduct signaled the collapse of the progressive, developmental, and (at least potentially) antislavery state that had been championed by Henry Clay, John McLean, and John Quincy Adams and the triumph of the conservative, antidevelopmental, and avowedly proslavery state of Andrew Jackson, Amos Kendall, and John C. Calhoun. This was a major shift in perspective and one of the principal legacies of Jacksonian Democracy. It was neither the Founding Fathers, nor the Adamsites, but the Jacksonians who forged the fateful link between proslavery and the Union, making a sectional clash inevitable and setting the country on a collision course that would culminate in civil war.

Conclusion

THE CHARLESTON post office break-in and the ensuing abolitionist mails controversy marked the end of an era in American public life. As perceptive insiders such as John Quincy Adams recognized, these events signaled the emergence of a new and potentially more dangerous phase in the simmering sectional conflict between the slaveholding and non-slaveholding states. "One can scarcely foresee," Adams confided in his diary shortly after news of the break-in reached Washington, "to what it will lead." Though the United States might appear to be peaceful and prosperous, the controversy that the break-in spawned was unmistakable evidence that the "elements of exterminating war" were in "vehement fermentation."[1]

At the core of this conflict was a new set of assumptions regarding the role of the central government in American public life. During the Sabbatarian controversy, the central government for the first time acquired an explicitly moral character. Following the ascendancy of the Jacksonians, it was stripped of its capacity to shift the balance of power from the slaveholding to the nonslaveholding states. With the abolitionist mails controversy, it assumed an explicitly proslavery cast.

For critics of slavery, this was profoundly disturbing. Prior to the 1830s, as Adams explained to a friend, even slaveholders professed to regard the institution as evil and seemed intent upon hastening its eventual demise, while its most outspoken critics pinned their hopes on legislative solutions rooted in the self-interest of the slaveholders, such as those that Adams had tried to implement during his administration. With the abolitionist mails controversy, everything changed. No longer could Adams confidently predict that in the United States, as in the

British West Indies, slavery might one day be peacefully set on the road to extinction. For abolitionists such as William Jay, this combination of circumstances helped to transform opposition to the institution into a religious principle that was not open to compromise. For champions of slavery such as George McDuffie, it emboldened them to defend the institution as a positive good.[2]

Adams's gloomy assessment furnished a revealing commentary on the changes in American public life that had occurred in the generation since Benjamin Rush had proclaimed the creation of an informed citizenry to be a cherished ideal. To help realize this ideal, Congress passed the Post Office Act of 1792, setting in motion a communications revolution that by 1828 had created a national market for commercial information and a public sphere for the discussion of national affairs. In addition, this revolution helped to establish the technical preconditions for the voluntary association and the mass party, two of the most notable institutional innovations of the age. In each of these developments, the central government was far more than an arena in which social groups jostled for advantage. On the contrary, it was an indispensable agent of change.

For a time, the communications revolution worked to thicken the bonds of Union. This was particularly true in the period prior to 1828, when postal policy helped to transform a loose federation of states along the Atlantic seaboard into a national community that stretched from the Atlantic to the transappalachian West. Tragically, however, the communications revolution also set in motion forces that worked after 1835 to put the Union at risk.

For many Americans, it was hard to understand how improvements in the means of communication could prove so divisive. After all, an entire generation of public figures had praised the unfettered movement of information as fundamental to the political, economic, and cultural well-being of the United States.

At least one contemporary, however, recognized the limitations of this popular view. On the eve of the passage of the Post Office Act of 1792, James Madison speculated that as long as the geographical extent of a republic was too large to hasten the rise of sectional factions, improvements in the means of communication would safeguard its future. Though Madison deliberately framed his analysis in theoretical terms, its import for the future of the Union was plain. For a time, public opinion could supplement force and self-interest as an agent of national integration. Geography, however, was not destiny. On the contrary, over time the very improvements in the means of communication that had helped to increase the importance of public opinion would decrease the effective size of the Union, narrow the orbit within which public life revolved, and set in motion an ever-widening sectional conflict that would lead inexorably to civil war.[3]

By 1835, the communications revolution set in motion by the postal system, the stagecoach industry, and the press had hastened the contraction of the Union that Madison had feared. Henceforth, the very improvements that had once knit the Union together would conspire to drive it apart. Here lay an irony that not even Madison could have foreseen. In the end, the Union would be saved neither by public opinion, as Madison had hoped, nor by self-interest, as Adams had dreamed. Rather, its salvation lay in the force of arms, an instrument of national policy that every public figure viewed with alarm, yet one that would prove at midcentury to be no less effective than the postal system had been during the early republic in shaping the boundaries of American public life.

ABBREVIATIONS

ABCFM-HU	American Board of Commissioners for Foreign Missions Records, Houghton Library, Harvard University
ASP:PO	*American State Papers: Post Office*
BLP-PU	Blair-Lee Papers, Princeton University
CSL-CMU	Cortland B. Stebbins Letterbook, Clarke Historical Library, Central Michigan University
EEP-MHS	Edward Everett Papers, Massachusetts Historical Society
EWP-WRHS	Elisha Whittlesey Papers, Western Reserve Historical Society
HCPO-NA	House Committee on the Post Office and Post Roads, National Archives
ILPO-NA	Incoming Letters, Post Office Department, National Archives
LDGP-LOC	Letterbook, Duff Green Papers, Library of Congress
LOC	Library of Congress
MHS	Massachusetts Historical Society
NA	National Archives
NYHS	New-York Historical Society
PMGL-NA	Postmaster General's Letterbooks, National Archives
SCPO-NA	Senate Committee on the Post Office and Post Roads, National Archives
USPSL	United States Postal Service Library

NOTES

Preface

1. See, for example, Lynn L. Marshall, "The Strange Stillbirth of the Whig Party," *American Historical Review,* 72 (1967): 445–468; and Matthew A. Crenson, *The Federal Machine: Beginnings of Bureaucracy in Jacksonian America* (Baltimore: Johns Hopkins University Press, 1975). Recent scholarship that draws on the Marshall-Crenson thesis includes Donald B. Cole, *The Presidency of Andrew Jackson* (Lawrence: University of Kansas Press, 1993), esp. p. 240; Gordon S. Wood, *The Radicalism of the American Revolution* (New York: Alfred A. Knopf, 1992), pp. 303–305; and James A. Morone, *The Democratic Wish: Popular Participation and the Limits of American Government* (New York: Basic Books, 1990), pp. 87–94.

2. Marshall, "Strange Stillbirth," p. 468.

1. The Postal System as an Agent of Change

1. Alexis de Tocqueville, *Journey to America,* ed. J. P Mayer, trans. George Lawrence ([1835; 1840]; Garden City, N.Y.: Doubleday & Co., 1971), p. 283.

2. Alexis de Tocqueville, *Democracy in America,* ed. J. P. Mayer, trans. George Lawrence (Garden City, N.Y.: Doubleday & Co., 1969), p. 304n. Unless otherwise specified, all quotations are from this edition.

3. Tocqueville, *Democracy,* p. 385.

4. Tocqueville, *Journey,* p. 355.

5. Tocqueville, *Democracy,* p. 303.

6. Ibid.

7. For a pioneering account of this phenomenon, see Robert G. Albion, "The 'Communication Revolution,' " *American Historical Review,* 37 (1932): 718–720.

8. Tocqueville, *Democracy,* pp. 384–385, 11.

9. *Historical Statistics of the United States: Colonial Times to 1970* (Washington, D.C.: Government Printing Office, 1975), pt. 2, p. 1103.

10. Ibid., p. 1142.

11. Pliny Miles, "History of the Post Office," *Bankers' Magazine,* 7 (1857): 363.

12. Pliny Miles, "Our National Post Office," *New-York Quarterly,* 3 (1854): 2.

13. John Barton Derby, *Political Reminiscences* . . . (Boston: Homer & Palmer, 1835), p. 171.

14. The post office totals for the United States, Great Britain, and France are, respectively, 7,651, (in 1828), 4,028 (in 1840), and 1,395 (in 1830). The British total includes Ireland. Miles, "History of the Post Office," p. 363; J. C. Hemmeon, *The History of the British Post Office* (Cambridge: Harvard University Press, 1912), p. 71; Susan Bachrach, *Dames Employees: The Feminization of Postal Work in Nineteenth-Century France* (New York: Haworth Press, 1984), p. 26. The population totals are derived, respectively, from *Historical Statistics,* pt. 2, pp. 8, 14; B. R. Mitchell, *British Historical Statistics* (Cambridge, England: Cambridge University Press, 1988), p. 11; and Mitchell, *International Historical Statistics: Europe, 1750–1988* (New York: Stockton Press, 1982), p. 4. The United States total excludes Indians and slaves; the British total includes Ireland.

15. William Smith, *The History of the Post Office in British North America, 1670–1870* (Cambridge, England: Cambridge University Press), p. 327.

16. K. V. Bazilevich, *The Russian Posts in the Nineteenth Century,* trans. David M. Shipton ([1927]; reprint, Rossica Society, 1987), p. 155.

17. Alfred D. Chandler, Jr., *The Visible Hand: The Managerial Revolution in American Business* (Cambridge: Belknap Press of Harvard University Press, 1977), pp. 50–78, 541.

18. Benjamin J. Klebaner, *American Commercial Banking: A History* (Boston: G. K. Hall, 1990), p. 16.

19. My understanding of the importance of the periodic character of postal communications owes much to conversations with Robert Dalton Harris and Milton Mueller.

20. Francis Lieber, *Encyclopaedia Americana* (Philadelphia: Carey and Lea, 1832), vol. 10, p. 289.

21. "The Post-Office Establishment," *Port Folio,* 3 (1809): 237. This is the second earliest magazine article I have located that deals specifically with the American postal system. The earliest is "Review of *List of Post Offices in the United States . . .,*" *Medical Repository,* 7 (1803): 174–176.

22. *Niles's Weekly Register,* 15 (Oct. 24, 1818): 133. This anonymous essay originally appeared in the *New-Hampshire Patriot,* which Hill edited.

23. *National Intelligencer,* Nov. 22, 1826.

24. For one exception, see Carl H. Scheele, *A Short History of the Mail Service* (Washington, D.C.: Smithsonian Institution Press, 1970), pp. 7–41.

25. "Post Office," *Ladies Literary Cabinet,* 2 (May 13, 1820): 4.

26. Leonard Bacon, "The Post-Office System as an Element of Modern Civilization," *New Englander,* 1 (1843): 10–13. For the attribution, see Theodore Davenport Bacon, *Leonard Bacon: A Statesman in the Church* (New Haven: Yale University Press, 1931), p. 169.

27. Miles, "History of the Post Office," pp. 337–338.

28. Albert Bigelow, "The Post Office System as an Element of Modern Civilization," *Yale Literary Magazine,* 16 (1851): 333–335.

29. Francis O. J. Smith, *A Letter Relating to the Administration and Present Con-*

dition of the Post Office Department of the United States under the Hon. William T. Barry, Postmaster General (Portland, Maine: I. Berry and Co., 1835), pp. 7, 9.

30. Bacon, "Post-Office System," p. 14.

31. *New York Times,* Oct. 20, 1852.

32. William D. Merrick, *Speech of Mr. Merrick, of Maryland, on the Bill to Reduce the Rates of Postage . . .* (Washington, D.C.: Gales and Seaton, 1845), pp. 3–4.

33. John C. Calhoun, "Speech on Internal Improvement," Feb. 4, 1817, in Robert L. Meriwether et al., eds., *The Papers of John C. Calhoun* (Columbia: University of South Carolina Press, 1959–), vol. 1, p. 401.

34. *Plough Boy,* 2 (Dec. 30, 1820): 243; "Letter Writing; in its Effects on National Character," *Ladies' Magazine and Literary Gazette,* 4 (1831): 242.

35. Bacon, "Post-Office System," p. 23.

36. James Rees, *Foot-Prints of a Letter Carrier* (Philadelphia: J. B. Lippincott & Co., 1866), pp. 6–7.

37. John McLean to Richard Rush, Feb. 22, 1828, *American State Papers: Treasury,* vol. 5, p. 1081.

38. James Holbrook, *Ten Years among the Mail Bags; Or Notes from the Diary of a Special Agent of the Post-Office Department* ([1855]; Philadelphia: Cowperthwait & Co., 1874), pp. 5, 302.

39. Miles, "Our National Post Office," p. 1. The rhetoric of the bureaucratic sublime has continued to inform popular discussions of the enterprise well into the twentieth century. To organize the *"whole* economy" along the lines of the postal system, declared Lenin in 1917, should be the Communists' "immediate aim . . . This is what will bring about the abolition of parliamentarism . . ." Vladimir I. Lenin, *The State and Revolution,* in *Selected Works* ([1917]; New York: International Publishers, 1971), p. 299.

40. *American Pioneer,* 1 (1842): 107.

41. Francis J. Grund, *The Americans in Their Moral, Social, and Political Relations* (Boston: Marsh, Capen, and Lyon, 1837), pp. 120, 389.

42. Absalom H. Chappell, *Magnetic Telegraph from Baltimore to New York,* 28th Cong., 2nd sess., 1845, H. Rept. 187 (serial 468), p. 2.

43. Francis Lieber, "Report of George Plitt . . .," *New York Review,* 9 (1841): 72–74. For the attribution, see Frank Freidel, *Francis Lieber: Nineteenth-Century Liberal* (Baton Rouge: Louisiana State University Press, 1947), p. 175.

44. Lieber, "Report," p. 73.

45. Lieber to Charles Wickliffe, April 15, 1841, Incoming Letters, Post Office Department, National Archives (hereafter ILPO-NA).

46. Grund, *Americans,* p. 119.

47. William Ellery Channing, "The Union," *Christian Examiner,* 6 (1829): 159–160. Channing's essay would almost certainly have been familiar to Samuel F. B. Morse and may well have inspired Morse's celebrated dictum that the electric telegraph had the potential to transform the United States into *"one neighborhood."*

48. Eli Bowen, *The United States Post-Office Guide* (New York: D. Appleton and Co., 1851), title page.

49. Ibid., pp. 5–6.

50. Ibid.

51. Morrell Heald, review of *The American Mail: Enlarger of the Common Life* by Wayne E. Fuller, *American Historical Review,* 79 (1974): 1242.

52. "Post Office Department," *Collections of Massachusetts Historical Society,* 3rd ser. 7 (1838): 48.

53. Rees, *Foot-Prints,* p. 5.

54. George Rogers Taylor, *The Transportation Revolution, 1815–1860* (New York: Holt, Rinehart, & Winston, 1951), p. 410.

55. Peter J. Coleman, "Beard, McDonald, and Economic Determinism in American Historiography," *Business History Review,* 34 (1960): 120.

56. Harry S. Stout, "Culture, Structure, and the 'New' History: A Critique and an Agenda," *Computers and the Humanities,* 9 (1975): 225.

57. Van Beck Hall, "A Fond Farewell to Henry Adams: Ideas on Relating Political History to Social Change during the Early National Period," in James Kirby Martin, ed., *The Human Dimension of Nation Making: Essays on Colonial and Revolutionary America* (Madison: State Historical Society of Wisconsin, 1976), p. 331.

58. George M. Frederickson, *The Arrogance of Race: Historical Perspectives on Slavery, Racism, and Social Inequality* (Middletown, Conn.: Wesleyan University Press, 1988), p. 133.

59. Carl W. Ernst, "American Postal Service, 1792–1845," *L'Union Postale,* 21 (Feb. 1, 1896): 22.

60. *Niles's Weekly Register,* 28 (July 23, 1825): 326.

61. Joseph Story, *Commentaries on the Constitution of the United States* (Boston: Hilliard, Gray, and Co., 1833), vol. 3, p. 23.

62. Jesse E. Dow, "The Progress and Present Condition of the Post Office Department," *United States Magazine and Democratic Review,* 6 (1839): 185. For the attribution, see *United States Postal Guide and Official Advertiser,* 2 (1851): 97.

63. "Post Office Establishment," *Farmer's Monthly Visitor,* 12 (1852): 183.

64. Eliza Quincy, *Memoir of the Life of Eliza S. M. Quincy* (Boston: n.p., 1861), p. 29.

65. One exception to this generalization are historians of technology, who have long stressed the importance of the federal armories in shaping the development of mass production.

66. John Murrin, "The Great Inversion, or Court versus Country: A Comparison of the Revolution Settlements in England (1688–1721) and America (1776–1816)," in J. G. A. Pocock, ed., *Three British Revolutions, 1641, 1688, 1776* (Princeton: Princeton University Press, 1980), p. 425.

67. Gordon S. Wood, "Framing the Republic, 1760–1820," in Bernard Bailyn et al., *The Great Republic: A History of the American People* (Lexington, Mass.: D. C. Heath and Co., 1977), vol. 1, p. 366.

68. David Brion Davis, *Antebellum American Culture: An Interpretative Anthology* (Lexington, Mass.: D. C. Heath and Co., 1979), p. 232.

69. James Sterling Young, *The Washington Community, 1800–1828* (New York: Columbia University Press, 1966), p. 27.

70. Edward Pessen, *Jacksonian America: Society, Personality, and Politics,* rev. ed. (Homewood, Ill.: Dorsey Press, 1978), p. 2.

71. Tocqueville, *Democracy,* p. 72. The final phrase is sometimes incorrectly translated not as "slips from notice" but as "is invisible." This is unfortunate, since it has

lent the weight of Tocqueville's authority to the mistaken idea that the central government in the early republic possessed no administrative apparatus at all.

72. Tocqueville, *Democracy,* p. 384. For a related discussion, see James T. Schleifer, *The Making of Tocqueville's* Democracy in America (Chapel Hill: University of North Carolina Press, 1980), p. 111. Tocqueville's underestimation of the role of the central government in American public life, Schleifer contends, was the "basic error" of his discussion of the nature and future of the American federation.

73. Peter B. Evans, Dietrich Rueschemeyer, and Theda Skocpol, "On the Road toward a More Adequate Understanding of the State," in Evans, Rueschemeyer, and Skocpol, eds., *Bringing the State Back In* (Cambridge, England: Cambridge University Press, 1985), p. 347.

74. Sean Wilentz, "On Class and Politics in Jacksonian America," *Reviews in American History,* 10 (1982): 52.

75. "Post Office Department," *Ariel,* 5 (June 25, 1831): 71; *United States Telegraph* (Washington, D.C.), May 28, 1831.

76. "Annals of the Post Office Department," Library of Congress (hereafter LOC); *American Pioneer,* 1 (1842): 107.

77. Dow, "Progress and Present Condition," pp. 177–204.

78. Peter G. Washington, ed., *United States Postal Guide,* 1–2 (1850–1852); Pliny Miles, "Our National Post Office," 1–19; Miles, "Post-Office Improvements," *New-York Quarterly,* 4 (1855): 21–52; Miles, *Postal Reform: Its Urgent Necessity and Practicability* (New York: Stringer & Townsend, 1855); Miles, "The Post Office in the United States and England," *American Geographic Society Bulletin,* 2 (1856): 158–188; Miles, "History of the Post Office," 337–365, 433–448; and Miles, "Our Postal System: Its Advantages, Requirements, and Shortcomings," *Bankers' Magazine,* 16 (1862): 577–588; Daniel D. T. Leech and W. L. Nicholson, *The Post Office Department of the United States of America* . . . (Washington, D.C.: Judd & Detweiler, 1879).

79. William Stickney, ed., *Autobiography of Amos Kendall* (Boston: Lee and Shepard, 1872).

80. Wesley Everett Rich, *The History of the United States Post Office to the Year 1829* (Cambridge: Harvard University Press, 1924); Leonard D. White, *The Federalists: A Study in Administrative History* (New York: Macmillan Co., 1948), pp. 176–198; White, *The Jeffersonians: A Study in Administrative History, 1801–1829* (New York: Macmillan Co., 1956), pp. 299–335; White, *The Jacksonians: A Study in Administrative History, 1829–1861* (New York: Macmillan Co., 1954), pp. 251–283; White, *The Republican Era: A Study in Administrative History* (New York: Macmillan Co., 1958), pp. 257–277.

81. Lynn L. Marshall, "The Strange Stillbirth of the Whig Party," *American Historical Review,* 72 (1967): 445–468; Matthew A. Crenson, *The Federal Machine: Beginnings of Bureaucracy in Jacksonian America* (Baltimore: Johns Hopkins University Press, 1975); and Allan R. Pred, *Urban Growth and the Circulation of Information: The United States System of Cities, 1790–1840* (Cambridge: Harvard University Press, 1973).

82. Richard B. Kielbowicz, *News in the Mail: The Press, Post Office, and Public Information, 1700–1860s* (New York: Greenwood Press, 1989); Oliver W. Holmes

and Peter T. Rohrbach, *Stagecoach East: Stagecoach Days in the East from the Colonial Period to the Civil War* (Washington, D.C.: Smithsonian Institution Press, 1983).

83. Wayne E. Fuller, *The American Mail: Enlarger of the Common Life* (Chicago: University of Chicago Press, 1972).

84. My decision to draw on general concepts like "network" and "infrastructure" has been influenced by the example of Alfred D. Chandler, Jr., who has long urged historians to frame their inquiries in broadly institutional terms. See, in particular, Chandler's "Business History as Institutional History" in Thomas K. McCraw, ed., *The Essential Alfred Chandler: Essays toward a Historical Theory of Big Business* (Boston: Harvard Business School Press, 1988), pp. 301–306.

85. For a more extended discussion of scholarship on the history of communications in the United States, including Chandler's treatment of the postal system, see Richard R. John, "American Historians and the Concept of the Communications Revolution," in Lisa Bud-Frierman, ed., *Information Acumen: The Understanding and Use of Knowledge in Modern Business* (London: Routledge, 1994), pp. 98–110.

2. The Communications Revolution

1. Jerrilyn Greene Marston, *King and Congress: The Transfer of Political Legitimacy, 1774–1776* (Princeton: Princeton University Press, 1987), pp. 228–231.

2. "TABLES of the Port of all Single Letters Carried by Post in the Northern District of North-America, as Established by Act of Parliament . . ." (Woodbridge, N.J.: James Parker, 1765); "TABLES of the Port of all Single Letters Carried by Post in the Northern District of North-America . . . as Established by Congress . . ." (n.p., 1775).

3. William Blackstone, *Commentaries on the Laws of England* ([1765–1769]; Chicago: University of Chicago Press, 1979), vol. 1, p. 312.

4. Gouverneur Morris, proposals on fiscal and administrative reform (June-July 1778?), in Paul H. Smith et al., *Letters of Delegates to Congress, 1774–1789* (Washington, D.C.: Library of Congress, 1976–), vol. 10, p. 206.

5. Thomas Jefferson to Joseph Habersham, March 24, 1801, Jefferson Papers, National Archives (hereafter NA); *Register of Debates,* Dec. 17, 1830, pp. 365–366.

6. The affinities between the American and British postal system have been challenged by a number of historians who stress the role of maverick printer William Goddard in setting American postal policy on a bold new course. Everyone agrees that in 1774 Goddard briefly established a subscription-based postal system to compete head-on with the Crown's. But questions remain about the influence of Goddard's venture on American postal policy. According to historian Daniel J. Boorstin, American policymakers used Goddard's abortive experiment to "free" the American postal system "from the domination of the government" by putting it on a "private enterprise" basis that was fundamentally different from the British model (p. 340). Boorstin's conclusion, however, is vulnerable on two counts. First, the Continental Congress chose Franklin rather than Goddard to head the new enterprise, which, given Franklin's prior involvement in the royal postal system, even Boorstin admits was an expression of its "conservatism"; and, second, there is no evidence that Goddard ever sought to adminster his postal system as a "private

enterprise" or, for that matter, that he envisioned it could remain for any length of time under nongovernmental control. Indeed, it is by no means certain that Goddard ever contemplated permitting printers to admit into the mail newspapers intended for ordinary subscribers, even though, as a newspaper printer, Goddard stood to benefit from such a policy himself. Daniel J. Boorstin, *The Americans: The Colonial Experience* (New York: Random House, 1958), pp. 338–340.

7. "TABLES of the Port" (1765).

8. For British North America and England and Wales, the totals are, respectively, 67 post offices for 1,478,037 people and 310 post offices for 6,805,200 people. The post office total for British North America is for the northern district only (see text) and may include some offices that had not yet gone into operation. In addition, it excludes North Carolina, South Carolina, and Georgia, since they fell outside of the northern district. The post office total for England and Wales is for 1761. The population total for British North America is based on a straight-line approximation of the totals for 1760 and 1770; Indians and blacks are excluded. The population total for England and Wales is based on a straight-line approximation of the totals for 1760 and 1770. If the British North American ratio is recomputed to include blacks, it decreases to 1 per 27,900, which is slightly lower than the comparable percentage for England and Wales. Source: post offices: "TABLES of the Port" (1765); Brian Austen, *British Mail-Coach Services, 1784–1850* (New York: Garland, 1986), p. 38; population: *Historical Statistics of the United States: Colonial Times to 1970* (Washington, D.C.: Government Printing Office, 1975), pt. 2 , p. 1168; B. R. Mitchell, *British Historical Statistics* (Cambridge, England: Cambridge University Press), p. 8 (Rickman's first estimate).

9. John Adams to Thomas Jefferson, May 26, 1777, in Smith, *Letters of Delegates to Congress,* vol. 7, p. 120; Cappon, *Atlas of Early American History: The Revolutionary Era, 1760–1790* (Princeton: Princeton University Press, 1976), p. 32.

10. John Adams to Thomas Jefferson, May 26, 1777, in Smith, *Letters of Delegates to Congress,* vol. 7, p. 120; Cappon, *Atlas of Early American History: The Revolutionary Era,* p. 32.

11. "List of Postmasters," 1788, Papers of the Continental Congress, NA.

12. Oliver W. Holmes, "Shall Stagecoaches Carry the Mail? A Debate of the Confederation Period," *William and Mary Quarterly,* 3rd ser. 20 (1963): 555–573.

13. Robert J. Stets, "U.S. Government-Authorized Private Mail Service, 1787–1800," *Chronicle of the U.S. Classic Postal Issues,* 44–45 (1992–1993): 233–237, 9–13, 83–97.

14. Alexander Hamilton, James Madison, and John Jay, *The Federalist,* ed. Jacob E. Cooke ([1787–1788]; Middletown, Conn.: Wesleyan University Press, 1961), p. 287.

15. Jack R. Pole, *The Gift of Government: Political Responsibility from the English Restoration to American Independence* (Athens: University of Georgia Press, 1983), p. 134, and Jack N. Rakove, *The Beginnings of National Politics: An Interpretative History of the Continental Congress* (New York: Alfred A. Knopf, 1979), pp. 354–355. On the relationship of the postal system and the press during the debates over the adoption of the federal Constitution, see "The Controversy over the Post Office and the Circulation of Newspapers," in Merrill Jensen et al., eds., *Documentary*

History of the Ratification of the Constitution (Madison: State Historical Society of Wisconsin, 1976–), vol. 16, pp. 540–596.

16. Carl F. Kaestle, *Pillars of the Republic: Common Schools and American Society, 1780–1860* (New York: Hill & Wang, 1983), p. 33.

17. Jack N. Rakove, *James Madison and the Creation of the American Republic* (Glenview, Ill.: Scott, Foresman, and Co., 1990), pp. 49, 90.

18. Benjamin Rush, "Address to the People of the United States," *American Museum,* 1 (1787): 8.

19. Ibid., p. 10.

20. Francis C. Huebner, "Our Postal System," *Records of the Columbia Historical Society,* 9 (1906): 138–139.

21. Wesley Everett Rich, *The History of the Post Office to the Year 1829* (Cambridge: Harvard University Press, 1924), p. 67.

22. *Gazette of the United States* (Philadelphia), July 16, 1791.

23. John Holt to Samuel Adams, Jan. 29, 1776, in Victor Hugo Palsits, "John Holt—Printer and Postmaster: Some Facts and Documents Relating to His Career," *Bulletin of the New York Public Library,* 24 (1920): 494.

24. James Madison, "Notes on Debates," Dec. 6, 1782, in William T. Hutchinson et al., eds., *Papers of James Madison* (Chicago: University of Chicago Press; Charlottesville: University Press of Virginia, 1962–), vol. 5, p. 372.

25. *National Gazette* (Philadelphia), Dec. 23, 1791.

26. Hazard, "Plan for Carrying Newspapers by Post," 1787, Papers of the Continental Congress, NA.

27. Hazard, "General Post-Office," March 19, 1788, in Jensen, *Documentary History,* vol. 16, p. 567.

28. Hazard to Jeremy Belknap, May 10, 1788, in ibid., p. 591.

29. Petition of Philadelphia newspaper printers, in ibid., p. 563.

30. *Annals of Congress,* 1st Cong., 2nd sess., July 10, 1790, p. 1680.

31. *Gazette,* March 9, 1791.

32. James Madison to Henry Lee, Jan. 21, 1792, in Hutchinson, *Papers of James Madison,* vol. 14, p. 193.

33. *National Gazette,* Dec. 26, 1791.

34. *Gazette,* June 27, 1792.

35. *Annals of Congress,* 2nd Cong., 1st sess., Dec. 28, 1791, pp. 289–290.

36. *General Advertiser,* Dec. 5, 1791.

37. Ibid., Dec. 1, 1791.

38. Ibid.

39. Ibid., Nov. 14, 1791.

40. Ibid.

41. *Gazette,* June 27, 1792.

42. *General Advertiser,* Dec. 1, 1791.

43. "History of the Post Office Department," *American Railroad Journal,* new ser. 5 (Nov. 29, 1851): 764.

44. *Columbian Centinel* (Boston), Sept. 12, 1792.

45. *National Intelligencer* (Washington, D.C.), Dec. 15, 1821.

46. Richard B. Kielbowicz, *News in the Mail: The Press, Post Office, and Public Information, 1700–1860s* (New York: Greenwood Press, 1989), p. 149.

47. Though the Post Office Act of 1792 officially admitted newspapers into the mail, postal officers continued to handle newspapers somewhat differently from letters and often excluded them from the official portmanteau. They were, however, handled with far greater care than they had been prior to this time and were far less likely to be lost or discarded en route.

48. For newspaper estimates, see William A. Dill, *Growth of Newspapers in the United States* (Lawrence: University of Kansas, 1928), p. 11.

49. "Cheap Postage," *National Era*, Oct. 18, 1849. The percentage was based on a calculation of Senator William Allen of Ohio, who estimated that the postal system transmitted 68 million of the 104 million country newspapers that city printers published for the rural market.

50. E. G. Bridge to Charles Wickliffe, Nov. 3, 1843, ILPO-NA.

51. "Comparison of the Products and Burthens of Letters and Newspapers in the Mail," 1796 (pp. 157–158), Postmaster General's Letterbooks, National Archives (hereafter PMGL-NA).

52. Felix Grundy, "Postage on Newspapers," May 19, 1832, *American State Papers: Post Office* (hereafter *ASP: PO*), p. 347.

53. Hill, *Speech of Mr. Hill, of New Hampshire . . . on Mr. Bibb's Amendment to the Bill . . . Proposing the Abolition of Postage on Newspapers* [Washington, D.C.: n.p., 1832], p. 1.

54. Amos Kendall, "Communication from the Postmaster General to Congress," undated, Miscellaneous Records, Post Office Department, NA.

55. "Taxes on Knowledge," *Atlantic Journal and Friend of Knowledge*, 1 (1832): 93–95.

56. Thomas W. Bacot to Philip Box, Aug. 8, 1814, Bacot Letterbook, South Caroliniana Library, University of South Carolina.

57. Richard B. Kielbowicz, "Mere Merchandise or Vessels of Culture? Books in the Mail, 1792–1942," *Papers of the Bibliographical Society of America*, 82 (1988): 169–200.

58. "A Friend to Improvement," *North American Review*, 1 (1815): 15–16.

59. John M. Duncan, *Travels through Part of the United States and Canada in 1818 and 1819* (New York: W. B. Gilley, 1823), vol. 2, p. 318.

60. Russel Blaine Nye, *Society and Culture in America, 1830–1860* (New York: Harper & Row, 1974), p. 372.

61. Amos Kendall to George W. Hopkins, Feb. 24, 1838, United States Postal Service Library (hereafter USPSL).

62. Leonard Bacon, "The Post-Office System as an Element of Modern Civilization," *New Englander*, 1 (1843): 26.

63. Leonard Bacon, "The New Post-Office Law," *New Englander*, 3 (1845): 541.

64. Memorial of the Mobile, Alabama, Chamber of Commerce, March 10, 1842, House Committee on the Post Office and Post Roads, National Archives (hereafter HCPO-NA); Memorial of the Savannah Chamber of Commerce, 1842, Senate Committee on the Post Office and Post Roads, National Archives (hereafter SCPO-NA).

65. Joseph Habersham, *The Post-Office Law . . .* (Washington, D.C.: Charles Cist, 1800), p. 53. Though historians have often assumed that the central government threw its support behind the country press only after the victory of Thomas Jeffer-

son in the election of 1800, in fact, Habersham's statement antedated Jefferson's inauguration by over a year, making this policy an achievement of the Adams Federalists, who helped in this way to institutionalize the changes in American public life that had been set in motion with the passage of the Post Office Act of 1792.

66. John Lambert, *Travels through Canada and the United States of North America in the Years 1806, 1807, and 1808* (London: C. Cradock and W. Joy, 1814), vol. 2, p. 498.

67. Alexis de Tocqueville, *Democracy in America,* ed. J. P. Mayer, trans. George Lawrence (Garden City, N.Y.: Doubleday & Co., 1969), p. 519.

68. David J. Russo, "The Origins of Local News in the U. S. Country Press, 1840s–1870s," *Journalism Monographs,* 65 (1980): 1–43.

69. For a related discussion, see Stephen A. Smith, "Promoting Political Expression: The Import of Three Constitutional Provisions," *Free Speech Yearbook,* 27 (1989): 1–32.

70. For a different interpretation, which credits the Federalists with having successfully established a court press, see Carl E. Prince, *The Federalists and the Origins of the U.S. Civil Service* (New York: New York University Press, 1977), p. 224. Prince neglects the extent to which Gerry's and Burke's objection was met with the passage of the Post Office Act of 1792.

71. Eliza S. M. Quincy, *Memoir of the Life of Eliza S. M. Quincy* (Boston: n.p., 1861), p. 152.

72. *Statutes at Large,* 1 (1792): 236.

73. James Holbrook, *Ten Years among the Mail Bags: Or Notes from the Diary of a Special Agent of the Post-Office Department* ([1855]; Philadelphia: Cowperthwait & Co., 1874), p. 6.

74. Francis Lieber, *Encylopaedia Americana* (Philadelphia: Carey and Lea, 1832), vol. 10, p. 293.

75. Francis Lieber, "Report of George Plitt," *New York Review,* 9 (1841): 78.

76. Thomas Jefferson to James Madison, Feb. 1, 1801, in Hutchinson, *Papers of James Madison,* vol. 17, p. 459.

77. *National Intelligencer,* March 30, 1820.

78. Kenneth Ellis, *The Post Office in the Eighteenth Century: A Study in Administrative History* (London: Oxford University Press, 1958), p. 139.

79. Dorothy Fowler, *Unmailable: Congress and the Post Office* (Athens: University of Georgia Press, 1977), p. 7.

80. John Jay to George Washington, Feb. 3, 1788, in Jensen, *Documentary History,* vol. 16, p. 19. Though the government permitted Jay to open letters under the ordinance of 1782, there is no evidence that he did. Richard B. Morris, *The Forging of the Union, 1781–1789* (New York: Harper & Row, 1987), p. 195.

81. *Niles's National Register,* 68 (Aug. 9, 1845): 364.

82. *Littell's Living Age,* 2 (Aug. 10, 1844): 28.

83. James Buchanan to Edward Livingston, Feb. 22, 1833, in John Bassett Moore, ed., *Works of James Buchanan* (Philadelphia: J. B. Lippincott Co., 1908), vol. 2, p. 320.

84. "The Post System," *DeBow's Review,* 5 (1848): 155.

85. Frederick Green to James Bryson, Oct. 23, 1786, Continental Congress Papers, NA.

86. *Gazette,* July 28, 1792. The article originally appeared in the *Columbian Centinel.*

87. Ibid., July 24, 1790.

88. *General Advertiser,* Feb. 2, 1791.

89. *Annals of Congress,* 1st Cong. 3rd sess., Jan. 31, 1791, p. 1887.

90. *General Advertiser,* Feb 2, 1791.

91. *Annals,* Jan. 31, 1791, p. 1887.

92. Hamilton to George Washington, Jan. 31, 1795, in Harold C. Syrett, ed., *Papers of Alexander Hamilton* (New York: Columbia University Press, 1961–1987), vol. 18, p. 239. See also Jefferson to Habersham, March 24, 1801, Jefferson Papers, LOC. Washington failed to act on Hamilton's proposal, which Jefferson had recommended as early as 1792. Following Jefferson's inauguration in 1801, however, it quickly became the law of the land.

93. This point is worth stressing, since postal historians Wesley Everett Rich and Wayne E. Fuller have long contended that the major postal policy debates in the early republic hinged on the competing claims of revenue and service. In fact, however, revenue generation remained, at best, but a minor refrain.

94. For a related discussion, see George L. Priest, "The History of the Postal Monopoly in the United States," *Journal of Law and Economics,* 18 (1975): 33–80.

95. Francis Lieber, *The Stranger in America* . . . (Philadelphia: Carey, Lea, & Carey, 1835), p. 41.

96. *Annals of Congress,* 1st Cong., 2nd sess., June 15, 1790, p. 1640.

97. "Post Office Bill [HR-74]," in Charlene Bangs Bickford and Helen E. Veit, eds., *Legislative Histories,* vol. 6, *Documentary History of the First Federal Congress of the United States of America,* ed. Linda Grant DePauw et al. (Baltimore: Johns Hopkins University Press, 1972–), p. 1698.

98. *Register of Debates,* 22nd Cong., 2nd sess., Jan. 2, 1833, p. 940.

99. Richard R. John, "Private Mail Delivery in the United States during the Nineteenth Century—A Sketch," *Business and Economic History,* 2nd ser. 15 (1986): 135–147. In the Trans-Mississippi West, in contrast, private mail delivery firms like the letter division of Wells, Fargo, & Company, would continue to carry a large percentage of the total letter mail until well after the Civil War.

100. Historical geographer Allan R. Pred has interpreted the spatial dynamics of postal policy in the early republic somewhat differently, contending that they remained subordinate to the preexisting pattern of commercial demand. This conclusion holds for the period prior to the Post Office Act of 1792, but it is misleading for the period following its enactment. Far more important were the political pressures that led Congress to expand service in the South and the West well in advance of what the market could bear.

101. *Annals of Congress,* 4th Cong. 2nd sess., Feb. 1, 1797, pp. 2057–2058.

102. This percentage is based on the ratio of payments to mail contractors to net postal revenue. The sectional percentages are: New England, 0.88; Mid-Atlantic, 0.53; South Atlantic, 1.52; Southwest, 1.67; Northwest, 1.10. John M. Niles, *Expenditures . . . Post Office Department—1840,* 26th Cong., 2nd sess., H. Doc. 120 (serial 386), pp. 4–23.

103. *Annals of Congress,* 10th Cong., 2nd sess., Nov. 8, 1808, p. 473.

104. See for example, Petition of citizens of Northampton, Lehigh, and Berks Counties, Pennsylvania, March 1830, HCPO-NA.

105. Petition of the inhabitants of Washington District, South Carolina, *State Gazette of South-Carolina* (Charleston), July 1, 1793, in Harvey S. Teal and Robert J. Stets, *South Carolina Postal History* (Lake Oswego, Ore.: Raven Press, 1989), pp. 23–24.

106. Petition of inhabitants of Reading, Connecticut, Dec. 22, 1809, HCPO-NA.

107. Petition of the residents of York County, South Carolina, Nov. 22, 1821, HCPO-NA.

108. *Statutes at Large,* vols. 1–5 (1792–1838).

109. Nathaniel Macon to Andrew Jackson, Feb. 14, 1800, in John Spencer Bassett, ed., *Correspondence of Andrew Jackson* (Washington, D.C.: Carnegie Institution of Washington, 1926–1935), vol. 1, p. 56.

110. *Congressional Globe,* 32nd Cong., 1st sess., July 6, 1852, p. 1664.

111. Lewis Williams, "To the Citizens of the Thirteenth Congressional District of North Carolina," Feb. 18, 1829, in Noble E. Cunningham, Jr., ed., *Circular Letters of Congressmen to Their Constituents, 1789–1829* (Chapel Hill, University of North Carolina Press, 1978), vol. 3, pp. 1489–1490.

112. Richmond *Enquirer,* Feb. 11, 1823.

113. Monroe to John McLean, July 15, 1825, John McLean Papers, LOC.

114. *United States Postal Guide and Official Advertiser,* 2 (1852): 200.

115. M. J. Daunton, *Royal Mail: The Post Office since 1840* (London: Athlone Press, 1985), p. 339. The British postal system would not run its first annual deficit until 1955.

116. Ibid, p. 41.

117. John Morley, *The Life of Richard Cobden* (Boston: Roberts Brothers, 1881), p. 313, cited in Linda Colley, *Britons: Forging the Nation, 1707–1837* (New Haven: Yale University Press, 1992), p. 372.

118. George Plitt, *Report of George Plitt, Special Agent,* 26th Cong., 2nd sess., 1841, S. Doc. 156 (serial 378), p. 15. The French total was Fr 4,000. The $200 total is based on a conversion rate of 20 francs per dollar.

119. The percentage is based on data for 1829, at which time 633 of the 7,826 post offices in the United States generated more than $200. This conclusion is, of course, based on the assumption that the French government did in fact shut down post offices in localities that could not generate the requisite revenue. William Barry, *Amount of Postages for One Year Prior to 31st March, 1829,* 21st Cong., 1st sess., 1830, H. Doc. 61 (serial 197). For a related discussion, see "The Post System," *DeBow's Review,* 5 (1848): 153–154.

120. Nathaniel Hawthorne, "A Virtuoso's Collection," in William Charvat et al., eds., *Mosses from an Old Manse* (Columbus: Ohio State University Press, 1974), p. 477.

121. Gideon Granger to James Jackson, March 23, 1802, in *ASP: PO,* p. 22.

122. Thomas Brown, "An Account of Lineage of the Brown Family," 1865, William R. Perkins Library, Duke University.

123. McLean to John Quincy Adams, March 9, 1825, PMGL-NA.

124. McLean to John Quincy Adams, Nov. 17, 1828, in *ASP: PO,* p. 183.

125. Pliny Miles, "Post-Office Improvements," *New-York Quarterly,* 4 (1855): 24.

126. Duncan, *Travels,* vol. 1, p. 231. For accounts of individual mail robberies, see Henry DeLeon Southerland, Jr., and Jerry Elijah Brown, *The Federal Road through Georgia, the Creek Nation, and Alabama, 1806–1836* (Tuscaloosa: University of Alabama Press, 1989), pp. 98–101; Lucius Wilmerding, Jr., "The Great Princeton Mail Robbery," *Princeton History,* 2 (1977): 18–33; and James Hadden, *A History of Uniontown, the County Seat of Fayette County, Pennsylvania* (n.p., 1913), pp. 623–636.

127. Miles, "Post-Office Improvements," p. 24.

128. Thomas Finlay to Charles Wickliffe, Nov. 22, 1843, USPSL.

129. In legal parlance, this meant that the postal system was not a common carrier. On this point, see *United States Postal Guide,* 1 (1851): 252.

130. "The Post Office," *Hazard's Register,* April 13, 1833, p. 240.

131. Benjamin Ficklin to Robert Jemison, July 18, 1836, Jemison Papers, University of Alabama.

132. Holbrook, *Mail Bags,* pp. 132–133. There is, of course, no easy way to determine the frequency with which merchants relied on banknotes, as opposed to other, less fungible kinds of money, such as promissory notes or bills of exchange. My discussion does, however, call into question the common assumption that merchants rarely sent banknotes in the mail.

133. For a related discussion, see Gordon S. Wood, "The Democratization of Mind in the American Revolution," in *Leadership in the American Revolution* (Washington: Library of Congress, 1974), pp. 63–88, and Michael Warner, *The Letters of the Republic: Publication and the Public Sphere in Eighteenth-Century America* (Cambridge: Harvard University Press, 1990). Warner's study focuses primarily on the heyday of the patrimonial public sphere in the period between 1765 and 1792, Wood on the early years of the disembodied public sphere in the 1790s.

134. William J. Gilmore, *Reading Becomes a Necessity of Life: Material and Cultural Life in Rural New England, 1780–1835* (Knoxville: University of Tennessee Press, 1989), p. 196.

135. Charles Augustus Murray, *Travels in North America During the Years 1834, 1835, and 1836* (London: Richard Bentley, 1839), vol. 2, p. 315.

136. Thomas Hamilton, *Men and Manners in America* (Edinburgh: William Blackwood, 1833), vol. 2, p. 78.

137. Thomas Ashe, *Travels in America, Performed in 1806* (London: Richard Phillips, 1808), pp. 140–141.

138. Thomas C. Leonard, *The Power of the Press: The Birth of American Political Reporting,* (New York: Oxford University Press, 1986), p. 74.

139. "Great Meeting in Favor of Post Office Reform," *New World,* Dec. 2, 1843; *Cheap Postage: A Dialogue on Cheap Postage* . . . [Washington, D.C.: n.p., 1849], p. 8.

140. F. O. J. Smith, "The Post-Office Department: Considered with Reference to Its Conditions, Policy, Prospects, and Remedies," *Hunt's Merchants' Magazine,* 11 (1844): 530–531.

141. Pliny Miles, "The Post Office in the United States and England," *American Geographic Society Bulletin,* 2 (1856): 180; Anthony Trollope, *North America* (New York: Alfred A. Knopf, 1951), p. 473.

142. *American Agriculturalist,* 3 (1844): 330.

143. "The Post System," *DeBow's Review,* 12 (1852): 253.

144. Washington, "Fifth Annual Address," 1793, in J. D. Richardson, ed., *Compilation of the Messages and Papers of the Presidents, 1789–1917,* 53rd Cong., 2nd sess., 1907, H. Misc. Doc. 210 (serial 3265), vol. 1, p. 142.

145. Rufus Putnam to Timothy Pickering, Aug. 30, 1794, in Rowena Buell, ed., *Memoirs of Rufus Putnam* (Boston: Houghton, Mifflin, and Co., 1903), p. 394.

146. James Madison, "Public Opinion," *National Gazette,* Dec. 19, 1791, in Hutchinson, *Papers of James Madison,* vol. 14, p. 170. Italics in original.

147. *Gazette,* Jan. 7, 1795. For a suggestive but not entirely persuasive attempt to portray the Federalists as opponents of the spread of political information, see Richard Buel, Jr., *Securing the Revolution: Ideology in American Politics, 1789–1815* (Ithaca, N.Y.: Cornell University Press, 1972). Buel exaggerates the contrast between the Federalists and the Republicans and neglects the extent to which both parties were responding to the new informational environment that had been created with the passage of the Post Office Act of 1792.

148. Madison, "Public Opinion," in Hutchinson, *Papers of James Madison,* vol. 14, p. 170.

149. Madison, "Address of the House of Representatives to the President," Nov. 9, 1792, in ibid., vol. 14, p. 404.

150. Madison, "Notes for the *National Gazette* Essays," c. 1791–1792, in Hutchinson, *Papers of James Madison,* vol. 14, pp. 158–159.

3. Completing the Network

1. John Quincy Adams, "Third Annual Message," Dec. 4, 1827, in J. D. Richardson, ed., *Compilation of the Messages and Papers of the Presidents, 1789–1917,* 53rd Cong., 2nd sess., 1907, H. Misc. Doc. 210 (serial 3265), vol. 2, p. 390.

2. The national postal network was one of several administrative networks that the central government established in the period between the adoption of the federal Constitution in 1788 and the election of Andrew Jackson in 1828. Others were the federal court system, the national banking system, and the mechanism for the distribution of the public lands. Taken together, the establishment of these administrative networks in the early republic deserves comparison with the establishment in the Progressive Era of the large-scale, science-based industrial combines that Samuel Hays has termed "technical systems." Both were genuinely new organizational forms, and both had far reaching implications for American public life. Samuel P. Hays, "The New Organizational Society," in Jerry Israel, ed., *Building the Organizational Society: Essays on Associational Activities in Modern America* (New York: Free Press, 1972), pp. 1–15, esp. pp. 2–5.

3. Martha Burri, "A New View of Blodget's Hotel," *Washington History,* 2 (1990): 103–104.

4. James Boardman, *America and the Americans* (London: Longman, Rees, Orme, Brown, Green, & Longman, 1833), p. 241.

5. McLean's last name, which was commonly pronounced "McLane," was sometimes spelled this way as well. *An Address to the People of Maryland . . . in the Late National Republican Convention* (Baltimore: Sands & Neilson, 1832), pp. 18–19.

6. Francis P. Weisenburger, *The Life of John McLean: A Politician on the Supreme*

Court (Columbus: Ohio State University Press, 1937), p. 35; Richmond *Enquirer,* June 10, 1823.

7. John Quincy Adams, *Memoirs of John Quincy Adams,* ed. Charles Francis Adams (Philadelphia: J. B. Lippincott & Co., 1874–1877), Nov. 30, 1827, vol. 7, p. 364.

8. My use of the phrase "national republican" deserves a word of explanation, in light of the expansive way in which this phrase has in recent years come to be used. For several recent historians, including Charles Sellers and Alexander Saxton, it has become customary to date the origins of the National Republican party to the years immediately following the War of 1812. While there can be little doubt that the public figures whom historians have identified as the leaders of this party— including John Quincy Adams, John C. Calhoun, and Henry Clay—did share an expansive view of the proper role of the central government in American public life, only rarely did they work together as members of a united group. Accordingly, it has seemed best to confine the party designation "National Republican" to the period following the election of 1828, when Clay and his allies attempted to organize a political party with this name to unseat Jackson in the election of 1832, and to use phrases such as "Adamsite," "Calhounite," and "Clayite" to describe the political allegience of public figures in the period prior to this.

9. McLean's tenure as postmaster general has long sparked controversy among historians and for this reason deserves comment. For the most part, the controversy has focused on whether McLean was a hypocrite for professing loyalty to President Adams while deviously manipulating postal patronage to Adams's disadvantage or a statesman who dispensed patronage in an impartial manner while making a number of praiseworthy improvements in postal administration. It is my contention that McLean was simultaneously a capable administrator *and* a political opportunist and that it was precisely McLean's success at combining his considerable adminis- trative ability with his covert support for Calhoun and himself that made him such a formidable figure on the national political stage.

10. Van Buren to Andrew Jackson, Oct. 11, 1831, in John Spencer Bassett, ed., *Correspondence of Andrew Jackson* (Washington, D.C.: Carnegie Institution of Wash- ington, 1925–1935), vol. 4, p. 355.

11. Frederick W. Seward, ed., *William H. Seward: An Autobiography* (New York: Derby and Miller, 1891), p. 89. William Seward wrote: "Mr. McLean was an ex- ceedingly popular man, and it seemed to us that his name, identified with the Anti- Masonic party, would secure it consideration and respect throughout the Union." Though McLean's refusal of the Anti-Masons' offer is forgotten today, it earned him a footnote in the history books: by forcing the Anti-Masons to scramble for a replacement, McLean left party leaders no alternative but to choose a candidate *during* their convention, establishing a precedent that would soon be emulated by the mass parties.

12. William E. Gienapp, *The Origins of the Republican Party, 1852–1856* (New York: Oxford University Press, 1987), pp. 314, 340.

13. William Plumer, *William Plumer's Memorandum of Proceedings in the United States Senate, 1803–1807,* ed. Everett Brown Somerville (New York: Macmillan Co., 1923), p. 130.

14. *National Intelligencer,* Feb. 27, 1829. McLean's success at thrusting himself

and the postal system into the public spotlight qualifies the contention of political scientist James Sterling Young that it was not until the victory of the Andrew Jackson in the election of 1828 that the Jacksonians solved the "problem" of "government at a distance and out of sight." To the extent that this problem can be said to have existed at all in the early republic, it had been solved *prior* to Jackson's election by John McLean. James Sterling Young, *The Washington Community, 1800–1828* (New York: Columbia University Press, 1966), p. 249.

15. Jeremiah Evarts to David Greene, March 5, 1829, American Board of Commissioners for Foreign Missions Records, Houghton Library, Harvard University (hereafter ABCFM-HU).

16. Anne Royall, *The Black Book: Or a Continuation of Travels in the United States* (Washington, D.C.: Printed for the author, 1828), vol. 3, p. 214.

17. McLean, *Report from the Postmaster General,* 20th Cong., 2nd sess., 1828, S. Doc. 1 (serial 181), pp. 179–181.

18. J. W. Campbell to Allen Trimble, Jan 6, 1827, in "Selections from the Papers of Governor Allen Trimble, 1823–1830," *Old Northwest Geneological Quarterly,* 10 (1907): 317.

19. Royall, *Black Book,* vol. 3, p. 214.

20. Adams, *Memoirs,* Oct. 23, 1827; Oct. 25, 1827; Nov. 30, 1827; vol. 7, pp. 343, 344, 364.

21. *Register of Debates,* 19th Cong., 2nd sess., Jan. 15, 1827, p. 64.

22. Adams, *Memoirs,* Oct. 23, 1827, vol. 7, p. 343.

23. Phineas Bradley to McLean, March 11, 1829, McLean Papers, LOC.

24. *Argus of Western America* (Frankfort, Ky.), March 18, 1829.

25. *Albany Argus,* March 11, 1829.

26. Adams, *Memoirs,* Sept. 14, 1831, vol. 8, p. 412.

27. Charles S. Bradley, "The Bradley Family and the Times in Which They Lived," *Records of the Columbia Historical Society,* 6 (1903): 123.

28. Charles W. Upham, *The Life of Timothy Pickering* (Boston: Little, Brown, and Co., 1873), vol. 2, p. 506; Timothy Pickering to Thomas Mifflin, Aug. 16, 1791, George Washington Papers, LOC.

29. Abraham Bradley, Jr., "Journal of the Proceedings of the Select Committee . . .," Feb. 1, 1831, *ASP: PO,* p. 331.

30. Abraham Bradley, Jr., *Map of the United States, Exhibiting the Post-Roads, the Situations, Connections, and Distances of the Post-Offices, Stage Roads* . . . (Philadelphia: n.p., 1796); Bradley, *Map of the United States, Exhibiting the Post-Roads, the Situations, Connexions, and Distances of the Post-Offices, Stage Roads* . . . (Philadelphia: F. Shallus, 1804).

31. Jedidiah Morse, *The American Gazetteer* . . . (Boston: S. Hall and Thomas and Andrews, 1797); Jedidiah Morse, *The American Universal Geography* . . . (Boston: Isaiah Thomas and Ebenezer T. Andrews, 1802).

32. John Melish, *The Traveler's Directory through the United States* (Philadelphia: John Melish, 1822), p. v; Oliver W. Holmes and Peter T. Rohrbach, *Stagecoach East: Stagecoach Days in the East from the Colonial Period to the Civil War* (Washington, D.C.: Smithsonian Institution Press, 1983), p. 96.

33. Richard H. Kohn, *Eagle and Sword: The Beginnings of the Military Establishment in America* (New York: Free Press, 1975), p. 419; Walter W. Ristow, *Amer-*

ican Maps and Mapmakers: Commercial Cartography in the Nineteenth Century (Detroit: Wayne State University Press, 1985), p. 71.

34. William Stickney, ed., *Autobiography of Amos Kendall* (Boston: Lee and Shepard, 1872), pp. 287–288.

35. Royall, *Black Book,* vol. 3, p. 214.

36. Ben: Perley Poore, *Perley's Reminiscences of Sixty Years in the National Metropolis* (Philadelphia: Hubbard Brothers, 1886), p. 218.

37. Stickney, *Autobiography,* p. 307.

38. Thomas B. Searight, *The Old Pike: A History of the National Road* (Uniontown, Pa.: Published by the author, 1894), p. 187.

39. *National Journal* (Washington, D.C.), June 30, 1829, Aug. 5, 1829.

40. *United States Telegraph,* Sept. 30, 1829.

41. Eli Bowen, *The United States Post-Office Guide* (New York: D. Appleton and Co., 1851), p. 16.

42. [William T. Barry], *Organization of the Post Office Department* [Washington, D.C.: n.p., 1830], p. 2; Alexis de Tocqueville, *Democracy in America,* ed. J. P. Mayer, trans. George Lawrence ([1835; 1840]; Garden City, N.Y.: Doubleday & Co., 1969), pp. 207–208.

43. I am grateful to Joan Zimmerman for suggesting this analogy.

44. The size of the clerical staff is calculated from the *Register of Officers and Agents* for 1827. Family size and slave ownership are calculated from the District of Columbia manuscript census for 1830 and the *Register of Officers and Agents* for 1829. Of the 25 postal clerks who could be positively identified in the 1830 manuscript census, 72 percent had children under the age of ten, 60 percent owned slaves, and 44 percent owned female slaves who were under twenty-four.

45. Joseph Habersham to Richard Dobbs Spaight, Oct. 2, 1801, Postmaster General's Letterbooks, National Archives (hereafter PMGL-NA).

46. *Post-Office Law, Instructions, and Forms* . . . (Washington, D.C.: Way and Gideon, 1825), p. 32.

47. Granger to postmaster at Middlebrook, Virginia, July 21, 1802, PMGL-NA. Granger's letter read, in part: "When I first entered upon the duties of this office, I felt strongly opposed to the system of distribution. I was soon convinced that the department was so extensive that the system was absolutely necessary to the existence of the department." For the standard view, see White, *Jeffersonians,* p. 307. Relying on published sources, White mistakenly credits the Jeffersonians with the establishment of the hub-and-spoke sorting scheme.

48. Joseph Habersham to William J. Hobby, Aug. 25, 1800, PMGL-NA.

49. Thomas L. Bacot to Abraham Bradley, Jr., Dec. 8, 1812, Letterbook, Bacot Papers, South Caroliniana Library, University of South Carolina. The establishment in 1800 of the three-tiered administrative hierarchy, with its cohort of middle managers, occured almost a half century before the completion in the 1850s of the transappalachian railroad network, the event that is customarily credited with having introduced the principle of middle management to the United States.

50. The establishment of this hub-and-spoke sorting scheme qualifies the common contention that it was the commercialization of the electric telegraph in 1844 that marked the decisive break in the link between transportation and communication. This link had already been broken more than forty years earlier with the

establishment in 1800 of a network of distribution centers to coordinate the movement of the mail. From this time on, postal officers routinely distinguished between the *conveyance* of the portmanteau that protected the mail and the *transmission* of the mail itself. And if, as sociologist Anthony Giddens has contended, the breaking of the link between transportation and communication is as significant as "any prior invention in human history," the establishment of the hub-and-spoke sorting scheme deserves to be remembered as a key event in the making of the modern world. To put it somewhat differently, with its establishment the United States witnessed a "revolution of 1800" that had nothing to do with the victory of Thomas Jefferson over John Adams, but which was no less far reaching in its implications for American public life. Anthony Giddens, *The Nation-State and Violence,* vol. 2 of *A Contemporary Critique of Historical Materialism* (Berkeley: University of California Press, 1987), p. 176.

51. McLean to James Hamilton, Feb. 22, 1828, in *American State Papers: Treasury,* vol. 5, p. 1081.

52. Daniel D. Leech and W. L. Nicholson, *The Post Office Department of the United States of America* . . . (Washington, D.C.: Judd & Detweiler, 1879), p. 18; F. O. J. Smith, "The Post Office Department, Considered with Reference to Its Condition, Policy, Prospects, and Remedies," *Hunt's Merchant's Magazine,* 12 (1845): 143; Joshua Leavitt, "The Practical Working of Cheap Postage," *Hunt's Merchant's Magazine,* 22 (1850): 51.

53. Peter G. Washington, "Post Office Department," *United States Postal Guide and Official Advertiser,* 2 (1851): 98.

54. *Post-Office Law, Instructions, and Forms* (1825); *Post-Office Laws, Instructions, and Forms* . . . (Washington, D.C.: Way & Gideon, 1828).

55. Adams, *Memoirs,* May 26, 1828, vol. 8, p. 12; Weisenburger, *McLean,* p. 57.

56. *Niles's Weekly Register,* 29 (Nov. 19, 1825): 181.

57. James Rees, *Foot-Prints of a Letter-Carrier: Or, a History of the World's Correspondence* . . . (Philadelphia: J. B. Lippincott & Co., 1866), pp. 314–315; James Holbrook, *Ten Years among the Mail Bags: or Notes from the Diary of a Special Agent of the Post-Office Department* ([1855]; Philadelphia: Cowperthwait & Co., 1874).

58. Adams, *Memoirs,* Jan. 17, 1828, vol. 7, p. 408.

59. See, for example, [Francis Lieber], "Dead Letters Opened and Burned by the Postmaster-General, Revived and Published by Timothy Quicksand," *New-England Magazine,* 1–2 (1831–1832): 505–511; 55–60. For the attribution, see Frank Freidel, *Francis Lieber: Nineteenth-Century Liberal* (Baton Rouge: Louisiana State University Press, 1957), p. 75.

60. McLean to Adams, Nov. 17, 1828, in *ASP: PO,* p. 184.

61. Leech and Nicholson, *Post Office Department,* pp. 38–39.

62. "The Defects of the Postal Service," *Nation,* Sept. 4, 1873, p. 158.

63. Woodson Wren to Jefferson Davis, Feb. 13, 1848, SCPO-NA.

64. McLean to John W. Taylor, March 14, 1826, in *ASP: PO,* p. 141.

65. McLean, *Report of the Postmaster General,* 19th Cong., 1st sess., 1825, S. Doc. 1 (serial 125), p. 168.

66. "To Give Dispatch and System to the Business of the Post Office Department . . .," 1823, McLean Papers, LOC. McLean's organizational manual is the earliest I have been able to locate. Its existence contradicts Crenson's blanket assertion that

McLean "never mentioned such bureaucratic abstractions as 'bureaus' or 'divisions' or 'offices.' " In his manual, McLean referred specifically to "divisions," though not to "bureaus" or "offices"; the latter two bits of nomenclature were introduced by Barry. Matthew A. Crenson, *The Federal Machine: Beginnings of Bureaucracy in Jacksonian America* (Baltimore: Johns Hopkins University Press, 1975), p. 113.

67. "Duties of Postmasters," *Niles's Weekly Register,* 33 (Oct. 6, 1827): 89–90.

68. McLean to Clay, Jan, 24, 1824; McLean to John W. Taylor, March 14, 1826; both in *ASP: PO,* pp. 114, 141.

69. Joseph Habersham to John Wheelock, Dec. 20, 1800, Gratz Collection, Historical Society of Pennsylvania.

70. *Post-Office Law, Instructions, and Forms* . . . (Washington, D.C.: Way & Gideon, 1825), p. 49.

71. *Post-Office Laws, Instructions, and Forms* . . . (Washington, D.C.: Way & Gideon, 1828), p. 7.

72. McLean to Lemuel Sawyer, Aug. 13, 1823, PMGL-NA.

73. McLean, "To the Citizens of Lebanon, Ohio," Aug. 19, 1827, McLean Papers, LOC.

74. *National Intelligencer,* Sept. 13, 1824.

75. William H. Gaines, Jr., *Thomas Mann Randolph: Jefferson's Son-in-Law* (Baton Rouge: Louisiana State University Press, 1966), pp. 146–147; Dumas Malone, *Thomas Jefferson: The Sage of Monticello* (Boston: Little, Brown, & Co., 1981), pp. 449–451; *National Intelligencer,* Sept. 13, 1824.

76. McLean to Monroe, Sept. 13, 1828, Monroe Papers, LOC. Characteristically, McLean took a very different position in public. In his eulogy for Monroe, for example, McLean claimed disingenuously that Monroe had never intimated a preference for any of the candidates whose names McLean laid before him. John McLean, *An Eulogy on the Character and Public Services of James Monroe* . . . (Cincinnati: Looker and Reynolds, 1831), p. 25.

77. Adams, *Memoirs,* Nov. 17, 1826, vol. 7, p. 180.

78. DeWitt Clinton to McLean, Oct. 11, 1825, Clinton Papers, Columbia University; Calhoun to Samuel L. Gouverneur, March 25, 1825, *Bulletin of the New York Public Library,* 3 (1899): 328.

79. McLean to Monroe, Sept. 19, 1828, Monroe Papers, LOC.

80. Adams, *Memoirs,* May 16, 1828, vol. 7, p. 544.

81. Van Buren to B. F. Butler, May 14, 1826, Van Buren Papers, LOC. For a different interpretation of this event, see Leonard D. White, *The Jeffersonians: A Study in Administrative History, 1801–1829* (New York: Macmillan, 1951), p. 319.

82. McLean to Everett, Aug. 8, 1828, in Worthington C. Ford, ed., "Use of Patronage in Elections," *Proceedings of the Massachusetts Historical Society,* 3rd ser. 1 (1907–1908): 367.

83. Ibid., pp. 366–367.

84. McLean to Everett, Aug. 27, 1828, in ibid., p. 384.

85. "An Ordinance for Regulating the Post Office in the United States," 1782, in Worthington C. Ford, et al., eds., *Journals of the Continental Congress, 1774–1789* (Washington, D.C.: Government Printing Office, 1904–1937), vol. 23, p. 670.

86. Richmond *Enquirer,* May 6, 1825, June 14, 1825.

87. McLean, "The Express Mail" [1827], McLean Papers, LOC.

88. Ibid., *National Intelligencer,* May 24, 25, 1825.

89. McLean to Skinner, April 27, 1825, PMGL-NA.

90. *Niles's Weekly Register,* 28 (May 28, 1825): 194.

91. *Enquirer,* June 3, 1825.

92. Skinner to Richard Douglass, May 25, 1825, ILPO-NA.

93. McLean, "Express Mail."

94. McLean to Mills, Dec. 4, 1826, PMGL-NA; Mills to McLean, Dec. 16, 1826, in *National Intelligencer,* June 27, 1827.

95. McLean, "Express Mail."

96. Martin Van Crevald, *Technology and War, from 2000 B.C. to the Present* (New York: Free Press, 1989), p. 155.

97. *National Intelligencer,* Dec. 28, 1807.

98. My calculation of the total number of newspapers in the period before 1820 with "telegraph" in the title is based on the list of American newspapers reported in Clarence Brigham, *History and Bibliography of American Newspapers, 1690–1820* (Worcester, Mass.: American Antiquarian Society, 1947), vol. 2, pp. 1343–1344.

99. Samuel F. B. Morse to Levi Woodbury, Sept. 27, 1837, *Telegraphs for the United States,* 25th Cong., 2nd sess., 1837, H. Doc. 15 (serial 322), p. 28.

100. Henry Clay to Alfred Vail, Sept. 10, 1844, Vail Telegraph Collection, Smithsonian Institution Archives.

101. "The Magnetic Telegraph: American and British," *American Railroad Journal,* 18 (April 17, 1845): 254; "Magnetic Telegraphs," *Niles's National Register,* 68 (July 4, 1846): 273–274; "Magnetic Telegraphs," ibid. (Sept. 26, 1846): 61. "All the other public journals that expressed opinions," wrote an editoralist in *Niles's* in September 1846, in surveying the public response to the new technology, "appeared to urge the government to make the telegraph a government monopoly. The principal motive leading to the advice was manifestly an impatience to have the lines of communication in all directions accomplished with the greatest expedition."

102. Petition of Baltimore merchants, Jan. 11, 1847, SCPO-NA.

103. Technically, the telegraph remained under the jurisdiction of the treasury secretary until March 1845, though this distinction had little practical import. Postal officers oversaw the construction of the Washington-Baltimore line and assumed control of its administration once it was complete. On this point, see John W. Kirk, "Historic Moments: The First News Message by Telegraph," *Scribner's,* 11 (1892): 652–656.

104. William B. Taylor, "History of the New York Post Office and Postal Arrangements," New-York Historical Society (hereafter NYHS).

105. Stebbins to Nathan Hall, Feb. 21, 1851, Cortland B. Stebbins Letterbook, Clarke Historical Library, Central Michigan University (hereafter CSL-CMU).

106. Mobile *Daily Advertiser,* Oct. 22, 1851.

107. Denys Peter Myers, "Historic Report of the General Post Office Building" (Washington, D.C.: General Services Administration, n.d.), p. 50.

108. *National Intelligencer,* May 14, 1823.

109. Ibid., Nov. 18, 1823.

110. *Niles's Weekly Register,* 25 (Oct. 4, 1823): 65. For circulation figures for *Niles's Weekly Register,* see Norval Neil Luxon, *Niles's Weekly Register: News Magazine of*

the Nineteenth Century (Baton Rouge: Louisiana State University Press, 1947), pp. 6–7.

111. *Niles's Weekly Register*, 29 (Oct. 1, 1825): 65.

112. Ibid., 36 (May 16, 1829): 178.

113. Mark Twain, *Old Times on the Mississippi* (Toronto: Belford Brothers, 1876), pp. 116–117.

114. *Register of Officers and Agents* (1827).

115. Arthur Hecht, "Government Owned and Operated Coastwise Mail Service of the Eighteenth Century," *American Neptune*, 22 (1962): 55–64; Holmes and Rohrbach, *Stagecoach East*, pp. 118–120.

116. McLean, *Report*, 1828, pp. 179–180; McLean, "Express Mail."

117. Holbrook, *Ten Years among the Mail Bags*, p. 221.

118. Adams, *Memoirs*, Dec. 26, 1839, vol. 10, p. 176.

119. Memorial of Benjamin Dearborn, Feb. 11, 1819, SCPO-NA; Samuel Melanchthlon Derrick, *Centennial History of the South Carolina Railroad* (Columbia: State Co., 1939), p. 90.

120. McLean to James Barbour, March 21, 1825, PMGL-NA.

121. Milton W. Hamilton, *The Country Printer: New York State, 1785–1830* (New York: Columbia University Press, 1936), p. 216; Leonard V. Huber and Clarence A. Wagner, *The Great Mail: A Postal History of New Orleans* (State College, Pa.: American Philatelic Society, 1949), p. 20.

122. "New York City Post-Office," *Harper's Magazine*, 43 (1871): 650.

123. Jonathan Elliot, ed., *The Debates in the Several State Conventions* . . . (Philadephia: J. B. Lippincott & Co., 1836–1859), vol. 4, p. 425; vol. 5, p. 441.

124. Granger to Nathaniel Irwin, March 23, 1811, Madison Papers, LOC.

125. Elisha Whittlesey to Polly Whittlesey, Nov. 5, 1841, Elisha Whittlesey Papers, Western Reserve Historical Society (hereafter EWP-WRHS).

126. *Independent Chronicle and Boston Patriot*, Aug. 31, 1831.

127. Cited in Henry DeLeon Southerland, Jr., and Jerry Elijah Brown, *The Federal Road through Georgia, the Creek Nation, and Alabama, 1806–1836* (Tuscaloosa: University of Alabama Press, 1989), p. 61.

128. McLean to James Hamilton, *American State Papers: Treasury*, vol. 5, p. 1080.

129. McLean, "Citizens of Lebanon, Ohio," McLean Papers, LOC.

130. "Justice" to G. and W. Robertson, 1826, ibid.

131. *National Intelligencer*, July 14, 1824.

132. McLean to James Hamilton, *American State Papers: Treasury*, vol. 5, p. 1080.

133. Adams, *Memoirs*, Oct. 18, 1827, vol. 7, pp. 340–341.

134. Huber and Wagner, *Great Mail*, p. 28.

135. McLean to John Gaillard, Jan. 7, 1824, PMGL-NA.

136. Southerland and Brown, *Federal Road*, p. 116.

137. Michael D. Green, *The Politics of Indian Removal: Creek Government and Society in Crisis* (Lincoln: University of Nebraska Press, 1982), p. 164.

138. Adams, *Memoirs*, Oct. 23, 1827, vol. 7, p. 343.

139. Edward Everett to McLean, Aug. 1, 1828, in Ford, "Patronage in Elections," p. 363.

140. Duff Green to Ninian Edwards, Dec. 10, 1823, in E. B. Washburne, ed., *Edwards Papers* (Chicago: Fergus Printing Co., 1884), p. 213; Duff Green, *Facts and*

Suggestions, Biographical, Historical, Financial, and Political . . . (New York: Richardson & Co., 1866), p. 27.

141. Adam Hodgson, *Letters from North America* . . . (London: Hurst, Robinson, & Co., 1824), p. 18.

142. John F. Stover, "Canals and Turnpikes: America's Early Nineteenth-Century Transportation Network," in Joseph R. Frese and Jacob Judd, eds., *An Emerging Independent American Economy, 1815–1875* (Tarrytown, N.Y.: Sleepy Hollow Restorations, 1980), p. 75.

143. Jordan Woolfolk Accounts, Woolfolk Papers, College of William and Mary.

144. J. F. Holton to Charles Wickliffe, Oct. 12, 1843, ILPO-NA.

145. James Graham to Willie P. Mangum and George E. Badger, Sept. 14, 1850, in Henry Thomas Shanks, ed., *Papers of Willie Person Mangum* (Raleigh, N.C.: State Department of Archives and History, 1950–1956), vol. 5, p. 189.

146. Frank A. Root and William Elsey Connelley, *The Overland Stage to California: Personal Reminiscences* . . . (Topeka: Published by the Authors, 1901), p. 488.

147. Cited in Raymond W. Settle and Mary Lund Settle, *War Drums and Wagon Wheels: The Story of Russell, Majors, and Waddell* (Lincoln: University of Nebraska Press, 1966), p. 111.

148. J. H. Keetley to Huston Wyeth, Aug. 21, 1907, in William Lightfoot Visscher, *A Thrilling and Truthful History of the Pony Express* (Chicago: Charles T. Powner, 1946), p. 33; Don Russell, *The Lives and Legends of Buffalo Bill* (Norman: University of Oklahoma Press, 1960), p. 47.

149. Samuel Osgood to Alexander Hamilton, Jan. 20, 1790, in *ASP: PO*, p. 6.

150. Bradley, *Map of the United States* (1796).

151. Root and Connelley, *Overland Stage*, p. 487.

152. John Marron to John W. Jones, April 28, 1840, ILPO-NA.

153. Royall, *Black Book*, vol. 1, p. 9.

154. Thomas W. Bacot to Bradley, Dec. 8, 1812, Letterbook, Bacot Papers, University of South Carolina.

155. Jesse Smith to Nathaniel Blake, Dec. 15, 1834, Nathaniel Blake Collection, Baker Library, Harvard Business School.

156. *Niles's Weekly Register,* 27 (Jan. 29, 1825): 341.

157. McLean to Calhoun, May 19, 1826, in *ASP: PO*, p. 141.

158. *Register of Debates,* 23rd Cong., 2nd sess., Dec. 29, 1832, p. 929.

159. "Letters from a Pennsylvanian . . .," *Columbian Magazine*, 3 (1789): 627.

160. Petition of the Proprietors of the Norfolk and Bristol Turnpike, Jan. 1818, HCPO-NA.

161. *Independent Chronicle,* Aug. 31, 1831.

162. Alexander Black, *Report, Exhibiting the Present State of the Work and Probable Progress of Operations of the Charleston and Hamburg Rail Road* (Charleston: William S. Blain, 1831), p. 13.

163. Carl David Arfwedson, *The United States and Canada in 1832, 1833, and 1834* (London: Richard Bentley, 1834), vol. 1, pp. 315–316.

164. [William T. Barry], *Organization of the Post Office Department.*

165. *Post-Office Law, Instructions, and Forms* (1825), pp. 53–60.

166. Pliny Miles, *Postal Reform: Its Urgent Necessity and Practicability* (New York: Stringer & Townsend, 1855), p. 88.

167. George Plitt, *Report of George Plitt, Special Agent,* 26th Cong., 2nd sess., 1841, S. Doc. 156 (serial 378), p. 6.

168. Stebbins to Chief Clerk, April 5, 1851, CSL-CMU.

169. Anthony Trollope, *North America,* ed. Donald Smalley and Bradford Allen Booth ([1862]; New York, 1951), p. 478.

170. Fernando Jones to ———, miscellaneous letters, Chicago Historical Society.

171. Pliny Miles, "Economical Advantages of Uniform Postage," *Hunt's Merchants Magazine,* 46 (1862): 528.

172. R. P. Duncan, "Post Office Reform," *American Whig Review,* 1 (1845): 205.

173. McLean to Theodorus Bailey, March 22, 1824, PMGL-NA.

174. *Niles's Weekly Register,* 25 (Oct. 25, 1823): 122. Niles doubted that this regulation could be carried into effect.

175. *Pittsburgh Recorder,* Nov. 6, 1823. From the *Massachusetts Yeoman.*

176. *Niles's Weekly Register,* 25 (Nov. 8, 1823): 148. McLean added, "This arrangement will supersede the post-bills, which have been forwarded with newspapers from some of the post offices."

177. Return J. Meigs, Jr., to Samuel Ingham, Feb. 5, 1816, in *ASP: PO,* pp. 50–55. Prior to Bradley's innovation, the general post office had frequently instructed mail contractors to draw on postmasters along the route for their pay. Bradley's innovation systematized the process and brought it under central control.

178. *National Intelligencer,* Sept. 26, 1829.

179. Meigs to Ingham, Feb. 5, 1816, in *ASP: PO,* p. 56.

180. Meigs to Thomas H. Hubbard, Feb. 11, 1819, in ibid., p. 66.

181. Leech and Nicholson, *Post Office Department,* p. 19.

182. Meigs to House of Representatives, Feb. 20, 1821, in *ASP: PO,* p. 87.

183. Monroe to McLean, Dec. 5, 1827, Monroe Papers, LOC.

184. William Barry, *Amount of Postage Paid into the Treasury,* 23rd Cong., 1st sess., 1834, H. Rpt. 285 (serial 261), p. 8.

185. Adams, "Fourth Annual Message," Dec. 2, 1828, in Richardson, *Messages and Papers,* vol. 2, p. 419.

186. Richard Rush, "Report . . . of the Public Revenue and Expenditure of the Years 1824 and 1825," Dec. 2, 1825, in *American State Papers: Treasury Department,* vol. 5, p. 240.

187. The cumulative surplus was calculated retrospectively from postal records. There is no evidence that the general post office itself compiled similar data, though postal officers probably had at least a rough idea of how much money they had on hand at any one time. In 1822, for example, Meigs estimated that the general post office had a surplus of $500,000, a figure that is quite close to my retrospective estimate of $481,000. Meigs to Philip Barbour, Feb. 25, 1822, in *ASP: PO,* p. 91; *Historical Statistics of the United States: Colonial Times to 1970* (Washington, D.C.: Government Printing Office, 1975), pt. 2, p. 805; Barry, *Amount of Postage Paid into the Treasury.*

188. Prior to McLean's appointment, Adams claimed that the postal system had cost the treasury nearly $100,000 for several years. It is likely that this transaction was a loan, since it was never mentioned in Congress, nor cited as a possible prec-

edent when the Jacksonians ran the postal system into debt, nor even recorded in the records of the postal system or the treasury department. Adams, *Memoirs,* Nov. 30, 1827, vol. 7, p. 364.

189. John McLean, *Report of the Postmaster General on the Subject of the Most Practicable Post Route from New Orleans to Washington City,* 18th Cong., 2nd sess., 1824, S. Doc. 4 (serial 108); John McLean, *Road—Baltimore to Philadelphia,* 19th Cong., 2nd sess., 1827, H. Doc 94 (serial 152).

190. Citizens of Dayton, Ohio, to John McLean, Jan. 10, 1827, Petitions, House Committee on Roads and Canals; John McLean to Charles Fenton Mercer, Dec. 20, 1827, Committee Papers, House Committee on Roads and Canals, National Archives. See also *National Intelligencer,* May 5, 1825; Jan. 26, 1826.

191. *National Intelligencer,* Jan. 1, 1827.

192. Adams, *Memoirs,* Oct. 23, 1827, vol. 5, p. 343; McLean, "Citizens of Lebanon, Ohio."

193. *National Intelligencer,* Jan. 1, 1827.

194. *Register of Debates,* 21st Cong., 2nd sess., Dec. 17, 1830, pp. 368–369.

195. Gideon Granger to Elisha Babcock, Jan. 12, 1802, John W. Taylor Papers, NYHS.

196. *National Intelligencer,* June 12, 1823.

4. The Imagined Community

1. For an introduction to the postal architecture of the Gilded Age, see Lois A. Craig, et al., *The Federal Presence: Architecture, Politics, and National Design* (Cambridge: MIT Press, 1984), pp. 164–169.

2. James Boardman, *America and the Americans* (London: Longman, Rees, Orme, Brown, Green, & Longman, 1833), pp. 218–219.

3. William B. Taylor, "The New York Post-Office in Olden Times," *Dollar Magazine,* 8 (1851): 231.

4. "The New York Post-Office," *Scribner's Magazine,* 16 (1878): 59.

5. "New York City Post-Office," *Harper's Magazine,* 43 (1871): 655–656.

6. Taylor, "New York Post-Office," p. 234.

7. In fact, this practice continued well into the twentieth century. Ross Allan McReynolds, "History of the United States Post Office, 1607–1931" (Ph.D. diss., University of Chicago, 1935), p. 512.

8. Cortland B. Stebbins to Second Assistant Postmaster General, April 2, 1851, CSL-CMU.

9. Mills's post office served as postal headquarters until the 1890s, when it was abandoned in favor of a squat fortresslike stone building that is now known as the Old Post Office. To this day, Mills's post office stands a few blocks north of the National Archives across the street from the National Portrait Gallery.

10. Alex Mackay, *The Western World: Or, Travels in the United States in 1846–47* (Philadelphia: Lea & Blanchard, 1849), vol. 1, p. 111.

11. Robert Mills to Levi Lincoln, Jan. 30, 1839, in Amos Kendall, *Post-Office Building,* 25th Cong., 3rd sess., 1839, H. Doc. 129 (serial 347), pp. 2–3.

12. "The Old Postoffice," *Yearbook, City of Charleston* (Charleston: Lucas & Richardson Co., 1898), p. 357.

13. "The Itinerant Post-Office," undated broadside (c. 1810), American Antiquarian Society.

14. "The Country Postmaster," *United States Mail and Post-Office Assistant,* 7 (1867): 1.

15. John Lorimer Graham to William Jones, June 3, 1842, Graham Papers, NYHS.

16. For reasons that will become plain in the text, I am assuming that postal officers and postal patrons were usually men.

17. Thomas Waterman Wood, *The Village Post Office,* 1873, New York State Historical Association, Cooperstown, New York.

18. Samuel Gwin to Amos Kendall, March 2, 1837, USPSL.

19. Catherine Sedgwick, "The Postoffice," *Graham's Magazine,* 23 (1843): 65.

20. T. C. Elliott, "Wilson Price Hunt, 1783–1842," *Oregon Historical Quarterly,* 32 (1931): 130–132.

21. Richard D. Miles, "The American Image of Benjamin Franklin," *American Quarterly,* 9 (1957): 134.

22. On the colonial postmaster-printer, see Charles E. Clark, "Boston and the Nurturing of Newspapers: Dimensions of the Cradle, 1690–1741," *New England Quarterly,* 64 (1991): 252–259. See also Clark, *The Public Prints: The Newspaper in Anglo-American Culture, 1665–1740* (New York: Oxford University Press, 1993), pp. 81–84, 119–122, 188.

23. Nonpolitical periodicals posed less of a problem. For example, no one seems to have been disturbed by the fact that John Stuart Skinner edited the *American Farmer* for many years while serving simultaneously as postmaster of Baltimore.

24. Timothy Pickering to Samuel Lyman, Dec. 21, 1793, PMGL-NA. See also Gideon Granger to William Loudon, Aug. 8, 1808, ibid.

25. Boston *Statesman,* March 9, 1829.

26. "Editors—Postmasters," *Kendall's Expositor,* Oct. 21, 1841; Kendall to H. A. Kerr, April 17, 1837, PMGL-NA.

27. John Barton Derby, *Political Reminiscences, Including a Sketch of the Origin and History of the "Statesman Party" of Boston* (Boston: Homer & Palmer, 1835), p. 42.

28. Thomas Brown, "An Account of Lineage of the Brown Family," 1865, William R. Perkins Library, Duke University.

29. For a related discussion, see Karen Orren, "The Work of Government: Recovering the Discourse of Office in *Marbury v. Madison,*" *Studies in American Political Development,* 8 (1994): 60–80.

30. William Stickney, ed., *Autobiography of Amos Kendall* (Boston: Lee and Shepard, 1872), pp. 153–160.

31. Ibid.; *Register of Officers and Agents* (1816). Kendall's appointment was an exception to the rule that, in general, postmasters were supposed to relinquish their editorships during their tenure in office.

32. Amos Kendall, *Letter of the Postmaster General Giving His Reasons for Not Removing the Postmaster at Bath* (n.p. [1836]), pp. 10–11.

33. C. P. Richardson to Charles Wickliffe, Jan. 7, 1844, ILPO-NA.

34. Woodson Wren to Jefferson Davis, Feb. 13, 1848, SCPO-NA.

35. Leander P. Richardson, "The New York Post-Office," *Appleton's Journal,* 5 (1878): 202.

36. *United States Postal Guide and Official Advertiser*, 1 (1851): 224.
37. Petition of Andrew S. Hart, June 9, 1852, SCPO-NA.
38. Timothy Pickering to Meriweather Morris, March 12, 1794, PMGL-NA.
39. *Register of All Officers and Agents* (1845).
40. "The United States Mail," *De Bow's Review*, 16 (1854): 563.
41. Ben: Perley Poore, *Biographical Sketch of John Stuart Skinner* (n.p. [1854]), p. 13.
42. *Paul Pry,* March 8, 1834.
43. Benjamin Lyon Smith, *Alexander Campbell* (St. Louis: Bethany Press, 1939), pp. 161–162.
44. Anne Royall, *Mrs. Royall's Southern Tour* . . . (Washington, D.C.: n.p., 1830–1831), vol. 1, pp. 118–119.
45. D. H. Sheldon & Co., "Circular to Agents" (c. 1855); Carroll & Co., "Mr. Postmaster," 1860; both in John F. Smith Papers, William R. Perkins Library, Duke University.
46. David Shields to John McLean, April 20, 1824, HCPO-NA; *Statutes at Large,* 4 (1827): 238.
47. *American Agriculturalist,* 6 (1847): 293.
48. William Leggett, *A Collection of the Political Writings of William Leggett,* ed. Theodore Sedgwick (New York: Taylor & Dodd, 1840), vol. 1, p. 244.
49. "Still an Inducement for Postmasters," *Godey's Magazine and Lady's Book,* 31 (1845): inside cover.
50. Thomas Whittemore circular, 1830, Charles Russell Paper, Massachusetts Historical Society (hereafter MHS).
51. Benjamin P. Thomas, "Lincoln the Postmaster," *Bulletin of the Abraham Lincoln Association,* 31 (1933): 3–9.
52. Edward R. Foreman, "Post Offices and Postmasters of Rochester," in Foreman, *Centennial History of Rochester* (Rochester: Rochester Historical Society, 1933), vol. 3, pp. 53–60.
53. Claude-Anne Lopez and Eugenia W. Herbert, *The Private Franklin: The Man and His Family* (New York: W. W. Norton & Co., 1975), pp. 53–55.
54. *Celebration of the Bi-Centennial Anniversary of the Town of Suffield, Connecticut* (Hartford: Wiley, Waterman, & Eaton, 1871), p. 58.
55. "Robert Patton," in James Grant Wilson and John Fiske, eds., *Appleton's Cyclopaedia of American Biography* (New York: D. Appleton and Co., 1888), vol. 4, p. 677.
56. *Annals of Congress,* 17th Cong., 1st sess., May 1, 1822, p. 1774.
57. Samuel R. Smith to the Postmaster General, Oct. 3, 1827, uninventoried records, Post Office Department Papers, NA; Andrew Coyle to William Barry, June 30, 1829, in *National Journal,* Aug. 5, 1829.
58. Stickney, ed., *Autobiography,* pp. 524–525.
59. Ibid., pp. 278, 511.
60. *Niles's Weekly Register,* 50 (July 16, 1836): 330.
61. Among the Washington postal officers to secure appointments in San Francisco were Jacob Bailey Moore and Charles Weller, who became the first and third San Francisco postmasters, and John Ferguson, who became the chief clerk.

62. On William A. Davis's career, see [J. L. Bittinger], *The Railroad Postal Service originated by William A. Davis* . . . (n.p., n.d.). Original at USPSL.

63. My emphasis on the cultural prerequisites necessary for officeholding is related to, but broader than, the stress that social historians have long placed on officeholders' social status.

64. On Ralph Allen's career, see Benjamin Boyce, *The Benevolent Man: A Life of Ralph Allen of Bath* (Cambridge: Harvard University Press, 1967).

65. On Parker, see Alan Dyer, *A Biography of James Parker, Colonial Printer* (Troy, N.Y.: Whitson Publishing Co., 1982).

66. Julian Ursyln Niemcewicz, *Under Their Vine and Fig Tree: Travels in America, 1798–1799, 1805* . . ., ed. Metchie J. E. Budka (Elizabeth, N.J.: Grassmann Publishing Co., 1965), p. 61.

67. William Goddard to Isaiah Thomas, April 15, 1811, American Antiquarian Society.

68. William Wirt to Heads of Departments, Oct. 17, 1828, Uninventoried Records of the Post Office Department, NA.

69. Samuel R. Smith to John McLean, Oct. 3, 1827, ibid.

70. Stephen Nissenbaum, "The Firing of Nathaniel Hawthorne," *Essex Institute Historical Collections,* 114 (1978): 77–78.

71. Samuel Mordecai, *Richmond in By-Gone Days: Being Reminiscences of an Old Citizen* (Richmond: George M. West, 1856), pp. 156–157, 163.

72. Charles Humphrey to Charles K. Gardner, July 3, 1839, Gardner Papers, New York State Library and Archives.

73. Marcus Morton to John Niles, Feb. 28, 1848, Marcus Morton Papers, MHS.

74. Solomon Van Rensselaer to William Barry, March 24, 1827; K. H. Van Rensselaer to Solomon Van Rensselaer, April 22, 1849; both in Catharina V. R. Bonney, *A Legacy of Historical Gleanings* (Albany: J. Munsell, 1875), vol. 2, pp. 58, 197.

75. Ronald Edward Bridwell, "The South's Wealthiest Planter: Wade Hampton I of South Carolina, 1754–1835" (Ph.D. diss., University of South Carolina, 1980), pp. 267–268.

76. On Franklin's role as a postal officer in popularizing the Gulf Stream, see Lloyd A. Brown, "The River in the Ocean," in *Essays Honoring Lawrence C. Wroth* (Portland, Maine: Anthoensen Press, 1951), pp. 69–84.

77. William Darby, *View of the United States, Historical, Geographical, and Statistical* (Philadelphia: H. S. Tanner, 1828), p. iv.

78. For relevant details, see Arthur Hecht, ed., "The Burr Conspiracy and the Post Office Department," *Missouri Historical Society Bulletin,* 12 (1956): 128–145.

79. W. C. C. Claiborne to Gideon Granger, June 7, 1805, in Dunbar Rowland, ed., *Official Letter Books of W. C. C. Claiborne, 1801–1816* (Jackson, Miss.: State Department of Archives and History, 1917), vol. 3, pp. 83–84.

80. James Beddo to John McLean, Sept. 6, 1824, Petitions, HCPO-NA.

81. Elam Langdon to Charles Wickliffe, Nov. 3, 1842, Robert Dalton Harris Collection, Wynantskill, New York.

82. Thomas B. Searight, *The Old Pike: A History of the National Road* (Uniontown, Penn.: Published by the Author, 1894), p. 186.

83. James Rees, *Foot-Prints of a Letter-Carrier: Or, a History of the World's Correspondence. . . .* (Philadelphia: J. B. Lippincott & Co., 1866), pp. 241–242.

84. Edward Everett to John McLean, Aug. 18, 1828, in Worthington C. Ford, ed., "Use of Patronage in Elections," *Proceedings of the Massachusetts Historical Society,* 3rd ser. 1 (1907–1908): 376.

85. Elam Langdon to Richard C. Langdon, April 24, 1841, Sutphin-Laws Papers, Cincinnati Historical Society Library.

86. *United States Postal Guide,* 2 (1851): 138–139.

87. Thomas Jefferson, "Draft of Instruction to the Virginia Delegates . . .," in Julian P. Boyd et al., eds., *The Papers of Thomas Jefferson* (Princeton: Princeton University Press, 1950–), vol. 1, p. 125.

88. Miles, "Image of Franklin," p. 123.

89. On Franklin's posthumous reputation, see Gordon S. Wood, *The Radicalism of the American Revolution* (New York: Alfred A. Knopf, 1992), pp. 283, 342.

90. Jesse E. Dow, "The Progress and Present Condition of the Post Office Department," *United States Magazine and Democratic Review,* 6 (1839): 180.

91. Ibid., p. 200.

92. *An Examination of the Probable Effect of the Reduction of Postage as Proposed to be Made by the Bill Introduced into the Senate of the United States by the Hon. Mr. Merrick, of Maryland* [Washington, D.C.: n.p., 1845]. By "Franklin." Original in the HCPO-NA.

93. Leavitt, "The Moral and Social Benefits of Cheap Postage," *Hunt's Merchants' Magazine,* 21 (1849), 601.

94. "Magnetic Telegraphs," *Niles's Weekly Register,* 68 (July 12, 1845): 304.

95. F. O. J. Smith, *The Secret Corresponding Vocabulary, Adapted for Use to Morse's Electro-Magnetic Telegraph, and also in Conducting Written Correspondence Transmitted by the Mails, or Otherwise* (Portland, Me.: Thurston, Ilsley & Co., 1844), pp. 236–237.

96. "Our Postal System," *Republic,* 1 (1874): 28.

97. Joseph Habersham to Isaac E. Gano, April 4, 1801, PMGL-NA.

98. For a related discussion, see Linda Kerber et al., "Beyond Roles, Beyond Spheres: Thinking about Gender in the Early Republic," *William and Mary Quarterly,* 3rd ser. 46 (1989): 578.

99. Richmond *Enquirer,* Aug. 4, 1835.

100. Salmon Bulkely to Gideon Welles, June 1, 1840, Welles Papers, Connecticut Historical Society.

101. For a related discussion, see Delsey Deacon, "Politicizing Gender," *Genders,* 6 (1989): 1–19.

102. *Enquirer,* Aug. 6, 1824.

103. Jacqueline Pendleton to Elizabeth Linn, June 20, 1845, Lewis F. Linn Papers, Missouri Historical Society.

104. "Our Post-Mistress, or, Why She Was Turned Out," *Godey's Magazine and Lady's Book,* 40 (1850): 90–92.

105. Cited in Claude Fuess, ed., *The Story of Essex County* (New York: American Historical Society, 1935), p. 498. The travel account, which was unidentified, dated from 1833.

106. Cortland B. Stebbins to Nathan Hall, April 26, 1851, CSL-CMU.

107. "Postmistresses," *Pennsylvania Freeman,* 9 (Sept. 4, 1852): 143.

108. Kenneth Ellis, *The Post Office in the Eighteenth Century: A Study in Administrative History* (London: Oxford University Press, 1958), p. 32; Susan Bachrach, *Dames Employees: The Feminization of Postal Work in Nineteenth-Century France* (New York: Haworth Press, 1984), p. 8.

109. Amelia Bloomer, *Life and Writings of Amelia Bloomer,* ed. D. C. Bloomer, intro. Susan J. Kleinberg ([1895]; New York: Schocken Books, 1975), p. 48. I am grateful to Nancy G. Isenberg for this citation.

110. Solomon Van Rensselaer to Jacob Collamer, April 2, 1849, in Bonney, *Legacy,* vol. 2, p. 195.

111. Foreman, "Post Offices and Postmasters," pp. 55–56.

112. *Statutes at Large,* 2 (1802): 191.

113. John McLean to Connecticut Postmaster, Dec. 10, 1828, *Niles's Weekly Register,* 35 (Jan. 10, 1829): 313.

114. Douglas R. Egerton, *Gabriel's Rebellion: The Virginia Slave Conspiracies of 1800 and 1802* (Chapel Hill: University of North Carolina Press, 1993), p. 67. See also the confession of William Young's Gilbert, Sept. 23, 1800, Executive Papers, Negro Insurrection, Virginia State Library. The slave testified that the "black man who carries the mail to Charlottesville had told him that he had convey'd the intelligence respecting the insurrection as far as Mr. Ross's Iron Works." I am grateful to Douglas R. Egerton for drawing my attention to this document.

115. Granger to James Jackson, in *ASP: PO,* March 23, 1802, p. 27.

116. Gideon Granger to Thomas Jefferson, April 19, 1806, Jefferson Papers, LOC.

117. Alfred Mordecai, "The Life of Alfred Mordecai, as Related by Himself," in James A. Padgett, ed., *North Carolina Historical Review,* 22 (1945): 72. I am grateful to Daniel A. Cohen for this citation.

118. John N. Niles, *Post Office Fines and Deduction,* 26th Cong., 2nd sess., H. Doc. 84 (serial 383), pp. 29, 67, 73.

119. *National Intelligencer,* March 31, 1821.

120. *Paul Pry* (Washington, D.C.), Feb. 1, 1834.

121. Constance McLaughlin Green, *The Secret City: A History of Race Relations in the Nation's Capital* (Princeton: Princeton University Press, 1967), p. 36.

122. William T. Steiger to Elizabeth Shriver, Aug. 11, 1835, in William D. Hoyt, Jr., "Washington's Living History: The Post Office Fire and Other Matters, 1834–1839," *Records of the Columbia Historical Society,* 46–47 (1947): 63.

123. "No Post-Mistresses," *United States Mail and Post-Office Assistant,* 2 (1862): 1; "Female Postmasters," ibid., 2 (1862): 2.

124. Frederick Douglass, "Self-Help," May 7, 1849, in John W. Blassingame, ed., *Frederick Douglass Papers* (New Haven: Yale University Press, 1979–), vol. 2, p. 168.

125. *United States Postal Guide,* 2 (1851): 97.

126. Pliny Miles, "The Post Office in the United States and England," *American Geographic Society Bulletin,* 2 (1856): 176.

127. Solomon Van Rensselaer to Amos Kendall, March 24, 1837, in Bonney, *Legacy,* vol. 2, p. 58.

128. *United States Postal Guide,* 9 (1850): 97.

129. Samuel Gridley Howe, "Postal Reform," *Massachusetts Quarterly Review,* 2 (1848): 95.

130. *Register of Officers and Agents* (1827–1851).

131. "Metropolitan Post-Offices: New York," *Illustrated Magazine of Art*, 1 (1853): 269.

132. Henry W. Connor, *Conflagration—Post Office Building*, 24th Cong., 2nd sess., 1837, H. Rpt. 134 (serial 305), app. B.

133. Neil Blue Diary, Dec. 25, 1847, Blue Papers, Alabama Department of Archives and History.

134. Petition of Joseph Timberlake, Dec. 7, 1818, SCPO-NA.

135. Petition of the Wheeling Board of Trade, Jan. 28, 1846, ibid.

136. George W. Thompson to Amos Kendall, Nov. 3, 1838, Petitions, HCPO-NA.

137. Stebbins to Hall, Oct. 8, 1850, CSL-CMU.

138. *United States Postal Guide*, 1 (1850): 94.

139. *Niles's Weekly Register*, 39 (Sept. 25, 1830): 73. Niles abbreviated the final phrase; I have filled in the missing letters.

140. Stebbins to First Assistant Postmaster General, April 2, 1851, CSL-CMU.

141. Basil Hall, *Travels in North America in the Years 1827 and 1828* (Philadelphia: Carey, Lea & Carey, 1829), vol. 3, p. 121–122.

142. Alfred Bunn, *Old England and New England, in a Series of Views Taken on the Spot* (London: Richard Bentley, 1853), pp. 278–279.

143. Rees, *Foot-Prints*, p. 349.

144. "New York City Post-Office," *Harper's Magazine*, p. 662.

145. Pliny Miles, "Our Postal System: Its Advantages, Requirements, and Shortcomings," *Bankers' Magazine*, 16 (1862): 579.

146. Charles Wickliffe to William Merrick, March 17, 1842, SCPO-NA.

147. *United States Postal Guide*, 1 (1851): 313.

148. Ibid., 1 (1850): 1.

149. *United States Postal Guide*, 2 (1852): 254. Peter G. Washington was not the first public officer to edit a journal of public administration. That distinction belongs to Charles Goldsborough, the editor of the *United States Naval Chronicle*, which was first published in 1824. Goldsborough, however, made no attempt to consider ongoing problems of public administration, while his *Naval Chronicle* consisted exclusively of a retrospective chronicle of past naval exploits.

150. Ibid., 2 (1852): 325–326.

151. Ibid., 2 (1851): 177.

152. Sedgwick, "Postoffice," p. 65.

153. Francis A. Richardson, "Recollections of a Washington Newspaper Correspondent," *Records of the Columbia Historical Society*, 6 (1903): 25.

154. [Alonzo B. Cornell], *"True and Firm": Biography of Ezra Cornell* (New York: A. S. Barnes and Co., 1884), p. 104.

155. Rees, *Foot-Prints*, p. 248.

156. Bayard Taylor, *Eldorado; Or, Adventures in the Path of Empire* (New York: G. P. Putnam's Sons, 1873), pp. 208–213.

157. Ibid., p. 209.

158. Ibid., p. 210.

159. Ibid., p. 211.

160. William Taylor, *Seven Years' Street Preaching* (New York: Carlton & Porter, 1850), p. 253.

161. Taylor, *Eldorado*, p. 212.

162. Henry C. Carey, *Principles of Social Science* (Philadelphia: J. B. Lippincott & Co., 1858), vol. 1, p. 211.

163. Habersham to postmasters of Philadelphia, New York, Boston, Salem, et al., Feb. 18, 1800, PMGL-NA. Habersham's letter read in part: "Receiving money for pigeonholes is . . . contrary to the spirit of the act for establishing the post office. It deprives the penny posts, who are very useful . . . of a portion of that compensation which they ought to receive. You are therefore instructed not to keep any such pigeonholes for private individuals and not to receive any pay for keeping such as may be deemed useful to public bodies."

164. "The Boston Post-Office," *Hunt's Merchants' Magazine*, 14 (1846): 135.

165. Charles Burrall to James McRea, Aug. 11, 1793, PMGL-NA. For a related discussion, see Robert J. Stets, "Penny Posts in the U.S. before 1809," *Penny Post*, 3 (1993): 4–12.

166. Grant Thorburn, *Forty Years' Residence in America* (Boston: Russell, Odiorne & Metcalf, 1834), p. 62.

167. Howe, "Postal Reform," pp. 98–99. For the attribution, see Joshua Leavitt, "The Practical Working of Cheap Postage," *Hunt's Merchant's Magazine*, 22 (1850): 46.

168. Miles, "Post Office in the United States and England," p. 162.

169. Leavitt, "Practical Working," p. 48.

170. Miles, "Our Postal System," pp. 577–580.

171. "The Lowell Post Office," *New England Offering*, 7 (1849): 191–192.

172. "Boston Post-Office," p. 135. For the history of one of the best known of these penny posts, see Elliott Perry and Arthur G. Hall, *One Hundred Years Ago, 1842–1942* (American Philatelic Society, 1942).

173. Pliny Miles, *Postal Reform: Its Urgent Necessity and Practicability* (New York: Stringer & Townsend, 1855), p. 46.

174. *New York Times*, June 7, 1852.

175. Henry E. Abt, "The New York Penny Post: The Beginning of the Story," *Collector's Club Philatelist*, 28 (1949): 100–105.

176. For the history of one of most successful of these city delivery firms, see Henry E. Abt, "Boyd's City Express Post," *Collector's Club Philatelist*, 28 (1949–1950): 163–171, 272–286, 13–29, 97–114, 159–174, 295–313.

177. Miles, *Postal Reform*, pp. 18–20, 38.

178. Howe, "Postal Reform," pp. 98–99.

179. Miles, "Post Office in the United States and England," p. 164.

180. Pliny Miles, "Advantages of Uniform Postage," *Hunt's Merchants' Magazine*, 46 (1862): 447.

181. William Barry, *Amount of Postages for One Year Prior to 31st March, 1829*, 21st Cong., 1st sess., 1830, H. Doc. 61 (serial 197).

182. Nathan O. Hatch, *The Democratization of American Christianity* (New Haven: Yale University Press, 1989), p. 145.

183. William Manning, "The Key of Liberty," in Michael Merrill and Sean Wilentz, eds., *The Key of Liberty: The Life and Democratic Writings of William*

Manning, "A Laborer," 1747–1814 (Cambridge: Harvard University Press, 1993), pp. 122–123.

184. *National Intelligencer,* Nov. 8, 1813.

185. Isaac Hill, *Speech of Mr. Hill, of New Hampshire, in Senate, May 10, 1832 . . .* [Washington, D.C.: n.p., 1832], p. 2.

186. *United States Postal Guide,* 2 (1852): 232.

187. *Argus of Western America* (Frankfort, Kentucky), May 30, 1817, cited in Lynn LaDue Marshall, "The Early Career of Amos Kendall: The Making of a Jacksonian" (Ph.D. diss., University of California, Berkeley, 1962), p. 136.

188. Jack Larkin, *The Reshaping of Everyday Life, 1790–1840* (New York: Harper & Row, 1988), p. 36.

189. The relative importance of newspapers compared with letters is worth stressing, given the common tendency to assume letter writing to be an old habit and the receipt of a newspaper to be relatively modern. In fact, the opposite is closer to the truth. Following the passage of the Post Office Act of 1792, with its generous subsidies for the newspaper press, thousands of Americans grew accustomed to receiving a newspaper through the postal system, while they seldom, if ever, received a letter that had been sent through the mail.

190. *National Intelligencer,* March 18, 1822.

191. Aaron Belknap to Selah Hobbie, Jan. 20, 1830, Belknap Papers, NYHS.

192. Elam Langdon to Josiah Langdon, Dec. 5, 1818, Suthpin-Laws Papers, Cincinnati Historical Society Library.

193. Whitfield Bell, Jr., "Dr. James Smith and the Public Encouragement for Vaccination for Smallpox," *Annals of Medical History,* 3rd ser. 2 (1940): 506.

194. Petition of William Barbour, et al., December 1812, HCPO-NA.

195. Memorial of James Smith, May 2, 1826, SCPO-NA.

196. Bell, "James Smith," p. 512.

197. "The Country Post Office," *Musical World,* 23 (Oct. 22, 1859): 5.

198. *National Intelligencer,* Dec. 24, 1830.

199. *Register of Debates,* 22nd Cong., 2nd sess., Jan. 2, 1833, p. 939.

200. Petition of Samuel Martin, Dec. 3, 1828, HCPO-NA; Petition of Samuel Martin, Jan. 10, 1830, SCPO-NA; Martin, *Petition of Samuel Martin, of Campbell's Station, Tennessee,* 22nd Cong., 1st sess., 1831, H. Doc. 19 (serial 219); Martin to Joseph Gales and William W. Seaton, July 20, 1853, MHS.

201. *Register of Debates,* 23rd Cong., 1st sess., Dec. 28, 1833, p. 927.

202. The constraints on letter writing that were imposed by the high cost of postage prior to 1845 raise important questions about the representativeness of the posted letter as a historical source. Even if one agrees that the revolutionary era of the 1770s and 1780s was the "greatest letter-writing era in American history," it should not be forgotten that the surviving correspondence provides a decidedly limited glimpse of the everyday concerns of the public at large and for that matter, of the private musings of public figures active at the state level, where so many of the vital political decisions of the day were made. Gordon S. Wood, "The Democratization of Mind in the American Revolution," in *Leadership in the American Revolution* (Washington, D.C.: Library of Congress, 1974), p. 65.

203. Anthony Trollope, *North America,* ed. Donald Smalley and Bradford Allen Booth ([1862]; New York: Alfred A. Knopf, 1951), p. 468.

204. Pliny Miles, "History of the Post Office," *Bankers' Magazine,* 7 (1857), p. 363.

205. Miles, "Post Office in the United States and England," p. 186.

206. Miles, *Postal Reform,* p. 33.

207. Miles, "History of the Post Office," p. 438.

208. Franklin to Henry Potts, April 23, 1761, in Leonard W. Labaree, et al., eds., *Papers of Benjamin Franklin* (New Haven: Yale University Press, 1959–), vol. 9, p. 303.

209. "The Penny Postage System," *American Railroad Journal,* 11 (1840): 131.

210. See the *National Intelligencer,* July 5, 1824, for the published list of dead letters on which my estimate is based.

211. "Letter Writing, in Its Effects on National Character," *Ladies' Magazine and Literary Gazette,* 4 (1831): 244. The author went on to say, "It is not the romance of political science to suppose private matters and sentiments are to have a powerful agency on our government. Public opinion rules, and what is that but the expression of those feelings and resolves which have been formed in the small, secluded circle of domestic life."

212. Carroll Smith-Rosenberg, *Disorderly Conduct: Visions of Gender in Victorian America* (New York: Oxford University Press, 1985), pp. 53–76.

213. William Johnson, *William Johnson's Natchez: The Ante-Bellum Diary of a Free Negro,* ed. William Ransom Hogan and Edwin Adams Davis (Baton Rouge: Louisiana State University Press, 1951), pp. 227, 244, 379.

214. Kate Harrington, "A Half Hour in the Post-Office," *Genius of the West,* 3 (1854): 100–103.

215. John Hemings to Thomas Jefferson, July 23, 1835, in John W. Blassingame, ed., *Slave Testimonies: Two Centuries of Letters, Speeches, Interviews, and Autobiographies* (Baton Rouge: Louisiana State University Press, 1977), p. 15; Randall M. Miller, ed., *"Dear Master": Letters of a Slave Family* (Athens: University of Georgia Press, 1990).

216. John M. Duncan, *Travels through Part of the United States and Canada in 1818 and 1819* (New York: W. B. Gilley, 1823), vol. 2, pp. 317–318.

217. James Fowler Simmons, *Remarks of Mr. Simmons, of Rhode Island, in Support of His Proposition to Reduce Postages to a Uniform Rate of Five Cents for a Single Letter, for All Distances* (Washington, D.C.: J. & G. S. Gideon, 1845), p. 12.

218. Petition of citizens of Huntington County, Pennsylvania, 1845, HCPO-NA.

219. *Cheap Postage: A Dialogue on Cheap Postage between Messrs. A. and B. in Washington City, 1849* [Washington, D.C.: n.p., 1849], p. 8.

220. James M. Campbell to Matthew M. Campbell, June 13, 1829, Campbell Papers, Filson Club.

221. *National Intelligencer,* March 15, 1839.

222. Jackson to James C. Bronaugh, July 18, 1822, in John Spencer Bassett, ed., *Correspondence of Andrew Jackson* (Washington, D.C.: Carnegie Institution of Washington, 1926–1935), vol. 3, p. 170.

223. Petition of the inhabitants of Pittsfield, Massachusetts [1828], HCPO-NA; petition of inhabitants of Albany, New York, December 1828, ibid.; petition of inhabitants of Elbridge, New York, December 22, 1828, ibid.

224. [Francis Lieber], "Dead Letters Opened and Burned by the Postmaster-

General, Revived and Published by Timothy Quicksand," *New-England Magazine,*
1–2 (1831–1832): 56.

225. Henry D. Thoreau, *Walden,* ed. J. Lyndon Shanley ([1854]; Princeton:
Princeton University Press, 1971), p. 94.

226. Though postal officers did not introduce the first postage stamp for national
distribution until 1847, a number of postmasters had issued postage stamps on their
own authority in the preceding years as a courtesy to their patrons, beginning with
New York postmater John Lorimer Graham in 1842.

227. For an introduction to the etiquette of nineteenth-century letter writing, see
Eliza Leslie, *The Behaviour Book: A Manual for Ladies* (Philadelphia: Willis P.
Hazard, 1853).

228. *The American Lady's and Gentleman's Modern Letter Writer . . .* (Philadephia:
Henry F. Anners [1847]), p. 4.

229. *The Art of Good Behavior; and Letter Writer . . .* (New-York: C. P. Huestis,
1846), p. 72.

230. Petition of John Julius Flourney, March 1852, HCPO-NA.

231. "The New Postage Law, and Its Advantages," *Hunt's Merchants Magazine,*
13 (1845): 75.

232. Basil Hall, *Travels in North America in the Years 1827 and 1828* (Edinburgh:
Cadell and Co., 1829), vol. 3, p. 142.

233. Thoreau, *Walden,* p. 168.

234. N. H. Carter to Solomon Van Rensselaer, Nov. 24, 1820, in Bonney, *Legacy,*
vol. 1, p. 357.

235. "Boston Post-Office," p. 129.

236. Frederick A. Whittlesey, "Remembrance and Prophecy: Tales of a Grandfather," in Foreman, *Centennial History,* vol. 2, p. 39.

237. Richardson, "New York Post-Office," p. 202.

238. Taylor, "New York Post-Office," pp. 232–233. For a related discussion, see
Benedict Anderson, *Imagined Communities: Reflections on the Origin and Spread of
Nationalism* (London: Verso, 1983), chap. 2.

239. For a related discussion, see Mary P. Ryan, *Women in Public: Between Banners
and Ballots, 1825–1880* (Baltimore: Johns Hopkins University Press, 1990).

240. John Lewis Krimmel, *Village Tavern,* [1814], Toledo Museum of Art.

241. Richard Caton Woodville, *War News from Mexico,* 1848, National Academy
of Design, New York.

242. William Alexander Percy, *Lanterns on the Levee: Recollections of a Planter's Son*
([1941]; Baton Rouge: Louisiana State University Press, 1984), pp. 5–6.

243. Foreman, "Post Offices and Postmasters of Rochester," vol. 3, p. 61.

244. *Paul Pry,* Dec. 27, 1834; W. Sherman Savage, *The Controversy over the Distribution of Abolitionist Literature, 1830–1860* (New York: Association for the Study
of Negro Life and History, 1938), p. 35.

245. Frederick Douglass, "Slavery and the Irrepressible Conflict," Aug. 1, 1860,
in John W. Blassingame, ed., *Frederick Douglass Papers* (New Haven: Yale University Press, 1979–), vol. 3, p. 382.

246. William B. Taylor to John Lorimer Graham, Dec. 3, 1843, Graham Papers,
Huntington Library and Archives.

247. Leslie, *Behaviour Book,* p. 150.

248. Lucy Skipwith to John Hartwell Cocke, Aug. 1, 1858, in Miller, *Dear Master*, p. 218.

249. William B. Taylor, "History of the New York Post Office and Postal Arrangements," NYHS.

250. Virginia Penny, *How Women Make Money, Married or Single* (Springfield, Mass.: D. E. Fisk and Co., 1870), p. 407.

251. Mary L. Wilbor Diary, 1822, in Emily Noyes Vanderpoel, *Chronicles of a Pioneer School from 1792 to 1833* . . . (Cambridge: Harvard University Press, 1903), p. 235.

252. Sedgwick, "Postoffice," p. 65.

253. Anne Royall, *The Black Book: Or, a Continuation of Travels in the United States* (Washington, D.C.: Printed for the Author, 1829), vol. 3, p. 213.

254. "Lowell Post Office," p. 192.

255. John G. Palfrey, *Speech of Mr. Palfrey, of Massachusetts, on Postage Reform* [Washington, D.C.: n.p., 1849], p. 7.

256. Howe, "Postal Reform," p. 99.

257. "A Street Picture," *Genius of the West*, 4 (1855): 251.

258. Penny, *How Women Make Money*, p. 407.

259. Unidentified newspaper clipping, *Papers, Documents, and Correspondence in the Case of Charles L. Weller* . . . (Washington, D.C.: William A. Harris, 1859), p. 87.

260. New York *Evening Post*, Aug. 18, 1835.

261. "Metropolitan Post-Offices: New York," p. 269.

262. New York *Evening Post*, Dec. 26, 1835.

263. "New Boston Post-Office Building . . .," *Ballou's*, July 31, 1858.

264. Nahum Capen, *Correspondence Respecting Postal Improvements and the Removal of the Boston Post Office* (Boston: n.p., 1858), p. 1.

265. Margaret Cockburn Conkling, *The American Gentleman's Guide to Politeness and Fashion* (New York: Derby & Jackson, 1858), p. 143.

266. "The Street Post-Office," *Scientific American*, 1 (July 9, 1859): 24.

267. Ibid.

268. Miles, "Our Postal System," pp. 581–582.

269. For a related discussion, see J. R. Pole, *The Gift of Government: Political Responsibility from the English Restoration to American Independence* (Athens: University of Georgia Press, 1983), p. 140. The phrases "politics of vigilance" and "politics of trust" are Pole's.

5. The Invasion of the Sacred

1. Lyman Beecher, "Pre-Eminent Importance of the Christian Sabbath," *National Preacher*, 3 (1829): 156.

2. The term "Sabbatarian" deserves a brief explanation. During the first half of the nineteenth century, it was often used to describe Seventh-Day Baptists and others who, like the Jews, observed the Sabbath on the seventh day (i.e., Saturday). In keeping with what has become the twentieth-century historical convention, I use the term to describe those who opposed the desecration of the first day (i.e., Sunday).

3. The first phase of the Sabbatarian protest has been almost entirely overlooked

by historians. For two exceptions, see Fred J. Hood, *Reformed America: The Middle and Southern States, 1783–1837* (University: University of Alabama Press, 1980), pp. 97–101, and Oliver W. Holmes, "Sunday Travel and Sunday Mails: A Question Which Troubled our Forefathers," *New York History,* 20 (October 1939): 413–415.

4. Granger to Wylie, July 25, 1808, PMGL-NA.

5. Granger to Wylie, Aug. 1, 1805, ibid.

6. Granger to William Hope, July 20, 1808, ibid.

7. Granger to Wylie, July 25, 1808, ibid.

8. Boyd Crumrine, ed., *History of Washington County, Pennsylvania* . . . (Philadelphia: L. H. Everts & Co., 1882), p. 487; *Register of Officers and Agents* (1816), p. 65.

9. *Records of the Synod of Pittsburgh* . . . (Philadephia: Luke Loomis, 1852), p. 62.

10. *Minutes of the General Assembly of the Presbyterian Church* . . . (Philadelphia: Presbyterian Board of Publication, [1847]), pp. 456, 508, 514.

11. Gideon Granger to Joseph B. Varnum, Jan. 30, 1811, PMGL-NA.

12. *Statutes at Large,* 2 (1810): 595.

13. Petition of members of the association of ministers in and about Boston, Dec. 26, 1811, William Ellery Channing Papers, MHS; Petition of citizens of New York (1810), HCPO-NA; Petition of James P. Wilson and others (1810), ibid.

14. Lyman Matthews, *Memoir of the Life and Character of Ebenezer Porter* (Boston: Perkins & Marvin, 1837), pp. 329–331.

15. Samuel Carswell to James Madison, June 16, 1810, Madison Papers, LOC.

16. Granger to House of Representatives, Jan. 31, 1811, *ASP: PO,* pp. 44–45.

17. *Records of the Synod of Pittsburgh* . . ., pp. 70, 73–74; Records of the Washington, Pennsylvania, Presbyterian Church, Washington County Historical Society.

18. *Minutes of the General Assembly of the Presbyterian Church,* pp. 514, 566–567.

19. *Proceedings of the General Association of Connecticut* . . . (Hartford: Peter B. Gleason and Co., 1814), pp. 12–13; *Extracts from the Minutes of the General Association of Congregational Ministers in Massachusetts* . . . (Boston: Samuel T. Armstrong, 1814), p. 3; Lyman Beecher, *The Autobiography of Lyman Beecher,* ed. Barbara M. Cross (Cambridge: Belknap Press of Harvard University Press, 1961), vol. 1, p. 197.

20. *Western Intelligencer* (Cleveland), Jan. 17, 1829.

21. John Garrett West, "The Politics of Revelation and Reason: American Evangelicals and the Founders' Solution to the Theological-Political Problem, 1800–1835" (Ph.D. diss., Claremont Graduate School, 1992), p. 207.

22. Petition of members of the Congregationalist Church in Monson, Massachusetts, Jan. 11, 1815, HCPO-NA.

23. Petition of inhabitants of Hollis, New Hampshire [1815], SCPO-NA.

24. "On Carrying the Mail upon the Sabbath," *Panoplist and Missionary Magazine,* 10 (1814): 438.

25. Petition of inhabitants of Bethlehem, New York, 1816, HCPO-NA.

26. "On Carrying the Mail," p. 436.

27. William Bentley, *The Diary of William Bentley* (Salem, Mass.: Essex Institute, 1914), vol. 4, p. 311.

28. Though the Disciples of Christ held their church services on the "First Day" (that is, Sunday) they treated the "Seventh Day" (that is, Saturday) as the Sabbath. Walter Wilson Jennings, *Origin and Early History of the Disciples of Christ* (Cincin-

nati: Standard Publishing Co., 1919), pp. 247–249. Interestingly, Wylie was sued for refusing to open his office "out of the hour" that Granger had specified, suggesting that there existed a certain amount of public pressure in Washington, Pennsylvania, to open the post office for the entire Sabbath. Gideon Granger to Robert Patton, Nov. 30, 1810, PMGL-NA.

29. John M. Duncan, *Travels through Part of the United States and Canada in 1818 and 1819* (New York: W. B. Gilley, 1823), vol. 1, p. 119.

30. P. T. Barnum, *The Life of P. T. Barnum* (New York: Redfield, 1955), pp. 64–65.

31. For a related discussion, see Daniel R. Ernst, "Church-State Issues and the Law, 1607–1870," in John F. Wilson, ed., *Church and State in America: A Bibliographical Guide: The Colonial and Early National Periods* (Westport, Conn.: Greenwood Press, 1986), pp. 331–336.

32. "On Carrying the Mail," pp. 436–437.

33. Petition of inhabitants of Hollis, New Hampshire.

34. Surprisingly little has been written about the history of Sabbath observance in the early republic. For a brief introduction, see Jack Larkin, *The Reshaping of Everyday Life, 1790–1840* (New York: Harper & Row, 1988), pp. 251–256, 275–281, 300–303.

35. Petition of inhabitants of Hollis, New Hampshire.

36. For a related discussion, see Stephen Botein, "Religious Dimensions of the Early American State," in Richard Beeman, Stephen Botein, and Edward C. Carter II, eds., *Beyond Confederation: Origins of the Constitution and American National Identity* (Chapel Hill: University of North Carolina Press, 1987), esp. pp. 321–322.

37. *Minutes of the Presbyterian General Assembly,* June 2, 1812, pp. 513–514.

38. "House Resolution," Jan. 20, 1815, in *ASP: PO,* p. 46.

39. Meigs to House of Representatives, Feb. 20, 1817, in ibid., p. 358.

40. *Annals of Congress,* 14th Cong., 1st sess., March 2, 1816, pp. 1123–1125; March 4, 1822, pp. 1189–1190.

41. Don E. Fehrenbacher, *The South and Three Sectional Crises* (Baton Rouge: Louisiana State University Press, 1980), p. 13.

42. Mills to House of Representatives, Mar. 1, 1817, in *ASP: PO,* p. 359.

43. The second phase of the Sabbatarian protest has received considerably more attention from historians than the first. For a variety of perspectives, see Robert H. Abzug, *Cosmos Crumbling: American Reform and the Religious Imagination* (New York: Oxford University Press, 1994), pp. 105–116; James R. Rohrer, "Sunday Mails and the Church-State Theme in Jacksonian America," *Journal of the Early Republic,* 7 (1987): 53–74; Paul E. Johnson, *A Shopkeeper's Millennium: Society and Revivals in Rochester, New York, 1815–1837* (New York: Hill & Wang, 1978), pp. 83–88; John Barkley Jentz, "Artisans, Evangelicals, and the City: A Social History of Abolition and Labor Reform in Jacksonian New York" (Ph.D. diss., City University of New York, 1977), pp. 66–111; and Bertram Wyatt-Brown, "Prelude to Abolitionism: Sabbatarian Politics and the Rise of the Second Party System," *Journal of American History,* 58 (1971): 316–341. For an earlier, more detailed, and somewhat different formulation of the argument of this chapter, see Richard R. John, "Taking Sabbatarianism Seriously: The Postal System, the Sabbath, and the Transformation of

American Political Culture," *Journal of the Early Republic,* 10 (winter 1990): 517–567. I am grateful to the editors for permission to draw on it here.

44. *Minutes of the General Assembly of the Presbyterian Church,* p. 183; *Proceedings of the General Association of Connecticut* (Hartford: Peter B. Gleason, 1826), pp. 6–7.

45. Charles G. Finney, *The Memoirs of Charles G. Finney: The Complete Restored Text,* ed. Garth M. Rosell and Richard A. G. Dupuis (Grand Rapids: Academie Books, 1989), p. 303.

46. Petition of citizens of Rochester, New York, Jan. 15, 1827, HCPO-NA. Another individual who responded to the Presbyterians' call was William Jay. See in particular William Jay, *Prize Essay on the Perpetuity and Divine Authority of the Sabbath* (New York: Sun Office, 1827). Jay's essay was awarded a $100 prize by the Albany synod of the Presbyterian Church.

47. Lyman Beecher to Lewis Tappan, May 21, 1828, Beecher Family Papers, Manuscripts and Archives, Yale University Library.

48. E. C. Tracy, *Memoir of the Life of Jeremiah Evarts* (Boston: Crocker and Brewster, 1845), p. 317.

49. *National Philanthropist,* May 23, 1828, cited in John L. Thomas, *The Liberator: William Lloyd Garrison: A Biography* (Boston: Little, Brown, and Co., 1963), p. 66.

50. "Minutes of the Convention," in [Lyman Beecher], *The Address of the General Union for Promoting the Observance of the Christian Sabbath . . .* (New York: Daniel Fanshaw, 1828), pp. 3–5. For the attribution of the *Address* to Beecher, see *Third Annual Report of the General Union for Promoting the Observance of the Christian Sabbath* (New York: Sleight & Robinson, 1831), p. 23.

51. Beecher, *Address,* pp. 11, 15, 16.

52. Beecher to Tappan, May 21, 1828, Beecher Family Papers, Manuscripts and Archives, Yale University Library.

53. Bruen, "Address," in *First Annual Report of the General Union for Promoting the Observance of the Christian Sabbath* (New York: J. Collord, 1829), pp. 11–12; [Beecher], *Address,* pp. 7–8, 11–12.

54. [Beecher], *Address,* p. 12.

55. Bruen, "Address," p. 11. Echoing contemporary anti-Sabbatarians, historian Paul Johnson has sharply distinguished Sabbatarians from temperance advocates by terming the latter voluntaristic and the former coercive. This distinction does not withstand close scrutiny. Both Sabbatarians and temperance advocates sought to change public opinion through a variety of means, including consumer boycotts. That some contemporaries found Sabbatarianism more coercive says less about the Sabbatarians' methods than it does about the nature of the grievance they sought to redress.

56. *Rochester Observer,* Jan. 2, 1829.

57. Richard F. Palmer, *The "Old Line Mail": Stagecoach Days in Upstate New York* (Lakemont, N.Y.: North Country Books, 1977), pp. 112–128.

58. John Fowler, *Journey of a Tour in the State of New York in the Year 1830* (London: Whittaker, Treacher, and Arnot, 1831), p. 157.

59. *Rochester Observer,* May 2, 1828.

60. Ibid., May 9, 1828.

61. Ibid., Dec. 12, 1828.

62. Finney, *Memoirs,* p. 303.

63. Tracy, *Memoir,* p. 318.

64. *Rochester Observer,* Dec. 12, 1828. Italics in original.

65. McLean to Bissell, Nov. 26, 1828, PMGL-NA.

66. McLean to Jason Parker, Dec. 31, 1828, ibid.

67. William Ellery Channing, "Associations," *Christian Examiner,* 34 (1829): 106–107.

68. Lewis Tappan, "Report of the Executive Committee," *Second Annual Report of the General Union for Promoting the Observance of the Christian Sabbath* (New York: Sleight and Robinson, 1830), p. 11.

69. "On Carrying the Mail," p. 440; *Niles's Weekly Register,* 37 (Oct. 24, 1829): 134. Italics in original.

70. *National Intelligencer,* April 18 and 28, 1829. Italics in original.

71. Bruen, "Address," p. 13.

72. On Evarts's long and distinguished public career, see John A. Andrew III, *From Revivals to Removal: Jeremiah Evarts, the Cherokee Nation, and the Search for the Soul of America* (Athens: University of Georgia Press, 1992).

73. Jeremiah Evarts to Rufus Anderson, Dec. 16, 1828, ABCFM-HU.

74. Printed petition, attached to a handwritten remonstrance from Oren S. Avery, postmaster, and others of Perryville, New York, Dec. 23, 1828, HCPO-NA.

75. My totals for Sabbatarian petitions cover the period between December 1828 and May 1831. The totals for the period between December 1828 and May 1829 are derived from Jeremiah Evarts, ed., *Memorials to Congress, Respecting Sabbath Mails* (Boston: Published at the Request of Many Petitioners, 1829), pp. 5–7. The totals for the period between December 1829 and May 1831 are based on my own count of the petitions in the National Archives. Sabbatarians continued to petition Congress long after the General Union disbanded in 1831; none of these later protests, however, generated as great a volume of public attention as did the petition efforts between 1810 and 1817 and 1828 and 1831.

76. The sectional breakdown is: New England, 316; Mid-Atlantic, 371; Northwest, 115; South Atlantic, 76: Southwest, 54; unspecified, 3. For a definition of the sections, see Chapter 6, Table 6.1. For a more elaborate quantitative analysis of the petitions, see West, "Politics of Revelation," pp. 247–305.

77. "Preface" to Richard M. Johnson, *Report of the Committee of the Senate . . .* (Baltimore: James Lovegrove, 1829), pp. 3–6.

78. *Niles's Weekly Register,* 35 (Jan. 10, 1829): 313.

79. Lewis Tappan Journal, Dec. 20, 1828, Tappan Papers, LOC.

80. Jentz, "Artisans," p. 81.

81. Robert T. Handy, *A Christian America: Protestant Hopes and Historical Realities,* 2nd ed. (New York: Oxford University Press, 1984), p. 45; William G. McLoughlin, *New England Dissent, 1630–1883: The Baptists and the Separation of Church and State* (Cambridge: Harvard University Press, 1971), vol. 2, pp. 1112, 1267; Barnabas Bates, *An Address Delivered . . . at Tammany Hall* (New York: Gospel Herald, 1830), p. 7.

82. Evarts, *Memorials,* pp. 15, 30.

83. Everett, "Sunday Mails," *North American Review,* 48 (1830): 154–167. For a

more critical assessment, see "Sunday Mails," *American Quarterly Review,* 8 (1830): 175–197.

84. Lewis Tappan, *The Life of Arthur Tappan* (New York: Hurd and Houghton, 1870), p. 101.

85. Samuel McKean to House of Representatives, Feb. 3, 1829, *ASP: PO,* p. 212.

86. Historian Paul Johnson has interpreted merchant support for the petition effort as evidence of the merchants' determination to coerce footloose artisans to adopt middle-class ways. A far simpler explanation for this admittedly puzzling phenomenon is that merchant support was deliberately cultivated by Sabbatarian organizers like Evarts, who hoped that the recruitment of an impressive array of merchant Sabbatarians would help convince a skeptical Congress of the commercial feasibility of the proposed reform. In this context, it is worth repeating that the strength of artisanal anti-Sabbatarianism is easily exaggerated. If we follow Johnson and agree to take the signatures on Sabbatarian petitions as a reasonable proxy for the relative support of the issue among various social groups, then even in New York City artisans solidly supported the Sabbatarians. For example, they made up almost 40 percent of the signers on the "monster" petition that Tappan helped to circulate among the public. Though artisans made up almost 50 percent of the working population of New York City at this time—and thus were slightly underrepresented on Tappan's petition—what seems even more notable is the magnitude of artisanal support for a cause that it is often presumed they overwhelmingly opposed. Jentz, "Artisans," p. 81.

87. Evarts, *Memorials,* p. 30.

88. Letter attached to memorial of inhabitants of Augusta, Maine, Jan. 21, 1829, HCPO-NA.

89. West, "Politics of Revelation," p. 262.

90. Jeremiah Evarts to David Greene, Feb. 15, 1829, ABCFM-HU.

91. James M. Campbell to Matthew M. Campbell, July 16, 1829, Campbell Papers, Filson Club.

92. Jeremiah Evarts to David Greene, Feb. 25, 1829, ABCFM-HU.

93. Anne Royall, *The Black Book: Or a Continuation of Travels in the United States* (Washington, D.C.: Printed for the Author), vol. 1, p. 171.

94. James Akin, *The "Holy Alliance," or Satan's Legion at Sabbath Pranks,* engraving, American Antiquarian Society, Worcester, Mass.

95. For a suggestive comparison, see Dorothy Ann Lipson, *Freemasonry in Federalist Connecticut* (Princeton: Princeton University Press, 1977), pp. 329–340.

96. Pliny Miles, "History of the Post Office," *Bankers' Magazine,* 7 (1857): 363.

97. Evarts, *Memorials,* p. 22.

98. Joseph Badger to Elisha Whittlesey, Feb. 20, 1830, EWP-WRHS.

99. Theodore Frelinghuysen, *Speech of Mr. Frelinghuysen on His Resolution Concerning Sabbath Mails* (Washington, D.C.: Rothwell & Ustick, 1830), p. 11.

100. For a related discussion that links the rise of humanitarian sentiment to the expansion of the market, see Thomas L. Haskell, "Capitalism and the Origins of the Humanitarian Sensibility," in Thomas Bender, ed., *The Antislavery Debate: Capitalism and Abolitionism as a Problem in Historical Interpretation* (Berkeley: University of California Press, 1992), pp. 107–160.

101. *Boston Recorder and Religious Telegraph,* Sept. 26, 1828; Evarts, *Memorials,* pp. 5–7.

102. Everett, "Sunday Mails," p. 161.

103. Evarts, *Memorials,* p. 15.

104. Ibid. p. 18.

105. Petition of citizens of Sullivan County, Tennessee, Mar. 2, 1830, HCPO-NA.

106. Evarts, *Memorials,* pp. 19, 21.

107. Petition of citizens of Sullivan County.

108. Thomas H. Baird, *An Essay on the Subject of the Transportation of the Mail on the Sabbath* (Pittsburg: Christian Herald [1830]), p. 5.

109. *National Intelligencer,* June 23, 1829.

110. Similar incidents occured in Trenton and Newark. See the *Western Intelligencer,* May 29, 1829, and July 7, 1829; and Frank J. Urquhart, *A Short History of Newark* (Newark: Baker Printing Co., 1908), p. 74.

111. *Third Annual Report,* p. 7.

112. *National Intelligencer,* April 2, 1829.

113. *An Address to the Committee . . . Held at Tammany Hall, January 31, 1829, to Express their Sentiments on the Proposition of the Sunday Union and Their Coadjustors . . .* [New York: n.p., 1829]; Fitzwilliam Byrdsall, *History of the Loco-Foco or Equal Rights Party* (New York: Clement & Packard, 1842), p. 37; Bates, *Address;* Preserved Fish, *"Preamble and Resolutions . . . against the Passage of Any Law Prohibiting the Transportation and Opening of the Mail on the Sabbath,"* Feb. 9, 1829, 20th Cong., 2nd sess., S. Doc. 64 (serial 181); Bertram Wyatt-Brown, *Lewis Tappan and the Evangelical War against Slavery* (Cleveland: Case Western University Press, 1969), pp. 68–69.

114. The sectional breakdowns for the anti-Sabbatarian petition effort are: New England, 19; Mid-Atlantic, 155; Northwest, 35; South Atlantic, 5; Southwest, 11; unspecified, 15. These totals are for the period between December 1828 and May 1831. They are based on my own count of the petitions in the National Archives.

115. Petition of Lewis Jenkins and others, Dec. 19, 1828, HCPO-NA.

116. George Savary to John Varnum, Jan. 3, 1829, ibid.

117. William B. Rochester and other merchants of Rochester to McLean, Dec. 10, 1828, ibid.

118. John McLean to Samuel McKean, Jan. 19, 1829, *ASP: PO,* pp. 214–215.

119. Petition of the Alabama Baptist Association, Oct. 10, 1831, HCPO-NA; *United States Telegraph,* Feb. 22, 1831.

120. Arthur Schlesinger, Jr., *The Age of Jackson* (Boston: Little, Brown, and Co., 1945), pp. 138–139; Sean Wilentz, *Chants Democratic: New York City and the Rise of the American Working Class, 1788–1850* (New York: Oxford University Press, 1984), pp. 160, 226.

121. *Argus of Western America,* Feb. 25, 1829.

122. Petition of inhabitants of Trumansburg, New York, December 1828, HCPO-NA; Petition of memorialists of Pulaski, Tennessee, February 1829, ibid.

123. James Holbrook, *Ten Years among the Mail Bags; Or Notes from the Diary of a Special Agent of the Post-Office Department* ([1855]; Philadelphia: Cowperthwait & Co., 1874), p. 219.

124. Bates, *Address,* pp. 3, 12.

125. Remonstrance of the postmaster and others of Perryville, New York, HCPO-NA; unidentified clipping attached to a petition from the inhabitants of Poughkeepsie, New York [1829], ibid.; unidentified clipping attached to a petition from the inhabitants of Poughkeepsie, New York, Jan. 13, 1830, ibid.

126. James Akin, *The "Holy Alliance."*

127. Anne Royall, *Mrs. Royall's Southern Tour, or Second Series of the Black Book* (Washington, D.C.: n.p., 1830), vol. 1, pp. 119–120, 125, 130, 150; Royall, *Mrs. Royall's Pennsylvania, or Travels Continued in the United States* (Washington, D.C.: printed for the author, 1829), vol. 1, p. 239.

128. Channing, "Associations," pp. 136, 122.

129. Richard M. Johnson, "Sunday Mails," Jan. 19, 1829, *ASP: PO,* pp. 211–212.

130. Ibid.; Johnson, "Sunday Mails," March 4 and 5, 1830, ibid., pp. 229–231. The antimajoritarian animus of Johnson's report sparked outrage among Sabbatarians. Huffed one Presbyterian minister from Virginia: "Mr. Johnson and his committee seem alarmed at the simultaneous exertions of citizens of every rank and denomination of Christians in our country—as if [a] union of multitudes must make a cause bad." *Niles's Weekly Register,* 36 (Feb. 28, 1829): 5.

131. Richmond *Enquirer,* Feb. 7, 1829.

132. Robert Richardson, *Memoirs of Alexander Campbell* (Cincinnati: Standard Publishing Co., 1897–1898), vol. 1, pp. 536–537; vol. 2, pp. 334–335n; Lyman H. Butterfield, "Elder John Leland, Jeffersonian Itinerant," *Proceedings of the American Antiquarian Society,* 62 (1952): 239.

133. *National Intelligencer,* Feb. 5, 1829.

134. William Stickney, ed., *Autobiography of Amos Kendall* (Boston: Lee and Shepard, 1872), p. 307.

135. Johnson, "Sunday Mails," p. 212.

136. *Religious Herald,* Aug. 5 and 26, 1860.

137. *Third Annual Report,* p. 24.

138. *Second Annual Report of the American and Foreign Sabbath Union* (Boston: T. R. Marvin, 1845), pp. 21–22.

139. *Railroads and the Sabbath* (New York: Edward O. Jenkins, 1858), p. 9.

140. Petition of Fred S. Wilson, National Association of Letter Carriers, Feb. 11, 1913, HCPO-NA.

141. *Boston Observer and Religious Telegraph,* Dec. 25, 1828.

142. *National Intelligencer,* Feb 5, 1829.

143. Johnson, *Report of a Committee of the Senate . . .* (Philadelphia: Reprinted for the Benefit of Mankind, 1829); Johnson, *Report of the Committee on the Senate . . .* (Baltimore: James Lovegrove, 1829); Johnson, *Shopkeeper's Millennium,* p. 87; Richardson, *Alexander Campbell,* vol. 1, p. 536; "Mr. Johnson's Report," broadside on silk (n.d.), American Antiquarian Society, Worcester, Mass.

144. Jacob Harris Patton, *A Popular History of the Presbyterian Church in the United States of America* (New York: D. Appleton & Co., 1903), pp. 350–351.

145. Harmon Kingsbury, *The Sabbath: A Brief History* (New York: Robert Carter, 1840), p. 35.

146. Baird, *Transportation of the Mail,* p. 3.

147. *Niles's Weekly Register,* March 13, 1830.

148. [Lyman Beecher], "Mr. Johnson's Report on Sabbath Mails," *Spirit of the Pilgrims*, 2 (1829): 142. For the attribution, see Jeremiah Evarts to David Greene, Feb. 5, 1829, ABCFM-HU. Beecher's essay was widely reprinted in pamphlet form, and includes one of the most notable statements of the Sabbatarian argument. In the spring of 1829, Evarts presented a copy to every member of Congress. *Review of a Report of the Committee . . . on the Subject of Mails on the Sabbath* (Boston: Peirce and Williams, 1829); Tracy, *Memoir*, p. 327.

149. W. Clarke to William McCoy, Jan. 21, 1829, HCPO-NA.

150. Evarts to David Greene, Mar. 5, 1829, April 10, 1830, ABCFM-HU.

151. Thomas Robbins to Francis Granger, Aug. 20, 1841, ILPO-NA. See also Richard J. Carwardine, *Evangelicals and Politics in Antebellum America* (New Haven: Yale University Press, 1993), p. 100. Interestingly, Granger signed an anti-Sabbatarian petition during the opening months of the second phase of the protest. See, for example, petition of Lewis Jenkins and others, Dec. 19, 1828, HCPO-NA.

152. Petition of Harmon Kingsbury, Dec. 1, 1841, HCPO-NA.

153. Joseph C. Hornblower to Charles Wickliffe, Oct. 25, 1843, ILPO-NA.

6. The Wellspring of Democracy

1. Alexis de Tocqueville, *Democracy in America,* ed. J. P. Mayer, trans. George Lawrence ([1835; 1840]; Garden City, N.Y.: Doubleday & Co., 1969), p. 384.

2. On the Jacksonians' support for states' rights, see Richard E. Ellis, *The Union at Risk: Jacksonian Democracy, States' Rights, and the Nullification Crisis* (New York: Oxford University Press, 1987).

3. Thomas Hart Benton, *Report of the Select Committee on Executive Patronage,* 19th Cong., 1st sess., 1826, S. Doc. 88 (serial 129), p. 11.

4. See, for example, *National Intelligencer,* Feb. 9, 1825, and May 5, 1825; John McLean, *Report of the Postmaster General, to Whom were Referred the Memorial of . . . Citizens of Maryland, in Relation to the Transportation of the Mail between Philadelphia and Baltimore,* 18th Cong., 2nd sess., 1825, H. Doc. 73 (serial 116); and Citizens of Philadelphia, *Memorial . . . upon the Subject of a Post Route between the Cities of Philadelphia and Baltimore,* 20th Cong., 1st sess., 1828, H. Doc. 203 (serial 173); and STATE *of the Application to Congress for Aid to Complete the Post Road from Philadelphia to Baltimore, and Observations Thereon* (n.p., n.d.). Original at the Library Company, Philadelphia.

5. Martin Van Buren, *Inquiry into the Origin and Course of Political Parties in the United States,* ed. Abraham Van Buren and John Van Buren (New York: Hurd and Houghton, 1867), p. 420; Ronald E. Shaw, *Erie Waters West: A History of the Erie Canal, 1792–1854* (Lexington: University Press of Kentucky, 1966; 1990), p. 192. The total cost of the Erie Canal was $7.1 million.

6. *National Intelligencer,* Jan. 30, 1825, and Feb. 9, 1825. See also John McLean, *Report of the Postmaster General on the Subject of the Most Practicable Post Route from New Orleans to Washington City,* 18th Cong., 2nd sess., 1824, S. Doc. 4 (serial 108); and John McLean to Charles Fenton Mercer, Dec. 20, 1827, Committee Papers, House Committee on Roads and Canals, NA.

7. John McLean, *An Eulogy on the Character and Public Services of James Monroe . . .* (Cincinnati: Looker and Reynolds, 1831), p. 24.

8. *Register of Debates,* 20th Cong., 2nd sess., Feb. 10, 1829, p. 347; John McLean, *Road—Baltimore to Philadelphia,* 19th Cong., 2nd sess., 1827, H. Doc 94 (serial 152).

9. See Charles Sellers, *The Market Revolution: Jacksonian America, 1815–1846* (New York: Oxford University Press, 1991); Alexander Saxton, *The Rise and Fall of the White Republic: Class Politics and Mass Culture in Nineteenth-Century America* (London: Verso, 1990), pp. 23–51; Sean Wilentz, "Society, Politics, and the Market Revolution," in Eric Foner, ed., *The New American History* (Philadelphia: Temple University Press, 1990), pp. 51–71; and Marvin Meyers, *The Jacksonian Persuasion: Politics and Belief* (Stanford: Stanford University Press, 1957).

10. Alexander H. Everett, *America: Or a General Survey of the Political Situation of the Several Powers of the Western Continent . . .* (Philadelphia: H. C. Carey & I. Lea, 1827), pp. 134–135; Jefferson to Madison, Dec. 24, 1825, in Paul Leicester Ford, ed., *The Writings of Thomas Jefferson* (New York: G. P. Putnam's Sons, 1892–1899), vol. 10, p. 348. See also Frederick Jackson Turner, *Rise of the New West, 1819–1829* (New York: Harper & Brothers, 1906), p. 288.

11. With the notable exceptions of Robert V. Remini, who has made Jacksonian antistatism a major theme of the second volume of his magisterial three-volume biography of Andrew Jackson, few American historians have taken seriously the antistatist thrust of Jacksonian ideology, choosing instead to interpret it as a covert critique of the market economy. See Remini, *Andrew Jackson and the Course of American Freedom, 1822–1832* (New York: Harper & Row, 1981), esp. pp. 29–31, 116. British historians, in contrast, have long recognized the significance of this key strand of Jacksonian thought. See, in particular, two valuable but neglected studies by M. J. Heale: *The Presidential Quest: Candidates and Images in American Political Culture, 1787–1852* (London: Longman, 1982), pp. 37–82; and *The Making of American Politics, 1750–1850* (London: Longman, 1977), chaps. 10–11.

12. Robert V. Remini, *The Election of Andrew Jackson* (Philadelphia: J. B. Lippincott Co., 1963), pp. 85–86.

13. For a related discussion, see John M. Murrin, "The Great Inversion, or Court versus Country: A Comparison of the Revolution Settlements in England (1688–1721) and America (1776–1816)," in J. G. A. Pocock, ed., *Three British Revolutions, 1641, 1688, 1776* (Princeton: Princeton University Press, 1980), pp. 425–429, and Heale, *Presidential Quest,* esp. pp. 57–76.

14. Remini, *Andrew Jackson and American Freedom,* p. 158.

15. Lambert A. Wilmer, *Our Press Gang: Or, a Complete Exposition of the Corruptions and Crimes of the American Newspapers* (Philadelphia: J. T. Lloyd, 1860), p. 21.

16. Kendall to Francis P. Blair, Feb. 3, 1829, Blair-Lee Papers, Manuscript Division, Princeton University Libraries (hereafter BLP-PU).

17. *United States Telegraph* (Washington, D.C.), Nov. 18, 1829.

18. Nathan Sargent, *Public Men and Events . . .* (Philadelphia: J. B. Lippincott & Co., 1875), vol. 1, pp. 157, 165.

19. Everett to McLean, Aug. 18, 1828, in Worthington C. Ford, ed., "Use of Patronage in Elections," *Proceedings of the Massachusetts Historical Society,* 3rd. ser. 1 (1907–1908): 376.

20. *United States Telegraph,* Nov. 3, 11 and 18, 1828.

21. Robert Mayo, *A Chapter of Sketches on Finance* (Baltimore: Fielding Lucas, Jr., 1837), pp. xii–xiii.

22. *National Intelligencer,* May 27, 1829.

23. Everett to McLean, Aug. 18, 1828, in Ford, "Patronage in Elections," p. 374.

24. Edward Everett to Alexander H. Everett, Feb. 15, 1829, Edward Everett Papers, Massachusetts Historical Society (hereafter EEP-MHS).

25. Kendall to Francis P. Blair, Feb. 14, 1829, BLP-PU.

26. John Barton Derby, *Political Reminiscences, including a Sketch of the Origin and History of the "Statesman Party" of Boston* (Boston: Homer & Palmer, 1835), p. 43.

27. Kendall to Blair, Feb. 3, 1829, BLP-PU.

28. Margaret Bayard Smith to Mary Ann Kirkpatrick, March 11, 1829, in Gaillard Hunt, *The First Forty Years of Washington Society* (New York: Charles Scribner's Sons, 1906), pp. 290–291.

29. Van Buren to James A. Hamilton, March 1829, in Hamilton, *Reminiscences of James A. Hamilton* (New York: Charles Scribner & Co., 1869), p. 129.

30. Everett to Alexander H. Everett, Feb. 15, 1829, EEP-MHS.

31. Henry Orne, *The Letters of Columbus . . . to Which Are Added Two Letters of Col. Orne to Gen. Duff Green* (Boston: Putnam & Hunt, 1829), pp. 80–81.

32. Webster to Achsah Pollard Webster, March 4, 1829, in Charles M. Wiltse et al., eds., *The Papers of Daniel Webster: Correspondence* (Hanover: University Press of New England, 1974–), vol. 2, pp. 405–406.

33. For more traditional accounts of the Jackson inauguration, see Edwin A. Miles, "The First People's Inaugural—1829," *Tennessee Historical Quarterly,* 37 (1978): 293–307, and Remini, *Election of Andrew Jackson.*

34. Derby, *Political Reminiscences,* p. 40.

35. Andrew Jackson, "First Inaugural Address," in J. D. Richardson, ed., *Compilation of the Messages and Papers of the Presidents, 1789–1917,* 53rd Cong., 2nd sess., 1907, H. Misc. Doc. 210 (serial 3265), vol. 2, p. 438.

36. Kendall to Francis P. Blair, March 10, 1829, BLP-PU.

37. Kendall to Blair, March 7, 1829, ibid.

38. Green to Samuel Ingham, May 6, 1829, Letterbook, Duff Green Papers, Library of Congress (hereafter LDGP-LOC).

39. Story to William Fettyplace, March 1829, in William W. Story, ed., *Life and Letters of Joseph Story* (Boston: Charles C. Little and James Brown, 1851), vol. 1, p. 564.

40. John Quincy Adams, *Memoirs of John Quincy Adams,* ed. Charles Francis Adams (Philadelphia: J. B. Lippincott & Co., 1874–1877), March 10 and 14, 1829, vol. 8, pp. 109–110, 112.

41. Everett to Alexander Hill Everett, March 18, 1829, EEP-MHS.

42. Sargent, *Public Men and Events,* vol. 1, p. 166.

43. Derby, *Political Reminiscences,* p. 49.

44. McLean to John Teesdale, Sept. 26, 1846, in William Salter, ed., "Letters of John McLean to John Teesdale," *Bibliotheca Sacra,* 56 (1899): 24.

45. John Holmes, *Post Office Inquiry: Mr. Holmes's Speech on Mr. Grundy's Resolution . . .* (Washington, D.C.: National Journal, 1831), pp. 9, 12.

46. Julius Franz Kany, "The Career of William Taylor Barry" (master's thesis, Western Kentucky State Teachers College, 1934).

47. *Paul Pry,* July 19, 1834.

48. John Pope to Jackson, Feb. 19, 1829, in John Spencer Bassett, ed., *Correspondence of Andrew Jackson* (Washington, D.C.: Carnegie Institution of Washington, 1926–1935), vol. 4, p. 8.

49. Story to William Fettyplace, March 1829, in Story, *Life and Letters,* vol. 1, p. 564.

50. McLean to Monroe, April 4, 1829, Monroe Papers, LOC.

51. McLean to Whittlesey, June 3, 1830, EWP-WRHS.

52. McLean to John W. Taylor, July 2, 1829, Taylor Papers, NYHS.

53. William T. Barry, "Circular to Postmasters," May 18, 1829, *Niles's Weekly Register,* 36 (May 18, 1829): 205–206; Bradley to President of the United States, October 1829, in John Clayton, *Speech of Mr. Clayton, of Delaware . . . on the Resolution of Mr. Grundy . . .* (Washington, D.C.: National Journal, 1831), pp. 27–28.

54. McLean to Duff Green, July 18, 1829, *Niles's Weekly Register,* 36 (Aug. 22, 1829): 422; James Rees, *Foot-Prints of a Letter-Carrier: Or, a History of the World's Correspondence. . . .* (Philadelphia: J. B. Lippincott & Co., 1866), p. 192n.

55. Smith to J. Bayard Smith, March 12, 1829, in Hunt, *Washington Society,* p. 299.

56. *National Journal,* Aug. 5, 1829.

57. Michael T. Simpson to McLean, May, 30, 1829, McLean Papers, LOC.

58. *Register of Officers and Agents* (1829–1835).

59. Adams to Charles Francis Adams, March 8, 1829, Adams Papers, MHS.

60. Henry Clay to Francis T. Brooke, March 12, 1829, in James F. Hopkins et al. eds., *The Papers of Henry Clay* (Lexington: University Press of Kentucky, 1959–1992), vol. 8, p. 8.

61. *National Intelligencer,* Sept. 19, 1829.

62. For a related discussion, see Richard B. Latner, "The Kitchen Cabinet and Andrew Jackson's Advisory System," *Journal of American History,* 65 (1978): 373.

63. Green to Jackson, April 23, 1829, LDGP-LOC; Kendall to Joseph Desha, April 9, 1831, in James A. Padgett, ed., "Correspondence between Governor Joseph Desha and Amos Kendall—1831–1835," *Register of the Kentucky Historical Society,* 38 (1940): 8.

64. Isaac Hill to McLean, Nov. 27, 1828, McLean Papers, LOC.

65. Meyers, *Jacksonian Persuasion,* p. 29. The phrase "dismantling operation" is Meyers's.

66. Abraham Bradley, Jr., Letter to the President, October 1829, in Clayton, *Speech,* p. 30.

67. Kendall to Francis P. Blair, April 30, 1829, BLP-PU.

68. "Messrs. Hawkins, Kendall, Bradley and Barry," *Niles's Weekly Register,* 37 (Oct. 3, 1829): 90.

69. Phineas Bradley to Elisha Whittlesey, Oct. 29, 1829, EWP-WRHS.

70. Ibid.

71. Kendall to Francis P. Blair, June 21, 1829, BLP-PU.

72. *Register of Officers and Agents* (1829; 1831); Abraham Bradley, Jr., "Testimony," in John Clayton, *Report . . . to Examine and Report the Present Condition of the Post Office Department,* 21st Cong., 2nd sess., 1831, S. Doc. 73 (serial 204), pp. 88–89.

73. Charles A. Wickliffe, *Post Office Department—Persons Employed,* 27th Cong., 2nd sess., 1842, H. Rpt. 170 (serial 404). Totals for 1835 are incomplete. The percentage is based on the number of post offices in 1829.

74. These totals were compiled from the *Register of Officers and Agents* (1829) and Wickliffe, *Post Office Department—Persons Employed.*

75. Green to Theodore Lyman, Dec. 14, 1828, LDGP-LOC.

76. Charles Lyell, *A Second Visit to the United States* (New York: Harper & Brothers, 1849), pp. 81–82.

77. Duff Green, *Facts and Suggestions . . .* (New York: Richardson & Co., 1866), pp. 30–33.

78. Green to Worden Pope, Jan. 4, 1828, LDGP-LOC; Michael D. Goldhaber, "The Tragedy of Classical Republicanism: Duff Green and the *United States Telegraph,* 1826–1837" (B.A. thesis, Harvard University, 1990), p. 31. For a different interpretation of Green's editorial strategy, and of this letter in particular, see Robert V. Remini, *The Legacy of Andrew Jackson: Essays on Democracy, Indian Removal, and Slavery* (Baton Rouge: Louisiana State University Press, 1988), p. 86.

79. Green to U. Updike, Feb. 1, 1829, LDGP-LOC.

80. Felix Grundy, *Speech of Mr. Grundy, of Tennessee, Relative to the Post Office Department* [Washington, D.C.: n.p., 1831], pp. 4–5.

81. Clayton, *Speech,* pp. 20–21.

82. *Register of Debates,* 22nd Cong., 1st sess., Jan. 25, 1832, p. 1325.

83. Joseph Story, *Commentaries on the Constitution of the United States* (Boston: Hilliard, Gray, and Co., 1833), vol. 3, p. 394; Alexander H. Everett, *The Conduct of the Administration* (Boston: Stimpson & Clapp, 1832), pp. 22–23.

84. Jackson to Andrew J. Donelson, April 11, 1824, in Bassett, *Correspondence of Andrew Jackson,* vol. 3, pp. 246–247.

85. Clayton, *Speech,* pp. 20–21.

86. Holmes, *Post Office Inquiry,* p. 17.

87. Abelard Reynolds deposition (1829), in Edward R. Foreman, "Post Offices and Postmasters of Rochester," *Centennial History of Rochester* (Rochester: Rochester Historical Society, 1933), vol. 3, p. 58.

88. Clayton, *Speech,* p. 11.

89. Alexander H. Everett, "Address of the National Republican Convention . . .," December 1831, in *Niles's Weekly Register,* 41 (Dec. 24, 1831): 309.

90. Bradley to President, October 1829, in Clayton, *Speech,* p. 28.

91. Coyle to Barry, undated and Aug. 14, 1829, in *National Intelligencer,* Aug. 3 and 17, 1829.

92. Catherine Maria Sedgwick, "The Village Post Office," in S. G. Goodrich, ed., *The Token and Atlantic Souvenir, A Christmas and New Year's Present* ([1837]; Boston: American Stationers' Co., 1838), pp. 164–184.

93. Bartleby's dismissal is not, as many critics have charged, unimportant to the story. In the opening paragraph, the lawyer-narrator clearly indicates that the explanation for Bartleby's curious conduct (which he slyly terms "one vague report") "will appear in the sequel." Herman Melville, "Bartleby the Scrivener: A Story of Wall Street," 1853, in Harrison Hayford et al., eds., *The Writings of Herman Melville* (Evanston: Northwestern University Press, 1968–), vol. 9, pp. 45, 13.

94. *Register of Debates,* 21st Cong., 2nd sess., Feb. 11, 1831, p. 195.

95. Francis P. Weisenburger, *The Life of John McLean: A Politician on the United States Supreme Court* (Columbus: Ohio State University Press, 1937), pp. 73–74.

96. Holmes, *Post Office Inquiry,* p. 15.

97. *Register of Debates,* 22nd Cong., 1st sess., Feb. 29, 1832, p. 1918.

98. John W. Forney, *Anecdotes of Public Men* (New York: Harper & Brothers, 1873), pp. 281–283.

99. Solomon Van Rensselaer to Rensselaer van Rensselaer, March 23, 1829, in Catharina V. R. Bonney, *A Legacy of Historical Gleanings* (Albany: J. Munsell, 1875), vol. 1, p. 470–471.

100. *National Intelligencer,* Aug. 8, 1831.

101. Ibid., April 5, 1830.

102. Jackson to William B. Lewis, Aug. 18, 1832, in Bassett, *Correspondence of Andrew Jackson,* vol. 4, p. 467.

103. Adams, *Memoirs,* 8 (Jan. 19, 1830): 176–177.

104. James Parton, *Life and Times of Andrew Jackson* (New York: Mason Brothers, 1861), vol. 3, pp. 669, 692.

105. Barry to Susan Barry Taylor, May 16, 1829, in "Letters of William T. Barry," *American Historical Review,* 16 (1911): 332.

106. *Niles's Weekly Register,* 36 (July 11, 1829): 315.

107. Ibid., 36 (May 9, 1829): 163.

108. [Charles Augustus Davis], *The Life of Andrew Jackson, President of the United States . . . by Major Jack Downing* (Philadephia: T. K. Greenbank, 1834), pp. 205, 207. The fullest account of this episode can be found in John Niven, *Gideon Welles: Lincoln's Secretary of the Navy* (New York: Oxford University Press, 1973), pp. 54–70.

109. Derby, *Political Reminiscences,* pp. 170–171.

110. Adams, *Memoirs,* Feb. 19, 1830, vol. 8, p. 192.

111. Barry to Charles P. Kirkland et al., June 8, 1829, *Niles's Weekly Register,* 36 (July 11, 1829): 314.

112. *National Intelligencer,* June 30, 1829.

113. Barry to Taylor, June 11, 1829, *American Historical Review,* p. 333.

114. J. G. A. Pocock, *The Machiavellian Moment: Florentine Political Thought and the Atlantic Republican Tradition* (Princeton: Princeton University Press, 1975), pp. 382–383, 393–394, 407, 414, 473, 519.

115. Barry to Taylor, June 11, 1829, *American Historical Review,* p. 333.

116. Jackson, "First Annual Message," in Richardson, *Messages and Papers,* vol. 2, pp. 448–449.

117. Everett, *Conduct,* p. 24. In an influential essay on the origins of the Whig party, social historian Lynn L. Marshall provides a different explanation for the Jacksonians' decision to adopt the doctrine of rotation in office. Drawing on the work of sociologist Max Weber and business historian Alfred D. Chandler, Jr., Marshall contends that Jackson's advisors, such as Amos Kendall, used the doctrine as a "cloak" to promote "organizational changes" that might otherwise have "appeared revolutionary." These organizational changes, in turn, marked the "point" around which the "colonial order" made itself over into "modern industrial America": "Political parties and government departments, especially the post office, were then the largest organizations in the country; the Jacksonian reorganization of them gave the first practical test to innovative techniques of large-scale rational organization on a peculiarly American model." While Marshall is correct to recognize that the Jacksonians' patronage policy marked a sharp break with the past, he exaggerates

when he contends that its outcome was "efficient" and thus "modern." In fact, rotation in office proved to be a relatively short-lived and largely unsuccessful experiment in public administration that sapped the esprit de corps of the staff and blunted the spirit of innovation. Few corporate managers followed the Jacksonians' lead, since, unlike Kendall, they recognized that no business could be successfully administered that routinely discarded its own personnel. Lynn L. Marshall, "The Strange Stillbirth of the Whig Party," *American Historical Review,* 72 (1967): 455, 455n32, 456, 465n51, 468.

118. For a related discussion, see three important works by Ronald P. Formisano: *The Transformation of Political Culture: Massachusetts Parties, 1790s–1840s* (New York: Oxford University Press, 1983), esp. pp. 16–17, 246–247; "Federalists and Republicans, Parties, Yes—System, No," in Paul Kleppner et al., *The Evolution of American Electoral Systems* (Westport, Conn.: Greenwood Press, 1981), pp. 33–76; and "Deferential-Participant Politics: The Early Republic's Political Culture, 1789–1840," *American Political Science Review,* 68 (1974): 473–487, esp. p. 486.

119. Tocqueville, *Democracy in America,* ed. Henry Reeve (New York: George Dearborn & Co., 1838), p. 110. Tocqueville omitted this discussion from later editions of his *Democracy,* very possibly in response to his American critics.

120. Thomas Hart Benton, *Thirty Years' View: Or, a History of the Working of the American Government for Thirty Years . . .* (New York: D. Appleton and Co., 1854), vol. 1, p. 163.

121. Robert V. Remini, *The Revolutionary Age of Andrew Jackson* (New York: Harper & Row, 1985), p. 80. To support his conclusion, Remini attributes to McLean the statement "For an administration to bestow its patronage without distinction of party is to court its own destruction." Such a sentiment is highly atypical of anything that I have come across in McLean's published or unpublished papers. Since Remini's book was intended for a general audience, it lacks footnotes, complicating the task of running it down. It is suggestive, however, that in 1828 Massachusetts congressman Edward Everett made an almost identical statement to McLean in a private letter; in reply, McLean declared that he could not accept Everett's position. Everett to McLean, Aug. 1, 1828; McLean to Everett, Aug. 8, 1828; both in Ford, "Patronage in Elections," pp. 361, 365–366.

122. Everett to McLean, Aug. 1, 1828, in Ford, "Patronage in Elections," p. 361.

123. Kendall to Francis P. Blair, July 2, 1829, BLP-PU.

124. Clayton to McLean, Oct. 14, 1833, McLean Papers, LOC.

125. B. B. Taylor to William Medill, March 30, 1845, Medill Papers, LOC.

126. New York *Enquirer,* cited in *United States Gazette,* March 12, 1829.

127. For a brief history of this episode, see Solomon Nadler, "The Green Bag: James Monroe and the Fall of De Witt Clinton," *New-York Historical Society Quarterly,* 49 (1975): 214–220.

128. *National Intelligencer,* May 13, 1830.

129. *Niles's Weekly Register,* 38 (June 26, 1830): 324–325.

130. Ibid., 39 (Jan. 29, 1831): 386.

131. Ibid., 45 (Oct. 12, 1833): 99.

132. Ibid., 45 (Nov. 30, 1833): 210.

133. Ibid., 40 (May 7, 1831): 164.

134. Ibid., 45 (Nov. 2, 1833): 147.

135. Martin Van Buren, *The Autobiography of Martin Van Buren,* ed. John C. Fitzpatrick (Washington, D.C.: Government Printing Office, 1918), vol. 2, p. 745.

136. *Register of Officers and Agents* (1822, 1833). In the period between 1823 and 1835, the price level remained virtually unchanged. *Historical Statistics of the United States: Colonial Times to 1970* (Washington, D.C.: Government Printing Office, 1975), pt. 1, pp. 201–202.

137. *National Intelligencer,* Aug. 11, 1831.

138. Henry W. Connor, *Examination of the Post Office Department,* 23rd Cong., 2nd sess., 1835, H. Rpt. 103 (serial 277), p. 51.

139. Van Buren, *Autobiography,* vol. 2, p. 745.

140. Phineas Bradley to William Allen, Woolfolk Papers, College of William and Mary.

141. Barry to Hamilton, March 15, 1834, in Hamilton, *Reminiscences,* p. 280–281.

142. *National Intelligencer,* Feb. 26, 1834.

143. Isaac T. Avery to Willie P. Mangum, March 8, 1834, in Henry Thomas Shanks, ed., *The Papers of Willie Person Mangum* (Raleigh, N.C.: State Department of Archives and History, 1950–1956), vol. 2, p. 119.

144. *National Intelligencer,* Aug. 29, 1834.

145. Ibid., Jan. 30, 1834. One group of New York merchants proposed establishing a special nonprofit, nongovernment express mail line on the critical New York–New Orleans route. They gave up the idea when the highly respected jurist James Kent declared the venture to be a violation of the postal monopoly. Postal law, Kent conceded, did permit individuals to send letters over postal routes via *"special* messenger." The proposed venture, however, did not fall within the meaning of this clause, since it was intended to be a "regular, established, periodical transmission." James Kent, "Opinion," *Niles's Weekly Register,* 47 (Oct. 25, 1834): 121.

146. *Paul Pry,* June 22, 1833.

147. [Davis], *Andrew Jackson,* p. 205.

148. Niles to Gideon Welles, Nov. 15, 1840, Welles Papers, NYHS.

149. *Paul Pry,* Nov. 9, 1833; John Floyd diary, Nov. 6, 1833, in Charles H. Ambler, ed., *The Life and Diary of John Floyd . . .* (Richmond, Va.: Richmond Press, 1918), p. 230.

150. *Niles's Weekly Register,* 45 (Jan. 11, 1834): 330.

151. Thomas Ewing, *Report . . . into the Condition of the Post Office Department,* 23rd Cong., 1st sess., 1834, Sen. Rpt. 422 (serial 242), p. 3.

152. "Articles of Agreement . . .," Aug. 31, 1832, in ibid., pp. 69–72.

153. *Register of Debates,* 23rd Cong., 1st sess., June 10, 1834, p. 1916.

154. Ibid., pp. 1927–1928. Though Jackson found the loans highly irregular, he did know of their existence prior to Ewing's investigation. Three months before Ewing made his report, Barry wrote Samuel L. Gouverneur that Jackson "begins to see things in their proper light . . . All can yet be saved, if wise councils prevail." Barry to Gouverneur, March 11, 1834, March 15, 1834, Gouverneur Papers, Rare Books and Manuscripts Division, New York Public Library, Astor, Lenox, and Tilden Foundations.

155. *Register of Debates,* 23rd Cong., 1st sess., June 10, 1834, p. 1933.

156. William Stickney, ed., *Autobiography of Amos Kendall* (Boston: Lee and Shepard, 1872), p. 336.

157. Isaac Hill, *Speech of the Hon. Isaac Hill, of New Hampshire, on the Motion of Mr. Southard . . .* (Washington, D.C.: Francis Preston Blair, 1834), p. 3.

158. *Niles's Weekly Register,* 46 (July 5, 1834): 313.

159. Ibid., 47 (Feb. 7, 1835): 395.

160. *Register of Debates,* 23rd Cong., 2nd sess., Feb. 6, 1835, p. 342.

161. Phineas Bradley to Elisha Whittlesey, April 28, 1835, EWP-WRHS.

162. On the history of Kendall's express mail, see James W. Milgram, *The Express Mail of 1836–1839* (Chicago: Collectors' Club of Chicago, 1977).

163. Jesse E. Dow, "The Progress and Present Condition of the Post Office Department," *United States Magazine and Democratic Review,* 6 (1839): 200–201; Phineas Bradley to Whittlesey, Nov. 2, 1835, EWP-WRHS.

164. Though few contemporaries gave the Post Office Act of 1836 more than a passing mention, it has recently been hailed by historians intent on playing up the innovative features of Jacksonian public administration. For this reason, it is worthwhile to remember how the act was viewed by informed contemporaries. According to Peter G. Washington, who as postal auditor presided over the largest of the administrative offices that the act created, the Post Office Act of 1836 did little to curtail the influence of the "political postmaster" over the contracting process, the "gradual result," Washington added, of the "almost inevitable concessions from the weak to the strong." Equally skeptical was postal historian Daniel D. T. Leech. Though Leech conceded that the act marked an "important epoch" in the history of the postal system, he added that the establishment of the auditor's office had failed to significantly curtail the postmaster general's discretion in the awarding of mail contracts, leaving him "pretty nearly 'master of the situation,' " just as he had been before. All told, there is no good reason to challenge the judgment of administrative historian Leonard D. White that the Jacksonians did little to change the basic contours of postal administration as they had existed in the period prior to Jackson's inauguration. Peter G. Washington, "Jurisdiction of the Accounting Officers of the Treasury," *United States Postal Guide and Official Advertiser,* 1 (1851): 351; Daniel D. Leech and W. L. Nicholson, *The Post Office Department of the United States of America . . .* (Washington, D.C.: Judd & Detweiler, 1879), pp. 22–24; Leonard D. White, *The Jacksonians: A Study in Administrative History, 1829–1861* (New York: Macmillan Co., 1954), p. 553.

165. Hiland Hall, "Opinion of the Second Comptroller of the Treasury," *United States Postal Guide,* 1 (1851): 371.

166. Kendall's role in the passage of the act has long been exaggerated by historians unfamiliar with the magnitude of the Barry scandals. Historians agree that Kendall assisted in the *drafting* of the legislation; this was expected of Cabinet officers, given the staffing limitations upon Congress. Numerous letters in the postmaster general's letterbooks attest to this fact. But there is little reason to suppose that Kendall played more than an incidental role in its *enactment,* notwithstanding Kendall's own account of his role in his *Autobiography.* Far more important was the work of congressmen Hiland Hall, George N. Briggs, and Abijah Mann.

167. Washington, "Jurisdiction of the Accounting Officers," 345.

168. Washington *Globe,* March 26, 1836. The legislation was also opposed by the influential Richmond *Enquirer,* the voice of Jacksonian orthodoxy in the South. Richmond *Enquirer,* April 14, 1835.

169. Story, *Commentaries,* vol. 3, pp. 387–388.

170. Calhoun, "Remarks on the Post Office Committee Report," Jan. 27, 1835, in Robert L. Meriwether et al., eds., *The Papers of John C. Calhoun* (Columbia: University of South Carolina Press, 1959–), vol. 12, p. 399.

171. *Register of Debates,* 23rd Cong., 2nd sess., Jan. 27, 1835, p. 252.

172. Royall to Mangum, Oct. 25, 1835, in Shanks, *Papers of Willie Person Mangum,* vol. 2, p. 362.

173. *Paul Pry,* Nov. 16, 1833.

174. *Huntress,* May 12, 1838.

175. Ibid., Feb. 1, 1840.

176. For a more detailed discussion of Whig ideology, see Daniel Walker Howe, *The Political Culture of the American Whigs* (Chicago: University of Chicago Press, 1979), and Major L. Wilson, *Space, Time, and Freedom: The Quest for Nationality and the Irrepressible Conflict, 1815–1861* (Westport, Conn.: Greenwood Press, 1974).

177. Van Buren, *Autobiography,* vol. 2, p. 745.

178. *Ohio State Journal,* April 9, 1834, cited in Francis P. Weisenburger, *The Passing of the Frontier, 1825–1850* (Columbus: Ohio State Archaeological and Historical Society, 1941), p. 308.

179. [Matthew St. Clair Clarke], *An Account of Col. Crockett's Tour to the North and Down East* (Philadelphia: E. L. Carey and A. Hart, 1835), p. 165. My attribution of the *Account* to Matthew St. Clair Clarke is based on a letter that Crockett wrote in 1835 in which Crockett attributed its authorship to a "Mr. Clark." This attribution has been disputed by Crockett's biographer James Atkins Shackford, who claims that Clarke could not have written the *Account* since he had "no conceivable business in Congress in connection with the post office committee." On this point Shackford is mistaken. In fact, Clarke was in Washington in the winter of 1834–1835, working as a secretary for Ewing on his post office committee. Thomas Ewing, *Report . . . into the Condition and Proceedings of the Post Office Department,* 23rd Cong., 2nd sess., 1835, S. Rpt. 86 (serial 268), pp. 222, 223, 230, 247, 250, 251, 349. James Atkins Shackford, *David Crockett: The Man and the Legend* (Chapel Hill: University of North Carolina Press, 1956), p. 185. Shackford reprints the "Mr. Clark" letter on pp. 184–185. Though Clarke had a large hand in writing the *Account,* there can be little doubt that the sentiments are Crockett's, since they resemble so closely the sentiments that Crockett had previously expressed in his own private correspondence. See, for example, Crockett to A. M. Hughes, Feb. 13, 1831, Tennessee Historical Society.

180. [Clarke], *Account,* pp. 162–163, 165, 166, 200–201.

181. Isaac Hill, *Speech of the Hon. Isaac Hill, of New Hampshire, on the Motion of Mr. Southard . . .* (Washington, D.C.: Francis Preston Blair, 1834).

182. *Niles's Weekly Register,* 46 (June 14 and 21, 1834): 273–280, 281–291; *Register of All Officers and Agents . . .* (Philadelphia: Key & Biddle, 1834), p. 269; *Post Office Department* [New York, 1834] (in LOC), pp. 1, 2.

183. J. B. Taylor to Ewing, June 21, 1834, Ewing Papers, LOC.

184. *Register of Debates,* 23rd Cong., 2nd sess., Feb. 14, 1835, pp. 1, 365.

185. "An Affecting Scene in Kentucky" (New York: Henry R. Robinson, 1836).

186. W. Babcock [?] to Whittlesey, Nov. 17, 1834, EWP-WRHS.

187. Willie P. Mangum, "Speech," Feb. 3, 1836, in Shanks, *Papers of Willie Person Mangum,* vol. 5, p. 610.

188. John P. Kennedy, "Defense of the Whigs," in *Political and Official Papers* (New York: G. P. Putnam & Sons, 1872).

189. William Leggett, *A Collection of the Political Writings of William Leggett,* ed. Theodore Sedgwick (New York: Taylor & Dodd, 1840), vol. 1, p. 246.

190. Ibid., vol. 2, pp. 194–196.

191. Ibid., vol. 1, p. 245.

192. Ibid., vol. 2, p. 192.

193. Ibid., vol. 1, p. 245.

194. *Register of Debates,* 24th Cong., 1st sess., May 19, 1836, p. 3785; John Bell, *Public Post and Conveyance of Letters,* 25th Cong., 3rd sess., 1839, H. Res. 16.

195. William D. Merrick, *Speech of Mr. Merrick, of Maryland, on the Bill to Reduce the Rates of Postage . . .* (Washington, D.C.: Gales and Seaton, 1845), p. 13.

196. Eli Bowen, *The United States Post-Office Guide* (New York: D. Appleton and Co., 1851), p. 27; "The Father of Cheap Postage," *United States Mail and Post Office Assistant,* 11 (1871).

197. James W. Hale, "History of Cheap Postage," *American Odd Fellow,* 10 (1871): 183.

198. A. L. Stimson, *History of the Express Business . . .* (New York: Baker & Godwin, 1881), p. 63.

199. On this debate, see Alison Goodyear Freehling, *Drift toward Dissolution: The Virginia Slavery Debate of 1831–32* (Baton Rouge: Louisiana State University Press, 1982).

7. The Interdiction of Dissent

1. Alfred Huger to Samuel L. Gouverneur, Aug. 22, 1835, in Frank Otto Gatell, ed., "Postmaster Huger and the Incendiary Publications," *South Carolina Historical Magazine,* 64 (1963): 201.

2. C. S. Hamilton to L. H. Hamilton, July 30, 1835, in Harvey S. Teal, ed., "Attacks on the Charleston, South Carolina, Post Office," *La Posta: A Journal of American Postal History,* 17 (1986), pp. 54–56.

3. Huger to Kendall, July 30, 1835, Richmond *Enquirer,* Aug. 25, 1835.

4. John Belton O'Neall, *Biographical Sketches of the Bench and Bar of South Carolina . . .* (Charleston: S. G. Courtenay & Co., 1859), vol. 2, p. 29.

5. Jacob Schirmer Diary, Aug. 21, 1835, South Carolina Historical Society.

6. Charleston *Southern Patriot,* Aug. 21, 1835. A further bit of circumstantial evidence that points to Wilson's participation in the break-in was Adams's conviction that the assault had been led by a South Carolina governor. Adams implicted Robert Hayne, an obvious mistake, since Hayne opposed the break-in as an outrageous violation of federal law. But it is suggestive that Adams thought a governor had been involved. Could it be that Adams misunderstood some bit of Charleston gossip that found its way to Washington in the weeks immediately after the event? John Quincy Adams, *Memoirs of John Quincy Adams,* ed. Charles Francis Adams (Philadelphia: J. B. Lippincott & Co., 1874–1877), Aug. 18, 1835, vol. 9, p. 255;

Theodore D. Jervey, *Robert Y. Hayne and his Times* (New York: Macmillan Co., 1909), p. 381.

7. *United States Catholic Miscellany* (Charleston), Aug. 1, 1835; John England to Paul Cullen, Feb. 23, 1836, *Records of the American Catholic Historical Society*, 8 (1897): 219–220.

8. Charleston *Mercury*, July 31, 1835.

9. C. S. Hamilton to L. H. Hamilton, July 30, 1835, in Teal, "Attacks on the Charleston, South Carolina, Post Office," pp. 54–56. Notable accounts of the controversy include Donna Lee Dickerson, *The Course of Tolerance: Freedom of the Press in Nineteenth-Century America* (New York: Greenwood Press, 1990), pp. 81–113; Leonard L. Richards, *"Gentlemen of Property and Standing": Anti-Abolition Mobs in Jacksonian America* (London: Oxford University Press, 1970); William W. Freehling, *Prelude to Civil War: The Nullification Controversy in South Carolina, 1816–1836* (New York: Harper & Row, 1965), pp. 340–348; Bertram Wyatt-Brown, "The Abolitionists' Postal Campaign of 1835," *Journal of Negro History*, 50 (1965): 227–238; and Clement Eaton, *The Freedom-of-Thought Struggle in the Old South*, rev. and enl. ed. (New York: Harper & Row, 1964), pp. 196–215.

10. Bertram Wyatt-Brown, *Lewis Tappan and the Evangelical War against Slavery* (Cleveland: Case Western University Press, 1969), p. 143.

11. Hartford *Times*, cited in Charleston *Courier*, Aug. 14, 1835.

12. *Mercury*, Aug. 17, 1835.

13. *Annual Report of the American and Foreign Anti-Slavery Society* (New York: American and Foreign Anti-Slavery Society, 1849), p. 65.

14. Amos Dresser, *The Narrative of Amos Dresser, with Stone's Letters from Vicksburg* (New York: American Anti-Slavery Society, 1836).

15. E. J. Shields, *Speech of the Hon. E. J. Shields, of Tennessee, on the Bill to Change the Organization of the Post Office Department and to Provide More Effectually for the Settlement of the Accounts Thereof* . . . (Washington, D.C.: National Intelligencer, 1836), p. 7.

16. William Jay et al. to Andrew Jackson, Dec. 26, 1835, in William Jay, *A View of the Action of the Federal Government in Behalf of Slavery* (New-York: G. F. Hopkins, 1839), p. 208.

17. "Alfred Huger," in N. Louise Bailey et al., eds., *Biographical Directory of the South Carolina Senate, 1776–1985* (Columbia: University of South Carolina Press, 1986), p. 767.

18. Huger to Samuel L. Gouverneur, Aug. 8, 1835, in Gatell, "Incendiary Publications," p. 198.

19. Huger to Gouverneur, Aug. 15, 1835, in ibid., p. 200.

20. Huger to Gouverneur, Aug. 6, 1835, in ibid., p. 196–197.

21. Huger to Gouverneur, Aug. 1, 1835, in ibid., p. 194.

22. *Mercury*, July 31, 1835; *Catholic Miscellany*, Aug. 1, 1835.

23. Huger to Gouverneur, Aug. 1, 1835, in Gatell, "Incendiary Publications," p. 194; *Catholic Miscellany*, Aug. 1, 1835.

24. Huger to Gouverneur, Aug. 6, 1835, in Gatell, "Incendiary Publications," p. 196.

25. Huger to Gouverneur, Aug. 22, 1835, in ibid., p. 201.

26. Huger to Amos Kendall, Aug. 10, 1835, *Enquirer*, Aug. 25, 1835.

27. Huger to Gouverneur, Aug. 1 and 8, 1835, in Gatell, "Incendiary Publications," pp. 195, 198.

28. Gouverneur to the President and Directors of the American Anti-Slavery Society, Aug. 7 and 9, 1835, *Niles's Weekly Register,* 48 (Aug. 22, 1835): 447–448.

29. New York *Journal of Commerce,* cited in Charleston *Courier,* Sept. 3, 1835.

30. Resolution of the Citizens of Charlotte County, Virginia, Sept. 8, 1835, in Samuel L. Gouverneur Papers, Rare Books and Manuscripts Division, New York Public Library, Astor, Lenox, and Tilden Foundations.

31. Forsyth to Martin Van Buren, Aug. 5, 1835, in William Allen Butler, *A Retrospect of Forty Years, 1825–1865* (New York: Charles Scribner's Sons, 1911), pp. 78–79.

32. Kendall to Jackson, Aug. 7, 1835, in John Spencer Bassett, *Correspondence of Andrew Jackson* (Washington, D.C.: Carnegie Institution of Washington, 1926–1935), vol. 5, p. 360.

33. Jackson to Kendall, Aug. 9, 1835, in ibid.

34. Terry L. Shoptaugh, "Amos Kendall: A Political Biography," (Ph.D. diss., University of New Hampshire, 1984), p. 210.

35. William Leggett, *A Collection of the Political Writings of William Leggett,* ed. Theodore Sedgwick (New York: Taylor & Dodd, 1840), vol. 2, p. 14.

36. Kendall to Geoge W. Hopkins, Feb. 24, 1838, USPSL.

37. Petition of Joshua M. Giddings and others of Jefferson, Ohio, Feb. 16, 1837, HCPO-NA.

38. Kendall to David A. Randall, Sept. 11, 1835, PMGL-NA.

39. Kendall to Gouverneur, Aug. 22, 1835, *Niles's Weekly Register,* 48 (Sept. 5, 1835): 8–9.

40. Kendall, *Report of the Postmaster General,* 24th Cong., 1st sess., 1835, Sen. Doc. 1 (serial 279), pp. 398–399.

41. George McDuffie, "Governor McDuffie's Message," 1835, in Albert Bushnell Hart and Edward Channing, eds., *American History Leaflets,* 10 (1893): 2, 12.

42. *Statutes at Large,* 5 (1836): 87.

43. The inclusion of a principled defense of the free press in the Post Office Act of 1836 has rightly puzzled historians unaware of Hiland Hall's key role in its passage. See, for example, William M. Wiecek, *The Sources of Antislavery Constitutionalism in America, 1769–1848* (Ithaca: Cornell University Press, 1977), pp. 177–178.

44. Hiland Hall, "Incendiary Publications," April 1836 ("corrected"), Hall Papers, Park-McCullough House Archive, North Bennington, Vermont. See also *National Intelligencer,* March 25, 1835, and April 6, 1836. The *Intelligencer* labeled Hall's report "proposed"; Hall himself said that it was "but an individual argument, divested of all official character."

45. Hall, "Incendiary Publications."

46. *Pennsylvania Freeman,* April 11, 1839.

47. Savage, *Abolition Literature,* p. 115.

48. John C. Calhoun, "Report from the Select Committee on the Circulation of Incendiary Publications," Feb. 4, 1836, in Robert L. Meriwether et al., eds., *The Papers of John C. Calhoun* (Columbia: University of South Carolina Press, 1959–), vol. 13, p. 65. For a related discussion, see Lacy K. Ford, Jr., "Inventing the Con-

current Majority: Madison, Calhoun, and the Problem of Majoritarianism in American Political Thought," *Journal of Southern History*, 60 (1994): 19–58.

49. Charleston *Courier*, July 31, 1835.

50. James Henry Hammond to Mordecai Noah, Aug. 19, 1835, draft, Hammond Papers, LOC.

51. Report of the Joint Committee of Federal Relations of the South Carolina Legislature, in *Niles's Weekly Register*, 49 (Jan. 9, 1836): 318–319.

52. Forsyth to Van Buren, Aug. 5, 1835, in Butler, *Retrospect*, pp. 78–79.

53. Richards, *Anti-Abolition Mobs*, pp. 47–130.

54. *Telegraph*, Sept. 4, 1835.

55. Legaré to Huger, Nov. 21, 1835, in Mary Swinton Legaré Bullen, *Writings of Hugh Swinton Legaré* (Charleston: Burges & James, 1846), vol. 1, p. 224.

56. William Seward to Thurlow Weed, n.d., in Frederick W. Seward, *Autobiography of William H. Seward from 1801 to 1834* (New York: D. Appleton and Co., 1877) p. 293.

57. Jay, *Federal Government*, p. 161.

58. New York *Evening Post*, Sept. 14, 1835.

59. *New Method of Assorting the Mail, as Practiced by Southern Slaveholders, or Attack on the Post Office, Charleston, S.C.* [1835]. Original at the American Antiquarian Society.

60. William E. Channing, *Slavery*, 3rd ed., rev. (Boston: James Munroe and Co., 1836), pp. 161–162.

61. William Goodell, *Slavery and Anti-Slavery: A History of the Great Struggle in Both Hemispheres* ... (New York: William Harned, 1852), p. 417.

62. Jay, *Federal Government*, p. 162.

63. Leggett, *Political Writings*, vol. 2, pp. 12, 14, 44, 50.

64. Harriet Martineau, *Society in America* (London: Saunders and Otley, 1837), vol. 1, p. 61.

65. Bradley to Elisha Whittlesey, Sept. 13, 1835, EWP-WRHS.

66. Adams, *Memoirs*, Aug. 12, 1835, vol. 9, p. 254.

67. *Congressional Globe*, Jan. 24, 1842, p. 978.

68. Nathan Sargent, *Public Men and Events from the Commencement of Mr. Monroe's Administration, in 1817, to the Close of Mr. Fillmore's Administration, in 1853* (Philadelphia: J. B. Lippincott & Co., 1875), vol. 2, p. 61.

Conclusion

1. John Quincy Adams, *Memoirs of John Quincy Adams*, ed. Charles Francis Adams (Philadelphia: J. B. Lippincott & Co., 1874–1877), Aug. 12, 1835, vol. 9, p. 254.

2. Adams to Charles Hammond, March 31, 1837, in William Henry Smith, *Charles Hammond and His Relations to Henry Clay and John Quincy Adams; or, Constitutional Limitations and the Contest for Freedom of Speech and the Press* (Chicago: Chicago Historical Society, 1885), p. 68.

3. James Madison, "Spirit of Governments," *National Gazette*, Feb. 18, 1792, in William T. Hutchinson, et al., eds., *Papers of James Madison* (Chicago: University of Chicago Press; Charlottesville: University Press of Virginia, 1962–), vol. 14, pp. 233–234.

SOURCES

The preparation of this study involved an extensive investigation of a wide range of sources, including published and unpublished government documents, the personal papers of contemporaries, pamphlets, newspapers, magazines, ephemera, and travelers' accounts. The most important sources are cited in the notes. This listing provides an overview of three of the most elusive of these sources: manuscript collections, the various editions of post office laws and regulations, and pamphlets.

Manuscript Collections

Academy of Natural Sciences Library, Philadelphia
Jacob Cist Papers

Alabama Department of Archives and History, Montgomery
Neil Blue Papers

American Antiquarian Society, Worcester, Massachusetts
Broadside Collection
Solomon Henkel Papers
Ralph Kellogg Papers
Paxton, Massachusetts, Post Office Records
Rutland, Massachusetts, Post Office Records
Stagecoach Firm Papers
Isaiah Thomas Papers
Ginery Twichell Papers
Waters Family Papers

American Philosophical Society, Philadelphia
Richard Bache Papers
Ebenezer Hazard Papers

Boston Public Library
Carl W. Ernst Papers
George Thacher Papers
Aaron Ward Papers

California Historical Society, San Francisco
Samuel Adams Papers
Milton S. Latham Papers

Central Michigan University, Clarke Historical Library
Cortland B. Stebbins Letterbook

Chicago Historical Society
George B. Armstrong Papers

Cincinnati Historical Society Library
Sutphin-Laws Papers

College of William and Mary
Maupin-Washington Papers
Woolfolk Family Papers

Columbia Historical Society, Washington, D.C.
Miscellaneous letters

Columbia University
DeWitt Clinton Papers

Connecticut Historical Society, Hartford
Gideon Welles Papers

Connecticut State Library, Hartford
Henry Leavitt Goodwin Papers
Gideon Welles Papers

Cornell University
Ezra Cornell Papers
Elizabeth Starkweather Papers

Duke University
Ambler-Brown Family Papers
Joseph Banner Papers
Eliza Bayles Papers
Campbell Family Papers
Erasmus H. Coston Papers
Richard Elwood Papers
Allen Hold and J. Holt Papers
Asa Holland Papers
Alfred Huger Papers
Albert Humrickhouse Papers
George Wesley Johnson Papers
Joseph Keeding Papers
William W. Reavis Papers
John F. Smith Papers
William G. Thompson Papers
Wilkes Family Papers
Winn Family Papers

East Carolina University
  John A. Clark Papers
  Hoyle J. Windley Family Papers
  Young-Spicer Family Papers

Essex Institute, Salem, Massachusetts
  John Dabney Account Books
  Ebenezer Putnam Post Office Account Book

Filson Club, Louisville, Kentucky
  William T. Barry Papers
  George M. Bibb Papers
  Matthew M. Campbell Papers

Georgia Historical Society, Savannah
  Joseph Habersham Papers

Granger Homestead, Canandaigua, New York
  Gideon Granger Papers

Hackley Public Library, Muskegon, Michigan
  Muskegon, Michigan, Post Office Records

Harvard Business School, Baker Library
  Nathaniel Blake Collection
  Cambridgeport, Massachusetts, Post Office Records
  N. F. M. and J. H. Dykeman Papers
  Hollis, Maine, Post Office Records
  William H. Moore Papers
  Phillipsburg, Maine, Post Office Records
  Post office circulars
  Gideon Welles Papers

Harvard University, Houghton Library
  American Board of Commissioners for Foreign Missions Records

Historical Society of Pennsylvania, Philadelphia
  James Buchanan Papers
  Tench Coxe Papers
  Gratz Collection
  William Pepper Papers
  William White Papers

Henry E. Huntington Library and Archives, San Marino, California
  John Sherman Bagg Papers
  William A. Brown Papers
  John Lorimer Graham Papers
  Francis Lieber Papers
  Robert Mills Papers
  Overland Mail Papers
  Russell, Majors, and Waddell Papers

Library of Congress
  Blair Family Papers
  Thomas Ewing Papers
  George William Gordon Papers
  Francis Granger Papers
  Gideon Granger Papers
  Duff Green Papers
  Nathan Hall Papers
  James Henry Hammond Papers
  James O. Harrison Papers
  Andrew Jackson Papers
  Thomas Jefferson Papers
  Amos Kendall Papers
  Horatio King Papers
  James Madison Papers
  John McLean Papers
  William Medill Papers
  Return Jonathan Meigs, Jr., Papers
  James Monroe Papers
  Samuel Morse Papers
  Lewis Tappan Papers
  Martin Van Buren Papers
  George Washington Papers

Maine Historical Society, Portland
  East Hebron, Maine, Post Office Records
  Francis O. J. Smith Papers
  Waldoboro, Maine, Post Office Records

Massachusetts Historical Society, Boston
  John Quincy Adams Papers
  Jeremy Belknap Papers
  William Ellery Channing Papers
  Alexender Hill Everett Papers
  Edward Everett Papers
  Marcus Morton Papers
  Timothy Pickering Papers
  Charles Russell Papers
  Theodore Sedgwick Papers

Michigan State University
  Cortland B. Stebbins Papers

Missouri Historical Society, St. Louis
  James O. Broadhead Papers
  Case Family Papers
  Hitchcock Collection
  Lamotte-Coppinger Papers

Lewis F. Linn Papers
Sappington Papers

National Archives
Continental Congress Papers
House of Representatives, Committee on Post Office and Post Roads, Petitions, Reports, and Committee Papers
House of Representatives, Committee on Roads and Canals, Petitions, Reports, and Committee Papers
Postmaster General's Letterbooks
Post Office Department, Letters Received
Post Office Department, Miscellaneous Records
Records of the Office of the Electro-Magnetic Telegraph
Senate, Committee on Post Office and Post Roads, Petitions, Reports, and Committee Papers
Senate, Committee on Roads and Canals, Petitions, Reports, and Committee Papers

New Hampshire Historical Society, Concord
Samuel Bell Papers
Hampstead, New Hampshire, Post Office Records
Isaac Hill Papers
Ephraim Hutchins Papers
Albert Mason Papers
Charles Hazen Peaslee Papers

New-York Historical Society, New York
Aaron Belknap Papers
Horatio Gates Papers
John Lorimer Graham Papers
Rufus King Papers
Henry Meigs Papers
Hezekiah Munsell Papers
Henry O'Reilly Papers
John W. Taylor Papers
William B. Taylor Papers
Gideon Welles Papers

New York Public Library
Gideon Welles Papers
Samuel L. Gouverneur Papers

New York State Library, Albany
Charles K. Gardner Papers

Ohio Historical Society, Columbus
Griswold Family Papers
John Allen Trimble Papers
Abraham Wotring Papers

Oneida County Historical Society, Utica, New York
Gideon Granger Papers

Park-McCullough House, North Bennington, Vermont
  Hiland Hall Papers

Presbyterian Historical Society, Philadelphia
  Ebenezer Hazard Papers

Princeton University Libraries
  Blair-Lee Papers

Rhode Island Historical Society, Providence
  John Wickes Greene Diary

Rochester Historical Society, New York
  John B. Elwood Papers

Rochester Public Library, New York
  Henry O'Reilly Papers
  Abelard Reynolds Papers

Smithsonian Institution, National Philatelic Collection
  Barnabas Bates clipping file
  Gideon Welles Papers
  Miscellaneous letters and post office records

Smithsonian Institution Archives
  Alfred Vail Papers

South Carolina Historical Society, Charleston
  Bacot Family Papers
  Robert Mills Papers

State University of New Jersey
  Imlay Family Papers

Tennessee State Library and Archives, Nashville
  Rhea Family Papers

University of Alabama
  Robert Jemison Papers

University of California at Berkeley, Bancroft Library
  Pacific Mail Steamship Company Papers

University of Georgia
  Joseph Wheaton Papers

University of New Hampshire
  Daniel Webster Papers

University of North Carolina, Southern Historical Collections
  John Bragg Papers
  Cameron Papers
  Felix Grundy Papers
  Duff Green Papers
  Maury Papers
  William P. Miles Papers

Nashville, North Carolina, Post Office Records
Reems Creek, North Carolina, Post Office Records
Rhett Papers

University of Rochester
Thurlow Weed Papers

University of South Carolina, South Caroliniana Library
Thomas W. Bacot Letterbook
Jacob Schirmer Papers

University of Texas, Austin
John Rice Jones Papers

University of Vermont
John Fay Papers

University of Virginia
Miscellaneous papers

U.S. Postal Service Library
Miscellaneous letters received

Virginia Historical Society, Richmond
Charles William Ashby Papers

Virginia State Library, Richmond
Kilby Family Papers

Western Reserve Historical Society, Cleveland
Elisha Whittlesey Papers

West Virginia University Library, Morgantown
William Sommerville Papers

Yale University Library
Beecher Family Papers

Postal Laws and Regulations (by date)

A Collection of the Statutes Now in Force, Relating to the Post-Office. New York: Hugh Gaine, 1774.
Instructions to Deputy Postmasters [Philadelphia: n.p., 1792]. Original at the Boston Public Library.
[*The Post-Office Law, Regulations, Forms, and Tables of Distances*] [Philadephia: n.p., 1794]. Incomplete edition, missing title page; original at the New York State Library.
The Post-Office Law, with Instructions, Forms, and Tables of Distances, Published for the Regulation of the Post Offices. Philadelphia: Charles Cist, 1798.
The Post-Office Law, with Instructions, Forms, and Tables of Distances. Washington, D.C.: Charles Cist, 1800.
The Post-Office Law, with Instructions and Forms, Published for the Regulation of the Post Offices. Washington, D.C.: General Post-Office, 1804.

The Post-Office Law, with Instructions and Forms, Published for the Regulation of the Post-Offices. Washington, D.C.: General Post-Office, 1808.

The Post-Office Law, with Instructions and Forms, Published for the Regulation of the Post-Office. Washington, D.C.: General Post-Office, 1810.

The Post Office Law, with Instructions and Forms, Published for the Regulation of the Post-Office. Washington, D.C.: General Post-Office, 1817.

The Post-Office Law, with Instructions and Forms, Published for the Regulation of the Post Office. Washington, D.C.: Lawrence & Wilson, 1818.

Post-Office Laws, Instructions, and Forms, Published for the Regulation of the Post-Office. Washington, D.C.: General Post-Office, 1820.

Post-Office Law, Instructions, and Forms, Published for the Regulation of the Post-Office. Washington, D.C.: Way & Gideon, 1825.

Post-Office Laws, Instructions, and Forms, Published for the Regulation of the Post-Office. Washington, D.C.: Way & Gideon, 1828.

Laws, Instructions, and Forms, for the Regulation of the Post-Office Department. Washington, D.C.: F. P. Blair, 1832.

Laws and Regulation for the Government of the Post Office Department. Washington, D.C.: Alexander and Barnard, 1843.

Laws and Regulation for the Government of the Post Office Department, With an Appendix. Washington, D.C.: John T. Towers, 1847.

Pamphlets

An Address Occasioned by the Opposition Which Originated in Cincinnati, Ohio, against the Attempts to Stop the Sabbath Mails, Delivered in the Associate Reformed Church, in Hamilton, on the Last Sabbath in Dec. 1829. Newburgh: C. U. Cushman, 1830.

An Address to the Committee Appointed by a General Meeting of the Citizens of the City of New York, Held at Tammany Hall, January 31, 1829, to Express Their Sentiments on the Proposition of the Sunday Union and Their Coadjustors to Stop the Transportation of the Mail and to Close the Post Offices on Sunday. [New York: n.p., 1829].

An Address to the People of Maryland from their Delegates in the Late National Republican Convention. Baltimore: Sands & Neilson, 1832.

The Akron Post-Office. Akron, Ohio: n.p., 1838. Original at the American Antiquarian Society.

American and Foreign Sabbath Union. *Second Annual Report of the American and Foreign Sabbath Union.* Boston: T. R. Marvin, 1845.

Austin, Arthur W. *A Memorandum Concerning the Charlestown Post Office.* [Boston: n.p., 1834].

Auxiliary Union of the City of Boston for the General Union for Promoting the Oservance of the Christian Sabbath. *Proceedings in Relation to the Formation of the Auxiliary Union of the City of Boston, for Promoting the Observance of the Christian Sabbath, with the Address of the General Union to the People of the United States.* Boston: T. R. Marvin, 1828.

Baird, Thomas H. *An Essay on the Subject of the Transportation of the Mail on the Sabbath.* Pittsburg: Christian Herald [1830].

Barry, William T. *Address of William T. Barry, Postmaster General, to the People of the United States.* Washington, D.C.: Francis Preston Blair, 1834.

————. *Letter of William T. Barry, Postmaster General, to the House of Representatives of the United States, Reviewing the Report of the Select Committee of That House Appointed to Investigate the Affairs of the Post Office Department.* Washington, D.C.: Blair and Rives, 1835.

[————]. *Organization of the Post Office Department and Assignment of Duties to the Officers and Clerks in Service, January 1830.* [Washington, D.C.: n. p., 1830].

[————]. *Organization of the Post-Office Department and Assignment of Duties to the Officers and Clerks, by the Postmaster General.* [Washington, D.C.: n. p., 1831].

Bates, Barnabas. *An Address Delivered at a General Meeting of the Citizens of the City of New York, Held at Tammany Hall, December 28th, 1829, to Express Their Sentiments on the Memorials to Congress to Prevent the Transportation of the Mail and the Opening of the Post Offices on Sunday.* New York: Gospel Herald, 1830.

————. *A Brief Statement of the Exertions of the Friends of Cheap Postage in the City of New York.* New York: William C. Bryant & Co., 1848.

Bayard, Samuel. *An Address Delivered on Thursday, the 14th August 1828, in the Presbyterian Church, at Princeton, N.J., at the Request of a Committee of the Society Auxiliary to the General Union for the Due Observation of the Lord's Day.* Princeton: Connolly & Madden, 1828.

[Beecher, Lyman]. *The Address of the General Union for Promoting the Observance of the Christian Sabbath, to the People of the United States.* New York: Daniel Fanshaw, 1828.

[————]. *Review of a Report of the Committee to Whom was Referred the Several Petitions on the Subject of Mails on the Sabbath.* Boston: Peirce and Williams, 1829.

[————]. *Review of the Hon. Mr. Johnson's Report, on the Subject of the Sabbath Mails.* [n.p., n.d.].

Black, Alexander. *Report, Exhibiting the Present State of the Work and Probable Progress of Operations of the Charleston and Hamburg Rail Road.* Charleston, S.C.: William S. Blain, 1831.

Bliss, George. *Reply to a Late Letter of the Postmaster General, and Report of the First Assistant Postmaster General.* Springfield, Mass.: Wood and Rupp, 1842.

Bond, William. *Speech of Mr. Bond, of Ohio, upon the Resolution to Correct Abuses in the Public Expenditures and to Separate the Government from the Press . . . April 1838.* [Washington, D.C.: n.p., 1838].

[Brown, Edmund F.] *The Postmaster General.* [Washington, D.C.: n.p., 1831]. "From the [Washington] *Globe*."

Brown, Obadiah B. *Address of Obadiah B. Brown, the Late Treasurer and Chief Clerk in the Post Office Department; Being a Vindication of the Charges Made against Him by a Majority of the Committee on Post Offices and Post Roads of the United States Senate.* Washington, D.C.: Blair & Rives, 1835.

A Candid Examination of Certain Doctrines Laid Down and Contended for by the Friends of Sabbath Mails: Or, a Brief Inquiry into the Religious Character, Obligations, and Powers of the Government of the United States. . . . Ithaca: Spencer & Chatterton, 1829. "By the Spirit of Seventy Six."

Capen, Nahum. *Correspondence Respecting Postal Improvements and the Removal of the Boston Post Office.* Boston: n.p., 1858.

Charles, Edmund. *Suggestions upon the Nature and Disadvantages of the Present Post*

Office Tariff Showing the Injurious Effects of the High Rates of Postage, Especially on Letters Containing Enclosures. . . . New York: n.p., 1844.

Cheap Postage: A Dialogue between Messrs. A. and B., in Washington City, 1849. [Washington, D.C.: n.p., 1849].

Clayton, John. *Speech of Mr. Clayton, of Delaware, in the Senate of the United States, Feb. 10, 1831, on the Resolution of Mr. Grundy.* . . . Washington, D.C.: National Journal, 1831.

Considerations on the Foundation, Ends, and Duties of the Christian Sabbath. . . . Utica: Northway & Porter, 1829.

Cooper, Thomas. *To Any Member of Congress.* . . . [n.p.: S. J. M'Morris, 1831].

Coyle, Fitzhugh. *Letter of Fitzhugh Coyle (Late a Clerk in the Auditor's Office on the Post Office Department) to the President of the United States.* . . . [Washington, D.C.: n.p., 1845].

Cushing, Caleb. *Speech of Mr. Cushing, of Massachusetts, on the Post Office Bill.* Washington, D.C.: Gales and Seaton, 1841.

Dresser, Amos. *The Narrative of Amos Dresser, with Stone's Letters from Natchez* . . . New York: American Anti-Slavery Society, 1836.

Evarts, Jeremiah. *The Logic and Law of Col. Johnson's Report to the Senate on Sabbath Mails.* Utica: G. S. Wilson, 1829.

———, ed. *Memorials to Congress, Respecting Sabbath Mails.* Boston: Published at the Request of Many Petitioners, 1829.

Everett, Alexander H. *The Conduct of the Administration.* Boston: Stimpson & Clapp, 1832.

An Examination of the Probable Effect of the Reduction of Postage as Proposed to be Made by the Bill Introduced into the Senate of the United States by the Hon. Mr. Merrick, of Maryland [Washington, n.p., 1845]. By "Franklin." Original in HCPO-NA.

Freedom's Defence: Or, a Candid Examination of Mr. Calhoun's Report on the Freedom of the Press. Worcester: Dorr, Howland & Co., 1836. By "Cincinnatus." Long attributed to William Plumer.

Frelinghuysen, Theodore. *Speech of Mr. Frelinghuysen on his Resolution Concerning Sabbath Mails.* Washington, D.C.: Rothwell & Ustick, 1830.

General Union for Promoting the Observance of the Christian Sabbath. *First Annual Report of the General Union for Promoting the Observance of the Christian Sabbath.* New York: J. Collord, 1829.

———. *Second Annual Report of the General Union for Promoting the Observance of the Christian Sabbath.* New York: Sleight and Robinson, 1830.

———. *Third Annual Report of the General Union for Promoting the Observance of the Christian Sabbath.* . . . New York: Sleight & Robinson, 1831.

Goddard, William. *To the Friends of Freedom.* Baltimore: n.p., 1775.

Goodwin, Henry L. *Memorial of the Penny Post Company of California, Praying Indemnity for Losses Sustained in Consequence of the Unlawful Detention of Letters at the Post Office in San Francisco.* Washington, D.C.: H. Polkinhorn's Steam Job Press, 1856.

Gordon, Samuel. *Speech of Hon. Samuel Gordon, of New York, on the Bill Making Appropriation for the Post Office Department.* Washington, D.C.: Globe, 1841.

Granger, Gideon. *A Vindication of the Measures of the Present Administration.* Wilmington, Del.: James Wilson, 1803.

Green, Duff. *Circular to the Presidents of Railroad Companies.* n.p., 1851.

Grundy, Felix. *Speech of Mr. Grundy, of Tennessee, Relative to the Post Office Department.* [Washington, D.C.: n.p., 1831].

Hazen, Abraham D. *The Post Office before and since 1860 under Democratic and Republican Administrations.* Hartford: Case, Lockwood, & Brainard Co., 1880.

Hill, Isaac. *Speech of Mr. Hill, of New Hampshire, in Senate, May 10, 1832, on Mr. Bibb's Amendment. . . .* [Washington, D.C.: n.p., 1832].

————. *Speech of the Hon. Isaac Hill, of New Hampshire, on the Motion of Mr. Southard. . . .* Washington, D.C.: Francis Preston Blair, 1834.

Holmes, John. *Post Office Inquiry: Mr. Holmes's Speech on Mr. Grundy's Resolution . . . .* Washington, D.C.: National Journal, 1831.

————. *Speech of Mr. Holmes . . . On His Resolutions Calling upon the President of the United States for the Reasons of his Removing from Office, and Filling the Vacancies thus Created.* Washington, D.C.: National Journal, 1830.

Jay, William. *An Essay on the Importance of the Sabbath, Considered Merely as a Civil Institution.* Geneva, N.Y.: James Bogert, 1826.

Johns, Evan. *A Review of the Layman's Essay on the Sabbath.* Canandaigua, N.Y.: Morse & Willson, 1829.

Johnson, Richard M. *Report of a Committee of the Senate of the United States on the Petitions against Sunday Mails.* Philadephia: Reprinted for the Benefit of Mankind, 1829.

————. *Report of the Committee of the Senate of the United States . . . on the Subject of the Transportation of the Mails on Sunday. . . .* Baltimore: James Lovegrove, 1829.

Kendall, Amos. *Address of the Central Hickory Club to the Republican Citizens of the United States, Adopted October 9, 1832. . . .* Washington, D.C.: n.p., 1832.

————. *Letter of the Postmaster General, Giving his Reasons for Not Removing the Postmaster at Bath.* [n.p., 1836].

————. *Mandamus Case: Letter of the Postmaster General and Opinion of the Attorney General. . . .* Washington, D.C.: Blair & Rives, 1837.

[————]. *Organization of the Post Office Department.* [Washington, D.C.: n.p., 1835].

King, John P. *Speech of Mr. King, of Georgia, on the Bill to Prohibit the Circulation of the Mails of Incendiary Publications. . . .* [Washington, D.C.: n.p., 1836].

Leavitt, Joshua. *Cheap Postage: Remarks and Statistics on the Subject of Cheap Postage and Postal Reform in Great Britain and the United States.* Boston: Cheap Postage Association [1848].

————. *The Moral and Social Benefits of Cheap Postage.* New York: George W. Wood, 1849.

Lieber, Francis. *Remarks on the Post Establishment in the United States.* [New York: n.p., 1841].

Ludlow, James C., et al. *Narrative of the Late Riotous Proceedings against the Liberty of the Press, in Cincinnati, with Remarks and Historical Notices Relating to Emancipation.* Cincinnati: Ohio Anti-Slavery Society, 1836.

The Mail Robbers: Report of the Trials of Michael Mellon, the Lancaster Mail Robber, and George Wilson and James Porter Alias May, the Reading Mail Robbers . . . Philadephia: J. Mortimer, 1830.

Mayo, Robert. *The Affidavit of Andrew Jackson. . . .* 3d ed. Washington, D.C.: Printed for the Plaintiff, 1840.

———. *The Misrepresentations of "A Member of the Hickory Club" in Reply to Dr. Mayo's "Sketches" &c., Refuted*. Washington, D.C.: Garret Anderson, 1837.

McLean, John. *An Address Prepared at the Request of the Union and Jefferson Societies, of Augusta College*. Cincinnati: John Whetstone, Jr., & Co., 1831.

———. *An Eulogy on the Character and Public Services of James Monroe*. . . . Cincinnati: Looker and Reynolds, 1831.

Merrick, William D. *Speech of Mr. Merrick, of Maryland, on the Bill to Reduce the Rates of Postage and to Regulate the Use and Correct the Abuse of the Franking Privilege*. Washington, D.C.: Gales and Seaton, 1845.

Miles, Pliny. *Postal Reform: Its Urgent Necessity and Practicability*. New York: Stringer & Townsend, 1855.

New York Cheap Postage Association. *An Address of the Directors of the New York Cheap Postage Association, to the People of the United States*. . . . New York: William C. Bryant & Co., 1850.

New York Sabbath Committee. *Railroads and the Sabbath*. New York: Edward O. Jenkins, 1858.

Orne, Henry. *The Letters of Columbus . . . to Which are Added Two Letters of Col. Orne to Gen. Duff Green*. Boston: Putnam & Hunt, 1829.

———. *Reply of Colonel Orne to the Attacks of Mr. Nathaniel Greene and David Henshaw and Others, in the Boston Statesman*. Boston: Putnam & Hunt, 1829.

Page, Horace F. *Argument before Hon. D. M. Key, Postmaster General*. . . . *The Origin, Method, and Important Public Uses of the Letter Service of Wells, Fargo, & Company*. Washington, D.C.: Judd & Detweiler, 1880.

Palfrey, John G. *Speech of Mr. Palfrey, of Massachusetts, on Postage Reform*. [Washington, D.C.: n.p., 1849].

Papers, Documents, and Correspondence in Relation to the Case of Charles L. Weller, Deputy Postmaster at San Francisco, Cal. Washington, D.C.: William A. Harris, 1859.

Pearl, Cyril. *The Sabbath a Divine Institution: A Reply to Arguments on the Negative on the Question "Ought the Law Requiring the Opening of Our Post Offices and the Transportation of Our Mails on the Christian Sabbath to Be Repealed?" Delivered before the Bangor Forensic Club, January 1831*. Boston: Peirce and Parker, 1831.

The Political Mirror: Or, Review of Jacksonism. New York: J. P. Peaslee, 1835.

Porter, Alexander. *Remarks of Mr. Porter, of Louisiana, in the Senate of the United States, on the Bill for Reforming the Post Office Establishment*. Washington, D.C.: Gales and Seaton, 1835.

Post-Office Department. [New York: n.p., 1834]. Original at LOC.

Proceedings of the Citizens of Charleston on the Incendiary Machinations Now in Progress against the Peace and Welfare of the Southern States. Charleston, S.C.: A. E. Miller, 1835.

Prohibition of Sunday Traveling on the Pennsylvania Rail Road. Philadelphia: Merrihew & Thompson, 1850.

"Proscription is Itself to be Proscribed." Washington, D.C.: Blair & Rives, 1844.

Quackenbos, M. M. *Proceedings of a Convention of Delegates from Several Wards in the City of New York on the Subject of the Location of the Post Office in That City*. . . . New York: James Van Norden, 1836.

Reeside, James. *Letters of James Reeside in Relation to the Charges Made against Him in the Report of the Majority of the Committee of the Senate on the Post Office and Post Roads.* Washington, D.C.: n.p., [1834].

A Reply to the Sketches of an Eight Years' Resident in the City of Washington. Washington, D.C.: n.p., 1837. "By a Member of the Hickory Club."

Seven Years in the Boston Post Office, by an Ex-Clerk. n.p., 1854.

Shields, E. J. *Speech of the Hon. E. J. Shields, of Tennessee, on the Bill to Change the Organization of the Post Office Department and to Provide More Effectually for the Settlement of the Accounts Thereof. . . .* Washington, D.C.: National Intelligencer, 1836.

Simmons, James Fowler. *Remarks of Mr. Simmons, of Rhode Island, in Support of His Proposition to Reduce Postages to a Uniform Rate of Five Cents for a Single Letter, for All Distances.* Washington, D.C.: J :& G. S. Gideon, 1845.

A Sketch of the Life of John McLean, of Ohio. Philadelphia: Grigg, Elliott & Co., 1846.

Smith, Francis O. J. *A Letter Relating to the Administration and Present Condition of the Post Office Department of the United States under the Hon. William T. Barry, Postmaster General.* Portland, Maine: I. Berry and Co., 1835.

Smith, Gerrit. *Abolition of the Postal System.* Washington, D.C.: Buell & Blanchard, 1854.

Smith, Truman. *Speech of Mr. Truman Smith, of Connecticut, on Removals and Appointments to Office.* Washington, D.C.: Towers, 1850.

South Carolina Canal and Rail Road Company. *Annual Report of the Direction of the South Carolina Canal and Rail Road Company, to the Stockholders, May 6th, 1834.* Charleston, S.C.: W. S. Blain's, 1834.

Spooner, Lysander. *The Unconstitutionality of the Laws of Congress Prohibiting Private Mails.* New York: Tribune Printing Establishment, 1844.

————. *Who Caused the Reduction of Postage in 1845?* Boston: A. J. Wright, 1849.

STATE of the Application to Congress for Aid to Complete the Post Road from Philadelphia to Baltimore, and Observations Thereon. n.p., n.d. Original at the Library Company, Philadelphia.

Sunday Mails: Or, Inquiries into the Origin, Institution, and Proper Mode of Observance of the First Day of the Week or Christian Sabbath. Philadelphia: Published for the Benefit of Sunday Mails, 1831.

Tappan, Lewis. *Letter to Eleazer Lord, Esq., in Defense of Measures for Promoting the Observance of the Christian Sabbath.* 2d ed. New York: John P. Haven [1831].

Taylor, John B. *Post Office Calendar, Containing a List of All the Post Offices in the State of Virginia, with the Distances from Richmond. . . .* Richmond: Shepherd & Pollard, 1825.

Thomas, William. *The Enemies of the Constitution Discovered, or an Inquiry into the Origin and Tendency of Popular Violence, Containing a Complete and Circumstantial Account of the Unlawful Proceedings at the City of Utica, October 21st, 1835.* New York: Leavitt, Lord, & Co., 1835.

Trial of the Mail Robbers, Hare, Alexander, and Hare. Baltimore: Howard J. Coale, 1818.

Trial of Reuben Crandall, M.D., Charged with Publishing Seditious Libels, by Circulating the Publications of the American Anti-Slavery Society. New York: H. R. Piercy, 1836.

Virginia Society for Promoting the Observance of the Christian Sabbath. *To the People of the United States.* [n.p., 1829].

A Voice from the West for John M'Lean of Ohio, for the Presidency. [n.p., 1847].

Wickliffe, Charles. *Speech of Mr. Wickliffe in the House of Representatives* . . . Washington, D.C.: F. S. Myer, 1828.

Willson, James R. *The Sabbath: A Discourse on the Duty of Civil Government, in Relation to the Sanctification of the Lord's Day.* Newburgh, N.Y.: Parmenter & Spaulding, 1829.

Woodbury, Levi. *Speech of Mr. Woodbury, of New Hampshire, Relative to the Post Office Department.* [Washington, D.C.: n.p., 1831].

Yeadon, Richard, Jr. *The Amenability of Northern Incendiaries as Well to Southern as to Northern Laws, without Prejudice to the Right of Free Discussion.* . . . Charleston, S.C.: T. A. Hayden, 1835.

INDEX

abolitionism, 13, 14; and American state, 177, 204–205, 281–282; and antiabolitionism, 272–273, 275–278; and Jackson administration, 269–272, 276–277; and mass mailing, 257, 260–263; and postal officers, 263–272

abolitionist mails controversy: and changing conceptions of American state, 279–280, 281–282; historians on, 259–260; and party politics, 276–277; and postal policy, 263–276; as public issue, 257–280

Adams, John, 27, 71, 110

Adams, John Quincy, 92; and Charleston post office break-in, 339n6; on embezzlement, 77; on Amos Kendall, 279; and John McLean, 69, 81; and national politics, 71, 203, 206–208, 215; on postal network, 64; on proslavery, 281–282; and the Union, 256, 280, 281

Adams, Samuel, 31

Adamsites, 82, 97; defined, 301n8; domestic agenda of, 206–207, 215, 256; in election of 1828, 211; opposition to, 207–210, 233

administration. *See* postal administration

administrative reform: under Jacksonians, 127–128, 218, 247–248, 255–256, 337n164; under John McLean, 79–81, 83–87, 95–97, 105–109

Akin, James, 189, 197

Alabama Baptist Association, 196

Albany Argus, 69

Allen, Ralph, 130

American Anti-Slavery Society, 257, 260–265, 271. *See also* abolitionism

American and Foreign Sabbath Union, 200

American postal system. *See* postal system, United States

American Railroad Journal, 88

American System, 206. *See also* internal improvements

American Temperance Society, 180, 181

Amis des Noirs, 263

ancients, 209; and moderns, 8–10, 14–15

antiabolitionism, 272–273, 275–277. *See also* abolitionist mails controversy

Anti-Masons, 66, 301n11

anti-Sabbatarianism, 193–200, 202–203. *See also* Sabbatarian controversy

antislavery, 256, 279–280; Duff Green on, 226. *See also* abolitionism

Anti-Slavery Record, 262

antistatism, 17, 19, 206–210, 290–291n71, 330n11

Arfwedson, Carl, 102–103

army: compared with postal system, 3–4, 283; and mail delivery, 134; and postal officers, 116, 134–135; in War of Independence, 27

Avery, Isaac, 244

Bache, Benjamin Franklin: on postal policy, 34, 35–37

Bache, Richard, 27, 130–131, 132

Bache, Richard, Jr., 77, 132

Bacon, Leonard, 9, 10, 11, 40

Bacot, Thomas W., 39, 75, 101

Badger, Joseph, 190

Bailey, Theodorus, 116, 162

357